Interpreting
Latin American History

From Independence to Today

Edited by
Ramón Eduardo Ruiz
University of California,
San Diego

HOLT, RINEHART AND WINSTON, INC.
New York, Chicago, San Francisco, Atlanta
Dallas, Montreal, Toronto

Preface

The republics of Latin America embrace a wide spectrum of peoples, customs, historical traditions, and geographical differences. To know intimately each of the twenty republics, its history, and its society represents a herculean challenge that only the brash amateur would accept. Yet, that is the goal of the average textbook, and it may partially explain the paucity of attempts by scholars in the field to write comprehensive surveys. The teacher in the classroom confronts a similar challenge in his attempt to teach a "history of Latin America." Text and classroom lectures, at best, offer only an outline of the history of each country. Ultimately, if the teacher seeks depth instead of broad coverage, he must assign priorities and stress what he decides is important and vital to an understanding of Latin American development. In the end he emphasizes, to the extent that his preparation permits, the history of the countries he has studied closely.

A similar dilemma confronted the editor of this reader. He could either select material on all of the republics and provide a superficial but total coverage, or he could emphasize particular topics and countries at the expense of others. The editor has chosen the second alternative. Although he made every effort to keep in mind the needs and interests of all teachers of Latin American history, his special predilections and biases obviously dictated the selection of his material. The editor apologizes for those countries or topics of special concern that he covered poorly or neglected completely.

The book is divided into three sections. Section One includes the histories of four republics: Argentina, Brazil, Cuba, and Mexico. The editor chose these countries because, in his opinion, Latin America embraces at least five peculiar historical currents. At one extreme lies what he would call the "European" republics where Europeans and their descendants account for nearly all of the population and where the culture and ideas of Europe predominate (though obviously modified by the American environment). From this category, which includes Uruguay and, in the minds of some scholars, Chile, the editor selected Argentina because of its historical significance and size.

A second category consists of the "mestizo" republics, where the Spanish conqueror superimposed his way of life upon large indigenous populations which, through the mestizo offspring of Spaniard and Indian, survived to modify not only the Spanish "race" but local culture and civilization as well. A majority of the countries founded by Spain fall into this category; from them the editor picked Mexico because of its historical significance since colonial days and the peculiarities of its national era.

Spaniard and Negro joined together to produce yet another historical current, particularly in the Caribbean and the Spanish Main. To the editor, Cuba seemed a logical example of this category. An island republic, distinct from the mainland colonies, Cuba remained under Spanish rule for four centuries and eventually developed a peculiar relationship to the United States that deserves careful scrutiny. Cuba is also the first socialist nation in the Western Hemisphere; no student of Latin American history can close his eyes to that fact.

Brazil, the sole Portuguese colony in the Americas, represents a fourth category. Its history has been influenced also by its pronounced African heritage.

Haiti, with its French and Negro heritage, forms a fifth category. Unfortunately for its students, Haiti is not included in this reader. Want of space and the scant attention given to Haiti in the teaching of Latin American history dictated this decision.

In Section Two, the editor has attempted to fill in some of the gaps left by the selection of only four countries. It contains topics of particular importance in the histories of Chile, Peru, Bolivia, and Venezuela which, at the same time, represent cross currents of Latin American growth. Students of Latin America can neither deny nor ignore the traditional political stability of Chile, the significance of the Peruvian Aprista movement (with marked impact on political events in countries as far off as Cuba), the Bolivian Revolution of 1952 (one of three socio-economic upheavals in the history of Latin America), or the issue of petroleum in Venezuela which, when viewed in the context of the Latin American struggle to eliminate or control foreign ownership of local resources and to emerge from the primary export stage, represents a hemispheric problem.

Section Three includes topical issues that cut across national boundaries and carry implications for each republic in the hemisphere. Of the many possible topics the editor chose five, again on the assumption that they represent major issues that no student should slight. These include the land question, economic development, the military problem, the role of one-man rule (the *caudillo* or, in current jargon, the "dictator"), and Latin American-United States relations couched in terms of the Alliance for Progress. Clearly, other topics of equal importance could have been selected.

Two principal objectives dictated the selection of all of the essays: first, that the readings will add depth to the coverage of a textbook and explore basic questions, problems, and ideas fleetingly discussed in any one-volume treatment that provides a historical framework of all of the republics; second, that the essays will furnish not only supplementary material required for a broader, more comprehensive view of Latin America, but the intellectual stimulation necessary to engage students in the study of history as well. The editor hopes that the essays will offer students and teachers significant and controversial topics for classroom discussion. "Articles About Latin American History that the Editor Has Read With Profit" could be the supplementary title of the reader. In essence, the editor speaks for the teacher who, in classroom lecture, in his office, or in private conversation, may recommend to students certain essays or books on the particular period of history that he is discussing in his course. The readings vary widely both in the nature of the issues raised and in their presentation, and all present a particular point of view. A basic premise of the editor is that students relish intellectual controversy, are stimulated by it, and can cope with it. Thus, both teacher and student profit from essays with a definite interpretation. The selections do not necessarily reflect the opinions of the editor; he chose them for their coverage, the nature of their ideas, and particularly for their interpretation which, he assumes, offer greater scope to a course on the history of Latin America. To complement the points of view included in the reader, a brief bibliographical essay on sources in English, which are readily available to students, is included at the end of each group of readings.

The reader is not a collection of source material; few primary documents are included. Instead, every effort was made to use historical interpretations that, when linked together, provide a chronological-topical discussion of the main outline of a country's history. When juxtaposed to the interpretations in the text, the secondary material in the reader should encourage the student to weigh a number of points of view. In this manner, the subjective nature of historical writing becomes clear, and the "truth" no longer lies in one book or in one historical version. We who teach know that historians rarely agree among themselves and that history often lends itself to conflicting interpretations. These facts should be made known early to students of history. Moreover, the editor has sought to include numerous works of Latin American scholars, not because their presentations are any more correct, but because they provide different viewpoints with a distinct emphasis.

Not all of the essays are by historians. Some are the contributions of economists, philosophers, and even novelists; these are included because history, in the opinion of the editor, is more than just political and institutional development or economics. History joins broad and complicated processes that deny the "truth" to any single discipline.

To save space, the footnotes that originally accompanied many of the essays have been eliminated. Nothing was done to alter or modify the interpretations of the authors.

R. E. R.
San Diego, California
January 1970

Contents

SECTION TWO

Chile, Peru, Bolivia, and Venezuela: The Particular Problems   305

SECTION THREE

Latin American Issues: The Problems of a Continent 367

Argentina, Brazil, Cuba, and Mexico

I

Argentina: The Story of a City

Since the fall of Juan Manuel de Rosas in 1853, the last of the Federalist *caudillos* (dictators), the city of Buenos Aires has dominated the history of Argentina. A modern, cosmopolitan metropolis, Buenos Aires is the economic, cultural, and political capital of Argentina. Directly or indirectly, the welfare of every section of the country depends on it. In an economic sense, the city provides the market for provincial goods, facilitates their export to foreign markets, and supplies the manufactured articles consumed in the interior. But this role, which explains the success of Buenos Aires, has hindered the development of the provinces.

This conflict between city and country began in colonial days. Buenos Aires, then a small provincial city, was the colony's commercial hub from which hides and tallow were shipped to foreign ports and European imports arrived for local sale. The provinces, however, developed their own economy which was closely linked to the viceregal capital of far-off Lima. Along the trade route between Buenos Aires and Lima, a long and perilous journey by mule or ox cart, centers of trade and manufacturing produced primitive goods for local consumption. Few of these merchants and artisans welcomed the competition of the imported goods supplied by Buenos Aires which, because of their better quality and price, had more popular appeal. Thus, a barrier rose between Buenos Aires, the import center of the colony, and the provinces,

3

which prospered in direct relation to their degree of isolation from the city and foreign goods.

Spanish restrictions on colonial trade with the outside world angered the merchants of Buenos Aires, but not the provincial merchants. Independence from Spain and the opening of the port of Buenos Aires increased trade, particularly with Great Britain, and European goods shipped through the city destroyed many of the provincial industries. Independence, therefore, widened the gap between the two Argentinas.

The contrast between the growing prosperity of Buenos Aires and the stagnation of the provinces explains much of the political conflict of the nineteenth century. The Rosas administration, although emanating from the Province of Buenos Aires and closely identified with it, spoke for the Federalist doctrines of the provinces, which advocated a large measure of local political autonomy and economic sovereignty. However, the needs of the city, as voiced by the Unitarians, eventually prevailed over the Federalism of Rosas and sealed the triumph of the *porteños*.

The remarkable development of Argentina in the latter half of the nineteenth century centered in Buenos Aires and, to a lesser extent, in the sister cities of the eastern seaboard. British capital and know-how provided a railway system that joined the provinces to Buenos Aires and the giant meat-packing plants. The railways, the opening of the British market to Argentine products, and new innovations (the barbwire fence, refrigerated ships, and pedigreed cattle) transformed a formerly backward cattle industry into a highly modern, efficient one producing beef for export. The meat industry furnished the foundations for the first stage of national growth, but before the end of the nineteenth century the production of wheat and other grains ranked first among exports. As the port from which the new products left for European markets and as the distribution center for imported goods purchased with profits from the sale of beef and grains, Buenos Aires reaped a rich harvest of benefits.

Argentina's expanding economy required a large labor force. To attract workers to the under-populated land, economic planners encouraged European emigration to Argentina. In the last three decades of the nineteenth century millions of Italians and Spaniards entered the country. Attracted by economic opportunities, the immigrant tide did not stop until the crash of 1930. However, the majority of immigrants settled in the coastal cities; only a few moved inland. The urbanization of Buenos Aires began with the coming of the immigrant.

An oligarchy of meat and cattle barons from Buenos Aires

established a political and economic hegemony over the nation. Heirs to the legacy of Domingo Faustino Sarmiento and the Unitarians, the oligarchy offered vigorous and enlightened leadership, provided an era of stability and order, and, on the surface, imposed the trappings of democracy. The oligarchy, bent on keeping control of the political apparatus and fearful that the immigrant and his children threatened it, closed its eyes to the profound changes taking place in the Republic. The new urban classes, which sought to win a political role commensurate with their increasing economic importance, eventually wrested control of politics from the conservatives in 1916. The Radical Party, representative of the urban middle sectors, governed Argentina until economic difficulties and a military coup returned the conservative oligarchy to power.

Argentina never fully recovered from the disastrous effects of the Great Depression, for the conservative response to national ills, like that of the Radicals, proved ineffectual. In 1943 the Argentines turned to military men, convinced that the traditional parties offered no viable solutions to the problems of the age. Three years later urban workers, disgruntled elements of the middle sectors, and military men elected president Juan Domingo Perón, a colonel in the army who offered a new deal. Perón's program, which virtually ignored the needs of the provinces, cured none of the traditional ills and created new ones. He used scarce national funds for the purchase of railways and other public utilities owned by foreigners in a time of declining production of agricultural products in the provinces and of markets in Europe, and he soon bankrupted Argentina. Perón fell in 1955. Since then, political troubles have plagued the nation, and military men have displaced civilian politicians as the arbiters of the Republic's destiny.

The political woes reflect socio-economic changes that have altered the face of the Republic since 1930. The economy no longer simply produces meat and grains for export. Three decades of industrialization have transformed it, and the value of industrial goods exceeds all others. Buenos Aires is highly urbanized, and the other coastal cities enjoy impressive growth. However, the economy lags, for neither Perón nor his successors have coped successfully with the Republic's problems. In the opinion of many scholars, the principal problems stem from imbalances in the economy created by the gap between Buenos Aires and the backward provinces. The industries of Buenos Aires produce more goods than the country can purchase, while production of agricultural goods for export (which would provide national income to finance further development) and for the home market stagnates. Meanwhile the coastal cities continue to grow as waves of rural people, lured by the promise of jobs in industry, leave the countryside where a small elite still exercises a monopoly of the land.

1

Conflict between province and city developed early in the history of Argentina. Many historians trace the origins of the Federalist cause to the economic isolation of the interior during the Confederation. In their opinion, self-sufficiency encouraged political isolation. Federalism, the product of an ignorant and poverty-stricken people, was neither a program nor a system and merely provided the provincial *caudillo* with an instrument of exploitation and oppression. To Miron Burgin, Federalism, although partly reflecting the disintegration of the national economy, stood for the economic and political integrity of country and nation and protected the economic and political autonomy of the provinces. Burgin concludes that Federalism and not Unitarianism stood "much closer to Argentine reality . . . for it showed a clearer insight into the complex fabric of Argentina's economy as well as into the processes of the country's economic development."

Miron Burgin:
Economic Aspects
of Argentine Federalism*

The rapid progress of political emancipation had little effect on the economy of the Interior. The mode and forms of production and distribution evolved under the colonial system continued, practically without change, to dominate the economic life of the prov-

* Reprinted by permission of the publishers from Miron Burgin, THE ECONOMIC ASPECTS OF ARGENTINE FEDERALISM, 1820–1852. Cambridge, Mass.: Harvard University Press, Copyright, 1946, by the President and Fellows of Harvard College.

inces. What the Revolution of 1810 did was to transform the political and geographic environment which conditioned the rise and development of the Interior economy. The Revolution abolished mercantilism as an instrument of economic policy; it substituted competition for paternalistic regulation and protection; it linked the economy of the country to overseas markets, at the same time that it separated the Interior from areas of which in the colonial era it formed an integral part. While these changes were in accord with the fundamental line of development of the eastern portion of the River Plate viceroyalty, they ran contrary to the needs and interests of the western provinces. For the growth and development of the economy of the Interior depended precisely upon keeping the pre-revolutionary political and administrative system intact. Given the natural resources and the geographical position of the Interior, its economy depended less upon foreign commerce than upon the preservation of political unity with contiguous areas. The interior provinces were interested in the opening of the country to foreign trade only in so far as it resulted in a more plentiful supply of manufactures at reasonable prices. But to the extent that direct commerce between the River Plate and Europe jeopardized the security of domestic industries, political emancipation in the interior provinces entailed economic and financial hardships. These hardships were further intensified by the circumstance that territories, which prior to the Revolution were economically complementary to the Interior, remained outside the Argentine Confederation. So the economy of the Interior was not only exposed to the devastating competition of overseas industries in the Eastern markets, but was also deprived of those markets in which European competition was least effective, namely, Bolivia and Peru. Adjustment to the new political environment might have been less difficult had the Interior been able to match the industry of Western Europe. But this was far from being the case. In methods of production and industrial organization the Interior remained rigidly colonial. To the Interior, therefore, emancipation and unrestricted commercial intercourse with Europe meant a considerable curtailment of production in some of its most important industries, the annihilation of its transandine commerce, and the contraction of its interprovincial trade.

The economic problem confronting the provinces of the Interior was fundamentally different from that confronting Buenos Aires. In Buenos Aires the solution of the problem entailed nothing more than the setting up of an appropriate administrative and fiscal structure. For the abolition of the colonial system was in itself a step forward in the economic development of the province.

In the Interior the problem was to conserve the pre-revolutionary *status quo,* or as much of it as possible. It was a problem of devising the proper means of defense against the encroachments of foreign industry and commerce, and of limiting the rate and scope of economic and financial decline. The Revolution and political emancipation had resulted in irreparable loss to the Interior. For example, it was impossible to revive the mule trade between the Litoral and Peru, or to restore commerce with Bolivia, Chile, or Peru to its pre-revolutionary level. The provinces could exercise some measure of control over internal markets. They could minimize the impact of foreign imports upon domestic industries and in this way effect a more orderly adjustment in the economic structure. The wine and brandy industries of Tucumán and the provinces of Cuyo, the manufacture of leather goods in Santiago del Estero and Córdoba, the cloth industry of Córdoba, and finally the handicraft-industry—in all these sectors of the national economy a policy of protection might at least mitigate the process of economic decline. Such a policy, provided it were national in scope, might not only save the native industry from ruin, but allow of a gradual modernization of the Interior's industrial plant. For it was reasonable to assume that with profits assured, domestic industries would be in a position to bid successfully for the capital resources and technical skill necessary to raise the standard of industrial production. Protection would undoubtedly raise the prices of consumers' goods, but it would also cause a shift in the distribution of the national income in favor of the Interior and so make for a better balanced national economy.

But a protective commercial policy on a national scale was unrealizable, and for the very reasons which led the Interior to demand such a policy. The control by Buenos Aires of the country's overseas port was the decisive factor here. Buenos Aires would accept protection only on one condition, that she gain as much from it as the Interior. But this was out of the question. Of all the provinces of the Confederation, Buenos Aires was least interested in fostering a restrictive commercial policy. In so far as a policy of high duties would result in a lower volume of overseas trade and higher prices on consumers' goods it was politically inexpedient and economically harmful. To the extent that an increase in the cost of living would result in higher money wages the burden of higher duties would fall upon the employers, that is, the cattle breeders, hide and meat producers, and merchants. Nor were these classes in the least inclined to submit to such an eventuality, the more so as it was highly improbable that the fall in the rate of profit had any chance of being compensated for by an increase in the volume of production or overseas trade. On the contrary, there was every reason to anticipate a reduction in both exports and imports, and hence in the volume of industrial production. The argument that the loss sustained by Buenos Aires would be more than offset by the revival of industrial activity in the Interior, and that ultimately the national dividend would gain on balance failed to convince the *porteños*. For it was not at all certain that a more stringent commercial policy would stimulate industrial expansion on a scale sufficient to counterbalance contraction of economic activity in Buenos Aires. Whether or not these doubts were well founded, one thing was clear: Buenos Aires had nothing to offer except the services of the middleman, and these under protection would become in large part superfluous. The economic future of Buenos Aires depended then upon strengthening its commercial relations with Europe rather than upon the expansion of the provinces in the Interior. The adoption of a policy of protection, such as the Interior demanded, held out the prospect for Buenos Aires of a restoration of pre-revolutionary conditions. Buenos Aires, therefore, had no other choice but to keep the port wide open.

Unable to secure the coöperation of Buenos Aires the provinces of the Interior attacked the problem of protection on the basis of provincial and sectional rather than national interests. Provincial tariffs and special regulations designed to protect local markets and native industries were introduced as a substitute for a national commercial policy. At the same time the provinces endeavored to encourage interprovincial trade by means of commercial treaties. By these methods the provinces of the Interior hoped to offset the commercial liberalism of Buenos Aires and to arrest the process of economic disintegration. In no condition to undergo a thorough social and economic reorganization, the provinces sought relief in economic isolation. However, they were not prepared to follow this policy consistently, for none could hope to attain self-sufficiency. Isolation, far from strengthening the economic position of the provinces, only intensified their dependence upon Buenos Aires. For this reason more perhaps than any other the provinces were anxious to finish with the task of political organization in a way that would guarantee their economic and political autonomy and at the same time stabilize interprovincial economic relations. . . .

The issues raised by the legislative assembly of Córdoba in its declaration of August 10, 1832 were not new. Ever since the rejection of the Constitution of 1819 the provinces had become increasingly aware that the constitutional question was as much an economic as a political question. The Constitution of 1819 made no attempt to deal with the economic and financial organization of the country, which was simply another way of sanctioning the post-revolutionary *status quo*. It had shown that so long as the central government remained under the influence of Buenos Aires the economic postulates of the Interior would in all probability be disregarded. It had shown, further, that in any central government the influence of Buenos Aires, given its superior economic and financial resources, was bound to predominate. If the provinces, therefore, were to escape the economic dominion of Buenos Aires it was essential that they retain some degree of economic and fiscal autonomy, and that the powers and authority of the central government should be more or less clearly defined. The rise of provincial governments during and after the crisis of 1820 was not only a reflection of social and economic disintegration; it was also a spontaneous protest against the complete subordination of local interests to those of Buenos Aires. By assuming control in matters of economic and fiscal policies the provincial governments laid down the fundamental principles of state organization. For whatever the ultimate form which the central government might take the provinces were determined to preserve their autonomy. Home rule was for the provinces a defense against further encroachments upon their economic *status quo*. At the same time it was indispensable, if the cost of economic adaptation was to be reduced to a minimum.

It was, indeed, immaterial to the provinces whether the solution of the constitutional question was along unitary or federalist lines. One solution was as capable as the other of satisfying the more fundamental demands of the provinces. Whether a province favored the federalist or the unitary form of state organization depended upon the extent to which the policies of the central government could be expected to meet the needs of that province, rather than upon the philosophical principles underlying the two ideologies. Thus, while the provinces had secured from the Congress recognition of their autonomous status, which was clearly a step in the federalist direction, they yet supported most of the unitary political program. That unitarism was not compatible with provincial autonomy nor capable of meeting the economic demands of the provinces became clear only later, when the unitary party assumed full control of the national government.

Within the provinces political division resembled that of Buenos Aires. As in Buenos Aires so in the provinces the unitary party addressed itself primarily to the small but highly articulate groups of wealthy merchants and intellectuals, whose economic interests and cultural inclinations blended nicely with the liberal and progressive tendencies of the unitary ideology. Contact between provincial and *porteño* unitaries was direct, unencumbered by interprovincial rivalries. For the unitaries the problem of specific provincial interests did not exist. Fully prepared to sacrifice the economic and financial integrity of Buenos Aires they were no less prepared to reject the demand for economic and fiscal autonomy in the provinces. Nor did the unitaries in the provinces insist upon home rule beyond what the Constitution of 1826 was willing to grant. On the contrary, their economic and political future depended precisely upon the abolition of interprovincial boundaries and upon the extension of the authority of the national government. They agreed, therefore, with the unitaries of Buenos Aires on the necessity of nationalization of land as well as of the most important sources of revenue, such as customs, stamp duties, license taxes, and other imposts.

The federalist parties lacked the unity of purpose so characteristic of their opponents. Concerned primarily with local problems, and with national problems only in so far as these affected provincial interests, the federalists of one province acted independently, and sometimes in opposition to the federalists of another. But while the various federalist parties differed among themselves on many important points of intra-provincial and national policy, they were nevertheless united on several fundamental issues. First, the federalists in every province recognized the importance of the constitutional problem, and were as anxious as the unitaries to see the country stabilized politically. Secondly, they were agreed that the political organization of the country must not be accomplished at the expense of provincial home rule. Finally, they held that the authority of the central government should be limited to matters of national concern, such as foreign affairs, peace and war, the collection and management of national revenues. The nationalization of customs revenues and their distribution on a pro rata basis among the provinces found enthusiastic supporters everywhere, except in Buenos Aires whose control over such revenue dated from the Revolution. The issue of protection vs. free trade aroused a good deal of controversy, and here, too, Buenos Aires differed from the majority. Again, contrary to the wishes of Buenos Aires, the federalists in the Litoral provinces insisted upon having the Paraná river open to foreign navigation. Frequently the provinces which suffered most from economic dislocation clamored for a national solution of their problems.

At no time during the Constituent Congress did the federalists succeed in formulating a consistent political and economic program.

When the Congress convened towards the end of 1824 in Buenos Aires neither the principles nor the implications of federalism as a political and economic doctrine were at all clear. The provinces came to the Congress hoping for a settlement of the constitutional question as would not only confirm the political *status quo* evolved in 1820, but mark out the basic lines of future development. The question of political stabilization was uppermost in the minds of the deputies, but problems of an economic and financial nature were equally urgent. In the few intervening years between 1820 and the opening of the Congress economic conditions in many provinces had gone from bad to worse. The picture painted by Manuel Antonio Acevedo, deputy from Catamarca, applied not only to his own province but to others as well.

> Fate [said the deputy], has brought about in Catamarca an
> ominous change. . . . Whether it is because of the extremely
> adultered currency, which has burdened these regions ever
> since the deplorable dissolution of the state, or because of foreign
> competition in all markets . . . Catamarca has had to stand by
> helplessly, while its agriculture is primitive and costly, its
> industry without consumers . . . and its commerce by now almost
> non-existent.

Catamarca was not even able to pay the living expenses of its representatives in Buenos Aires. Misiones, Santiago del Estero, and other provinces in the Interior were in a similar position. The Constitutional Committee of the Congress to which the question of the representatives' salaries was referred argued that the provinces should be able to bear the expense, first, because the prospects of economic revival had improved considerably with the termination of the war against Spain, and second, because the provinces had appropriated revenues once belonging to the state. To the provinces these arguments must have sounded hollow (the representative of Misiones considered them insulting) for the prospects of economic expansion were not as bright as the Committee liked to believe, nor were the provinces receiving their full share of the Confederation's revenue. The reasoning of the Constitutional Committee consisted in generalizing the experience of Buenos Aires, and the reasoning was therefore specious. It revealed how profoundly the unitary leaders misunderstood both the nature and scope of the problem facing the provinces. The war of emancipation was neither the only nor even the most important cause of the economic ills of the Interior. The real cause was emancipation itself, and the consequent separation of Buenos Aires from the rest of the country. The Constitutional Committee's faith in the economic resurgence of the Interior following the termination of the war against Spain was baseless, as the economic situation of the provinces amply proved. There the struggle was not against the ravages of war nor against a wasteful administration, but against the strangling effects of foreign and *porteño* competition. The provinces believed, not without reason, that Buenos Aires gained much of its wealth at the expense of the country. Were they not entitled to a share of this wealth? Indeed, the basic task of the Constituent Congress was to set up a political system which would assure a more equitable distribution of the national dividend. The very life of the Constituent Congress as well as of the regime it endeavored to establish depended upon carrying out this task.

That the Congress failed to carry it out was perhaps to be expected. The majority of the Congress followed the leadership of the national government rather than the instructions of their constituents. And the political and economic program of the national government practically ignored the demands of the provinces. Nor is this surprising. The demands of the provinces not only ran counter to some of the major principles of the unitary doctrine but threatened to undermine the economic position of those classes whose interests the unitary party championed.

For one thing the unitary party was traditionally opposed to protectionism. So far from heeding the demand of the provinces for higher duties on commodities which could be produced at home, the unitaries leaned towards further liberalization of the commercial policies of Buenos Aires. At the same time the Congress and the national government assumed sole authority in the formulation of foreign commercial policies. So the revenues derived from customs duties were brought under the national government's control. But the nationalization of customs duties was only the first step towards the solution advocated by the provinces. That solution called for the distribution of the proceeds among the provinces. The unitary party refused to take this next step. For it was clear that the distribution of customs revenues among the provinces was incompatible with the unitarian doctrine of centralization. A national government financially dependent upon the generosity of the provinces would of necessity remain politically impotent. On the other hand, the unitary solution which would place all revenues recognized as national under the unconditional control of the central government could not but arouse strong opposition in the provinces. Together with the nationalization of the city of Buenos Aires such an arrangement would not only enormously increase the political power of the national government, but would leave the economic supremacy of Buenos Aires intact. In an effort to placate the provinces the unitaries argued that the establishment of a national capital in Buenos Aires would destroy the economic and political power of the province of Buenos Aires. Whether deliberately or not what the unitaries failed to see was that the country was less afraid of the province than of the city of Buenos Aires. This was made clear by Salta's representative, Juan Ignacio Gorritti, who opposed the federalization of Buenos Aires on the ground that as the center of the nation's resources the city would attract wealth from the provinces. Gorritti was only voicing the attitude of the provinces, for the provinces had been complaining of the concentration of wealth in Buenos Aires ever since the establishment of the viceroyalty. Had the national government been willing to open the Paraná river to foreign navigation thereby deflecting a portion of the nation's overseas commerce to the provinces it would have probably allayed a good deal of the suspicion and fear of the provincial governments. But on this question as on so many others the unitary party was unwilling and unable to make concessions. Lacking the political support of the majority of the population it was essential for the unitary regime, still in process of organization, to exercise as rigid a control as possible over the economic and financial resources of the country. It was mainly for this reason that the unitary leaders in the Constituent Congress remained deaf to the protests and entreaties of the few representatives who took the instructions of their constituents seriously.

The Congress of Buenos Aires was a constituent assembly. Its primary task was the drawing up of a constitution, subject to the approval of the provincial legislatures. Yet, for nearly two years, the Congress postponed consideration of this fundamental problem. Early in April of 1826, i.e., after the Congress had been in session for fifteen months, President Rivadavia demanded immediate consideration of the constitution, for "nothing disturbed the provinces so much as the lack of a law which would delimit the powers and authority of the (central) government, and would at the same time guarantee their most valued rights. Such is the uniform demand of the people, and there is no reason why the representatives should disregard this demand." Nevertheless, it was not until September of 1826 that the constitutional debate got under way, and by that time the question lost much of its poignancy. For in the intervening twenty months of legislative activity the Congress had shown unmistakably its preference for the unitary political system. In nearly all its measures dealing with national problems the Congress had anticipated the outcome of the constitutional discussion. With the outcome well known in advance the interest of the provinces in the discussion could have been hardly more than academic.

President Rivadavia was not mistaken when in his letter of April 4 he called the Constituent Assembly's attention to the growing restlessness of the population. But he was mistaken in ascribing this restlessness to the Assembly's procrastination with respect to the constitutional question. Ever since the partition of Buenos Aires and the nationalization of the provincial capital, an act which was in patent contravention of the law of January 21, 1825, the provinces regarded the Congress with suspicion. They were anxious to do away with the Congress which far from reflecting the sentiments of the majority of the population had become instead an instrument of political oppression in the service of the unitary party. And when at last the constitution was submitted to the provinces, early in 1827, province after province refused to approve it. The unitary party acknowledged the defeat. The president resigned and the Constituent Congress voted its own dissolution. The provinces reverted to their pre-congressional status, eager to begin anew the task of the political organization of the country. But taught by bitter experience they were no longer willing to leave the question of the system of government to the discretion of a national congress. Acceptance of federalism as the basis of political organization became the *conditio sine qua non* of all interprovincial discussion. Argentina was a confederation of provinces *de facto,* and such it had to remain *de iure.* And the solution of the economic and financial problems facing the provinces had to be sought within the federalist framework.

2

In their conflict with the Unitarians of the city of Buenos Aires, the provincial Federalists called upon Juan Manuel de Rosas to lead them. A charismatic *caudillo,* Rosas won the support of a majority of the poor and of the middle class in the city and province of Buenos Aires. He also spoke for the provinces, because, as head of the Argentine Federation, he respected the independence of the provinces and their leaders. He reserved for himself a free hand in foreign affairs but left domestic questions to local *caudillos*. In addition, Rosas often heeded the economic complaints of the provinces, even offering their industries protection from foreign competition. In time the provincial regimes matured, grew more stable, and consequently less dependent upon Rosas. In the opinion of an English scholar, Henry S. Ferns, Rosas' formula eventually created the conditions for a "successful federal government."

Henry S. Ferns:
Britain and Argentina*

The Rosas régime . . . endured for more than twenty-one years. The modesty and moderation which attracted [Sir Woodbine] Parish's attention did not, however, become the leading characteristics of that régime. Rosas's political techniques and the institutions he developed were more typical of the twentieth than the nineteenth century. He preserved the institutions of government which had been designed by the liberals of the revolutionary period. Indeed, he was described as the restorer of the laws in order to distinguish him from what his party described as the anarchists, who had tried to destroy the constitutional foundations of society. But with Rosas neither the legislature nor even his cabinet were the respositories of final authority nor were they the architects of policy. At the beginning of his career Rosas had hung back from a public assumption of final authority and he had let others negotiate on his behalf and accept responsibility. At the end of his career he still employed the tactics of reluctance and remoteness. In January 1851, a year before his overthrow, the British Minister reported that Rosas had not seen his Foreign Minister for more than two years. At the height of the political terror of 1841-2 he told the British Minister that he did not know what was happening nightly in Buenos Aires and in the military prison at Santos Lugares. When, in response to the British Minister's protests, he visited Buenos Aires, he professed to be shocked by what he had learned about the wholesale killing of the opposition then in progress. It is, perhaps, a sufficient comment to say that the political murders ceased once he had personally received the British protest.

* From Henry S. Ferns, BRITAIN AND ARGENTINA IN THE NINETEENTH CENTURY, by permission of the Clarendon Press, Oxford.

Like a skilful monarch Rosas left much formal authority and nearly all the details of government to subordinates, whom he could change according to whim or circumstance. Power he retained in his own hands so that the Provincial Assembly of Buenos Aires, the cabinet, the staff of the Army, the Navy, and the militia, the Police, and his secret political society, the Mazorca, were all instruments for his use, and none of them, save perhaps the Mazorca, was a source of policy or of decision. There can be little doubt that Rosas willed it so. Repeatedly during his career he appeared before the people as a reluctant leader. His favourite device in any difficulty was a threat to retire, and in fact he did retire at the end of his first term of office. But he always managed to acquire greater power after each threat of retirement, whether he carried it out or not. He was convinced that the Argentine Republic 'could not be governed by European methods,' by which he meant that no power of policy-making could be left to the legislature and that it should have no influence upon the personnel or path of the Government. Its business was to register popular assent and to strengthen the hand of authority. Elections served the same purpose. They were not conceived of as a social device for establishing a government for a limited period of time and for limited purposes. Rosas asked for the widest powers to serve the most general purposes. When the Provincial Assembly voted him dictatorial powers for five years in March 1835, they did so for two purposes: firstly, to save and defend the Roman Apostolic and Catholic religion and, secondly, to defend the Argentine Confederation. Not content with receiving dictatorial powers from the Assembly by a vote of thirty-one out of thirty-three (the two voting against him were his brother and his business partner, who out of an excess of delicacy voted for Rosas's cousin Nicolás Anchorena), he held a plebiscite, which ratified the action of the Assembly by 9,320 votes to 4.

The original source of Rosas's power was the gaucho militia which he had commanded for many years prior to his emergence on the political stage. We have already observed how this militia was employed to defeat the party of Rivadavia which depended upon the regular army. Rosas employed the militia again to displace his successor General Balcarce when that unfortunate man permitted liberal elements to gain too much authority in his Goverment during the years 1832-3. But Rosas did not rely exclusively upon the gaucho militia. Indeed, in the end the militia and the regular army which he built up after the dissolution of Lavalle's forces came to occupy a subordinate place in his apparatus of power. Rosas had always inclined strongly towards the Church as a bulwark against liberal courses, so much so that British Ministers in

Buenos Aires frequently referred to Rosas's supporters as the Apostolical Party. Parish reported in 1831 that Rosas's Government was pursuing an active policy of paying priests, erecting new parishes, building churches, and rebuilding old ones. One British Minister, at least, did not regard the clerical side of Rosas's policy with so much indulgence as Parish. Hamilton, who served in Buenos Aires while Rosas was establishing his dictatorship, spoke of the Governor's supporters as 'the bigoted and besotted remnant of the old Spanish dominion', and he described 'some of his alterations . . . [as] far from being improvements [and] calculated rather to restore and perpetuate . . . uncivilized manners and mental prostration . . . namely the revival of the bull fight, and the re-opening of the convent of the Dominicans'. There was as much of design as of piety in Rosas's policy, for he was firmly Erastian. One of his last and, perhaps, fatal political encounters was with the Holy See. In 1851 he emerged the victor in a trial of strength with Count Bessi, Archbishop of Canopo, a delegate sent from Rome to assert the Church's authority in the selection of a new bishop and the disciplining of an old one.

In order to buttress his power originally acquired through the agency of the gaucho militia, Rosas developed a political party operating directly among and upon the populace both as a means of expressing enthusiasm and suppressing the lack of it. All the British representatives in Buenos Aires agreed in their observation that Rosas was supported by a 'majority of the middle and lower classes of the inhabitants, both of the Capital, and of the Province of Buenos Aires'. One representative described the Province as one of the 'Democracies of the purest, but of the lowest description', and another declared that the régime excited little enthusiasm among those 'of any rank and consideration in society'. In order to bring this support of the lower strata to bear there was brought into being the secret political society, the Mazorca. This organization acted to stimulate mass enthusiasm by such devices as making obligatory under pain, not of official but of popular reprisal, the wearing of the crimson colour of the Rosas party. The Mazorca selected and killed the enemies or supposed enemies of the régime in moments of crisis such as that which existed during the French and again during the Anglo-French intervention. The Argentine Foreign Minister once admitted that 'in these cases the Police are as much afraid as any other person, or as I am'. The Mazorca even imposed itself upon the armed forces to the extent that on one occasion the guards at the Fort stopped the British Minister and denied him entry because he did not wear a crimson emblem. On that occasion Hamilton seized the opportunity to insist that British subjects were entitled and indeed bound by Treaty to maintain political neutrality, and he secured an apology from the Government which subsequently was interpreted not merely as the immunity of a diplomat but as a guarantee to British subjects of liberty to abstain from political demonstrations.

Rosas, of course, controlled the press and the organs of public information. He was aware of the advantages of employing competent journalists and propagandists to place the case for the régime before not only the Argentine people but those foreigners both at home and abroad who were interested in the politics of the River Plate. An Italian immigrant scholar, Pedro de Angelis, emerged as the most persuasive and learned apologist for the régime. de Angelis sought to explain Rosas simply by presenting to the world the history of Argentina. His *Archivo Americano* is a permanent contribution to any serious consideration of Argentine development. But de Angelis leaves the impression of being a sophisticated European whose racial and national memories had rendered him impervious alike to enthusiasm or indignation and who could see nothing novel or horrible in the history of Buenos Aires or anything attractive or enlightened in the activities and objectives of Rosas's liberal critics. That Rosas should have abandoned not only the plans but the hopes of universal education and that he should have impoverished and controlled the University of Buenos Aires in the interests of economy and the Roman Catholic Church did not seem crimes to a man who set his sights as low as de Angelis.

Rosas's propaganda was prepared for two classes of consumers. de Angelis presented the serious case, which was based upon an experience of man and particularly man on the pampas in the first half of the nineteenth century. In essence de Angelis, like Rosas, argued that the policies of the régime were necessities springing from the ungovernable wickedness of man and society. The popular case was stated otherwise in glaring black and white. Rosas and his allies in the Argentine Confederation manned the armed fortress of righteousness. This armed camp was beset by criminals who appeared in various guises sometimes as Frenchmen, atheists, North Americans, liberals, monarchists, old Spaniards, and foreigners. These criminals, though numerous and dangerous, were but the allies, however, of a comprehensive class of the most debased, treacherous, and insinuating murderers who ever threatened an ordered Christian community, namely, the vile unitarians, a misbegotten band of lying, libellous, cut-throats who wished to seize the Government for the purpose of oppressing the humble folk who worked in Buenos Aires and the free and noble

plainsmen of Buenos Aires Province. Not only this. Having seized
Buenos Aires they would impose upon the other provinces a rule
even more oppressive than that with which they would afflict
Buenos Aires itself. Like any effective propaganda the arguments
of the Rosista journalists and pamphleteers contained a kernel of
truth. There *was* a contradiction between the professions of Rosas's
critics and their actions. Parish once described the unitarian party
as 'in general a brawling, worthless set of unemployed Officers and
broken Speculators'. But the passage of time rendered the stereo-
types of Rosas's propaganda flat and ineffective. By the time of his
overthrow, the memories of Dorrego's martyrdom and Lavalle's
revolt were dim. Even the memory of the French intervention was
not green enough to dazzle the popular vision.

Rosas belonged to that class of politician which specializes
in bold simple alternatives in order both to get power and to keep
a free hand for its exercise. He always tended to suggest that the
alternative to Rosas was chaos. And he was widely believed. As
late as 1851 the British Minister, Henry Southern, as cool an
observer as one could encounter, reported to Palmerston:

> It is not wise to judge lightly the motives of a man who
> has discovered the means of governing one of the most turbulent
> and restless People in the World, and with such success that,
> though there is much cause for complaint, and not a little
> discontent, still the death or fall for General Rosas would be
> considered by every man in the Country as the direst misfortune.
> It certainly would be the signal of disorder and of intestine
> quarrels which could reduce the Country to misery.

By the time Southern wrote these words, Rosas was no longer
the indispensable alternative to chaos. He had created the conditions for his own suppression. When he swore to defend the Argentine Federation he had undertaken to respect the independence of
the Argentine provinces, and by that fact to acknowledge a sever-
ality of authorities within the Republic. Rosas assumed that each
provincial Governor would share his vision of a federal state, would
not strive to assert an authority outside the boundaries of his own
province, and would give to the Governor of Buenos Aires a free
hand in foreign affairs. Eventually Rosas's conditions for successful federal government were realized. The unitarian politicians
and armies were rooted out of the provinces. The economic complaints of provinces like Mendoza were given a hearing, and protection from foreign competition was accorded to some of their
industries.

As the provincial régimes grew stronger and more stable

tion, the already sparse population was dispersed along valleys and river banks. The trend toward urbanization which played such a fundamental role on the coast did not extend to the interior. Here few forces drew people together in cities. The provincial capitals, invariably towns established during the Spanish conquest, met the modest administrative and commercial needs of the area. Except for the special cases of Mendoza and Tucumán, they expanded no more rapidly than the surrounding countryside. The extraordinary growth of the coastal cities caused the overall proportion of rural population to fall from three-quarters in 1869 to less than one-half in 1914. But in all the interior provinces except Tucumán the rural population (classified as living in settlements of less than two thousand inhabitants) numbered between 70 and 85 per cent of the total.

The railroads did bring about an increase in commerce, mining, and agricultural production, and, as a result, a few secondary centers arose in the interior after 1900, but there was nothing to compare with the spread of towns on the coast. The 1914 census clearly illustrated the extent of the division. Outside of the federal capital, the urban population of the province of Buenos Aires had increased since the previous census (1895) from 61 towns with 316,000 inhabitants to 147 towns with 1,120,000 inhabitants. On a smaller scale, the same development occurred in Santa Fe, Entre Ríos, Corrientes, and Córdoba, and, as might be expected, in Tucumán and Mendoza. Elsewhere, the capitals—usually containing 10 to 20 per cent of the provincial population—provided almost the only exception to a rural environment dominated by farms and small villages. Besides the city of San Juan, that province boasted only two small towns. In the extreme northwest, Jujuy's urban population numbered 15,000, divided among the capital and three towns. Even Santiago del Estero possessed only three towns besides the capital, a total urban population of 35,000.

The cities and towns of the interior provided an accurate reflection of the colonial past, not only in numbers but also in composition of population, class structure, way of life, social customs, and intellectual activities. Here little had changed since the eighteenth century, when the decline of Potosí's silver wealth and the emergence of the port of Buenos Aires began to cast a shadow over the interior. While French ideas, Italian blood, and English capital inundated the coast, the impact of European influences in the interior was limited to Mendoza and Tucumán. Elsewhere, except for migrants from Chile and Bolivia, foreigners added little to the population. As a result, the growth that occurred in the interior came largely from natural increase. In these provinces large families with an average of four to six children continued to predominate, unaffected by the contemporary trend toward smaller families in the coastal cities. San Juan, Tucumán, Jujuy, and Santiago del Estero boasted the highest birth rates in the nation—between thirty-nine and forty-one per thousand inhabitants. Yet this was balanced by high rates of infant mortality and by a life expectancy that ranged from thirty-five to thirty-nine years in most of the northwestern provinces.

In the interior towns a traditionalist type of society continued to hold sway, untouched by the radical transformations taking place in the coastal region. The majority of provincial capitals remained small cities, built in accord with the plans of their conquistador-founders. By 1914 only two had expanded significantly: Tucumán with 91,000 inhabitants and Mendoza with 59,000. The rest had grown slowly: Salta, 28,000; Santiago del Estero, 23,000; San Juan, 17,000; San Luis, 15,000; Catamarca, 13,000; and La Rioja and Jujuy with 8,000 each. Although size was not the whole story, these figures suggest severe limitations on any efforts to bring progress, change, or prosperity to provincial capitals. The smallness of the urban center placed effective checks on educational facilities, community services, local revenues, and opportunities for exchange, consumption, or advancement.

All provincial capitals were founded and continued to exist as centers of administration and trade. These cities controlled large, sparsely settled territories, as in colonial times, and provided the only markets for the exchange of goods. Yet in the interior these functions remained modest. The governor of Buenos Aires might almost equal the president in power and prestige, while the size of Buenos Aires' provincial budget compared favorably with that voted by the national congress. But many a governor in the interior disposed of budgets smaller than those allocated by town councils on the coast and presided over the barest of provincial assemblies, law courts, and police forces. The gradual disappearance of local autonomy turned much of provincial government into a bureaucratic extension of national authority—posts to be sought as stepping stones to higher power or, more often, as comfortable, undemanding sinecures. The possibilities for commercial expansion were likewise limited. A mass of population which lived at little more than subsistence level topped by a tiny elite class provided neither producers nor consumers to swell the flow of trade through the interior.

Perhaps most resistant to change in these interior cities was the class structure. The descendants of the conquistadors still constituted the elite. For three centuries they had maintained a pure

lineage, marrying only within their class and rejecting any introduction of new blood within their society. Here the immigrant or
middle-class person found himself excluded from upper-class homes
even more effectively than on the coast. The very smallness of this
elite in the capitals, rarely numbering more than a few hundred
persons, led to considerable inbreeding, further aggravated by the
fact that the most ambitious and talented were almost invariably
drawn away to the coast by opportunities in government service,
the professions, or business. Symptomatic of the social cleavages
in interior cities was the arrangement found at La Rioja for the
biweekly evening band concerts in the plaza: the town's aristocracy
enjoyed an enclosure with garden, reclining seats, and promenade
in the center of the plaza from which the police barred all others.
Throughout the interior the arrangements for any ball or celebra-
tion always included a place from which the common people could
watch without being admitted to the festivities.

The elite of the interior supported itself from large landholdings, supplemented by occupations in government, Church, law,
medicine, and commerce. Compared with the *estancieros* and landowners of the pampas, those of the interior were poor. Rarely did
they expend either capital or effort on their holdings, and since land
was valued for social prestige and political influence at least as much
as for economic gain, owners contented themselves with paltry returns from grazing and tenant farming. This elite also monopolized
political power and, by the end of the nineteenth century, was satisfied to divide, rather than to fight over, political spoils. The
Church likewise continued to be a bulwark of the aristocracy, for
religion played a more vital role in the interior than on the "liberal"
coast. The position of the cathedral on the main plaza facing the
cabildo represented a very real share of temporal power carried
over from the days of the Spanish Empire. The membership and
control of convents, monasteries, private schools, the priesthood,
and all high Church offices belonged to the aristocracy, and, as
such, represented an important part of its economic and political
dominance. The favored profession of law, necessitating university
training in Buenos Aires, Córdoba, or, after the turn of the century,
in La Plata or Santa Fe, tended to draw off the talented toward the
coast. After a few years in these urban centers many preferred to
escape the provincial atmosphere permanently or at least to seek
a career in politics that might soon return them to the coast. Commerce still enriched many an aristocratic creole family, although
care was exercised not to dirty one's hands with the actual dis-
pensing of merchandise. The elite dominated the wholesale trade:
the import of fine European consumer goods; the sale of mules for

work in the Bolivian mines; the export of boots and sandals for the Indian miners; the shipment of agricultural and mineral raw materials to the coast; and the handling of carriages, woolen homespun, and such native manufactures which had not succumbed to outside competition.

The middle class in the interior had to be considered as a social rather than as an economic group, since many of its members were as well off as the sometimes impecunious but proud descendants of the conquistadors. As on the coast, this was a wholly urban class comprised mostly of foreigners. In size it was, if anything, smaller than the elite, and its position hardly justified the description "middle." Isolation, division, and transiency were its predominant characteristics. Rejected by the upper class, its members in turn held themselves aloof from the masses. Yet, unlike the elite which did form a powerful, well-integrated class closely linked by family ties, the middle-class inhabitants possessed no common bond beyond occasional national loyalties—an Italian mutual aid society, a Basque association, or a Syrian social center. Furthermore, few of the middle class developed any attachment to the particular capital or town in which they found themselves. Whether descendants of creoles or immigrants, or recent arrivals from Europe, their principal motivation was economic advance. For the moment they had no political power, and socially they had not arrived. Consequently, the drive was to gain acceptance and position through wealth wherever opportunity arose.

Retail commerce, technical services, and certain management functions provided occupations for the middle class. Every interior capital and town had its pharmacist, barber, and baker. The Andean cities usually boasted a handful of mining engineers and office managers of British companies. After the arrival of the railroad, most towns needed station managers, telegraphers, and dispatchers. Rare was the urban center that could not claim a French hotel keeper or a German merchant. The school systems, provincial courts, and administration added a corps of poorly paid teachers and clerks to this amorphous middle group. Most of the middle class were immigrant Spaniards and Italians, while after 1900 increasing numbers came from the Levant.

The urban lower class, as in colonial times, numbered 80 to 90 per cent of the city population and was composed of all those who labored with their hands, performed menial services, or otherwise did not qualify for the elite or middle classes. The amalgam of several centuries produced a dark-skinned yet thoroughly Europeanized individual who spoke—but rarely read—Spanish and bore little cultural or even racial resemblance to his Indian or Negro

ancestry. These were not a downtrodden people, but they sorely
lacked the education, sanitation, and nutrition to improve their
situation. Disease, unhealthy diets, economic stagnation, and a
rigid caste system bred a quiet, resigned, and indolent lower class.
Malaria and tapeworm were endemic in most of the northern provinces; goiter afflicted the inhabitants of Mendoza and Santiago del
Estero; and tuberculosis and influenza flourished, due to the inadequate housing and malnutrition. This class contributed in large
measure to the high infant mortality rates and the short life expectancy of the interior provinces. Here also starvation was far
more prevalent than on the meat- and grain-producing coast. Even
in the mountain valleys, Nature was a hard master, and the verdure
of irrigated farms and orchards only emphasized man's dependence
on water. More injurious than starvation was the constant malnutrition. Boiled corn or boiled rice constituted the universal diet of
the interior—not always in the tasty regional dishes now served in
porteño restaurants. Vegetables, fresh meat, and milk remained
beyond the reach of urban masses. The chewing of fresh sugar-
cane stalks and the excessive consumption of *caña,* or alcohol, frequently indicated the shocking lack of any other nourishment. In
the *puna* of the northwest, as in Bolivia, the chewing of coca leaves
was frequently all that made life endurable.

Urban residence provided access to more social services than
could be obtained in the country, but in the interior this advantage
was hardly significant. By the first decades of the twentieth century the interior capitals had no more than a handful of doctors,
and these were more than occupied with the 10 per cent of the
population who were well enough clothed, fed, and sheltered to
have a chance for recovery, and who could also afford to pay. Municipal and Church hospitals, as a general rule, provided little more
than a place to die, and no one entered them until all hope was lost.
The middle and upper classes had their own wells, collected rain-
water from their roofs, or in some capitals connected into municipal
water systems, but the poor relied on public wells or irrigation
ditches. Since few towns had any adequate means for disposing of
sewage, the incidence of typhoid fever and dysentery within the
lower class was high.

The Church was omnipresent in these provincial capitals, and,
even in a city as closely linked to the coastal economy as Córdoba,
its influence remained paramount. Yet its responsibility for the
well-being of the community had been reduced by national legislation in the 1880's, and reform elements which emerged in the 1890's
were unable to revive the Church's social mission until after World
War I. Eliminated from the public school system in 1884, supple-

mented by the state in matters of civil registers, marriages, and burials, and removed from overt political control, the Church became a conservative body struggling to preserve vestiges of its former glory. The wealth remained: in Córdoba the Church owned at least one-quarter of the city's real estate; in Catamarca its magnificent and imposing cathedral, built over a span of several decades beginning in the 1850's, contrasted strangely with the poor and backward urban center; in all the capitals it maintained large and frequently luxurious convents and monasteries. The masses and, above all, the women, supported the Church, but only in an occasional hospital or orphanage or among a few parish priests did one find the zeal and abnegation which had once spread the Catholic faith into the remotest regions of the continent.

The interior suffered from poor educational facilities, at least in comparison with the coast. Diligent efforts by Argentina's statesmen, led by Sarmiento himself, reduced the illiteracy rate from more than two-thirds in 1869 to a little over one-third by 1914, encouraged the building of primary schools by the provinces, established a secondary school system under the supervision of the national government, and created a university structure second to none in Latin America. But as with immigration, foreign investments, and living standards, the effect of these measures was overwhelmingly concentrated on the coast and in the cities of Buenos Aires, La Plata, Rosario, Santa Fe, and Córdoba. Decades of anarchy and civil strife, the poverty of provincial treasuries (aggravated by an inevitable tendency to consider education as the part most easily sacrificed in any budget), and the logical tendency of national authorities to place funds, teachers, and efforts in areas where obstacles seemed less staggering, robbed the interior of any fair share in Argentina's educational campaign. By 1914 only 48 per cent of school-age children attended school in Salta and Jujuy and 44 per cent in Santiago del Estero, as contrasted with 61 per cent in the city and province of Buenos Aires. Despite the legal requirement of school attendance through the age of fourteen, it was well into the twentieth century before many children of the lower class in the interior cities and towns completed more than a couple of years of instruction. Elementary education thus became largely the privilege of the middle class and the elite.

Although education was tuition-free, access to the secondary level in the interior was even more restricted than to the primary grades. By the last decades of the nineteenth century, *colegios* and normal schools had been established in each of the provincial capitals, but they were poorly attended in comparison to similar institutions on the coast. At least the normal school served the educational process by providing slightly trained men and women for the elementary school system. But the *colegio*'s emphasis on university preparation tended to limit attendance to the sons of the wealthy who had the time and opportunity to pursue the university studies of law and medicine. To fill the gap, the national government opened several secondary institutes in agronomy, animal husbandry and viniculture. Lower-class parents, however, lacked the resources to send their children through even these courses of study, while the middle classes aspired to the professions as the only path to success and status.

Investments, government expenditures, and intellectual opportunities similarly distinguished between two Argentinas: one of progress and development, the other of conservatism and stagnation. In Mendoza and Tucumán, French and Italian capital built several of the important wineries and sugar mills. But beyond that, the interior provinces had only unproven mineral resources to attract foreign investors. Silver, gold, and copper were exploited on a small scale in Catamarca and La Rioja. In Mendoza and Salta surface seepage indicated the presence of oil. Antimony, manganese, iron, lead, tungsten, and coal, along with marble and slate, were known to exist in varying quantities and qualities along most of the Andean chain and eastward as far as the Córdoba hills. But such prospects were overshadowed by the dazzling investment opportunities on the pampas. In view of the long and costly freight hauls to the coast, the legal wrangles surrounding all mining claims, and the inadequate supply of capital, machinery, and trained workers, it seemed simpler to buy coal and metals from Europe and oil and kerosene from the United States. To attain self-sufficiency in oil (as Argentina finally did early in the 1960's), to reach the remote coal deposits, or to develop a significant extraction of metallic ores would have required major investments and probably major sacrifices. For the moment neither the ruling elite nor British entrepreneurs saw any purpose in developing the interior's rich but distant potential. Only when oil was accidently struck at Comodoro Rivadavia on the coast in 1907 did the national government reserve certain subsoil rights to itself and subsequently create a federal oil agency. Even then, exploitation languished for another half century.

The interior provinces secured equally few benefits from government expenditures. The area suffered from a lack of taxable resources. Landowners ruled provincial councils even more absolutely in the interior than on the coast, and they refused to allow themselves to be burdened with fiscal demands. Commerce and the tiny middle class provided only a trickle of revenues from license, stamp, and produce taxes. In 1910 the budget for the province of Mendoza totaled 5 million pesos, for Santiago del Estero 3 million, for San Juan 1.5 million, and for La Rioja 0.3 million, at a time when the province of Buenos Aires was spending 38 million pesos. Provincial capitals received water systems at national expense, government-built railroads reached into the remoter provinces, and irrigation projects were discussed for several of the Andean provinces. But, as with education, appropriations for public works tended to favor areas that could show immediate benefits and results. Millions were spent (ironically by presidents and congressmen from the interior) to modernize the new federal capital, Córdoba received the bulk of irrigation funds, and an army of federal experts and engineers remained concentrated in the coastal cities.

It is almost superfluous to point to the intellectual desert in the interior. Many of Argentina's great men of letters and arts were born outside the coastal fringe, but almost without exception they were drawn to the city of Buenos Aires. A veritable flowering of artistic and intellectual potential during the first decades of the twentieth century contrasted with the occasional masterpieces of Sarmiento and Hernández in the nineteenth. But this spiritual and cultural achievement of nationhood was built on the porteño monoply of the country's talents. Provincial capitals remained oases where men of promise tried out their abilities, wrote and edited the daily or weekly newspapers, printed their verses, painted or composed while pursuing success in politics, law, or commerce. But only in Buenos Aires could these men find communion with kindred talents and the necessary contact with European ideas and models.

Life in the interior capitals moved in the leisurely pace of the colonial centuries. Hotels and restaurants were inferior and expensive. Amusements were few, limited to cockfighting and gambling, an occasional band concert in the plaza, or the gathering of upperclass men at the town's principal cafe for an evening of talk, billiards, or cards. May 25 was celebrated with fireworks, speeches, brightly lit houses, and the fresh whitewashing of buildings. A wedding or wake provided an excuse for dancing and drinking at all social levels, while many of the lower class lapsed into a drunken stupor each Sunday. Everywhere the condition of streets was abominable; they were almost always unpaved except for those near the central plaza. Electric street lights replaced the flickering tallow wicks in the main plaza and along a couple of the principal streets. But the power came from steam plants run on imported coal rather than from the energy of nearby mountain streams.

Beyond the provincial capitals and the infrequent secondary towns lived the 70 to 85 per cent of the population that provided the labor for the interior's agriculture and mining. There was no upper or middle class here save for an occasional patriarchal landowner who chose to live on his holdings, a wandering peddler, or a country storekeeper. The centuries apparently had stopped for the rural interior and for remote regions of the littoral such as Corrientes.

Even in the late nineteenth century Indians figured among the rural masses far more than porteños cared to admit. In Salta, Jujuy, Santiago del Estero, and Corrientes, pure-blooded Indian communities lived much as they had before the Spanish conquest, exposed only to occasional contacts with Argentine economy and society. The Quechua or Guaraní language, the diet of corn or potatoes, the dress, religion, and social customs had changed but little. The village economy was based on subsistence agriculture and raising goats and sheep. The Indian entered the mestizo-Hispanic environment only in the sugar fields of the northwest or in the lumber camps of the Chaco. From this brief exchange he acquired some superficial aspects of a new culture: a pair of pants or a shirt, a mirror or a hat, a fondness for cane alcohol, and an understanding of Spanish. Such limited acculturation did not immediately destroy the Indian way of life or the deep distrust of Hispanic and foreign peoples, but it facilitated eventual absorption within the formless lower class of rural Argentina.

Throughout most of the interior, however, the Indian element had blended into the mestizo lower class. From these people came the herdsmen, gauchos, miners, tenant farmers, contract laborers, peons, and squatters of the interior. After 1900 coastal Argentina also began to draw on this poorly paid, ignorant labor force to help with cereal harvests, railroad building, and construction projects. The census of 1914 registered a marked increase in migration toward the coast from La Rioja, Catamarca, and San Luis—amounting to as much as 30 per cent of the population in those provinces.

The same aspects of malnutrition, poor housing, and lack of ambition that characterized the urban workers in the interior afflicted the rural lower class. Social services of government and Church totally bypassed them. Not until well into the twentieth century would schools reach out into the remote regions and make the white smocks of school children a familiar sight along the paths and roads of rural Catamarca, Santiago del Estero, or Corrientes. As in pre-Conquest times, medical care was in the hands of healers whose art alternated between an expert use of native herbs and a mystical faith in strange concoctions of dried monkey brains, powdered snake skins, and the like. Religion frequently combined a fanatic acceptance of Catholicism with the superstitions, deities, and lore of Indian heritage. Promiscuity and loose family attachments helped to blend the racial strains but contrasted sharply with the isolation of middle- and upper-class women.

Such, therefore, were the aspects of a world which existed beyond the coastal cities, the pampas, and the railroad net of late-nineteenth-century development. In the capitals, towns, and countryside of the interior provinces and even in the remote regions of the littoral lived a people almost a century removed in tradition, culture, and way of life from the coast. Gradually the coast would absorb this other Argentina. Better communications would link the nation together. Economic opportunities or military conscription would draw individuals to the coast and open their eyes to a different existence. Other provinces would follow the lead of Córdoba, Tucumán, and Mendoza and prosper on the basis of integration with the coastal economy. Urban centers in the interior would expand. Even the countryside would finally feel the effect of roads, schools, dams, doctors, and priests. The gap, nevertheless, was not one that could be closed easily or quickly, and the dichotomy between porteño and provincial, betwen coast and interior, between urban and rural, remains to trouble Argentina today.

4

Out of the Unitarian triumph in 1853 there emerged a remarkable era of growth and development. With capitalism as their economic pattern and funds and know how from Great Britain, the Unitarian leaders of Argentina linked the provinces to Buenos Aires by a system of railroads, claimed the best lands for their great estates, and imported immigrants from Europe to make the land productive. To many Argentines, therefore, the victory of city over country proved profitable and providential. But, the new leaders converted themselves into an oligarchy of cattle and grain barons who, in their haste to modernize Argentina and to wax rich in the process, corrupted themselves and the national political fiber and subjugated the entire nation to their will. José Luis Romero, an Argentine scholar, writes that blind class interest dominated the thinking of the oligarchy which, because of its betrayal of the liberal republican ideals of 1853, eventually succumbed to the attacks of the Radical Party, spokesman of the immigrant and of popular democracy in the early twentieth century.

José Luis Romero:
A History of
Argentine Political Thought*

It was in politics that the old ideals of liberalism fell victim to class interests. As early as the first days of the struggle for economic aggrandizement, the oligarchy learned that if it should succeed in retaining power, it might hope for important benefits and attractive privileges. But the rulers realized that no political instrument should slip out of their hands, and they prepared to do whatever might be necessary, with or against principle, to strengthen their positions. From this political attitude, fed by its easy justification as patriotism, was born what would be called shortly after 1880 the "unicato" (one-party rule), and still later, the "Organization."

Julio A. Roca and Miguel Juárez Celman were the pre-eminent leaders of the *unicato*. This was an elemental political system in which one could distinguish the former tendencies toward native authoritarianism, now restrained by the strong brakes of constitutional order; and it was a system that led to both a solemn affirmation of juridical principles and to their constant, systematic violation by fraud and violence. The core of the system was an absolutist conception of the executive branch, determined perhaps by the political instability of the country, but strengthened by the desire for centralization shown by Roca and Juárez Celman and, to a lesser degree, by those who followed them in the presidency, such as Pellegrini, Quintana, and Figueroa Alcorta. Within this concept, republicanism was negated in various ways by the decisive influence exercised over politics by the president of the republic. Voluntarily or involuntarily, all the devices for controlling the institutional life of the country were in his hands, not excluding those that ought

* Reprinted from A HISTORY OF ARGENTINE POLITICAL THOUGHT, by José Luis Romero; introduction and translation by Thomas F. McGann with permission of the publishers, Stanford University Press. © 1963 by the Board of Trustees of the Leland Stanford Junior University.

to have ensured a federalist form of government. As Congressman
Olmedo wrote in a letter to Juárez Celman, referring to the kind
of authority that General Roca was already exercising in 1882:

> Yesterday it was the province of Corrientes; Entre Ríos fol-
> lowed; today it is Santiago del Estero that is falling or will fall
> under the sword of the Consul, who aims to hold undivided
> power, no doubt in order to be Caesar, at least for six years. An
> error! A fatal error! It is not possible for a government to exist
> without public opinion and legal machinery, but only his per-
> sonality and power are keeping General Roca in office. What is
> the point of this boss rule, which is full of peril, makes his
> friends uneasy, and worse yet, renders his authority useless
> against the day when he will need it? If he wishes power, is it
> not his in its highest and most ample form, that given him by the
> laws, that with which he is armed by the constitution? Must he
> be the cause of soldiers taking up their *machetes*? Does he need
> the cheap words of mercenary reporters to prop up his authority,
> which no one disputes and which we all wish to fortify legally?

If a co-regionalist, ashamed of the obsequiousness demanded
by the president, could make such complaints, it is not strange
that opponents painted the situation in still darker colors. Some
years later, during the troubled days preceding the revolution of
1890, Joaquín Castellanos would tell a meeting of the Civic Union:

> National life is paralyzed as far as the functioning of its estab-
> lished organs is concerned. An all-encompassing centralism such
> as could not have been imagined by the most fanatical defenders
> of the Unitarian regime has been substituted for our constitu-
> tional forms of government. The president of the republic is
> exercising *de facto* total public power. He has in his hands the
> reins of municipal authority, the keys to the banks, tutelage over
> the provincial governors, control of the voices and the votes of
> the members of congress, and he even manages the judicial
> machinery. Furthermore, he has become what is called the boss
> of the ruling party, a party whose members are passive bodies
> who neither deliberate nor decide anything nor exercise public
> functions, and who have become accustomed to begging as favors
> from the boss the positions they rightfully should attain at the
> polls. The president makes *de facto* use of the Special Executive
> Powers which were placed in the constitution because of earlier,
> notoriously unhappy events of our political life, despite the fact
> that the document provides that those who wield these powers
> in favor of any one provincial governor should be considered as
> infamous traitors to the nation. No one has expressly asked him
> to exercise the Special Powers, but without intent they have been
> surrendered to the head of the executive branch by the tacit re-
> nunciation which other branches of the government have made
> of their attributes and prerogatives.

These complaints and diatribes reveal the interior dynamics of the *unicato*, which not only established itself as a centralized regime to the degree required by the defense of its privileges, but became more and more exclusive, as though moved by a blind force that impelled the oligarchy to confide *de facto* dictatorial power to a savior capable of containing the threats that loomed in the distance. Thus, against all logic, the elite began to demand unanimous support from its own followers in the legislatures, even to the point of humiliating the representatives, which, at the same time, humiliated all representative assemblies. As Osvaldo Magnasco said in 1891:

> The Argentine congress, during two administrations and
> throughout the last ten years, has let itself become a vassal to
> the pernicious influence of the chief executive. Congress has
> accepted political slavery and has worked to bring about its cur-
> rent loss of prestige, which demeans a body that, in these hours
> of unparalleled trials, could have rallied support and the force
> necessary to make it a focus of resistance, as in other times it
> has been the solid and unmovable bulwark against the excesses of
> insolent and autocratic executives.

And who could be surprised at this situation if the most enlightened men were corroded by skepticism and if there was none among the oligarchy to preserve the traditional devotion to the people that had nurtured the republican fervor of Sarmiento or of Mitre? Eduardo Wilde, a liberal *por excelencia*, did not hesitate to write these revealing words: "The candidate whom General Roca designates will be the president. The General has made himself responsible for this course and he must accept the honor with a clear conscience: he has gained it legitimately. . . . It seems as though General Roca must have an oracle hidden some place, which puts the most patriotic ideas into his head every night and places the most just and proper words in his mouth." And once when he was asked to define universal suffrage, Wilde replied: "It is the triumph of universal ignorance."

This opinion of the right to vote explains the imperturbable boldness with which the government and party officials arranged and carried out electoral frauds. Mitre, who had remained on the margins of the oligarchy as an illustrious member of the old republican elite, said at the political meeting of April 13, 1890: "Since the lists of registered voters are falsified and the polling places are closed by fraud as the result of this plot by administration officials against popular sovereignty, the people are divorced from their government, excluded from public life, and expelled from the protection of the constitution." A full-scale system was rigged up to dominate the political situation in every part of the country, and no method was left unexploited to ensure victory. Venality, tricks, fraud, and force were all exercised both by hired thugs and by government forces. The popular Argentine folk-figure, Juan Moreira, was in reality nothing more than one of the bravos who put themselves at the service of the government in order to win elections. While public faith was being insolently violated in every hamlet and city ward, government circles continued dreaming about the uncontainable progress of the country, the unending growth of national wealth, and the perfecting of the juridical devices needed for orderly national life. Nor were solemn and emphatic declarations lacking, such as that made by President Quintana, the most autocratic of the leaders produced by the oligarchy, when he took office in 1904: "Far from being timid, I vehemently desire peaceful, democratic activity for my country, and one of my greatest ambitions is to evoke debate between opposing doctrines and to preside from the presidency with impartiality over the encounter of two great, organic parties."

Surely nobody was confused by these words: the convictions behind them were notorious. The oligarchy was certain that it was not facing an organized opposition but, rather, a heterogeneous mass that had scarcely begun to outline its vague aspirations. Juárez Celman maintained that a party fit to govern could not be created by the masses, and Mitre himself declared that the Radical Civic Union lacked the characteristics necessary for such a function. The attitude reflected in this conviction could therefore be only that of ensuring the monopoly of power to the oligarchy, which was convinced that it comprised a "party of government," that is, a group of men who knew what they wanted and what suited their interest.

DEFENSE OF THE OLIGARCHY'S INTERESTS

If, in politics, the oligarchy displayed blind conservatism—blind and suicidal—it maintained only a portion of the dignity of its principles in accomplishing its ideals of economic progress and reform. Before long, the oligarchy saw that the enrichment of the country and of its own members could get out of hand, but it lacked the austerity to orient its steps toward the sole objective of the general welfare of the country. Thus it pursued its policies with cool calculation, and it did not waver in disowning its traditional principles in order to benefit its new privileges.

The oligarchy's great treasure, its starting point in the race to riches, was the land, of which its members possessed vast expanses. By 1880, almost all usable public land had been taken up, but the landowners were obtaining only slim returns from their property. It should be said that the enormous task that the oligarchy accomplished through the government toward modernizing the country and incorporating recent technical advances was stimulated and guided by the intention to obtain the increment of wealth from these expanses of land. It was not only essential to import laborers who would work the land; it was imperative to make it productive, and above all to bring it near to the centers of distribution. Thus the oligarchy began to stimulate immigration and to construct numerous public works, seeking to have the benefits of such measures redound on their lands.

The immense majority of the immigrants remained localized in the Littoral region, and the public works doubtless benefited the areas where the return was greatest. But to achieve those results the oligarchy dispensed with systematic planning and did not hesitate to concede to foreign capital immoderate advantages, which compromised the national patrimony. While it may have been necessary to grant concessions for the construction and exploitation of specific services, the terms offered to the consortia that agreed to do the work were usually extremely advantageous, even when there were no equivalent risks. The construction of certain railway lines brought awards of enormous tracts of land to the concessionaires; even so, the generosity of the capitalists who were risking their money seemed to be admirable.

In 1887, General Roca, speaking in London after a banquet that was offered to him by the investment house of Baring Brothers, said: "I have always had the greatest affection for England. The Argentine Republic, which will one day be a great nation, will never forget that its present state of progress and prosperity is due, in great part, to English capital, which does not fear distance and which has flowed into Argentina in substantial quantities in the form of railroads, streetcar lines, settlements of colonists, the exploitation of minerals, and various other enterprises." But these English capital investments took the form of loans on which it was necessary to pay interest. Argentina's foreign debt quickly reached fabulous figures that threatened the financial stability of the State and its very autonomy. In 1896, Juan Bautista Justo, the founder of the Socialist Party in Argentina, wrote in an article in *La Nación:*

> English capital has done what their armies could not do. Today our country is tributary to England. Every year many millions

of gold pesos leave here and go to the stockholders of English enterprises that are established in Argentina. No one can deny the benefits that the railroads, the gas plants, the streetcars, and the telegraph and telephone lines have brought to us. No one can deny to English companies the right to possess vast expanses of land in our country, since the Argentine lords of the land have the right to live on their income wherever it most pleases them. But the gold that the English capitalists take out of Argentina, or carry off in the form of products, does us no more good than the Irish got from the revenues that the English lords took out of Ireland. The money might as well be blown up or sent to the bottom of the sea. We also suffer from absentee capital; without opposing its coming, we ought not to regard as a favor the establishment in the country of additional foreign capital. It is this capital that largely prevents us from having sound money and obliges our financial market to submit to a continuous drain of hard currency. May capital come in all good time—but the capitalists ought to come with it. . . .

Despite the activity of this capital in the country, the servicing of the loans increasingly unbalanced the financial structure, while at the same time the abundance of money rapidly created a climate favorable to business deals, especially to financial undertakings whose expansion was shown by the speculative enterprises entered into by large segments of *porteño* society. During 1889 and 1890 the stock exchange was the scene of feverish activity. "There," Julián Martel wrote, "the cream of Buenos Aires society was mixed, so to speak, with the dross of the foreign newcomers, who were trying to disguise their origins." The speculative fever had in fact penetrated all levels of society, and it was not long before it led to the economic cataclysms that could be foreseen as a consequence of sudden enrichment in the uncontrolled "game of the millions." The State and private persons suffered grave losses, which, of course, had an impact on the entire economy. The oligarchy, on the brink of disaster, tried to ride out the storm by protecting foreign credit, in defense, certainly, of the good name of the nation, but also with the hope of being able to count in the future as in the past on the support of foreign capital. Carlos Pellegrini, to whom fell the arduous task of leading the country after the crisis of 1890, said later:

When I became president of the republic, I was certain that with the resources which the country possessed at that moment, and as long as no new sources of income were obtained or developed, it would not be possible to service the foreign debt. But I believed that the credit of the nation was worth any sacrifice. Many people criticized me then for what I did. In the midst of the financial anguish, when there was not even money to pay government salaries, I sent the last peso to Europe to pay the interest on our debt for the period from October 1, 1890, to January 1891. Along

with the money to pay the interest—which pointed up what
sacrifices the government was capable of making in order to
maintain its credit—I sent Doctor de la Plaza to meet with the
committee of the Bank of England, which at that time had been
constituted under the name of the Baring Committee and was headed
by Baron Rothschild.

After some harsh lessons the country entered on a moderate
course. Without completely abandoning its program, the oligarchy
tried not to exceed the national economic potential, but since it
was important not to cut off foreign capital, the leaders wished to
strengthen confidence in the seriousness of the government and
planned, during the second presidency of General Roca, to unify
the nation's debts by putting up the customs revenues as security.
Without any doubt, the plan was too much of a compromise of
national rights, since it authorized foreign intervention in the supervision of national finances. It was violently rejected by the
public, and the government soon had to withdraw the proposal.
From then on, it became a mark of sound policy to try to limit
borrowing. In the end, prosperity began to return, and foreign
capital, sure of obtaining huge profits, began to flow in again. In
1908, Figueroa Alcorta was able to say:

> The balance sheet from our last harvest, our trade statistics and
> those representing the growth of our industries, in general, every
> factor relevant to the material progress of the country, demon-
> strate that the prosperity we have attained exceeds the most
> favorable forecasts, and that these labors to build a great nation,
> which are founded on the efforts of a hard-working and pro-
> gressive people, have an unshakable foundation and an extraordi-
> nary future.

In the same year, when announcing the slate of Socialist candidates, Justo said:

> Many of the great landlords do not even know where their prop-
> erties are located—land they bought at the laughable price of
> four hundred pesos per square league, which today is worth more
> than two hundred thousand pesos per league. The work of the
> bourgeoisie has been to increase the value of their lands by means
> of concessions and guarantees for railroad construction. They
> have propagandized for immigration by paying agents in Europe
> with public funds in order to attract laborers who would cultivate
> their fields and keep salaries down, a condition made possible only
> by the increase of available workers.

The accusation was valid. The oligarchy was working for the
country's material progress, but its objective was to satisfy its own
interests.

The oligarchy's conservatism was made categorically clear with the appearance of the first organized labor forces. In 1902, mindful of the spread of resistance to low salaries and to the surplus of workers, congress approved the Residence Law, basing it on a plan drawn up years earlier by Miguel Cané, the subtle humorist of *Juvenilia*. The law gave the government authority to expel foreigners who were active in provoking social conflict. At the same time, police repression increased. Demonstrations by workers were violently broken up, and the police furiously pursued the laborers who took part in the strikes that occurred frequently after 1904. In 1909 and 1910 labor agitation was renewed, and severely repressed. The anarchists' answer was to attempt to assassinate the chief of police of Buenos Aires, and a short time later they placed a bomb in the Colón Opera House. The government reacted immediately; in June 1910, congress voted the so-called Law of Social Defense, which applied severe measures to organized labor. Nonetheless, the men who made this answer to such a natural social development were the same men who had contributed toward endowing the country with legislation that was in other respects modern and progressive. . . .

VICISSITUDES OF LIBERALISM

The widening breach between liberal principles and democratic principles led the oligarchy to a crisis. Because of its attitude toward the creole-immigrant mass and because of its marked tendency to pull in and close its ranks, the oligarchy gradually weakened its foundations without most of its members noticing that fact. But not all of them failed to see the portents. Mitre deserves credit for having kept up the struggle against the antidemocratic trend; he saved his own reputation and, with him, other men later saved their names—men who once belonged to the oligarchy and were eminent representatives of its principles, but who came to have sharp insights into the formless political and social panorama of the republic. . . .

Thus liberal ideas—generous, humane, full of democratic understanding—flourished again in the oligarchy. And this trend influenced many men of strong moral fiber, to whom the divorce between progress and democracy had begun to be insupportable.

With its class consciousness weakened, and a breach opened in the ideological structure that supported it, the oligarchy lost its impetus and agreed to its own surrender. There was a unanimous demand for a law that would rectify the electoral system, and when

Roque Sáenz Peña came to power in 1910, he prepared to satisfy the demand, the justice of which was no longer doubted. He promptly sent to congress the draft of an electoral law establishing the secret, compulsory ballot, with representation for both majority and minority groups. At that time Sáenz Peña stated in a document of great significance:

> At this unique and decisive moment we are balancing the present and the future of our institutions. We have arrived at a point where our road divides into two distinct routes. Either we must proclaim ourselves incapable of developing a democratic system, which depends totally upon free suffrage, or we must do our job like Argentines, by solving the chief problem of our times despite the temporary special interests that now promise only unlimited arbitrary rule without future solutions to our ills.

Sáenz Peña well knew that the interests of the oligarchy were doomed by the approval of the law of secret and obligatory voting. But his appeal to patriotism was backed by threatening public opinion, while the oligarchy, for its part, had begun to lose faith in its exclusive right to govern a country that was growing and changing from moment to moment. So it happened that there was no force able to oppose approval of the law, which in 1912 was added to the institutional framework of the country as an effective instrument for perfecting its democracy.

As soon as the new electoral machinery began to function, the oligarchy lost its political strongholds. In 1916, the Radical Party candidate, Hipólito Irigoyen, became president of the republic. The conservative groups continued to hold some of their positions in certain provinces, but their strength decreased visibly before the drive of the new, free forces. The ideology of the elite was by this time only a shadow of its former liberal conservatism, impoverished as it was by the narrow, limited ambitions of the most reactionary groups. From this ideological posture it was not difficult to make the transition to what was called "nationalism" —the adaptation of the fascist ideology that began to take root among some of these people after 1922.

Nonetheless, the liberal tradition was not entirely lost; it was included in parts of the diffuse program of the Radical Party and was embodied principally in some men who repudiated the excessive personalism that could be noted among the Radicals after they came to power. But it was among other men and other parties that liberalism again bore fruit and regained constructive force by being adapted to new demands and new realities. It was Lisandro de la Torre, the continuer of the inspired work of Aristóbulo del Valle and the founder of the Progressive Democratic Party, who became the bold leader of the march toward material progress and civic betterment. And in the end it was Alfredo L. Palacios who tried to infuse into Socialist thought whatever could be preserved that was at the same time alive and creative in the liberal tradition and compatible with basic Socialist ideology.

5

In 1916 the Conservative oligarchy, heir to the men of 1853 who defeated Rosas and the Federalists, relinquished its political control of Argentina to the Radical Party. Led by Hipólito Irigoyen, a taciturn politician who governed with a firm hand, the Radicals dictated policy until 1930. Unfortunately for the provinces and ultimately for the entire nation, the Radicals represented no drastic change from the past. An urban party of shopkeepers, bureaucrats, white-collar employees, and workers of recent immigrant origin, the Radicals made no changes in economic policy and quickly mastered the rules of the politics of corruption and cynicism. Nothing altered the traditional hegemony of city over provinces. In 1930 the military toppled Irigoyen's second administration which, graft-ridden and paralyzed by the economic crisis, fell in a matter of hours. Behind the military, says Felix Weil, an Argentine economist of that day, stood the old landed gentry, eager to defend the economic formulas of earlier years.

Felix J. Weil:
Argentine Riddle*

Argentine politics have always been permeated with graft. What induces an Argentine to choose politics as a career is not alone the prestige commonly associated with public office, but the

many privileges inherent therein. He acquires *fuero*, that is, privileges denied the hoi polloi, to an extent that sets him above the
average citizen as the old Indian caste system set the Brahmins
above the "untouchables." His is the delightful sensation of merely
having to flash his genuine gold official badge to make police officers
jump to attention and government employees spring to their feet.
The *chapa blanca* (white license plate) on his car gives him carte
blanche in traffic. He may park before a fire hydrant, drive the
wrong way on a one-way street and exceed speed limits. Not that
this privilege is legally inherent to his office,—but woe to the poor
cop who would dare to interfere with somebody who has that much
of "pull" as the display of these coveted symbols of authority
indicates. The politician, excluding ostentation, becomes imbued
with his own importance to a point where he even awes himself.

From freedom from restraint in small matters which frustrated ordinary citizens do not enjoy, there is only a short step
to accepting free passes for small favors and bribes for more important ones. If it were not for these aspects of the position, for
the chance of using official influence for private gains, small or
large, many politicians would not consider public office worth
while.

There are those politicians, however, who, either wealthy in
their own right or executives of large concerns, are in politics
to further certain special interests. What is more, they are apt
to make no bones about it, except "for the record" where the national interest is made to seem uppermost in their mind. I recall
an "off the record" conversation with a Conservative Deputy who
represented a group of interests in the North. His support was
needed in the Chamber to put through an amendment essential
to the income tax law. In reply to my efforts, in the government's
behalf, to show him that this amendment was in the national interest and not at all a partisan matter, he replied: "National interest or not, I know the measure cannot be passed without the
five 'Yeas' my friends and I represent. I'll block it unless you
change the sales tax bill now under discussion so as to exempt
our interests." The government had no choice but to accept the
deal. It was quite a chore to draft the exemption in acceptably
legal terms. It would have been much simpler to say: "In compensation for services in passing the income tax amendment, the interests represented by Deputy X. are herewith exempted from the
sales tax."

An "old hand" in the political game differs from the new-
comer in that he can afford to be careless about accepting graft.
In the course of holding office he has accumulated so much incrim-

inating information—the proof of which he has carefully tucked away somewhere—about other officeholders, that none of them would dare to bring charges against him in the fear that the investigation might backfire. Occasionally a novice is caught who lacks this "secret weapon" and consequently lands in jail or commits suicide, but this is the exception confirming the rule. Graft is taken for granted. Irigoyen's administration was notorious for being the most corrupt in Argentine history, but he was not ousted because of that. Alvear's government gained a reputation for "honesty"—since no "juicy" scandals occurred during his term—but actually his administration was no more honest than that of the Conservatives.

The difference between a "corrupt" and an "honest" Argentine government is one of degree. In a corrupt administration one can offer bribes to a Minister of State or a Division Chief freely and without ado. An "honest" administration necessitates subtler methods, like getting acquainted with the Minister's brother and throwing a lucrative legal case his way. Contributions "for the party treasury" or for "charitable purposes" are helpful, too.

Irigoyen's administration had a particularly unsavory reputation because it was graft-ridden from top to bottom, instead of just at the top,—with the one ironical exception of Irigoyen himself. During his administration, it was impossible even to get a passport or another simple document without bribing every lower official concerned, beginning with the attendant in the waiting room. Strictly speaking, this was not even corruption in the accepted sense of paying a government official for doing what he is not supposed to do. The lower officials seldom exacted payments to "accommodate" people. They only did what it was their duty to do, except that they had to be bribed to do it. If not forgiveable, this is at least understandable in view of the fact that government salaries remained unpaid for long periods of time, because treasury funds were either unavailable or had been diverted to other purposes. In the case of schoolteachers, for instance, salaries sometimes remained unpaid for as long as a year. One can't blame an official for wanting to keep alive.

Irigoyen's ministers were mainly newcomers, chosen not for their administrative talents but as yes-men. Some of them seem to have been fast grabbers; they believed in "making hay while the sun shines." Irigoyen's case illustrates, incidentally, that an honest president may be much more expensive for the country in the course of time than a "run-of-the-mill" politician. Ordinarily, the average politician, whether Minister or President, will, in deciding on a course of action, ask only, "what is in it for me?"

and proceed accordingly. But if a President is honest, his corrupt
advisers may have a hard time convincing him of the "public
necessity and convenience" to grant, let us say, a railroad concession. They must beat around the bush, for they cannot admit that
their personal interests are at stake. This is tedious and ultimately
much more expensive. Irigoyen's honesty caused him to move so
cautiously and slowly in following his advisers' recommendations
that as a result the government machinery almost came to a standstill. "Doctrinaires of clean government are expensive to deal with,"
a railway executive once said to me. "In the long run the corrupt
politician is better for the country because he gets things done,
though sometimes the wrong ones—the honest one stalls everything."

LOOKING BACK: URIBURU'S "REVOLUTION" OF 1930

If Argentine revolutions are not caused by popular indignation which, deprived of a democratic way to express itself, grows
and grows until it finally overflows, what explanation is there for
the fact that the last two revolutions succeeded in a couple of
hours, almost without bloodshed?

Of the 1930 "revolution" it has been said that "it was not a
particularly unpleasant revolution as revolutions go." It has also
been called a "bloody uprising," but this description is in no way
warranted by the facts. True, a few lives were lost in 1930 as well
as in 1943, but not those of resolute defenders of the government.
The victims were innocent bystanders, a few soldiers, some taxi
drivers. Many of the casualties occurred two days after the coup
d'état, in the "battle" between the *Casa Rosada* ("Pink House,"
the government palace) and the General Post Office which I wit-
nessed myself.

The "revolutionary" troops were jittery because they had not
expected to win so quickly. When a tire of a passing car blew out
or its motor backfired, troops guarding the government palace,
believing themselves attacked by the *Radicales*, fired some shots
in the direction of the sound and hit the post office a mile away.
The detachment of revolutionary troops holding the post office
returned the fire. For hours on end they shot at each other, finally
even resorting to cannon. The shells ripped some big holes into
the post office building. Then somebody brightly thought of tele-
phoning to find out why they were fighting each other. Everything
was cleared up with apologies on both sides, and everybody found
it extremely hilarious—except the victims. The official version of
the fracas was that "the partisans of Irigoyen staged a counter-

revolt. They entered the central section of the city, armed with machine guns . . . Uriburu's armed forces quickly subdued the opposition." This was a "cover up" for the blundering commanders whose hasty firing orders had caused the death of several people.

Behind the comic opera character of these revolutions lies tragic reality.

On September 6, 1930, General Uriburu's troops, consisting of a few thousand soldiers and cadets of the Military Academy, marched against the government. One could not say that the soldiers "rose" against the President. The cadets, who mostly belong to Conservative families, probably were "in the know." But the soldiers just obeyed orders and marched, as others like them marched again in June, 1943. A "revolutionary" soldier, asked for whom he was about to fight, would have answered: "I don't know, you have to ask the officers." In this manner, a President elected by one of the largest majorities in Argentine history was deposed by a few thousand cadets and soldiers. Nobody, either in the capital or in the provinces, raised a hand to defend the legal government. The workers were disinterested, apathetic, no strike was called, no demonstrations held, no plant or shop closed; one heard in the morning that a revolution was expected in the afternoon and waited for the evening papers to find out who was the new President. With so many government employees, especially police and army officers, unpaid for some time, the military and civilian bureaucracy didn't mind exchanging the legal but insolvent, vitiated government of a senile, dreamy, insincere reformer for a general's government which could be expected to be favored by the banks, pay salaries on time and reward its followers handsomely. Uriburu kept his promises. Some time after he came into power, he had the Treasury distribute over 7 million pesos among the army officers to pay their private debts, "one of the cleverest wholesale bribery schemes ever invented in South America."

By this revolt "big-money interests overthrew the liberal regime of the Radical party." But the leaders of the insurrection succeeded in creating the impression among some observers that the movement was "a popular one," carried out "with almost the unanimous consent of the country."

Actually the people had nothing to do with it, and it was no more "popular" than the despairing silence, lethargy and hopelessness were "consent."

True, Critica, an independent, liberal afternoon paper of sensational, tabloid character, with a large circulation, allegedly angered by Irigoyen's inability to stave off depression and to get rid of the grafters, helped prepare the revolt by violently attacking the Radical government during its last few weeks. (Gratitude not being a political habit, Uriburu soon turned against *Critica*.) But many Argentines have voiced their suspicion that *Critica*'s denunciation of the liberal government was inspired not so much by unselfish concern over the nation's fate as by good business reasons. It has been observed, too often, that violent attacks on certain "trusts" made by papers of this kind ceased abruptly, to be followed by handsome ads paid for by these same "trusts." Nor would this have been the first time that backers of a revolution were able to enlist the aid of a popular newspaper for "good business reasons."

It is also true that "furniture was dragged from the presidential mansion, the homes of numerous Radical leaders were invaded, and the *confiteria El Molino*, opposite the Congress, where the Radicals had been wont to congregate, was so smashed up that it did not open its doors for almost a year," and that the offices of the leading Radical newspapers were ransacked and burned.

But, strangely enough, this all happened the evening after the "revolution" had already succeeded. Surveying the scene after an unexpectedly rapid victory, Uriburu's henchmen seem to have realized that the "popular touch" was lacking. Raiding and burning posses were quickly organized to give the day the proper "revolutionary fireworks," as several of the participants, later in high government positions, themselves told me, and as I saw others of my acquaintances doing. It was easy to recruit members of the posses among the few hundred juveniles, unemployed and hoodlums who found amusement in milling around the government palace, overturning and burning buses and trolley cars (which belonged to foreign-controlled companies, anyway), and in shouting themselves hoarse without exactly knowing why. As the police had orders from the new government to look the other way, the brave hoodlums and upper-class students were very successful in destroying sundry undefended offices, shops and residences and in setting fires which the fire department was prevented from putting out.

The entire revolt, directed as it was against a popular liberal leader, was characterized by the strenuous efforts of the wire-pullers to have it appear in the annals of history as a "popular" uprising to "right the wrongs inflicted upon the people by a bunch of unscrupulous, grafting demagogues." The leaders of the uprising passed the word among the thousands made unemployed by the depression and among the numerous unpaid government employees that jobs were to be had for the first ones to "welcome the Army." They thus succeeded in rounding up a crowd of job-seekers to greet the troops at the outskirts of the city. Furthermore, "the leaders of the opposition political parties had gone to *Campo de Mayo* [Army Headquarters several miles from the city] at Uriburu's request and accompanied him on the march into the capital, in order to make the revolution look like a civilian uprising instead of a military one. Although Uriburu had been plotting the revolt for weeks, he always maintained the fiction that his march on Buenos Aires was in response to the urgent request of the leaders of the political parties who had gone to *Campo de Mayo* and asked the co-operation of the army."

Who were the groups behind the revolt? Undoubtedly it was fathered by the landed gentry. They had long waited for an occasion to correct their mistake of 1916 in permitting honest elections. The Conservatives were well aware that the Radicals' belief in honest majority rule through the ballot boxes was just as much "bunk" as their own; that they had no chance ever to return to power the democratic way. In 1930, the depression created a difficult situation for Irigoyen's popular government. The Conservatives used this golden opportunity for the comeback by a shortcut.

The revolt was mothered, so to speak, by the banks, big business and the employers' associations, who were enraged by Irigoyen's clumsy attempts to "do something" about the depression at their expense, without any real constructive plan. I recall a characteristic episode. Irigoyen called the members of the Grain Exporters Association before him and ordered them (sic!) to pay more for wheat. When their spokesman replied that supply and demand on the world market made a raise impossible, Irigoyen answered: "I don't believe you. The law of supply and demand is an old fairy tale. I know for sure that you can pay the farmer more if you really want to, and you are going to do it, or else. . . ." Is it any wonder that the grain exporters favored a change?

Also, Irigoyen's attempts failed to satisfy the poor farmers and workers, for whom timid half measures were of little help.

To carry the allegory further: the midwife for the insurrection seems to have been the foreign oil interests, which is not surprising in Latin America. There is no evidence in the legal sense to substantiate this assertion. But I have reliable inside information to the effect that negotiations between the Soviet Trade Delegation and the *YPF* (*Yacimientos Petrolíferos Fiscales*, the official organization running the government-owned oil wells) were successfully completed shortly before the revolt. A contract had been drawn up and was ready for signature whereby *YPF* undertook to buy exclusively from Russia all oil needed for Argentine consumption and not produced by the domestic wells. The Russians agreed to supply this oil at a certain discount below current and future world market prices. Such an agreement would have had far-reaching effects on Argentina. It would have enabled *YPF* to regulate the import of oil with the view of fully developing domestic production. With the discount, *YPF* would have had a practical monopoly of oil imports, shutting out all other competitors. Reason enough for the foreign oil interests to favor a change of government! The contract was never signed. Instead, one of the first acts of the newly installed Uriburu government was the ousting of the Soviet Trade Delegation, with the age-old accusation that it spread "Communistic propaganda."

6

Although the city consolidated its hold on Argentina, fate intervened in the 1940s to impose on the *porteños* a leader who linked his name with Rosas. Juan Domingo Perón hardly favored the provinces, but his reliance on worker and military recalled the days of the Gaucho-military rulers of the early nineteenth century. Two factors made possible Perón's success: first, the growth of the eastern seaboard cities, particularly Buenos Aires; second, increased demands for cheap labor by the new urban industries. With the industrialization of Argentina, urban jobs attracted waves of rural workers from the backward provinces, providing a pool of cheap labor for industry and creating masses of restless and alienated workers eager for social benefits denied to them. Tomás Roberto Fillol, an Argentine scholar, writes that the migrant workers, hungry for a security absent in urban life, turned to Perón who spoke for an Argentina no longer totally dependent on the export of grains and beef. In the process, many workers had their day in court at the expense of the old oligarchy and the Radicals.

Tomás Roberto Fillol:
Social Factors in
Economic Development*

In political life, *personalismo* expresses itself as "the exalta-tion of, and identification with, the leader—el 'caudillo'—at the ex-pense of principles or party platforms." It is obvious that this is simultaneously the best definition of "Peronism"—loyalty to the man, Perón, rather than formulation *by* the working masses of their own political and economic goals. To some extent, the same definition applies to the masses' idolization of Irigoyen a generation earlier. The scope and consequences, however, of "Irigoyenism" and "Peronism" bear no comparison with each other, as has been mentioned earlier. Apart from the obvious differences between the methods, ambitions, and honesty of the two leaders, Perón came to power at an extremely propitious time; he found the country in the midst of a process of social transformation which made the masses far "readier" to receive him and his demagoguery than they had been in Irigoyen's time.

During the period 1937–1947, the number of workers employed in secondary industries increased annually by an average of 42,000, while the number of persons entering the total labor force each year averaged only about 40,000. Furthermore, tertiary industries showed during the same period a pronounced increase in employ-ment: between 1940–44 and 1945–49, for instance, employment indices rose from 125.8 to 142.9 in commerce, and from 167.4 to 250.7 for state employees (1925–29 $=$ 100). Also taking into account the fact that immigration stopped for all practical purposes after 1930 (it did not resume until 1947), this means that during the period under consideration secondary industries by themselves absorbed more than the total number of persons entering the labor force, while the total demand for labor exceeded by at least 80 or 100 per cent the supply determined by normal demographic growth in the absence of any immigration. This process had two obvious consequences: first, full employment; and second, the mass emigra-tion of rural workers to the cities.

* Reprinted from SOCIAL FACTORS IN ECONOMIC DEVELOPMENT: THE AR-GENTINE CASE, by Tomás Roberto Fillol by permission of The M.I.T. Press, Cambridge, Massachusetts.

In September 1940, a Department of Labor study indicated that there were 180,700 unemployed workers in the Republic, more than half of them in the city of Buenos Aires: 60,000 in industry and commerce, 21,000 in transportation and communications, 15,000 in the building-construction and metal trades, etc. Percentagewise, these figures were still high, since the maximum number of unemployed workers registered during the depression hardly reached 260,000 (in 1932). Full employment had already been reached, however, by the end of 1942, at least six months before the 1943 military revolution and ten months before an obscure Army colonel, Juan Perón, was made director of the national Department of Labor. It was maintained through 1947–48, when immigration resumed.

Full employment, besides affording opportunities for vertical and horizontal social mobility, directly contributes to improving workers' living standards. Most importantly, however, it greatly strengthens the workers' bargaining power. Conceivably, given this basic position of strength, workers could have gained, if properly organized, and without government help, the same or even greater benefits than they actually received under Perón's "protection." In 1943, however, the government took over the direction of the labor movement. As a result, workers regarded the benefits they received as coming from the state, a homage it did not fully deserve.

Until around 1930, the increases in population—over and above normal demographic growth—of the larger Argentine cities were mainly the consequence of European immigration. Between that period and 1947, however, European immigration was replaced as a source of city growth by the massive influx of internal migrants. Between 1943 and 1947, about 900,000 to 1,000,000 persons, or 20 per cent of the rural population in 1943, are believed to have moved into urban areas. During the same period, Greater Buenos Aires (including the capital and seven centers within the urban agglomeration) gained approximately 750,000 inhabitants, nearly 600,000 of them internal migrants, and by 1947 it contained 29 per cent of the national population.

Two main consequences can be attributed to this exodus to the cities. First, the largest cities, and particularly Buenos Aires, experienced acute housing shortages. The situation was worsened by rent controls instituted by the revolutionary government in 1943 as a means of redistributing national income in favor of urban areas. This measure, of course, completely discouraged new private construction for rental. Therefore, high percentages of migrant workers were forced into peripheral shantytowns, locally called *villas miseria*. Adequate housing was not available despite relatively high incomes. The extent of this problem was only made public after the fall of Perón by the National Housing Commission. It revealed that although government-assisted construction of dwellings *for sale* had been belatedly undertaken, black-market practices (not always unofficial) had become common in housing transfers, and that it had been almost impossible for low-income migrant families without savings to find new dwellings. According to the same report, the *villas miseria* of Greater Buenos Aires still housed about 100,000 persons (2 per cent of the city's population) in 1956. Several of these shantytowns had risen on land otherwise unused because it was subject to flooding or near garbage dumps.

Second, urbanization greatly contributed to the formation of an amorphous human mass in and around the large cities (and especially Buenos Aires) which built the basis for the greatest socio-political mass movement the country had yet undergone. Undoubtedly, the amount of social adjustment necessary through an industrialization and urbanization process is far smaller in Argentina than elsewhere in Latin America. The lack of any sharp ethnic or cultural contrasts between rural and urban Argentines, together with the fact that the nation's labor supply, either directly or indirectly, is derived to a great extent from southern Europe, has made Argentine labor more adaptable to the requirements of industrialization than working forces of other Latin American countries with large percentages of Indian population and well-entrenched native traditions and ways of life. Furthermore, official Argentine publications suggest that a high percentage of the population that migrates to the big cities comes from populated centers with more than 2,000 inhabitants and from the small cities (generally from the suburbs and outskirts), which means that they adapt themselves very soon to the environment of the large cities.

This does not mean, however, that the process of industrialization and urbanization during the period under consideration was exempt from social consequences. Actually, less than 200,000 workers out of 1,000,000 migrants were absorbed by industry between 1943 and 1947. A great percentage of the rest had to find work as porters, hawkers and petty traders, construction workers, domestic servants, and the like—all low-paid activities plagued by underemployment or irregular employment. In any case, and whatever type of work they found in the large city, internal migration to industrial centers entailed a change to a different socio-economic environment. Therefore, besides their lack of training and technical skills, workers very often had to change their former occupation; and more often than not they were also forced to adhere to principles of regularity and punctuality at work and in general to the more rationalized and orderly ways of life of a large industrial city.

To these factors we should also add the usual psychological readjustments accompanying any acculturation process. The loss of traditional forms of security makes migrant workers eager to find new reference groups with which to identify. Their self-image and sense of identity will be the more undermined if they are forced by seemingly uncontrollable circumstances into conditions of underemployment and unhealthful living quarters, as was the case in Buenos Aires. The result is the formation of a rootless human mass eager to follow any leader capable of supplying them with a new and attractive set of values and ideals. For such people, Perón's demagoguery had an almost compulsive appeal: not only did it satisfy their high need dependency, but it also furnished the migrant masses with a seemingly new and obviously attractive social and political philosophy; with a new, perfectly compatible reference group (the peronist unions) ; and with the necessary scapegoats (*yanquis* and *oligarcas,* among others) to make them rally behind a common banner and against whom they could vent their rage and thus satisfy their need aggression. It should be noted here that our statement that peronist unions were readily accepted as a new "reference group" does not violate our assertion that Argentine workers, being "personalists," have a basic distrust in any kind of organization. Each individual, whether or not he is a "personalist," needs to see his behavior, which gives him a satisfying identity, validated by the acceptance of it by a "reference group," *his* reference group. In the absence of recognized acceptance, the individual would become socially alienated and thus susceptible to influence and change.

Furthermore, the mass movement of population from rural areas to the cities, and the spread of mass media among them, greatly contributed to the creation of a new spirit of angered nationalism which swept the country during the mid-1940's. This emergence of *modern* nationalism, which has been defined as "the collective demand of frustrated people for direct action by the State," was partly due to the migrant's emotional need to replace the broken sense of local or provincial identification with new symbols of group membership at a higher, national level. This new type of nationalism gave Perón the opportunity to associate the old ruling élite with foreign exploitation and the agricultural economy, while presenting himself as the promoter of native values and a modern diversified economy.

Of course, these commentaries should not be interpreted as a suggestion that Perón's popularity was restricted to the migrant masses. We are only suggesting that these masses constituted the necessary basis and support on which Perón was able to build his unquestionably great and widespread popularity. The rest of the *peronista* electorate succumbed by conviction, apathy, interest, propaganda, frustration, or outright coercion. In 1947, for instance, a delegation of the American Federation of Labor visiting Argentina found that "it is not certain whether the apparent popularity of ... Perón is due to the satisfaction of the working masses or ... to the various techniques of psychological intimidation or coercion to which Mr. Perón has resorted." Actually, the emergence of the *peronista* labor masses was the joint product of *both* the factors mentioned in the A.F. of L. report.

The main elements determining the unquestionable satisfaction of the working masses with Perón's social and economic policies are patent. The first factor is purely monetary. The average industrial worker made five times as much money in 1950 as in 1943. Of course, it did not follow that he was able to buy five times as much with this income. But wage levels of industrial (urban) workers increased more than consumer price levels from 1943 to 1948, and although their real incomes began to fall in 1949, workers did experience an increase of about 50 per cent in purchasing power between 1937 and 1948. Second, and more important, Perón gave the worker *recognition,* the *feeling of being valued,* and the conviction that the government was genuinely interested in his needs and wishes. We will of course not discuss here how well- or ill-founded these feelings were. It is important, however, to realize that during the dictatorship, the Argentine worker saw for the first time his drive for recognition, accentuated by his basic Being-orientation, at least partially fulfilled. He felt important, someone to be catered to, someone whose wishes the government apparently respected. Not only was the worker given an extra month's pay but he also received the ostentatious protection of all sorts of laws. Every corner newsstand sold the text of these laws; the worker who carried one in his pocket felt for the first time in his life that he held a whip hand over his employer. This situation had pernicious consequences for the economic life of the nation. And the reasons for it must again be found in the value-orientation profile of the society.

The Argentine worker was driven by his cultural traits to solve the new problem, in which the authority relationship had not yet been defined, in terms of power; to take advantage of the new situation to maximize his short-run benefit without giving any consideration to the effect his actions would have on the community at large and over the long pull; and to try to assert—obviously by aggressive means—his newly acquired status against those who questioned the legitimacy of it. This latter point should be particularly stressed. We must not forget that it was the *government* that claimed to recognize labor's status, rights, and privileges—*not the employer*. In other words, recognition and the feeling of being valued came from a force alien to the worker's prime source of (low) status in the society—his occupation. Moreover, this force was only indirectly responsible for his job, the axle on which his life and that of his family turned. It is therefore only natural that the worker should have sought to pin increased responsibilities for his job on the new and unexpected source of social recognition. On the other hand, at least unconsciously, the worker must have realized *himself* that his new position in society was illegitimate and artificial, since it was questioned by those who, in his eyes, bore prestige in society and particularly in the industrial environment. This feeling was a main source of internal conflict and anxiety which, by definition, would not have appeared had the worker been granted recognition *at work* rather than only by a force alien to it. As it happened, encouraged by their leader, workers not only sought increased protection from the government but overtly turned against the main barrier to general social recognition. Thus, employers were converted into one of the popularly sanctioned targets against which the working masses discharged their (cultural) rage and anxiety. This had, of course, direct effect on every phase of Argentina's economic life and particularly on industrial relations and the productivity of the labor force.

7

Perón's economic program, which favored industry at the expense of agriculture, further increased the imbalance between city and countryside. While Buenos Aires and the coastal cities enjoyed a boom and expanded, the agricultural and pastoral interior lagged behind, unable to match either the volume or value of urban production. Urbanization brought modernization to the coast, but in the interior the land tenure system kept back most of the provinces. Although a few provinces tasted the fruits of economic growth, all became more closely linked to the metropolis of Buenos Aires and more dependent on federal funds to finance the cost of administration and public-works projects. Unhappily for the nation at large, as the Argentine economist, Aldo Ferrer, points out, Buenos Aires had exhausted its capacity to carry the burden of the entire economy. The emphasis on development that centered on Buenos Aires had created a "national economy . . . incompatible with realizing the development potentialities of Argentina." Recent political unrest reflects that economic malady.

Aldo Ferrer:
The Argentine Economy*

The concentration of population in the Federal District and its environs has been the most striking feature of Argentina's population distribution in recent decades. The large metropolitan area known as Greater Buenos Aires comprises 3,600 square kilometers, that is, 1.3 percent of national territory. In 1914, 25.8 percent of Argentina's population lived in that area; in 1947, 29.7 percent; and in 1960, 38.8 percent. In 1960, the population of Greater Buenos Aires was almost 7 million inhabitants. From 1914 to 1960, it increased 232 percent, whereas the country's total population went up 126 percent. The difference between the growth rates became more pronounced after 1947, when the population of Greater Buenos Aires expanded 43 percent as compared to the country's over-all rate of only 12 percent. It is interesting to note that while the population of the whole metropolitan area increased rapidly, that of the Federal District increased slowly and even declined slightly from 1947 to 1960. This was the result of the process of suburbanization typical of large cities in the United States.

From 1914 to 1960, population in towns of over 2,000 inhabitants rose from 52.7 percent to 65 percent of total population. On the other hand, two thirds of the urbanization that has taken place in Argentina in the last forty-six years is explained by the expansion of Greater Buenos Aires.

* From Aldo Ferrer, THE ARGENTINE ECONOMY, translated by Marjory M. Urquidi (Berkeley and Los Angeles: University of California Press, 1967), pp. 179–184, 203–205.

Although this pattern of demographic growth is by no means new in Argentina in view of the growth of population in Greater Buenos Aires from 11 percent of the total in 1869 to 25.8 percent in 1914, the reasons for such concentration changed after 1914. Until that date, a large part of the immigrants entering the country remained in the Federal District and surrounding areas. The census of that year showed that 49 percent of the total population of Greater Buenos Aires was of foreign extraction. The subsequent slowing down of immigration reduced the proportion of foreign population in Greater Buenos Aires to only 36 percent in 1936. In that year a new force emerged that was to have a profound influence on the distribution of population in the country as a whole and on the social and political characteristics of Argentina's development: the massive migration from the countryside to Greater Buenos Aires. From 1936 to 1960, about 2 million people from the interior of the country settled in the metropolitan area, raising the proportion of this sector of inhabitants from 12 percent to 40 percent of total population in Greater Buenos Aires.

Most of the migration to Greater Buenos Aires between 1936 and 1960 originated in the provinces of the Pampa region. The provinces of the Northwest (Santiago del Estero, Tucumán, Catamarca, Jujuy, La Rioja, and Salta) were net exporters of population, but in absolute amounts they contributed relatively little because in 1914 these provinces contained only 13 percent of the country's total population. The province of Córdoba maintained its relative share of total population from 1914 to 1947 at about 9.3 percent; however, in spite of its recent industrial development, its share fell to 8.8 percent in 1960. Apart from Greater Buenos Aires, the only regions to increase their relative share were Cuyo (provinces of Mendoza and San Juan), Patagonia (provinces of Santa Cruz, Chabut, Neuquen, Río Negro, and Tierra del Fuego) and the Northeast (provinces of Chaco, Formosa, and Misiones). Cuyo's population ascended from 5 percent of the total in 1914, to 5.3 percent in 1947, and to 5.9 percent in 1960; the share of Patagonia in total population rose from 1.4 percent in 1914, to 2.2 percent in 1947, and to 2.5 percent in 1960; the Northeast's share went up from 1.5 percent in 1914, to 5 percent in 1947, and to 5.5 percent in 1960. The circumstances affecting the relative shares of the various regions will be discussed later, but in any case the combined population of these three regions is only 13.9 percent of the total, which means that its upward trend could not counteract the general imbalance between regional populations.

CONCENTRATION IN GREATER BUENOS AIRES

After 1930, the concentration of population in Greater Buenos Aires, which had begun in the primary-exports period, was intensified. Industry and services began to absorb an increasing share of the country's labor force and, at the same time, urbanization was accelerated because such activities were carried out in urban centers. In the last few decades, Greater Buenos Aires has been the focal point of the establishment of industry and the expansion of services by virtue of the following attractions: a greater availability of basic utilities and services such as water and sewage disposal, urban transport, electric energy, schools, and hospitals; the location of most of the national market in an area which by 1930 contained 30 percent of Argentina's population representing the sector with the highest income level; the city of Buenos Aires as port of entry for a large proportion of the raw materials, intermediate products, machinery and equipment, and fuels needed for many industrial activities; an abundant supply of labor with an above-average level of training; the employment and income afforded by a vastly expanded program of public expenditures in that area, especially after 1945.

Most of these forces were already operating by 1930 and were decisive in the subsequent location of economic activity and population. This is typical of the cumulative nature of the development process, in which certain original causes become self-reinforcing and strengthen the pre-established trends.

At the same time that Greater Buenos Aires attracted population, the latter was actually expelled from other parts of the country. The stagnation of agricultural and livestock output in the Pampa region and the concentration of land in the hands of a few property owners limited employment opportunities and reduced relative income levels. The settlement of most immigrants in urban centers, especially Greater Buenos Aires, was largely the result of the land-tenure system, which also prevented the emergence of a class of medium landholders. After 1930, the shift of rural population to urban centers was more rapid than it would have been if the producer had had a more stable relationship with the land he was cultivating.

The "expulsion" effect of the land-tenure system in Argentina after 1930 was especially important in the Litoral and the Pampa. The share of these provinces in the country's total population decreased from 44.3 percent in 1914 to 37 percent in 1947, and by 1960 it had fallen to 32.4 percent. Thus, the land-tenure system hastened the decline in the relative importance of the agricultural and livestock sector which was implicit in the process of development. It not only drove away labor but hindered the adoption of higher levels of technology which would have offset this loss. Unlike the United States and the more advanced countries of Europe, in Argentina the shift from farm to city did not coincide with but preceded the technological revolution in agriculture, and this helps to explain the stagnation in output over the last thirty years. The problem must be solved by improving agricultural techniques and mechanizing rural activity rather than by redirecting the urban population to the countryside.

CHANGES IN THE INTERIOR REGIONS

Elements existed which, although they were not sufficient to offset the concentration of population and economic activity in Greater Buenos Aires, enabled some provinces to maintain their share in the country's total population and, in the case of Cuyo, Patagonia, and the Northeast, even to improve it.

Industrialization and the decline in imports, due to the fall in Argentina's capacity to import, opened up a domestic market for lines of production that had not figured in the over-all economy or had scarcely developed. For example, output of certain farm products for domestic consumption increased as follows: cotton, 432 percent; sugar, 64 percent; wine grapes, 108 percent; and yerba maté, 495 percent. Most of these crops, for ecological reasons, are grown outside the Pampa region, so that agricultural and livestock output in the rest of the country (including those crops and others for domestic consumption) expanded its share in total agricultural and livestock output from 22 percent in 1925–1929 to 32 percent in 1955–1957.

On the other hand, the development of mining and of petroleum production, although never very important in this stage, did attract economic activity to areas distant from Greater Buenos Aires, for example, Patagonia.

Provinces like Cuyo, where output for the domestic market increased, were able to diversify their economic structure on the basis of the dynamic nucleus of their exports to the national market. Industries were established to supply the regional markets insofar as the availability of natural resources, manpower, and the basic services, together with growth in local demand, made this feasible. A substantial part of the income generated by these export activities spilled over into the region itself and led to economic diversification, new activities and investment opportunities, and a general rise in employment and income.

In other provinces, where basic conditions for the "take-off" of industrial activities and services for the regional markets were not present, the increased income generated by the dynamic export activities was spent on imports from the rest of the economy. This prevented the increment in income from having an impact on the internal economic structure of the regions and kept them as essentially primary-producing areas.

Some provinces had an appreciable expansion, particularly in recent years, of industries producing for the national market, for example, the metallurgical industries in Córdoba. But in several provinces of the Northwest, no activity producing for the national market was established, and the consequent stagnation completed the decline of that reigon which had begun in the colonial period.

In any event, although some regions of the country have developed to a certain extent in the last thirty years, they are dependent and increasingly so on Greater Buenos Aires as the dynamic center of the domestic market for their exported output. Furthermore, most of the industrial commodities they import from the rest of the economy are supplied by industries within Greater Buenos Aires. There continues to be little communication between the various Argentine regions because the transport system still fans out from the port of Buenos Aires. It was inherited from the primary-exports stage, and is one of the fundamental obstacles to the geographical integration of Argentina.

In each province, fiscal resources are closely linked to the development trend. In the traditionally dynamic provinces like Buenos Aires, Santa Fe, and Córdoba, or in those like Mendoza where some development has occurred, the local government can draw on a substantial volume of revenues to implement its policy. Furthermore, given their relative importance, these provinces are entitled to the largest shares in federal-tax proceeds. An analysis of local budgets and investment programs reveals that a sizable percentage of public investment, as well as the basic services of education, health, social security, and so on, is financed out of local resources.

The relatively stagnant provinces, on the other hand, have to rely on grants from the federal government to finance their administrative expenses and to carry out their public works. The performance of the public sector in the dynamic provinces as contrasted with its performance in the stagnant provinces testifies once again to the cumulative effects typical of economic and social development.

Therefore, the nonintegrated industrial economy which began in 1930 has sealed the doom of the old "economic federalism" and has decisively strengthened the role of Greater Buenos Aires as the focus of economic and social development in Argentina. This process of centralization, however, seems to have reached its saturation point owing to population expansion and the accumulation of shortages in housing, sanitary facilities, schools, hospitals, urban transport, and other general services. It is no accident that the stagnation of the national economy after the late 1940's coincided with exhaustion of the capacities of Greater Buenos Aires. Clearly, the present structure of the national economy is incompatible with realizing the development potentialities of Argentina.

THE REDISTRIBUTION OF INCOME

The third and last objective of the economic policy followed after 1955 was to reduce the share of labor in the national income in order to free resources for investment. The transfer of income to the rural sector and the impact of a number of official measures designed to keep wage demands down in the face of rising prices have been, since 1950, the principal determinants of the share of labor in net domestic income. As indicated before, this share reached a maximum of 56.9 percent in 1952 and declined to 52 percent in 1958. But from 1958 to 1959, the share fell precipitously from 53.1 percent to 45.8 percent, and in 1960 it was still only 45.9 percent. Inasmuch as net domestic income declined more than 5 percent in 1959, the total wage bill decreased almost 20 percent in that year.

Furthermore, there was a sharp reduction in real wage rates. In 1955 they were 23 percent below the 1948 level. Real wages have continued their downward trend and at present are 40 percent below the 1948 average. The contraction was especially severe from 1958 on. In 1959 wages dropped 20 percent, and they have not recovered this loss.

In his study, Dr. Olivera brings up an interesting point in connection with the remuneration of labor and capital. He states that in some branches of production there has been a fall in real wages per man-hour; on the other hand, the income of capital and entrepreneurs (profits, interest, and rent) maintained a comparatively stable ratio to the stock of capital in the period 1949–1959. In other words, whereas the earnings of capital remained constant and even increased toward the end of the period, the remuneration of labor plummeted. To quote Olivera: "Relative factor prices moved against labor during the last decade." The remuneration of capital undoubtedly was affected by the higher income accruing to capital invested in agriculture and livestock.

The ratio of gross domestic investment to product in a five-year period when labor's share of income was rising may be compared with a more recent period when the opposite occurred. It will be seen that between 1947 and 1952, 23.7 percent of gross product went into capital investment (including replacement of existing capital) and that between 1958 and 1961 the percentage declined slightly to 23.3. Irrespective of the allocation of capital between the different sectors of activity, there is no evidence of any correlation, unless an inverse one, between the share of capital in national income and the proportion of gross product used for capital formation.

CONTINUED STAGNATION AND THE PRESENT CRISIS

The policy followed since 1950 to overcome the stagnation of the Argentine economy has not been successful. Per capita product has not gone up and during most of the period has remained below the 1948 level. The basic structural problems of the economy, far from being solved, have gradually become worse. Recently, a more restrictive monetary policy and the uninterrupted transfer of income to the rural sector through devaluation have brought about an increasing underutilization of installed capacity and unemployment of labor and have worsened the living conditions of the urban masses.

At the same time that real deflation takes place through growing unemployment of productive factors, the inflationary process is speeded up by continued depreciation of the peso and transfer of income to the export sector. In fact, the worst of all possible worlds has been reached: real deflation with monetary inflation.

The Argentine experience is a logical consequence of a policy that has disregarded the prevailing conditions of the economic and social reality of the country and of the international economy. Before concluding the analysis of the stage of a nonintegrated industrial economy, those conditions may be briefly recapitulated.

First, since 1930 the demand for agricultural and livestock products has been at a standstill, partly because of the trend in the demand for these commodities and partly because of the protectionist policies of the countries that are traditional importers of primary products, particularly Western Europe and countries like the United States that are competitors of Argentina. Second, the international flow of private capital has shifted to investments totally different from those it entered before the great depression; foreign capital from public sources is replacing private capital in certain sectors, especially in social overhead investment. Third, the land-tenure system sterilizes price incentives to the agricultural and livestock sector and limits the possibility of expanding farm output through higher yields. Fourth, the increase in employment in the public sector is mainly the result of the inability of the basic sectors of the economy to absorb the increment in the labor force. As long as alternative occupations do not exist, the public payroll cannot be cut without depressing the level of employment and domestic income. Fifth, inflationary pressures actually stem from the inability of the economy to expand the supply of goods and services in order to meet rising demand; and monetary expansion, in conditions of full employment, may accentuate this structural rigidity. Sixth, the transfer of income to the rural sector as an incentive to agricultural output leads to strong inflationary pressures that cannot be alleviated by merely limiting the money supply and wages. Seventh, the economic system cannot automatically make the necesary adjustments for steady growth.

The contradiction between the policy described above and the prevailing objective conditions proves the impossibility of regressing to the primary-exports economy.

It can easily be understood that in a country in which 75 percent of the population lives in urban areas and in which almost all of the manpower is employed in industries and services, this type of readjustment of the structure of output would inevitably run into serious difficulties. Urban population will not return to the countryside merely because of a worsening of living conditions; not only is the rural sector structurally incapable of absorbing a higher share of the labor force, but also it is well known that population that migrates to the cities never returns to rural activities.

The solution to the long stagnation of the Argentine economy is not to be found in a return to the old economic model, but in the integration of the various economic sectors by means of the development of basic industries, the expansion of social overhead capital, and a correction of the geographical imbalance in the distribution of output. In fact, any economic policy must be judged by its effects on the process of integrating the economic structure of Argentina.

Suggestions for Further Reading

For a picture of the provincial *caudillo* and his links with the local landed elite in the days of Rosas, see Roger M. Haigh, "The

Creation and Control of a *Caudillo,*" *The Hispanic American Historical Review,* XLIV (November, 1964), 481–490. An excellent analysis of the Gaucho, as man, myth, and loyal supporter of *caudillos* is Madaline W. Nichols' *The Gaucho* (Durham, 1942). The classic study of the conflict between city and country in the early half of the nineteenth century, written by a politician-intellectual with an axe to grind, is Domingo F. Sarmiento, *Life in the Argentine Republic in the Days of the Tyrants* (New York, 1961). But Sarmiento's views must be tempered with Allison W. Bunkley's *The Life of Sarmiento* (Princeton, 1961), who esteems the noted Argentine but is not unaware of his limitations and prejudices. In *Argentina, the United States, and the Inter-American System, 1880–1914* (Cambridge, 1957), Thomas F. McGann provides a thoughtful and sympathetic account of the generation of the 1880s. Although outdated in some respects, Ysabel F. Rennie, *The Argentine Republic* (New York, 1945), still offers the most cogent socio-economic analysis of Argentine development, in particular the crises of the Radical Party in 1930. The early years of the Perón period are covered by Robert J. Alexander, *The Peron Era* (New York, 1951), while Samuel L. Baily, *Labor, Nationalism, and Politics in Argentina* (New Brunswick, 1967), discusses Perón's decade through his study of labor. In *Peron's Fall and the New Republic* (New York, 1956), Arthur P. Whitaker offers a brief account of Peróns' drop from power. The best comprehensive study of relations between Argentina and the United States is Harold F. Peterson, *Argentina and the United States, 1810–1960* (New York, 1963).

II

Brazil: The Foundations of Empire and Republic

Brazil is a unique country in Latin America. It is the giant of South America and the third largest nation in the Western Hemisphere after the United States and Canada. The offspring of Portugal, Brazilians speak Portuguese in a continent dominated by the Spanish-speaking republics. In addition, Brazil is a melting pot—some 40 per cent of its population, the largest in Latin America, is Negro or mulatto.

Brazil retained a monarchical form of government in the nineteenth century, which lasted until 1889. Amidst the political chaos and economic turmoil in the Spanish American republics, Brazil enjoyed more than four decades of peace and order under the benevolent rule of Dom Pedro II, the Emperor of Brazil from 1841 to 1889. Dom Pedro's rule not only represented a successful historical experiment, but fostered a generation of often able and distinguished public figures. The Empire survived with the support of the sugar barons of the Northeast who formed a slavocracy that merits careful study by scholars not only because of its size and duration but also for the light that it can shed on other systems of slavery in the Western Hemisphere, particularly that of the Southern United States.

Besides questions of slavery, a number of other issues, such as religion, played a role in the collapse of the Empire. Dom Pedro's downfall, as the readings demonstrate, ended the dominance in Brazil of a generation of public figures whose accomplishments partly account for Pedro's political success. Historians may discover the Emperor's formula for successful rule by studying the leading figures of this time, both in and out of government; the career of Viscount Mauá is described in one of the following readings.

The society of the Empire, sugar-based and coastal-oriented, mimicked European ways and ideas and generally ignored the hybrid population of the hinterland. The First Republic marked the shift from empire to republic and from sugar to coffee and coincided with an intellectual awakening that stressed the need for a recognition of "true" Brazilian values. Intellectuals of the era explored the question of nationality, emphasizing the importance of the *sertanejos* in whom the intellectuals discovered the "real" nation. In his famous work, *Os Sertoes*, Euclydes da Cunha presented this novel thesis with eloquence and spirit and made himself the leading writer of his age. In the 1920s, Da Cunha's beliefs received support from a school of intellectuals (among whom Gilberto Freyre figures prominently) who, in their zeal to describe in flattering terms the contribution of Africans to Brazilian development, pictured Portuguese slavery in an almost idyllic sense.

Unfortunately for Brazil's future, the Republic produced few politicians whose deeds matched the rhetoric of the new intellectuals. Despite the strenuous efforts made to build a sound economy, Republican leaders merely substituted the politics of coffee for those of sugar. Instead of an Emperor who spoke for the sugar aristocracy, the Republican bosses represented the politics of coffee planters and the states they dominated, especially São Paulo and Minas Gerais, the largest and most powerful.

In 1930 the political clique from São Paulo, then in control of the presidency, brushed aside the claims of Minas Gerais to that office, which the traditional pact between the two states had guaranteed. Aided by the worsening economic situation produced by the Great Depression and the fall of coffee prices, Getulio Vargas, a political figure from Rio Grande do Sul, took advantage of the quarrel to organize a successful revolution. By 1937 he had discarded all democratic pretenses and ruled as a dictator. Patterned after the corporate state idea of Fascist Italy, Vargas' *Estado Novo* survived until 1945 when his foes forced his resignation. Still, the dictator's elaborate programs of social welfare, a response to the increasing urbanization of Brazil, had won the support of urban labor and large segments of the new middle sectors. In 1950, his popularity only slightly tarnished, Vargas again declared himself a candidate for the presidency and won the election.

His second term proved less successful. Older and perhaps less able to manipulate the rival political factions, he failed to cope with the new political and economic problems. Confronted with the threat of a military coup, a tired and discouraged Vargas committed suicide in 1954, leaving behind a farewell note that blamed his international enemies and their collaborators in Brazil for his failure. Any analysis of recent Brazilian history must begin with a careful study of the Vargas years.

In 1964 a military coup ended the life of the Second Republic and ushered in an era of rule by generals, which the controlled election of 1966 legitimized. However, the political events of the last decade cannot be understood, as historians and economists point out, without an analysis of Brazil's changing economic picture. The country underwent a period of remarkable economic growth in the 1950s, which drastically transformed the nature of Brazilian society. Brazil is no longer just a coffee exporter; though coffee still ranks as the leading export, the nation has made vast strides toward the goal of industrialization. To the economist Werner Baer, for example, the difficulties underlying the transition to a modern industrial economy explain the failure of the Goulart administration and the military coup that toppled it.

1

The nature of the system of land ownership and the legacy of three hundred years of colonial development represent, along with the importation of a vast population of Africans, one of the two major forces shaping the character of nineteenth-century Brazil. Although masters of a huge colony, the Portuguese effectively colonized just the narrow coastal belt on the Atlantic. Only occasionally did colonists push inland. Regardless of where they settled or whether they cultivated sugar cane with black slaves in the Northeast or became stockmen in the São Francisco Valley, explains the sociologist T. Lynn Smith, the colonists claimed enormous expanses of territory. The owners of the great estates controlled not merely the economy of the Empire, but its social and political life as well. The masters of the land, almost always a minority of whites set among a black majority, remained the bulwark of the Empire and unchallenged rulers of Brazil until well into the twentieth century.

T. Lynn Smith:
Brazil*

The system of landownership and control established by the Portuguese colonists in Brazil represented a very sharp break with the traditional small-farm agricultural pattern of Portugal. This is only one of the many aspects of rural social organization that underwent radical changes in the colonization of Brazil. Before the establishment of its colonies in America, Portugal had developed the sesmaria as an institution for seizing concentrations of landed property and distributing them among persons who would cultivate the land. In this way it had preserved, for the most part, a system of small farms. From this tradition the land system established in Brazil represented a decided departure. Says Oliveira Vianna relative to the introduction of and role played by the large estate in Brazil:

> In our country . . . agriculture had its beginning in the large state. The Romans evolved the large property from the small. . . . Other peoples developed in a similar manner. In contrast with this we have been since the beginning a nation of latifundia: among us the history of the small farm can be said to go back only a century. All the long colonial period is one of the splendor and glory of the immense territorial property. In this period it alone appeared and shone; it alone created and dominated; it is the central theme interwoven throughout the entire drama of our history for three hundred fecund and glorious years.

The same writer, after pointing out that the region of northern Portugal from which the colonists came was then, as now, one of small farms, analyzes the reasons for the break with the traditional cultural pattern. He emphasizes the importance of two factors: (1) The colonists were not ordinary citizens (*homens do povo*) but adventurers from the lower and even the upper segments of the nobility who migrated in order to restore depleted fortunes. For the most part plebeians came only in later years, after the discovery of gold and diamonds and the economic development of the country had made a place for small manufacturing and trading

---

* From T. Lynn Smith, BRAZIL: PEOPLE AND INSTITUTIONS (Baton Rouge: Louisiana State University Press, 1963), pp. 321–329.

enterprises. (2) Lands were granted only to persons who could convince the authorities that they were from "good" families and that they had the slaves, finances, and other requisites to develop sugar plantations and mills. Even those members of the lower classes who reached Brazil and sought lands were careful to represent themselves to the authorities as coming from old established families and possessed of ample means for developing the concession.

But the establishment of a sugar plantation and mill required a considerable amount of capital, and it was not always possible for the impoverished noble or aspiring plebeian to borrow this from the Jewish moneylenders of the coastal towns. But the establishment of a curral for cattle surrounded by vast acreages of pasture lands was much less costly. Hence many who could not obtain the coveted social and economic status of the sugar planter turned their steps inland and carried the pastoral enterprises to the interior—the curral preceded the fazenda and the sugar plantation. Although it took less capital, the development of a curral, later a fazenda, for cattle also served to diffuse the large estate throughout Brazil. Whereas it was considered necessary to have a grant of at least two leagues (some eight miles) square in order to have sufficient land for a sugar plantation, an extension of 10 leagues, or about 40 miles, on each side was the customary size of the sesmaria that was granted for purposes of raising cattle. And even those who were unable to secure concessions of land and rented the areas on which they grazed their cattle leased areas at least one league square.

The diffusion of the large landholding throughout Brazil proceeded very rapidly. Along the entire coastal area the sesmaria was the instrument for the spread of the large estate devoted to sugar production. Few persons of the farmer class gained a foothold there. Nor did small farms develop in the hinterland to constitute a "shelter belt," protecting the plantations from the natives, as was the case in the southern part of the United States. Owing in a large measure to the intrepid Paulistas of the seventeenth century, the menace of Indian attacks from the interior was largely eliminated and the lands themselves appropriated in extremely large tracts for the purposes of cattle raising. Accompanied by their numerous slaves and agregados, these Paulista bandeirantes went on long exploring and Indian-hunting expeditions; but they also drove their herds of cattle before them in a species of "combined operations," and upon this economic base they established nodules of settlement, throughout the entire length and breadth of Brazil. One can hardly overstress the contribution of the small handful of adventurers from São Paulo. They pushed south through what is now Paraná and Santa Catarina to the great plains of Rio Grande do Sul; they spread westward into Mato Grosso and northwest into Goiás; they introduced their particular variety of European civilization, or better, the new American variety, based on pastoral activities, into Minas Gerais, pushed on down the São Francisco through Bahia, and then spread out onto the areas of the great sertão in Pernambuco, Ceará, Piauí, and Maranhão.

Furthermore, they were just as bold in asking for lands in sesmaria as they were in penetrating new areas and enslaving the Indians. As a rule they petitioned for grants of the maximum size, asking them not only for themselves but for all the members of their numerous families. No doubt they felt entitled to the possession of vast expanses of territory by virtue of being the explorers, the first to reduce the natives, the founders of the settlements, and the owners of the herds which formed the economic basis of the economy. Oliveira Vianna cites the case of Brito Peixoto, who was not content with a sesmaria for himself, but requested His Majesty the King to grant one to each member of his family. In the mining regions the royal letters confirming the possession of the owners ordered that the lands be distributed to the discoverers and their associates. From the south a governor reported that there were families in possession of 15 and 16 leagues of land, "the fathers have three leagues, and the sons, still living with the father, have secured the remainder."

The valley of the São Francisco River formed a center of dispersion for these Brazilian stockmen and frontiersmen. Here they established strongholds, built up their breeding stock, and then continued their migrations, so that this great valley served as a second point of irradiation in the conquest of Brazil. From here in 1590 Christovão de Barros opened Sergipe for the Portuguese; from here other sertanistas, driving their herds before them and supported by their warriors, made their way along the Rio São Francisco to near the place where Cabrobo, Pernambuco, now stands, and then spread out over the interior parts of Pernambuco, Paraíba, Rio Grande do Norte, Ceará, Piauí, and Maranhão. "For the most part, the villages existing in the high sertões of the northeast, from Bahia to Maranhão, have for this reason their origins in former cattle fazendas," says Oliveira Vianna. Even today, as has been mentioned elsewhere, "Bahiano" is a synonym of "countryman" in the cattle-grazing portions of Maranhão and Piauí.

The manner in which the large concentrations of grazing lands came into private possession, the vicissitudes through which some of the large estates passed, and the central fact that there was no tendency for them to be broken up as one generation succeeded another are brought out in the following quotation:

> Domingos Jorge, a Paulista, and Domingos Affonso, from Maffra, in Portugal, were the first persons who began the conquest of this province (Piauí). Towards the year 1674, the latter possessed a fazenda for breeding cattle on the northern side of the river St. Francisco. The great injury which he there sustained from the central Indians, and the desire of augmenting his fortune with similar possessions, urged him to undertake the conquest of the northern country, for which object he assembled all the people he could accumulate, and having passed the serra of Dois Irmaos, (Two Brothers), towards the north, he, fortunately for himself, encountered the Paulista before mentioned, who was in the process of reducing Indians to captivity, and they afforded mutual succour to each other. Having ultimately captured a considerable number, and caused the remainder to retire, the Paulista returned to his country with the greater part of the captive Indians, and the European remained the master of the territory. Other companies made similar entries into this district, the said Affonso always remaining supreme captain of the whole, and the vast possessions thus acquired by the entrance of various parties, received the denomination of Certam. It is said that he established above fifty fazendas for the breeding of large cattle, and that he gave away and sold many during his life. It is however certain, that at his death, he left thirty, and appointed the Jesuits of the College of Bahia administrators of them, ordering the revenues of eleven to be appropriated for dowries to young virgins, to the clothing of widows, and to succour other necessities of the poor. With the rest they were to augment the number of fazendas, but it is said that they only established three more. With the extinction of this sect, the whole passed under the administration of the crown, and are preserved in the same state by the inspection of three administrators, each having eleven fazendas in his jurisdiction, with three hundred milreas of salary. They occupy the territory through which the rivers Piauhy and Caninde flow, from the boundary of the province to the north of the capital, in the vicinity of which there are some principal ones. The privilege of forming establishments within their lands is not granted to any one, where the slaves of the fazendas work alone for their subsistence and clothing. The cattle arriving at a certain age are conducted by the purchasers principally to Bahia and its reconcave. Those of the northern district descend to Maranham, others are driven to Pernambuco.

The literature is filled with other references to and descriptions of Brazil's tremendous landed properties. At the opening of the nineteenth century one of these in the province of Paraíba, belonging to the Albuquerque do Maranhão family, was said to extend fourteen leagues along the road leading from Natal to

Recife. "Besides this prodigious property the owner possessed estates in the *Sertam,* which were supposed to be from thirty to forty leagues in extent, . . . such leagues as, if measured by time, are each three or four hours' journey."

In the concentration of landownership that prevailed in Brazil, however, there is a distinguishing feature—the role played by the Church was a very modest one. Never did the Church become famous in Brazil, as it has elsewhere, for the control of broad acreages. At most, some of the priests were said to have transferred to mulatto offspring a number of the best engenhos in such provinces as Bahia. In fact, in Brazil the chapel usually seems to have been an adjunct to the engenho or the fazenda, and the priest to have been there at the sufferance of its aristocratic owner. Only the lay brotherhoods were noted for their extensive holdings. The key to this situation, so different from that in Spanish-American countries such as Mexico, is to be found in a royal letter of February 23, 1711, which stipulated that "in the concessions of land in the State of Brazil there shall always be the condition of it never passing by any title to the dominion of Religions."

By 1800 Brazil was already cut to the pattern of the large estate. Although there were few landholders, there were not many unclaimed acres. This point needs emphasizing because of the tendency to think of Brazil as a young country. It is not; its cultural patterns are deeply rooted in tradition and in a tradition that grew out of the social relationships in the large landed estate. Brazil's coastal fringe was dotted with sugar plantations, and most of its vast interior was thinly veneered with a pastoral culture long before our thirteen colonies gained their independence. However, this culture merely occupied the country; it did not settle it. And Brazil is still engaged in the process of settling its vast territory.

After the first century or so the settlement process proceeded, and the density of population was increased by the development of new fazendas in established districts, rather than by the occupation of more territory. . . .

The concentration of landownership, resulting from the grants of sesmarias, had already reached a high degree in 1822, when Brazil gained her independence. Ruy Cirne Lima states that the results have never been summarized better than by Gonçalves Chaves, who wrote anonymously at the time of the independence:

> *1.* Our population is almost nothing in comparison with the immensity of the territory which we have already occupied for three centuries.
>
> *2.* The lands are almost all divided and there are few left to distribute, except those subject to invasion by the Indians.

3. The monopolists possess up to 20 leagues of land and rare are the times that they consent for any family to establish itself on any part of their lands, and even when they do consent, it is always temporarily and never by a contract which would permit the family to remain several years.

4. There are many poor families wandering from place to place, following the favor and caprice of landowners and always lacking the means of obtaining some ground on which they could make a permanent establishment.

5. Our agriculture is as backward and unprogressive as is possible among any agricultural people, even the least advanced in civilization.

Similar generalizations about the high concentration of land-ownership, unused lands, and the consequent loss to the nation are abundant in other writings. In perusing this literature one soon comes to appreciate the special Brazilian flavor given to the term "latifundium," that the principal element in the concept is the withholding from productive uses of extensive tracts of land. An official report to the Minister of Agriculture made in 1873 described the manner of giving lands in sesmaria that once prevailed and then added:

> From this amplitude of liberty it resulted that all the lands about the cities and important villages on the coast fell into private ownership, with the result that today it is not possible to find in the populous cities close to the markets and along the great lines of communication a single palm of land that belongs to the state and could be converted into a nucleus of colonization or distributed to immigrants. Since the owners do not possess the necessary means of cultivating such vast extensions of land, much of it remains uncultivated and lacking in villages or houses.
>
> From this concentration of property in the hands of a few comes the abandonment of agriculture in the country districts, the stagnation or lack of development in urban constructions, the poverty and dependency of a large part of the population, who do not find a field for their activity nor means to become proprietors, and finally the difficulties that today surround the public administration in offering immigrants a commodious and appropriate location.

Gilberto Freyre has done much to delineate social development among the aristocratic families of the Northeast. In his works are presented a wealth of material dealing with the latifundium in Pernambuco. Not of least significance are some extracts from Recife newspapers and periodicals which he has reproduced. Particularly important for those interested in the land system are such articles as one by A. P. Figueiredo published in 1846 in *O Progresso* of Recife.

The major part of the land in our province is divided into great properties, remains of the ancient sesmarias, of which very few have been subdivided. The proprietor or the renter occupies a part of them and abandons, for a small payment, the right to live on and cultivate the other portions to one hundred, two hundred and sometimes to four hundred families of free mulattoes or blacks, of whom he becomes the protector but from whom he demands absolute obedience and over whom he exercises the most complete despotism. From this it results that the guarantees of the law are not for these unfortunates, who compose the greater part of the population of the province, but for the proprietors, of whom three or four, united by the ties of blood, of friendship, or of ambition, are sufficient to annihilate, in a vast expanse of territory, the forces and influence of the government.

It is essential that people of slight means shall be able to obtain lands and cultivate them with the certainty of enjoying the products, conditions which do not exist today, because the senhores de egenhos or fazendas obstinately refuse to sell any portion of their lands, source and guarantee of their feudal power, and because the unfortunate morador who takes the risk of planting remains at the mercy of the proprietor, who may expel him from the land inside of twenty-four hours.

Even more detailed and caustic is another and longer article published by Figueiredo, under the pseudonym Abdalah-el-Kratif, in the *Diario de Pernambuco,* March 24, 1856.

What destiny has the continued increase of population in the interior? Will they come to be employed in agriculture? No; the best elements will leave for Recife to seek their fortune, to solicit a ridiculous employment; the remainder will move to the vilas and other population centers to pass a life of misery, because we have no industry which offers the free worker steady work and regular pay.

This is the source of those masses of men without secure means of subsistence which in certain blocks feed the politics of the parties and in the inferior parts of society practice robbery in all of its varieties.

What is the reason that these grossly dissolute families do not engage in agriculture instead of entering into the precarious careers in public services? Why, instead of leaving to be tailors, masons, and carpenters, do not the sons of families little favored by fortune return to the interior; why also do they not become agriculturists? Why do the inhabitants of the forests not cultivate the soil if they are not forced to do so? Why do their children seek out the vilas? For all of this we do not see more than a single answer, and disgracefully it is fully complete.

In the social state in which we live, the means of subsistence of a father of a family do not increase in proportion to the number of children with the result that, in general, the children are poorer than the parents and possess less capital. Now agriculture is encircled by a barrier that makes it inaccessible for the man of modest means; for all those who do not possess a certain number of contos de reis. However, she is the productive function par excellence, the mother (dead soul) of the nations, and it is here that reside the vital interests of our country; but since it is found encircled by a barrier, it is necessary that this barrier fall, cost what it may.

And what is this barrier? The great territorial property. This terrible entity which has ruined and depopulated . . . [illegible] and many other countries.

This region which includes all the littoral of our province and extends to a depth of ten, twelve, and sometimes fifteen or eighteen leagues into the interior, is found divided into engenhos or properties whose dimensions vary from one fourth of a league square to two, three and even four and five leagues square.

Here because cane growing demands a quantity of certain soil which is not found everywhere, it follows that, besides the cane lands, the woods that they must have, and the lands which they require for their oxen and for planting mandioca, indispensable for feeding the slaves, the greater part of the engenhos possess vast extensions of unopened lands, lands that would be eminently suited for small farming, and which, were they cultivated, would be sufficient to furnish an abundance of mandioca flour, beans, and corn to all the population of the province and neighboring provinces, and even for export.

The proprietors refuse to sell these lands and even to rent them. If one possesses thirty or forty contos de reis, then he may buy an engenho; but if you are poor and would like to buy or rent a few acres of land you will not find them.

This is what produces the unproductive population of the cities, the class in search of public employment that increases every day, that makes the crimes against property become more frequent every day, and the country poorer day by day, because of the increased number of consumers while the number of producers remains stationary or at least increases at a slower rate.

But the large proprietors say, we are far from refusing poor people the land they need to cultivate; let them come, and for a modest charge, and sometimes even for nothing, we will give them, not only lands to plant, but wood to build houses. Very well; but this enjoyment only lasts at the pleasure of the large proprietor.

However, whenever they do not please the landowner, because of some small capriciousness, or because they refuse to vote for his candidates, or for failing to comply with an order, they are ejected without recourse. How can these unhappy ones be brought to plant if they are not certain of harvesting? What incentive is there to induce them to improve land of which they may be dispossessed at any moment?

On the lands of the large proprietors, they do not enjoy any political rights, because they have no free opinion; for them the large proprietor is the police, the courts, the administration, in a word, everything; and outside the right and the possibility of leaving him, the condition of these unhappy ones differs in nothing from that of the medieval serfs.

Sugar estates, whether in Pernambuco, Rio de Janeiro, Bahia, or São Paulo, were very much of a kind. It is not necessary to multiply instances to show the concentration of land that prevailed in the areas producing cane. But elsewhere the evidences of concentrated ownership are similar. Cattle estates, fazendas or estâncias, occupied even greater acreages than the sugar engenhos, and, because of the extensive nature of the enterprises, cattle sections were also much more sparsely populated. Nineteenth-century visitors to Rio Grande do Sul even hesitated to report the size of the estâncias they found, for fear their veracity might be challenged. John Luccock, who traveled throughout the province on horseback, wrote: ". . . indeed, the reported extent of farms in this part of the American Continent can scarcely be mentioned with boldness, by one who has himself little doubt of the truth of the accounts. The smallest are stated at four square leagues, or more than twenty thousand acres; the largest are said to reach to a hundred square leagues, or near six hundred thousand acres. To each three square leagues are allotted four to five thousand head of cattle, six men, and a hundred horses."

An official source, dated 1904, says:

> These plains are divided up into "Estancias" or "Fazendas," the medium superficial area of an "Estancia" being 1 square League (4356 Hectares or 10,760 Acres), many of them however being 3 to 6 times that size. Wherever possible, natural limits were chosen in the division, such as rivers and brooks, which, besides avoiding all questions and doubts as to the boundary lines, serve as natural fences for keeping in the cattle. Where this has not been possible, strong wire fences serve now almost everywhere the same purpose. Internally the "Estancias" are divided into various enclosures called "Invernadas," to separate the breeding cattle from that to be fattened for sale. The house of the proprietor, more or less modest and simple, according to his means, generally stands on some elevation, near the center, overlooking the surrounding country, and around it are the huts or "ranchos" of the "peons." Agriculture on these estancias is as a rule conducted only to the extent of supplying the wants of the owner and his vassals.

A similar pattern of concentration in landownership prevailed throughout most of the interior of Brazil, including the western portions of Santa Catarina, Paraná, and São Paulo; much of Minas Gerais; Mato Grosso and Goiás; all except the coastal fringes of the states from Bahia to Maranhão; and even the populated portions of the Amazon Valley. (Of course in all of these, collecting and mining activities competed for the available labor, but they did little or nothing to affect the concentration of landownership.) One of the most extreme cases encountered is reported from the state of Paraná by the English engineer Bigg-Wither.

> A few more such fazendas as the Forteleza, . . . would turn the whole province of Paraná into a desert. . . .
>
> The whole estate occupies no less than 340 square miles of the zone or belt from whence, as I have shown, all the prosperity of which the province can boast has been primarily derived. Yet its owner will neither use it himself, except to an insignificant extent, nor will he sell any portion of it to others. On both sides, . . . it is flanked by the chief agricultural districts of the province, supporting between them a large population, while itself, it supports just a dozen persons, eight of whom are slaves. . . .

Except in the south, where the program of colonization was making real headway, Brazil entered the twentieth century as a nation in which the large estate ruled supreme.

2

Without labor to cultivate it, the land proves useless. That axiom of economics shaped the nature of the demographic pattern of colonial and imperial Brazil, where a few white landlords imported a vast population of blacks to till their huge plantations. Black slaves constituted the chief source of cheap labor in Brazil until their emancipation in 1889. Most blacks cultivated and cut sugar cane in the *fazendas* of the Northeast. Stanley J. Stein, a professor of Latin American history at Princeton University, explains that slaves also made possible the development of the early coffee plantations in the south. But Stein demonstrates more than the simple fact that coffee as well as sugar provided the economic base for the Empire. His study of Vassouras coffee plantations presents a vivid picture of slavery that contrasts sharply with the idyllic version of Brazilian slavery popularized by its apologists. Stein's monograph, a careful and detailed account, makes self-evident that slavery, whatever the nationality of the European owner, ruthlessly exploited black slaves for the benefit of white masters in Imperial Brazil as well as in English America.

Stanley J. Stein:
Vassouras*

"Greater or lesser perfection . . . of discipline determines the greater or lesser degree of prosperity of agricultural establishments." Constant supervision and thorough control through discipline joined to swift, often brutal punishment were considered an absolute necessity on coffee plantations. Proper functioning of a fazenda varied directly with the steady application of the working force; in an epoch of little machinery, slave labor or what Brazilians termed "organized labor," had to be guided carefully and supervised closely.

It seemed that apparently slow-witted slaves had to be driven to produce. In a day's work conscientious planters had to "look for a fugitive slave, consider punishing a second, decide to send a third to help a neighbor—check the weeding . . . complain about the escolha . . . explain each morning in detail to a flock of slaves the nature of extremely simple tasks they were to accomplish, check each evening to see if they have been barely achieved." In their reasoning, the needs of production dovetailed with concepts of slave character. "Only with constantly exercised vigilance under military-like discipline" would slaves work hard and earnestly, was a widespread opinion. The Negro slave was "by nature the enemy of all regular work," the "passive partner" in the transaction that entrusted him to his owner at the time of purchase. His salary? The purchase price and food and clothing provided by his master.

Those Brazilian planters who failed to find in the nature of their plantation economy sufficient justification for slavery could find support in the writings of foreigners, both resident and transient. In 1839 planters were informed, for example, that the Negro was a "man-child" with the mental development of a white man fifteen or sixteen years of age. To the French émigré, Charles Auguste Taunay, the "physical and intellectual inferiority of the

* Reprinted by permission of the publishers from Stanley J. Stein, VASSOURAS, A BRAZILIAN COFFEE COUNTRY, 1850–1900, Cambridge, Mass.: Harvard University Press, Copyright, 1957, by the President and Fellows of Harvard College.

Negro race, classified by every physiologist as the lowest of human races, reduces it naturally as soon as it has contact and relations with other races (especially the White race) to the lowest rung and to society's simplest tasks. One searches in vain for examples of Negroes whose intelligence and works merit admiration." He felt that Negroes' inferiority obliged them to live in a state of perpetual tutelage and that therefore it was "indispensable that they be kept in a state of servitude, or near servitude." Another Frenchman assured Brazilian slaveholders that the Negro was intellectually inferior to the white because the Negro's cranium was smaller and therefore he could not develop his "moral intelligence to a comparable degree." In defense of these writers it must be noted that their line of reasoning was akin to that of many Brazilian slaveholders who taught their sons that Negroes were not humans but different beings "forming a link in the chain of animated beings between ourselves and the various species of brute animals." This conception of Negro inferiority was generally universal, although some planters and town residents did not share it. A description of a Parahyba Valley planter published shortly before the abolition of slavery, underscores the prevalence of prejudices, the effect of routinism, and the absence of scientific knowledge. Though a planter might be capable of displaying compassion and pity for whites, toward his slaves he was "harsh and very cruel" for he refused to see in them the "nature and dignity" of men. The slave was little more than an "animated object, a tool, an instrument, a machine."

On isolated fazendas, amid numerous slaves, planters perceived the precariousness of their situation. Many declared openly "The slave is our uncompromising enemy." And the enemy had to be restrained and kept working on schedule through fear of punishment, by vigilance and discipline, by forcing him to sleep in locked quarters, by prohibiting communication with slaves of nearby fazendas, and by removing all arms from his possession. Where fazendeiros judged that one of their number did not maintain adequate firmness toward his slaves, they applied pressure, direct or indirect. Manoel de Azevedo Ramos discovered this when he brought charges against the overseer of a nearby plantation for beating unmercifully one of his slaves. Neighbors testified that Azevedo Ramos enforced little discipline on his establishment, and the case was dropped since witnesses refused to testify in his behalf. To judge by tasks assigned him, the model planter was an omnipotent, omnipresent, beneficent despot, a father to his "flock" of slaves when they were obedient and resigned, a fierce and vengeful lord when transgressed. And, unlike the urban slaveholder whose punishments were somewhat regulated by law, "on the fazendas of the interior the master's will decided and the drivers carried it out." Lightest of punishments might be the threat "Mend your ways or I'll send you to the Cantagallo slave market," more serious might be the age-old instruments of corporal punishment.

Most visible symbol of the master's authority over the slave, the whip enjoyed several names: there was the literate term *chicote* for what was usually a five-tailed and metal-tipped lash, colloquially known as the "codfish" or "armadillo tail." Probably because Portuguese drivers went armed with such cat-o'-nine-tails, slaves tagged it with the name of the favorite article of Portuguese diet —codfish. It was felt that sometimes it was used too much, sometimes too little, for often masters had the "very poor habit of failing to whip on the spot, and prefer to threaten the vexatious slave with 'Wait, you'll pay for this all at once' or 'The cup is brimming, wait 'til it pours over and *then* we'll see'—and at that time they grab and beat him unmercifully; why? because he paid for his misdeeds *all at once!!!!*" It was difficult to apply legal restraints to the planters' use of the lash. When one of the founding fathers of Vassouras, Ambrozio de Souza Coutinho, proposed, as one of the municipal regulations of 1829, that "Every master who mistreats his slaves with blows and lashes, with repeated and inhuman punishment proven by verbal testimony. . ." be fined, fellow-planters refused to accept it. Not sheer perversity but the desire to drive slaves to work longer and harder motivated liberal use of the lash. "Many inhuman fazendeiros," wrote Caetano da Fonseca, more than thirty years after Souza Coutinho, "force their slaves with the lash to work beyond physical endurance. These wretched slaves, using up their last drops of energy, end their days in a brief time." And, he added, "with great financial damage to their barbarous masters." Indeed there were masters who believed "their greatest happiness was to be considered skillful administrators, men who force from their slaves the greatest amount of work with the smallest possible expense."

Whipping was not done by the senhor himself who "ordered his overseer to beat the slaves." The whipping over, overseers rubbed on the open wounds a "mixture of pepper, salt and vinegar," probably as a cauterizer but interpreted by slaves as "to make it hurt more." An ingenious labor-saving variation of the whip was reported by ex-slaves. This was a water-driven "codfish" by which a whip secured to a revolving water-wheel lashed slaves tied to a bench. So widespread was use of the lash, that terms such as "fulminating apoplexy" and "cerebral congestion" were employed as medical explanation for death induced by whipping. Typical is an eye-witness account of a beating told by an ex-slave. On orders from the master, two drivers bound and beat a slave while the slave folk stood in line, free folk watching from further back. The slave died that night and his corpse, dumped into a wicker basket, was borne by night to the slave cemetery of the plantation and dropped into a hastily dug grave. "Slaves could not complain to the police, only another fazendeiro could do that," explained the eye-witness

Only slightly less brutal than the whippings were the hours spent by male and female slaves alike in the *tronco,* a form of heavy iron stock common on plantations. Arms and legs were imprisoned together forcing the victim to sit hunched forward with arms next to ankles, or to lie on one side. This was the *tronco duplo;* the *tronco simples* merely imprisoned legs. One ex-slave claimed that she had been told that the fazendeiro placed her to her mother's breast to nurse while her mother served her punishment in a tronco duplo. Another variation was the long wooden stock (*tronco de pau comprido*) into which were locked the feet of four or five slaves. For inveterate offenders an iron hook or collar (*gancho*) was used to encircle the neck. For less important offenses the slave's open palm was slapped with a hardwood palm-slapper (*palmatorio*). Inveterate runaways were chained to each other and put into field gangs, or forced to wear a heavy iron weight on one foot. Such chain gangs were part of the *pena de galés* prescribed by the Imperial Criminal Code of 1830. This form of punishment may have inspired the jongo:

> Pretty little canary, kept in a cage
> Why the little chain on your leg, please tell why?

The worst offender of all was the unregenerate, rebellious slave. If the planter did not kill him outright, he wisely preferred to sell him far away. With evident regret at losing a field hand as well as a skilled artisan, F. P. de Lacerda Werneck wrote his Rio factor: "I authorize you to sell my slave Ambrosio for the highest price you can get. He is a first-class carpenter, axman and field hand, with health like iron; you may say I sell him because he refuses to work for me." If a planter owned more than one establishment, often it proved feasible to shift the offender to another fazenda to conserve among slaves "ideas of order and obedience." Wrote the Baroneza do Paty: "I decided to transfer our mulatto slave, Ciro, because he is a pernicious influence on the maintenance of good discipline." Zeferina Adelaide das Chagas Werneck sold an African slave south to Rio Grande do Sul because "it is necessary to remove him from the fazenda and to sell him because he is insubordinate and will not work and he may serve as a bad example to the other slaves."

As a complement to supervision, to discipline, and to fear of corporal punishment, fazendeiros hoped that the local priest, on visits to plantations of his parish, would use the sermon to "rehabilitate the Negro's condition, to consecrate his relations with his master, who would thereby no longer appear as proprietor or tyrant but rather as father, as a portrait of God whom he should love and serve with the sacrifice of his toil and sweat." The Barão do Paty suggested that the conscientious confessor instil in the slave "love for work and blind obedience to his masters and to those who control him." Such an attitude other Vassouras planters expressed laconically as "religion is a restraining force and teaches resignation" and therefore planters should "push by every means the development of religious ideas." Planters were not to quibble over the costs of the visiting priest, for "in addition to being necessary for the good, the spiritual grazing of souls, such expenses contribute heavily to maintain the morality, order, submission and proper discipline of . . . slaves who cannot be kept in hand and controlled merely by temporal punishment." Padre Caetano da Fonseca advised that "confession is the antidote of slave insurrections," that the confessor was to teach the slave to see in the master a father and therefore owed him "love, respect and obedience." Through the confessor, explained this priest, the slave learned that "this life is as nothing compared to eternity" and that "the slave who bears his captivity patiently finds recompense in the heavenly kingdom where all are equal before God." Reflecting his nineteenth-century liberal outlook, Ribeyrolles demanded sarcastically: "And what do these pastors of the Negroes preach? Absolute obedience, humility, work, resignation. Some go as far as to say that Negroes are the sons of Cain—sons of the accursed—and that there is no possible rehabilitation for their condemned race."

In a society, half free and half slave, many Vassouras planters maintained harmonious relations with the individual members of their labor force. Strong attachments based upon affection and mutual respect often obscured the harsh reality of slavery. A notable difference developed between the affluent planters and the proprietors of small holdings with regard to this relationship. While the large planter had to employ intermediaries to direct the activities of his labor force, the sitiante directed his few field hands personally, resided in unpretentious quarters hardly better than those of his slaves, even "maintained his slaves as part of his family and fed them on the same fare."

It appears, however, that slaves bore perennial animosity toward planters as a group. While slaves in general accommodated themselves to the conditions of their existence, few were ever reconciled to them. Range of reaction was wide—from merely verbal acquiescence to masters' orders to violent, organized insurrection.

To defend themselves against masters trained to "absolute dominion" who were always ready to interpret independent thought as insubordination, slaves responded automatically "Sim-Senhor" to any positive command or opinion and "Não-Senhor" to the negative. "Slaves never resist outwardly" and although "apparently obsequious and attentive, refusing to argue over an unreasonable order . . . they use any means at their command to defend themselves," Couty observed. Where a command demanded no immediate execution, "the slave considers it a law permitting him to do nothing." Mistresses knew they could not order a cook to perform other household tasks. Slave washerwomen or nurses "refuse to wash floors, or they will do so sloppily, soiling walls and curtains; their retort is ready: 'that's not my work.' " Or, in more subtle form of reaction similar to a slowdown in effect, they forced the master "to repeat several times each new detail."

Not always as subtle or restrained was the reaction to a regime where "fear and coercion" were believed the only techniques for obtaining work. Portuguese overseers, as symbols of authority constantly in the view of slaves, suffered much violence. "A slave of the widow, Dona Joaquina, shot Manoel, overseer of the house and land of the widow, and it is necessary that he be severely punished to avoid repetition of similar acts which are extremely poor examples especially in places where the slave population considerably exceeds the free," was reported in Vassouras in 1837. On the São Roque plantation a slave who "lost control over his feelings when his overseers refused to stop beating his wife, seized a shotgun and shot him." In the last two decades of slavery, attacks on overseers mounted as rumor spread that imprisoned slaves received food and clothing without work. Such ideas could not be extirpated and the local newspaper advised its readers that "there is an erroneous belief that under the penalty of perpetual 'pena de galés', which is almost always imposed for slave crimes, slaves' existence is less harsh than that which they bear under private ownership." When a crime was committed, slaves surrendered voluntarily to the police, confessed the crime "with cynical disdain and tranquilly awaited inevitable condemnation." Thus, Faustino, "slave of Dr. Antonio José Fernandes, killed his overseer with a billhook at 8:30 P.M. and then gave himself up," recorded the same local newspaper which concluded: "Rare is the week when such facts are not registered."

Where slaves could not bring themselves to react by passive resistance or violence, many committed suicide. "Eva, slave of Francisco Soares Torres, a planter of the parish of Mendes, committed suicide on April 7th with a knife blow in the abdomen." Similarly, "on the morning of November 3rd, Maximiano, slave of José Manoel Teixeira Coelho, committed suicide by cutting open his stomach." According to an ex-slave, some slaves hung themselves "to avoid a beating" and others "to make themselves useless to the master." "On May 23rd, on the left side of the Commércio road in land belonging to Senhora D. Maria Francisca das Chagas Werneck, there was found hanging the corpse of Henrique, who belongs to Senhora D. Zeferina Adelaide das Chagas Werneck, also a fazendeira of the same locality."

Many slaves escaped to the woods until accidentally discovered or rounded up by local police and planters helped by agregados and slaves. Since coffee groves were usually prepared near virgin forest, slaves working in gangs asked permission to leave to attend to physical necessities then fled. Others chose to flee in the dusk as gangs returned from the fields. Others managed to crawl from their locked quarters during the night. As early as 1824 so troublesome were slave flights that planters requested the Câmara Municipal to hire a slave-catcher (*capitão do mato*) to hunt down and recapture fugitives. Once in the woods, the fugitive built a shelter and might prepare a small patch for growing corn and beans. It was probably more common to obtain supplies by stealing from nearby plantations. Hunting parties might run across a slave refuge, as occurred when several free men encountered "a rancho which seemed to have a fugitive slave, and there they waited to ensnare anyone who came. Shortly there appeared a Black man and, when José Barboza tried to hit him, the said Negro resisted. The Negro fell on the ground. Barboza shouted to his companion to help, bashed in the Negro's head while his companion knifed him twice . . ."

Individual slave reactions to discipline could readily be kept within manageable proportions. It was the haunting fear of mass reaction, insurrection, that terrorized masters and their families throughout the period of slavery. Many could recall the revolting slaves of Manoel Francisco Xavier who formed an organized group more than 300 strong in 1838 and supplied with "all the tools sufficient to form a new fazenda . . . withstood the musket fire" of local police and planters until troops from Rio under the command of the then Marquez de Caxías defeated them on the Fazenda Maravilha. The dramatic impact of this episode brought the adoption of a stringent slave code in the same year, regulating the movement and assembly of slaves and their possession of any arms. These measures failed to inhibit repeated abortive uprisings during the forties, the decade when the largest number of Africans arrived at Vassouras plantations. What one aged resident of Vassouras termed a "zum-zum" or threatened insurrection was noised abroad by slaves in 1848, then quickly squelched by masters who circulated warning letters to neighbors. Mindful of the violent slave revolts in Bahia during the 1830's, Vassouras planters dreaded that among the northern slaves sold southward when African importations ceased, unscrupulous planters would include those who "least suit their owners because of their evil disposition and incorrigible comportment." The commission of Vassouras planters formed in 1854 instructed its members to use every means to convince planters of the "danger of insurrections and of the need to take measures which hinder and prevent so terrible a misfortune as soon as possible." "If the fear of a general insurrection is perhaps still remote, nevertheless the fear of partial uprisings is always imminent, particularly today when our plantations are being supplied with slaves from the North who have always enjoyed an unfortunate reputation. We have had partial insurrections in various spots, and unfortunately they will not be the last." In following years isolated references in municipal archives to group resistance may be largely attributed to the exaggerated fears of planters, to malicious statements by quarreling slaves eager to settle accounts with their fellows, or to incitement by a few slave leaders. Despite planters' fears, Vassouras slaves are reported to have harbored animosity toward the northerners or *Bahianos*, who felt themselves culturally superior. To this element of division among slaves may be added the activity of slaves who curried favor with their masters by offering to help catch fugitives or by informing on their companions. Slaves are reported to have ostracized the slave tale-bearers (*chaleiras*), refusing to speak to them or to aid them in their work. Furthermore, when the chaleira could be enticed from under the overseer's eye, a group of slaves might maul him unmercifully.

Passage of the Rio Branco law (1871), the rising tide of abolitionist sentiment, and discussion of abolition at masters' dinner tables and over the counters of country saloons and stores frequented by slaves, spread among slaves "hopes never before felt, spurring them with the prospect of a smiling future around the corner" and apparently made slavery less tolerable. The worsening situation forced a newspaper of the province of Rio to announce in 1877 that in one town "all planters and their families dread attacks at any moment. In view of the attitude of the slaves their existence and personal security run great risk." By the early 1880's, Couty, undoubtedly bearing in mind the social ferment in Europe at that period, expressed fear of a "frightening . . . social revolution" foreshadowed by the isolated slave attacks everywhere, particularly frequent assassinations of overseers. There was a permanent undercurrent of insubordination ("refusals to obey, passive disobedience") that slaveholders tolerated to avoid "aggravating the crisis." "The slave no longer obeys or obeys reluctantly, and even runaways are protected by the tacit or avowed complicity of a large segment of the population."

At this point, the problem of mounting slave reaction to forced labor and to the master became more than a matter for local repression. It became the problem of Brazilian labor in general, linked closely to the spread of transportation lines, decline of older coffee plantations, and the rise of an urban middle class. The protest of slaves against their status in a changing society now became part of the nationwide movement for abolition.

3

Of the rulers of Latin America, none had a longer or more successful tenure of office than Dom Pedro II, the Emperor of Brazil from 1841 to 1889. Yet his regime collapsed almost without protest; the change from monarchy to republic occurred in a matter of hours. The fall of the Empire is the subject of Anyda Marchant's essay. It is part of a biography of Irineu Evangelista de Sousa, Viscount Mauá, one of the legendary entrepreneurs who surrounded Dom Pedro during his long reign. In her study, the author explains that history overtook the monarchy and its supporters. In the triumphal days of the Empire, Viscount Mauá exemplified the resourceful, daring, and successful tycoons of the imperial business and political world. Viscount Mauá, an "old gentleman with thick, snow-white hair closely trimmed and a short snow-white beard," died just nine months before the fall of the Empire. With his death the strength of the Empire, which Mauá epitomized so well, passed into history.

Anyda Marchant:
Viscount Mauá and the
Empire of Brazil*

In 1885 an old gentleman with thick, snow-white hair closely trimmed and a short snow-white beard was frequently to be seen in the commercial and financial center of Rio. In spite of his age—he was more than seventy—and the fact that he had become somewhat more portly than he had been when younger, Mauá still walked with an upright carriage and a brisk step. He was dressed in the stout, sober black broadcloth which, in spite of the tropical climate, was then considered to be the only proper garb for a man of important affairs. He had kept the friendly sympathetic manner that had always been his towards friends and strangers, but his dark eyes, once so sparkling with visions of new enterprises, were inclined to brood or flash suddenly with resentment against the disappointments of his old age. It was a quickly changing world in which he was living out his last years. All about him there was evidence of things he had done to bring about some of that change: tramlines; at night, lighted streets; a constant flow of visitors to the capital, arriving by train from various parts of the country formerly inaccessible; news in the newspapers scarcely a day old, received by cable from the great cities of Europe and North America. Yet in the midst of all this he was almost unknown except to various elderly people who were aging with the empire and to the English businessmen come to Brazil to carry on enterprises which as likely as not had been founded by Viscount Mauá.

Thirty-five years had passed since he had been Senhor Irineu to the merchants who made up the commercial life of Rio. In those thirty-five years he had made several fortunes and spent several fortunes in a constantly growing financial and industrial domain. All that was gone now. During the years between 1878, when he had been declared a bankrupt, and 1884, when his discharge in bankruptcy had been granted, he had made earnest efforts to rally his last remaining resources. He had, at the insistence of the other

---

* From Anyda Marchant, VISCOUNT MAUÁ AND THE EMPIRE OF BRAZIL: A BIOGRAPHY OF IRINEU EVANGELISTA DE SOUSA (1813–1889) (Berkeley and Los Angeles: University of California Press, 1965), pp. 258–272.

shareholders, continued as manager of the prosperous Companhia Pastoril Agrícola. He had been abroad to try to collect something on the old debt owed him by the São Paulo Railway. Now he was reduced to earning commissions in the handling of exchange transactions for the customers of his modest stockbroker's office.

The contraction in his manner of living meant no great hardship for him personally. In spite of the great sums of money with which he had been accustomed to deal during his active life, he had never acquired a taste for luxurious display. Unlike most of the men ennobled by the Emperor, he built no great palaces, imported no great store of expensive house furnishings and trinkets from Europe, and when he went abroad, did not imitate the majority of the Brazilian sugar and coffee barons who in Paris gained a reputation for fabulous wealth. Not that he did not know how to use money for such adornments. When the occasion demanded, he could make a display of luxury equal to the best. Complaints were made, in fact, of the amount of money he spent on banquets for the Princess Imperial on her visit to London in the early 1870's, especially at a time when the darkest rumors were afloat about the soundness of his finances. He knew how to choose the expensive and the ornate when he made a gift to such lovers of luxury as General Urquiza or some of the Emperor's public men. But such things, in private, held little charm for him.

Chiefly the reason why the narrowness of this new life irked him was the loss of the power to launch new enterprises. A man whose thoughts were in the custom of ranging daily over financial affairs covering a good part of Europe and South America was reduced to the trivial routine of small negotiations. His discharge in bankruptcy in 1884 was a great satisfaction to him. There were still some old friends remaining who could sincerely rejoice with him in this removal of what he considered the deepest mark of ignominy. And the occasion was made the sweeter by the thought that he had paid off more than 90 percent of his debts. Few bankrupts had achieved such a record. But though the discharge was something gained, it left him with no future. There could be no future for a man seventy-one years of age, who had once been the wealthiest and most powerful banker and industrialist in Brazil and who now was forgotten and unrecognized in the midst of all the tangible evidence of his achievements.

He was forgotten because, his financial world gone, he was swallowed up in the events that were hurrying the empire into its grave. By 1885 it was not only Mauá who was reaching the end of his road. The empire and the Emperor had entered their last decade. The Emperor had outlived most of the men upon whom he relied throughout his long reign. Viscount Paraná, Euzébio de Queiroz, Mont'Alegre had long since left the stage. Viscount Bom Retiro, his dearest friend and boyhood chum, was to die within the year. The remaining old men of the days of the Regency, Antônio Paulino Limpo de Abreu (Viscount Abaeté, in 1883), Joaquim José Rodrigues Torres (Viscount Itaboraí, in 1872), Pedro de Araújo Lima (Marquess Olinda, in 1870), José Antonio Pimenta Bueno (Marquess São Vicente, in 1878), were all dead. Luiz Alves de Lima e Silva, the Duke of Caxias, the military mainstay of the empire, had died May 7, 1880, six months before José Maria da Silva Paranhos, Viscount Rio Branco. These men were not only the principal pillars of the regime of Dom Pedro II, but they also represented the social and economic forces that supported his throne.

Among the men who survived none was more sympathetic to the Emperor than Baron Cotegipe, who entered politics very young and soon found a comfortable niche in the Emperor's confidence. He was born João Maurício Wanderley, November 1, 1815, in the province of Pernambuco, the descendant of a Dutch nobleman who had settled there in the seventeenth century and had married into a Brazilian family. He was educated in Baía at a time when the old northern slave port was still the social arbiter of the country, the Baía described by the Frenchman Alcides d'Arbigny, in 1838, as the home of a society, "gentle, affable, and renowned in Brazil for its good manners," and above all luxurious.

Young Wanderley had the usual gentleman's education of his day in Brazil—Latin, French, rhetoric, rational and moral philosophy, arithmetic and geometry. He graduated in law from the Law Faculty at Recife, with a class of brilliant men, but he left more of a reputation as a connoisseur of the opera and the theatre than as an assiduous student. Indeed, he did not need to study carefully to do well; his brilliant, facile mind took in at a glance all he needed or wanted to know of a subject. But this ease gave him negligent habits and a predilection for rule-of-thumb methods the weakness of which his political enemies were not slow to seize upon. Zacarias de Góes e Vasconcelos, for instance, found him fair game for satirical comment in parliament:

> The noble minister gets up late, more or less at ten o'clock in the morning. He dresses with great care, which takes him the better part of an hour; he breakfasts at 11, chats with his friends. He arrives at the Senate at 12 o'clock; he goes to the House or responds here to questions concerning the cabinet's actions. He is free at four o'clock; he finds his house full of people; he stops to chat with his intimates; he dines at half-past seven; he gambles at his inevitable game of ombre; he goes to the

theater at ten; he comes out at eleven; he goes here, there, and
everywhere; and finally he goes home after midnight or even later.

It was obvious, was the implication of this vignette, that the
noble minister had no time in which to discharge the duties of his
cabinet post. He was an extrovert, a sybarite. His bath was perfumed; he wore silk underwear; he smoked only the best Havana
cigars. His old friend Francisco Octaviano called him the "chief
butterfly of the empire." Yet all this did him no harm in the staid
atmosphere of the imperial court, for in the Emperor's eyes his
background was the right one, his political viewpoint correct, his
devotion to the interests of the old slaveholding society secure.
Politics was to him a game, the chief amusement of life. Rarely did
the political questions of the day arouse any real warmth in him.
In 1857, at forty-one years of age and after an active political
career of some years, he married, retired to his native north to be
a *fazendeiro*, a power in local affairs, and father of a family. But
when his wife died in 1864, he returned to Rio, to a splendid house
in Botafogo, where, perhaps not as gay as he had been in his bach-
elor days, still he maintained the worldly court of a *grand seigneur*.
Politically he shone out from among his contemporaries purely
through his gifts of manner. No one else had quite his vivacity, his
quickness, his grace, his fondness for solving a difficult situation by
a brilliant improvisation. The Emperor rewarded these virtues with
frequent political appointments of the highest importance. In 1860,
when the Emperor had paid a visit to Baía, he had conferred on
João Maurício the title of Baron Cotegipe.
From July to September, 1868, he was Minister of the Navy
and *ad interim* Minister of Foreign Affairs in the cabinet of Viscount Itaboraí (whom, at this anxious stage of the Paraguayan
war, the Emperor had called to form a Conservative cabinet after
the dismissal of Zacarias). In 1875 he was for a second time (the
first time had been in 1853 to 1855) the Minister of the Treasury in
the Caxias cabinet which succeeded that headed by Viscount Rio
Branco. In June, 1875, he added the post of Minister of Foreign
Affairs to that of Minister of the Treasury, both of which he held
until 1877. Finally, when he was seventy-three years of age, the
Emperor named him to form a new cabinet. Thus between August
20, 1885, and March 10, 1888, he governed Brazil in a period that
embraced the last critical years of the empire. The air was full of
violent change—demands for absolute abolition, the rise in power
of the army as an independent force, the increasing clamor for a
republic. The Emperor, in ill-health and old before his time, went to
Europe in search of medical treatment and some mental diversion.

Early in 1883, Carl von Koseritz, a German military man who had settled thirty years before as a colonist in Rio Grande do Sul, paid his second visit to Rio. He was a newspaperman most of his life and a principal figure in the German colony in the south of the country. He kept a diary when he visited Rio in 1883, which he published in German. His observation was sharp and his method of expressing himself candid and even caustic, and he did not think the capital of the empire came up to his home city of Pôrto Alegre.

He arrived in a Rio in which, he pointed out, sixty or seventy people died a day of yellow fever. It was April, and "the heat was insupportable, at a time when we already enjoy, in Rio Grande, a cool temperature." The noise was tremendous—horse-drawn streetcars passing in all directions, multitudes of people walking, the ubiquitous newsboys and streetvendors crying their wares in an incessant clamor; there was everything, to his mind, to prove the advantage of a small city. It was not without cause that Rio was interesting but not agreeable to live in. One could feel the pulse of the empire there—"here we find ourselves at the central and most important point of it and in the Rua do Ouvidor there may be seen daily the men who govern the country and lead public opinion; but the general character of the local society is very special and almost what I should call frivolous."

> Whoever wishes to learn the manner in which Brazil is governed and public affairs conducted, has only to walk about for a few hours a day in the Rua do Ouvidor. It is one of the oldest streets in the city; it goes from the Rua Direita (where the stock exchange is), runs parallel to the Rua da Alfandega and other streets, and cuts across the Rua dos Ourives and yet more streets, all of which belong to the old part of the city and which are narrow, dirty, and crooked as they have been for the last two hundred years. Wide, regular streets, like those of the new Porto Alegre or especially pretty Pelotas [a town in Rio Grande do Sul near the Uruguayan border], there are not many such in Rio. In this narrow and almost always shady street is found the better part of the retail trade of Rio; brilliant show windows display products of European industry and innumerable articles of luxury are set out in them. The great dress-making houses, like the "Notre Dame de Paris" or the "Grande Magico" can compete with the best of Paris and Berlin; the jewelry shops are brilliant with gold, silver, and precious stones. Fruit shops exhibit fruits from all regions—pineapples and mangos side by side with grapes from Portugal and pears from Montevideo. Book shops and shops selling objets d'art call one's attention by their de luxe editions, their steel and copper tables, etc. However narrow and dark the old street may be, the shops are brilliant in their contents and mode of presentation. An immense crowd of people wander about it from morning till night, and on each corner a club forms, where the talk is of politics and life abroad.

Certainly a great change had come about in the retail trade of the city since the boy Irineu had first arrived from the south sixty years earlier.

The Emperor's style of living did not impress the visitor from the south. In a city where great sums of money were carelessly spent in luxurious living, Dom Pedro lived in the greatest simplicity. His old palace near the waterfront, the Paço that had housed his grandfather and greatgrandmother when they had taken refuge in Rio, was a regular barracks, "like a government house in Pôrto Alegre, only five times bigger." It was old, ruinous, badly kept, never freshly painted. The Emperor had no personal fortune and he devoted a great share of his civil list to charity. He was averse to spending any of it in keeping up a princely state and to furbishing up his palaces. A wealthy planter like Baron Friburgo might construct a mansion costing eight thousand contos, a real fairy-tale palace in the Pompeian style, with sweeping staircases, bronze statues, and seven drawingrooms on the first floor, furnished with tall looking glasses, crystal chandeliers, blue velvet carpets. [On the establishment of the republic, this palace became the new president's office building, the Catete Palace.] But Dom Pedro continued to live in a couple of old houses. Certainly this was praiseworthy in the man, but it added little to the prestige necessary to an emperor. The old Paço, for instance, had still the makeshift galleries to connect it with its adjoining buildings, hastily built before Dom João's arrival to make room for his retinue. The lower floor of these galleries was rented out to small shopkeepers and barbers, giving an odd impression to the European visitor.

Even when the Emperor went to open the new Congress, he was not able to mtaintain a properly splendid royal state:

> Strange spectacle! First passed, at a gallop, a unit of cavalry, brandishing unused and unsheathed sabres, and soon after came four carriages of the Court, with gentlemen and ladies in waiting. Court carriages, I said, but of what a variety! Everything looked as if it belonged to the past century and was more or less in the style in which Marie Antoinette made her entrance into Paris. The gilding had become very black, the padding had come out, everything was in the saddest condition.

In fact, the whole thing made Koseritz think of carnival—the black coachmen in antiquated trappings, the elderly *grandes dames* in equally antiquated finery. The Princess Imperial and her husband, Count d'Eu, made a better impression.

> One can see in him the soldier and the pride of his princely origin (which, nevertheless, does not prevent him from having

a penny-pinching preoccupation with money) is written in his
face. The Princess is growing old quickly and her features have
acquired a certain hardness, but her blond hair always goes
well with her healthy skin and her full figure. She was dressed
with considerable simplicity and wore only a few diamonds. The
people allowed her to pass between ranks of the most absolute
silence, and only here and there could be heard some sarcastic
remarks about the Count, who does not enjoy any great esteem.

Then the worthy Empress arrived. Her carriage was a
little better, but it too is quite worn and dilapidated. She stepped
down with effort and was conducted to the entrance by pages.
She wore a low-necked dress, ceremoniously sewn with brilliants,
and in her hair, which is completely white, scintillated a diadem
of brilliants, while on her breast she wore the famous diamond
collar which constitutes her principal treasure. On the kindly
features of the Empress, who was greeted with every mark of
the most profound respect, there was a shadow of fatigue.
Finally the Emperor appeared. Four horse-guards in new livery,
on fine horses with rich trappings, and carriage, if not new, at
least completely renovated, decorated and ornamented with silver
and the imperial crown on the door, announced his arrival. No
applause greeted him, not even a simple "viva." He himself
seemed to notice this, because, after getting down from the carriage, he straightened up to his full height and plunged a long,
sharp glance over the people surrounding him. I could not find
him majestic, in his buckled shoes, silk stockings, short breeches,
cape of green velvet trimmed with a band of feathers, under
which shone his gold decorations. The curious ornament of
feathers especially produces an almost carnival-like impression.
[These feathers are from the throat of the toucan bird, a brilliantly colored inhabitant of the Brazilian jungles; the Emperor's
state dress for the opening of parliament may be seen by the
modern visitor in the Imperial Museum in Petrópolis.] The Emperor walked a little bent over and lately he has aged considerably. Also he is getting perceptibly bald, and his great cares,
perhaps also his physical sufferings, have made furrows in his
cheeks. Servants carried his crown and sceptre before him, and
his sword hung at his left side. After having thrown a long
glance over the silent people, who had been accumulating there,
he directed his steps, with considerable rapidity and his head
held high, to the entrance, and with that the spectacle was ended
for us.

Later Koseritz had an opportunity for a closer view of the
Emperor, when he was received in audience at the Quinta da Boa
Vista, or the palace of São Christovão in the suburbs of the city.
The *quinta* (park) itself presented pretty views, but it was not well
cared for, partly because of the Emperor's poverty and partly because he permitted hundreds of families to grow their cabbages
within his grounds. There were about twenty people, chiefly government officials, waiting to see the Emperor that afternoon. The

Emperor walked into the reception room with no ceremony, only preceded by a few minutes by his gentleman-in-waiting for the day. He knew how to be friendly, said Koseritz. Koseritz went to visit him again some days later and reported:

> The truth is that the Emperor is not amongst those princes who are adored by their peoples, but he is also not hated and can live without a guard. However, it should be realized that he is not as ingenuous as he appears, because there are few princes in the world whose will intervenes so much in the destiny of their nations as does Dom Pedro's, who in the true meaning of the expression "reigns, governs and administers."

Such was the pass that the empire had reached in the 1880's. The Emperor was not hated, partly because the Brazilians were not a people much given to hating and partly because they did not suffer that last degree of misery that produces hatred.

"Whoever wants to work can always get his daily bread. That worst element, neediness, is therefore lacking; a people relatively well-dressed and fed, whom the climate permits to sleep, if necessary, on a park bench, doesn't throw dynamite. They are much more likely to laugh easily, make good or bad jokes and not have much respect for kings."

Koseritz pointed out that in Europe itself the age of royalty was passing. Royalty, to be majestic, must conform to the times; the Emperor would have been better advised to have appeared on state occasions in a field marshal's uniform and in a more up-to-date equipage. Furthermore, in Brazil, monarchy had always been exotic, for Brazil was part of the New World, of the hemisphere that had revolted against the idea of kingship. Thus, to have a throne, the Emperor had been obliged to create his own nobility, to fashion his own court out of the material at hand, the sugar barons and the coffee barons. He had modified the concept of title-holding to some extent. Titles were strictly a reward for services given to the throne, and they were not inheritable; each generation had to earn its own. This odd mixture of the aristocratic and the democratic gave a distinctive flavor to Dom Pedro's peerage, as distinctive as the barbaric Indian names of many of the baronies, viscounties, counties, and marquisates he created: Baron Cotegipe, Viscount Itaboraí, Viscount Inhomerim, Marquess Paraná, Marquess Tamandaré.

It was a court, however, that lived in a glass case, well-insulated from the economic realities of the country. So long as the great landowners received princely incomes from their *fazendas*, that elegant, sophisticated world of society in Rio could survive, centering on the Emperor and his appendages, the parliament, and the cabinet. Men like Mauá might complain that in this state of affairs the country was forgotten and neglected, that all the money went to maintain the brilliance of the capital, that the provinces were left in a state of backwardness convenient to the *fazendeiros,* who, as slaveholders, saw only trouble in material improvements. A slave regime had no use for a modern economy, and as late as 1860 one quarter of the population of Brazil were slaves.

Certainly the Emperor, aware of foreign opinion concerning Brazil and sensitive to aspersions on his country as backward, must have regretted the foundation of his empire on a slave state. But the fact remained that to abolish slavery meant to disrupt the entire economic structure of the empire, and, as Koseritz remarked, the Emperor was not as ingenuous as he sometimes appeared. He was thoroughly in agreement with Baron Cotegipe, when that clever man pointed out that the question of emancipation was dangerous. Tackling it was like rolling a rock down a mountain: "We must not give it a push or we may be hurt."

In Cotegipe, however, the Emperor had one of the few of his statesmen who were fully aware of the economic changes, emanating from the south, that were pressing so inexorably on the life fashioned by the old habits of the north. Cotegipe recognized the fact that, if the eighteenth century lingered longer in Brazil than in other parts of the world, the new forces of the nineteenth could not be indefinitely resisted, and it was in the south that these forces flourished.

In the south, in the province of São Paulo, there were also *fazendas,* growing coffee instead of sugar. But São Paulo was not in the tropics, and the pace of life was faster. It was too fast, in fact, for slave labor to keep up with. The climate was attractive to free white labor; it became the mecca for European immigrants, seeking better opportunity outside of an overpopulated Europe. Likewise, the growing of coffee presented problems different from those of the growing of sugar. It took more capital to begin with and it was sometimes grown on small plantations, interspersed among the great *fazendas.* It needed quick transport to the seacoast from the interior of the province, for it was more perishable than sugar. Besides, the greatest customer for Brazilian coffee was the United States, another new land that was rapidly being transformed from a purely agricultural country to one where industry flourished and where African slavery had been recently abolished, at the expense of a bloody war. All these things combined to make the *fazendeiro* of the south much more a man at home in the nineteenth century than his brother from the north. The great wealth that the Paulistas accumulated went into railroads, cities, industries, modern machinery—it created what J. F. Normano had defined as the Brazilian *homo economicus*—"that Yankee of the southern continent, whose ancestors were the *bandeirantes*, the equivalent of the pioneers of the United States."

It was the rise of a new civilization, a civilization innately at odds with the empire. The new age was not static. Koseritz declared that 25,000 immigrants came to Brazil in 1882, less than 200 of whom went to the northern provinces. Nor were they in the majority Portuguese, with a traditional respect and habit of allegiance to the Bragança dynasty. About 9,000 were Portuguese; the rest were Italians, Spaniards, Germans, Frenchmen, Englishmen, and other nationalities. These people were in search of economic independence, and, if farmers, wanted small land-holdings of their own. Slaveholding did not form an element in their plans for the future. Thus the city of São Paulo, which in 1875 had had 20,000 inhabitants, in 1884 had 35,000, at a time when Rio, the imperial capital, had grown to 500,000. By 1888 the stream of immigrants to Brazil had grown to more than 133,000 in one year, 90,000 of whom went to São Paulo.

Further south still conditions were even less favorable to the maintenance of an empire based on a slave state. The original settlers of Rio Grande do Sul had been Portuguese colonists from the Azores and migrants from the province of São Paulo. They were industrious people, used to working for themselves. Early in the nineteenth century they were joined by a constantly growing stream of German settlers, who spread out into the neighboring provinces of Paraná and Santa Catarina. In 1874 came the Italians in almost as great numbers, and Poles, and from Montevideo a constant supply of Basques. None of these people were slaveholders and as free workmen disliked and feared the slave regime.

The emancipation program was early claimed by the Liberal party as its own particular property, nor were the Liberals pleased when, to forestall more sweeping reforms, the Conservative party then in power undertook measures to bring about gradual abolition. At the close of the Paraguayan war, the Emperor named a Conservative cabinet, going counter to the popular opinion that a Liberal cabinet, with Nabuco de Araújo at its head, would be more representative of the majority view. He named first Pimenta Bueno (Viscount São Vicente). If there was any emancipating to be done—and the Paraguayan war had aroused a good deal of pro-abolitionist sentiment, strengthened by the presence of thousands of slaves who had been sent south in the imperial army on the promise of freedom—a Conservative cabinet would do the job more to the liking of the *fazendeiros*. Pimenta Bueno was soon only too glad to hand his job over to Viscount Rio Branco. Rio Branco, also, had been originally opposed to abolition, but he was preëminently a practical man and he read the signs of the times with care. Emancipation could not be ignored, so he introduced into the lower house of parliament a bill based on some of the recommendations made by the committee headed by Nabuco de Araújo. In general the bill provided that children of slave mothers should be free when they reached the age of twenty-one. This was the law of September 27, 1871, which was signed by the Princess Imperial as Regent in the absence of her father. Dom Pedro was in Europe, no doubt aware that such a law, signed by his daughter, who was known to have ardent opinions in favor of absolute abolition, would not, perhaps, draw too much unpopularity against himself, if he were far from the scene.

It was a difficult law to execute, however, especially in the remoter regions of the country. Thus, neither the *fazendeiros* nor the abolitionists were satisfied, and agitation for complete abolition, without compensation for the slaveholders, proceeded during the following decade. Enlightened men like Baron Cotegipe favored reforms to be carried out by local governments, such as the emancipation decrees issued by municipalities within the various provinces. Thus the province of Ceará abolished slavery in 1881 and the province of Amazonas in 1884. But a new problem then arose—the shipping of supplies of slaves from one province to another within the empire. A bill prohibiting this interprovincial traffic was introduced into the parliament during the incumbency of the Liberal cabinet under Sousa Dantas in 1884, but the opposition it stirred up among the pro-slavery group caused the Emperor to dismiss the cabinet and call on José Antônio Saraiva to form a new one.

Saraiva was always willing to take on a difficult task—as he had demonstrated twenty years before in the troubles in the River Plate. He formed a new cabinet on May 6, 1885, but again the task proved too much for simple good will. He was succeeded by Baron Cotegipe, who with a Conservative party cabinet obtained the passage of a new emancipation law on September 28, 1885, a law which this time was signed by the Emperor himself. This law, like its predecessor, satisfied neither side, for the *fazendeiros* made every effort to evade it and the abolitionists saw no hope for effective enforcement. The Emperor was tired of the vexed question; it had provided the most serious problems of his whole reign, in both national and international affairs. He was exhausted and old, suffering from diabetes, malaria, and congestion of the liver. Again he went to Europe in search of medical treatment, calling home his daughter, the Princess Imperial, from Paris to take charge of the government. His popularity was reaching its lowest point; the newspapers said he was getting old and doddery and no longer fit to be Emperor.

Princess Isabel, his heir, lost no time in falling in step with the spirit of the times. She was ultramontane in her sympathies, well aware that Pope Leo XIII had made a pronouncement against slavery, and much under the influence of her French husband, to whose European ideas slavery was an anachronism not to be tolerated. It was obvious that she and Baron Cotegipe, whose divided sympathies made him favor gradual emancipation, could not continue to run the government together for long. In March, 1888, he resigned and Princess Isabel named a new cabinet under João Alfredo Corrêa de Oliveira. The new law providing for absolute abolition was passed May 9, 1888, by an overwhelming majority in the Chamber of Deputies and signed by the Princess on May 13.

Baron Cotegipe, in the Senate, was not so joyous; he had lived a long political life and he had no illusions about the durability of the glass case under which the Emperor's government lived. Abolition, he said, would overthrow the monarchy, but his remarks were drowned out by the enthusiastic voting in favor of the bill and by the shouting of the crowds in the street outside. Cotegipe was right. No compensation had been provided for the slaveholders, and in the north of the country, his own native land, there would be an acute labor shortage, for the free slaves would set out at once for the cities and the European immigrants were not attracted to the tropical zone as they were to the milder climate of the south of the country. Cotegipe had not long to live to see his prophecy come about. On February 13, 1889, nine months before the empire collapsed, he died the way he had lived, in ease and grace, without so much as a groan, as he stepped out of his perfumed bath.

Dom Pedro himself returned from Europe on August 22, 1888, somewhat restored in health, but not in popularity. His French son-in-law was no help in mending the situation, for Count d'Eu had always been viewed with suspicion in Brazil. He was a good soldier, but he had no great opinion of things Brazilian, was always aware of the precarious state of royalty in the world of the nineteenth century (as a relative of Louis Philippe and a descendant of the Bourbons could well be), was close with money, was deaf, and above all was a foreigner. In the newspapers and in popular complaints he was sarcastically referred to as the "Third Sovereign" and the "French Sovereign," and the idea that his wife, notably under his thumb, should succeed Dom Pedro, aroused no enthusiasm.

4

The Empire and the Republic derived their strength from the coastal cities and towns. Don Pedro II spoke for the sugar planters of the Northeast; Republican leaders reflected the rising economic power of the coffee barons of São Paulo and Minas Gerais. Both imperial and republican societies condemned to oblivion the backland people, the mestizo or mulatto *sertanejos*. Blind to local values, Brazilian society mimicked European ways and ideas and decried the *sertanejos* as barbarous and unimportant. *Os Sertões* published in 1902, questions in forceful and moving language traditional concepts of Brazilian culture. Written by Euclydes da Cunha, *Os Sertões* describes the Canudos rebellion of 1896–97 that federal troops harshly put down, challenges old prejudices, and calls attention to the long-neglected reservoir of cultural strength of the *sertanejos*. Da Cunha's masterpiece won fame as the "Bible of Brazilian nationality."

Euclydes da Cunha:
Os Sertões*

THE DROUGHT

And then, of a sudden, there comes a tragic break in the monotony of their days. The drought is approaching.

Thanks to the singular rhythm with which the scourge comes on, the sertanejo is able to foresee and foretell it. He does not, however, take refuge in flight, by abandoning the region which is being little by little invaded by the glowing inferno that radiates from Ceará. Buckle has a striking passage in which he draws attention to the strange fact that man never learns to accustom himself to the natural calamities which surround him. There is no people more

* Reprinted from OS SERTÕES (REBELLION IN THE BACKLANDS) by Euclydes da Cunha, trans. with Introduction and Notes ·by Samuel Putnam, by permission of The University of Chicago Press.

afraid of earthquakes than is your Peruvian; yet, in Peru, children in the cradle are rocked by the earth's tremors. The sertanejo, on the other hand, is an exception to the rule. The droughts do not frighten him; they serve merely to round out his tormented existence, framing it with tremendously dramatic episodes. And he confronts them stoically. Although this grievous ordeal has occurred times without number, as is borne out by traditions which he knows well, he is nonetheless sustained by the impossible hope of being able to hold out against it.

With the scant help afforded him by his own observations and those of his ancestors, in which common-sense directions are mingled with extravagant superstitions, he has studied this affliction as best he could, in order that he might understand it and be able to bear or to avert it. He equips himself for the struggle with an extraordinary calmness. Two or three months before the summer solstice, he props and strengthens the walls of the dams or cleans out the water pits. He looks after his fields and plows up in furrows the narrow strips of arable land on the river's edge, by way of preparing these diminutive plantations for the coming of the first rains.

Then he endeavors to make out what the future holds in store. Turning his eyes upward, he gazes for a long time in all directions, in an effort to discover the faintest hints which the landscape may have to offer him.

The symptoms of the drought are not long in appearing; they come in a series, one after another, inexorably, like those of some cyclic disease, some terrifying intermittent fever on the part of the earth. The brief period of October rains, the *chuvas do cajú*, goes by, with numerous showers that are quickly evaporated in the parched air, leaving no trace behind them. The caatingas are "mottled," here, there, and everywhere, speckled with grayish-brown clusters of withered trees, and the number of these splotches, which look like the ash heaps left by some smothered conflagration, without flames, all the time increases; the ground cracks; and the water-level in the pits slowly sinks. At the same time it is to be noted that, while the days are scorching-hot, even at dawn, the nights are constantly becoming colder. The atmosphere, with the avidity of a sponge, absorbs the sweat on the sertanejo's brow, while his leathern armor, no longer possessing the flexibility it once had, is stiff and hot on his shoulders, like a breastplate of bronze. And, as the afternoons, growing shorter every day, fade into evenings without twilights, he sorrowfully contemplates the first flocks of birds leaving the region and flying away to other climes.

This is a prelude to the trouble that is coming. And the situation is destined to grow more acute until December.

The vaqueiro takes his precautions and anxiously looks over his herds, making a tour of the far-lying pasture grounds, until he comes to those more fertile bottom lands, between the sterile uplands, where he turns his cattle out to feed. And he waits resignedly for the thirteenth day of this month; for on that day ancestral usage will enable him to sound the future and interrogate the designs of Providence.

This is the traditional experiment of Santa Luzia. On December 12, at nightfall, he sets out six lumps of salt in a row, where they will be exposed to the action of the dew; they represent, respectively, from left to right, the six coming months, from January to June. At daybreak the next morning, he observes them. If they are intact, it presages drought; if the first has dissolved somewhat, has been transformed into a soggy mass, he is certain of rain in January; if this happens to the second, it will rain in February; if it happens to the majority of the lumps, the winter will be a kindly disposed one.

This experiment is a most interesting one. Despite the stigma of superstition which attaches to it, it has a positive basis and is acceptable when one stops to consider that from it may be gathered the greater or less amount of vaporized moisture in the air and, by deduction, the greater or less probability of barometric depressions capable of bringing rain.

Meanwhile, although this test is a traditional one, it leaves the sertanejo still uncertain. Nor does he invariably lose heart, even when the signs foretell the worst. He waits patiently for the spring equinox, to consult the elements again. He spends three whole months in anxious expectation, and then, São José's Day, March 19, he has recourse to one last augury.

This day is for him an index to the following months. Within its span of a dozen hours, it will show all the climatic variations that are to come. If it rains during the day, the winter will be a rainy one. If, on the contrary, the blazing sun makes its way across an unclouded sky, it means that all hope for the earth is gone. The drought is inevitable.

ISOLATION IN THE DESERT

He thereupon becomes another being. No longer is he the incorrigibly indolent and violently impulsive individual who spends his days in galloping over the cattle trails. He now transcends his primitive state. Resigned and tenacious, with that superior placidity which is characteristic of the strong, he looks the fatality, about which he knows he can do nothing, squarely in the face and prepares to meet it. The heroism of the backlands, the frightful tragedies which there take place, are a theme forever lost to us; they cannot be made to live again, nor can they be told in episodic form. They arise from a struggle which no one has described—the insurrection of the earth against man. At first, eyes turned heavenward, the vaqueiro prays. His first reliance is his religious faith. With their miracle-working saints in their arms, with raised crosses, image-carrying litters borne aloft, and holy pennants fluttering, whole families may be seen—not merely the strong and healthy but the aged and infirm, the sick and the lame, as well—walking along with the stones of the road on their heads and shoulders, as they transport the saints from one place to another. For long days the backland wastes echo to their mournful litanies, as the propitiatory processions slowly wend their way; and for long nights the plains are aglow with the tapers of the penitents as they wander here and there. But the skies remain sinister, devoid of clouds, and the sun blasts the earth, as the dreaded spasm of the drought comes on. The backwoodsman looks at his offspring. Sadly, he looks at his cattle, huddled down there in the marshy bottoms, or straying slowly at a distance, necks drooping, heads to the ground, bellowing plaintively as they "smell out the water." And without relaxing his faith, without doubting the Providence which crushes him, muttering the same customary prayers at the same hours, he prepares himself for the sacrifice. With hoe and spade he attacks the earth, seeking in the lower-lying strata the water which may have fled the surface. Sometimes he finds it; other times, after an enormous amount of exertion, he strikes a rock which renders useless all the labor he has expended. Yet again, and this is what happens most frequently, he lays bare a subterranean bed of water, only to see it disappear in a day or two, evaporated, or sucked into the ground. He keeps after it, stubbornly, deepening his excavation in quest of the fleeing treasure, to reappear finally over the brim of the pit he has dug, like one coming back from the dead. But inasmuch as a rare frugality enables him to go for days on a few handfuls of passoca, he is not so readily disheartened.

Here round about him is the caatinga, his own wild granary. He cuts up into bits the thirst-quenching mandacarús, or the greenish boughs of the joaz trees, which serve to nourish the lean and famishing members of his herd. He digs up the roots of the urucuris, scrapes them, bruises them, and then cooks them, making out of them a sinister bread which he calls *bró,* and which bloats the bellies of those who eat it in an illusory manner and gives to a starving person the sensation of being glutted. He fills the food containers with little coconuts. He excavates, also, the swollen roots of the umbú. These are to quench his children's thirst; for himself he reserves the astringent juice from the leaflike branches of the "chique-chique," which makes the one who drinks it hoarse or causes him to lose his voice entirely. In short, he labors excessively, making indefatigable use of every resource—a strong and affectionate being, looking out for himself, for his downcast progeny, and for the herds intrusted to his superhuman energy.

All his efforts, nevertheless, meet with frustration. He is put to it, in combating Nature with the desert. The seriemas have fled to other *taboleiros* (tablelands), and the parakeets have taken flight to the distant seashore, while he is left to contend with a cruel fauna. Myriads of bats now come to aggravate "lean days," swooping down on the cattle and decimating them. In the patches of scorched weeds, the sound of innumerable rattlesnakes may be heard—the more intense the summer heat, the greater their number.

By night, the treacherous, thieving puma, which robs him of his calves and steers, comes up to the very threshold of his humble cottage. It is one more enemy with which he must cope. He attempts to frighten it off by running out into the yard with a lighted firebrand in his hand. If it does not beat a retreat, he attacks it. He does not, however, fire upon it, for he knows that, should he miss his aim, or should the bullet fail to finish off the beast, the puma, "coming in on top of the puff," is invincible. The bout is a more exciting one than that. The weakened athlete, with a pitchfork in his left hand and his knife in his right, now irritates and challenges the intruder, provoking it to spring; he then wards it off in mid-air and dispatches it at a single blow.

Not always, though, does he dare risk such an exploit; for, to add to his other troubles, he suffers from a very strange malady— hemeralopia. This pseudo-blindness is due, paradoxically, to a reaction to the light; it is born of bright, hot days, gleaming skies, and the lively swaying of the currents of heated air above the barren earth. It is due to a plethora of sight. No sooner does the sun set in the west than the victim stops seeing; he is blind. Night swoops down upon him all of a sudden, before enveloping the earth. On the following morning, his extinguished vision is revived at the first ray of dawn, only to vanish once more, in the late afternoon, with a painful regularity.

With his sight, his energy comes back. He does not yet consider himself beaten. For quenching the thirst and satisfying the hunger of his young ones, there still remain the tender stocks of plants, the "truffles" of the wild bromelias, and with these barbarous messes he affords himself the illusion of satiety.

On foot now, for it tears his heart out so much as to look at his horse, he goes to the pastures, there to behold the ruins of his ranch: steers that look more like ghostly cattle, still alive, no one knows how, lying beneath the dead trees and barely able to raise their withered carcasses upon their thin legs, as they stagger about slowly and aimlessly; others that have been dead for days and are still intact, since, no matter how much they may peck, not even the vultures are able to pierce these sun-parched hides; cattle that are about to breathe their last, gathered about the clearing of clotted earth where their favorite drinking pool once stood; and, what grieves him more than anything else, those that are not yet wholly exhausted now come up to him and surround him confidently, bellowing piteously all the while, as if they were weeping.

Not even a cactus is left in the vicinity; the last green leaves of the joaz trees have long since been nibbled away.

However, there are still the impenetrable macambira thickets. They are a last resort. He proceeds to set fire to their dead and withered foliage, by way of stripping them of their thorns as speedily as possible; and, as the smoke comes puffing up and spreads out on the limpid air, there may be seen running up from all sides a sad-looking troop of sickly cattle, lean and famished, in search of one last meal.

Finally, all his resources are exhausted, and the situation remains unchanged. There is no likelihood whatsoever of rain. The marizeiros are the harbingers of rain, and their trunks are not oozing moisture. The northeast wind continues to blow intensely, roaring over the plains, rustling and howling in the noisy foliage of the caatingas; and the flashing sun in a cloudless sky pours down the irresistible heat of the dog days. Done in with all his adversities, the sertanejo at last gives up.

One day he sees going past his door the first lot of "quitters." With deep forebodings, he watches the wretched throng as they cross the village terrace and disappear in a cloud of dust, around the bend of the road. The next day there are more of them, and still more. It means that the region is being evacuated. He can hold out no longer but joins one of these bands, which leave their bones along the wayside as they go. He goes with them on this painful exodus to the coast, to the distant mountains—any place where life's primordial element is not denied to man. He reaches such a place. He is saved.

Months go by, and the scourge is at an end. Overcome by homesickness for the backlands, he returns. He comes back happy, reinvigorated, singing; forgetful of his misfortunes, he comes back in quest of the same brief hours of unstable fortune, the same long days of anguish, of trials and tribulations long drawn out.

5

The first Brazilian Republic covered the era from 1891 to 1930. In 1894, after two military men had governed the country, civilian politicians, none of whom left a strong imprint on the history of the period, assumed control of the government. The administration of Manuel Ferraz de Campos Sales (1898-1902), which the Brazilian historian José María Bello discusses in the next essay, helped to set the tone for the succeeding administrations. Believing that agriculture was the "true source" of national wealth, Campos Sales followed a program that discouraged industrialization yet accepted the nineteenth-century liberalism of the industrial nations that stressed private enterprise and social Darwinism. The landed interests dictated national policy while the desires of the majority of the population were largely ignored. Powerful cliques of landed "colonels," particularly in the states of São Paulo and Minas Gerais, decided elections and turned national control of the political processes over to the state oligarchies.

José María Bello:
A History of Modern Brazil*

[President Manuel Ferraz de] Campos Sales's [1898–1902] inauguration was attended by representatives of nearly all the great powers; this impressive showing tickled the vanity of Brazilians,

* Reprinted from A HISTORY OF MODERN BRAZIL, 1889–1964, by José Mariá Bello; translated from the Portuguese by James L. Taylor with the permission of the publishers, Stanford University Press. © 1966 by the Board of Trustees of the Leland Stanford Junior University.

who were generally regarded as incorrigible revolutionists. On assuming the presidency, Campos Sales found the nation wearier than ever. The Republic's first civilian government had not succeeded in restoring internal harmony; the strife that had torn the country had prevented the reconstruction of its administration. What hopes could the new President hold out? What would his financial plan mean for the weakened nation?

During the first republican decade, conditions in Brazil were not much different, after all, from those during the twilight years of the Empire. After the Encilhamento's [era of boom and collapse] short spell of euphoria had vanished, the Brazilian privileged classes had returned to their former way of life. The rural middle classes, their dreams of easy riches shattered, went back to their abandoned fazendas, where they could enjoy at least a degree of self-sufficiency. Even the great mass of former slaves, who, intoxicated by their unexpected freedom, had deserted the old feudal estates, once more sought the shelter of the "big house."

But the fazendas had lost their former plenty. The downfall of sugar, reduced to serving the modest domestic markets, had ruined the Northeastern sugar barons, and paralyzed their initiative. The crisis in coffee prices was threatening the fazendeiros in the South with a like fate. The extraordinary boom in Amazon rubber bolstered the sick national economy a little, and proved the salvation of the *nortistas* who had been reckless in risking their lives in the malarial swamps of the jungles and in selling their souls to the greedy rubber extractors.

The remarks with which Joaquim Murtinho had begun his report as Minister of Transportation at the beginning of the Prudente de Morais [first civilian president of the Republic, 1894–98] administration were no doubt a guide for Campos Sales. Analyzing Brazil's general economic and financial situation, Joaquim Murtinho did not merely criticize the policies followed until then by the Republic. He also outlined a plan of government based on the formal logic of the nineteenth-century liberal economists. The republican policy, according to Murtinho, embodied two dangerous illusions, a belief in the extraordinary riches of Brazil and confidence in the dynamic capacity of inconvertible paper, which in the final analysis were only different aspects of the same error.

Beginning with the first idea, the republican statesmen had believed it possible to industrialize the country rapidly. An increase in tariffs and steady emissions of inconvertible currency by both the Treasury and the banks were naturally the means by which the government could foment material progress. Since the Brazilians did not possess the initiative and work habits of the North

Americans, and Murtinho did not mention the basic elements of heavy industry found in the United States, such as coal and iron, all attempts at industrialization were doomed to failure. The new industries did not get beyond the planning stage. They merely immobilized a part of the capital in circulation, stimulated urbanism, and increased imports, all to the detriment of agriculture, the true source of Brazil's national wealth.

Inflationism spurred speculation and gambling, and, worst of all, depressed the rate of exchange, for to Murtinho, as to all subscribers to the quantitative theory of money, the rate of exchange was tied almost wholly to the volume of paper in circulation. As a logical consequence of the protectionist and industrializing policies, there arose a mania for public jobs and government controls. These in turn were transforming the government into an entrepreneur of works and services, thus [said Murtinho] paving the way for the advent of the greatest plague of modern societies: socialism.

There was nothing new in the doctrine outlined by Murtinho. It could be found in any manual of political economy, and corresponded perfectly to the individualistic conception of the nineteenth-century philosophers. Cold, skeptical, a man of affairs, a Darwinist by instinct and education, Joaquim Murtinho was the most self-consistent of the Republic's ministers. Diagnosing Brazilian life, he also prescribed the remedy, but as a homeopathic physician accustomed to treating symptoms, he applied the same technique to his handling of Brazil's finances.

Brazil's problem was essentially to balance the Treasury's finances. It was therefore absolutely necessary to deflate the currency, cut expenses, increase taxes, abandon public works, return to agriculture, and withdraw the government from industrial activity, which could flourish only under free, individual enterprise. In his rigid understanding of liberal economics, Murtinho dissociated the financial problem from the economic one. Once the government was able to restore the soundness of its money, which would raise exchange rates and balance the budget, the reconstitution of economic forces would come about automatically, without dangerous official interference. The weakest, those least able to adjust, would perish in the competition to survive. Darwin's theory of natural selection was regarded at the time as almost infallible scientific dogma. The state, a mere juridical expression of the social superorganization, should not be influenced by sentimental considerations.

It was easy at first for Campos Sales to adhere strictly to his administrative plans and to carry out the terms of the funding loan. Beginning in January 1899 the government would deposit with the British and German banks in Rio, which would act as trustees, the paper currently withdrawn from circulation according to the terms of the loan. The Chamber, in agreement with the administration, chose to have the paper burned rather than kept on deposit, in order to prevent its possible use in banking transactions that might stimulate speculation in foreign exchange.

A gold reserve fund for the outstanding paper currency was set up; the gold was to be accumulated from customs duties. A fund for the redemption of Treasury bills was also set up. It was to be supported by the revenue from leased federal railroads, budget surpluses, and any other available resources. The government's plan was capped by an increase in taxes.

The percentage of customs duties that had to be paid in gold was raised from 10 to 15 per cent, and in the next year the tariff was thoroughly revised. The government, which had earlier been so adverse to a protectionist policy, now went much further in that direction than any of its predecessors, although it announced the tariff increase simply as a revenue measure. Stamp and excise taxes on domestic goods were also created, as well as stamps for direct taxation of income. The Union's fiscal net spread over the entire country; it included all visible sources of revenue and assessed numerous additional tax liabilities. The states copied the federal example, increasing especially the taxes on the exports allotted to them by the Constitution. The already debilitated Brazilian economy, precariously supported by São Paulo's coffee and Amazonia's rubber, had to hand over its meager surpluses to the three overlapping fiscal systems of the Union, the states, and the municípios.

Joaquim Murtinho's deflationist policy was having its first full effect on business and banking credit, both inadequately established in the first place. Bankruptcies followed one after another, culminating with that of the Banco República, which had been created by a merger of the Banco do Brasil and the Banco da República do Estados Unidos do Brasil. In September 1900 the semiofficial bank suspended payments, which set off a tremendous panic. In keeping with his doctrine of the survival of the fittest, the Minister of Finance let the bank go under.

The reestablishment of credit abroad and the rise in the exchange rates were compensation enough for the domestic hardships. The quantitative theory of money had won a great victory in actual practice. In the four years 1898–1902, while the total of inconvertible paper dropped from 780,000 to 679,000 contos, the rate of exchange rose from 8½ to 12½ pence to the milreis. The national budget showed a surplus, and the government was piling up gold in the London banks.

By the end of these four years, 116,000 contos of Treasury paper had been redeemed. In 1901 it had been possible to resume paying the service on the foreign debt in gold. The government had paid off the Treasury loan of £1,120,000 contracted by Prudente de Morais. The Treasury owed nothing and had a credit balance in its accounts. The market price for the government's foreign and domestic bonds was rising; public revenues had also increased. Campos Sales and Joaquim Murtinho could claim that they had achieved their goal.

But Brazil had grown even poorer. The sugar barons of the Northeast had been ruined; their lands had gone to the money-lenders in the cities. A similar fate menaced the coffeegrowers in the South. The old hopes of urban industrialization had gone glimmering, binding the economy to monoculture and exports. The increased taxes raised the living costs Murtinho had promised to reduce. But the Treasury, saved by the people's increased poverty, had been refilled, and the European bankers had regained their confidence in Brazil as a field for profitable investment.

The Rothschilds were sincere in their praises of Campos Sales at the end of his term of office. The flow of capital from Europe to Brazil, now that the country had been saved from bankruptcy, began once more and continued until after World War I, when American competition appeared on the scene. The Treasury's restored finances would enable Campos Sales's successor, the prudent and clear-sighted Rodrigues Alves, to inaugurate a period of national development.

The execution of the financial plan completely monopolized the attention of Campos Sales's administration. But in order to execute it, Campos Sales first had to tone down party conflicts, diminish Congress's itch for greater independence, and restrain dissension in state politics. The conservative reaction that arose during and persisted after the adoption of the Constitution of 1891 had shown how the chief executive, even without military dictatorship, could run the country with no great hindrance. Using different methods, Campos Sales would arrive at a like position.

The top priority of the financial problem had naturally made Joaquim Murtinho, as Minister of Finance, the cabinet's leading figure. Epitácio Pesoa, who had made a name for himself in the Constituent Assembly while still quite young, and who had been Florian Piexoto's unrelenting foe, had been made Minister of the Interior and of Justice. Severino Vieira, a politician from Bahia, was Minister of Transportation and Public Works, and Olinto

Magalhães, Minister Plenipotentiary in Switzerland, was Minister of Foreign Affairs. General Medeiros Mallet and Admiral Pinto da Luz had taken their posts as War Minister and Navy Minister, respectively. By thus selecting his cabinet from among the various republican factions and freeing himself from any possibility of partisan control, Campos Sales had caused what was left of the PRF and of the Republican party organized by followers of Prudente de Morais to rapidly dissolve, though he did not succeed in eliminating the rancor that divided them.

The approaching elections for a new Chamber and one-third of the Senate in 1900 served to restrain the politicians, who were eager to remain in the government's good graces. Each of the two large, disintegrating groups created by the splintering of the PRF [Partido Republicano Federal] was hoping to win the government's favor, which would make the reelection of its members certain. The state parties presented their own complete tickets, hoping to win at the third and final scrutiny of the mandates, made by Congress and following the one made by the tally boards. There was even some consideration given to electing two chambers in order to force the government to choose between the opposing factions.

To prevent the threatened confusion, the government secured a revision in the rules of the Chamber to provide that the actual mandates would result from the final vote counts signed by a majority of the municipal chambers in each electoral district. It further proposed that the temporary presidency of the newly elected Chamber would be held, not by the oldest member of the previous body, as was then the practice, but by its former president, provided he had been reelected, of course. The new president was to appoint a five-man committee to pass on the validity of the credentials. The committees of inquiry into contested elections would be chosen by lot. Thus, by means of the powerful "Committee of Five," the government could arbitrarily recognize or repudiate the mandates that were presumably from the people.

As an extension of his political plan, Campos Sales secured the support of some large states, principally Minas Gerais, whose governor declared his support to be unconditional. In exchange, the recognition of mandates in the new Chamber and partly reelected Senate would favor the local parties that sided with the government. By serving their interests, Campos Sales won their backing for the execution of his financial policy. Thus any evidence of victory at the polls by the opposition in the states was disregarded in advance; the candidates put up by the local governments were automatically seated. The old comedy of democratic elections in Brazil was being officially sanctioned.

However, the most serious consequence of Campos Sales's political horse-trading with the governors was the immediate consolidation of the state oligarchies. The groups that had gained control of the states were made up mainly of former members of the monarchic parties. They calmly went about setting up powerful machines devoted to graft, bribery, and violence. Although the Congress of 1900 had the same vicious origins as the Congresses, including the imperial Parliaments, that preceded it, it was the one that gave up its last pretense of free political power.

The Union was converted into feuding groups, large and small, concerned much more with their regional interests than with those of the nation as a whole. Their demographic and economic superiority gave São Paulo and Minas the leading positions in political control. Rio Grande do Sul, with Borges de Medeiros at its head, but still under the powerful discipline imposed by Júlio de Castilhos, was another decisive element. It was represented on the federal level by the increasingly prestigious Pinheiro Machado. Pernambuco, Bahia, and the state of Rio de Janeiro were the other "big states" that had numerous representatives in the legislative bodies. The small states gravitated into the orbits of the big ones, as if imitating the international balance-of-power game.

The priority he had given financial problems, and his solution of them, did not exempt Campos Sales from the political difficulties that had plagued his predecessors. His control of politics through the state governors had apparently given him almost unanimous support by Congress, but his hopes were quickly dashed. Partisan feelings were only waiting for an opportunity to explode. Opposition in the newspapers grew from day to day, criticizing the extortionate tax regulations and the scandalous "recognition of mandates." Some former monarchic leaders, unreconciled to the Republic, tried to use the growing discontent as an opportunity for revolution and restoration, but the government, without resorting to a state of siege, easily thwarted their plots.

The opposition political movement headed by Rosa e Silva, the Vice-President, was more serious. It recreated the situation that had arisen between Deodoro [da Fonseca, Marshal of the army and first President of the Republic, 1899–91] and Floriano [Peixoto, general and President of the Republic, 1891–94], and between Prudente de Morais and Manuel Vitorino. Under Rosa e Silva's leadership, the congressional blocs from Pernambuco and Maranhão, allied to the opposition in some of the states, came out against the government's financial policies, especially on the leasing of the railroads [to foreigners].

In September 1901 political dissension by Prudente de Morais broke out in São Paulo, some of whose brilliant and active deputies threw their support to the opposition in Congress. For some years deep, unspoken grounds for misunderstanding had seemed to exist between Campos Sales and Prudente de Morais. Certain groups were naturally interested in stimulating the dissension, when it had come to light, over the question of choosing a governor for São Paulo. In spite of conciliatory efforts by Governor-elect Rodrigues Alves, Campos Sales's rigid criterion for the recognition of mandates by the Congress had been rejected immediately by some Paulista deputies closely tied to Prudente de Morais. Shortly afterwards, the Paulista faction set forth in a manifesto their reasons for dissent, insisting, as a point of doctrine, on the necessity for a constitutional revision that would moderate the excessive powers held by the President of the Republic.

National public opinion, insofar as such a term applies to Brazil's disjointed immensity, held Campos Sales's severe fiscal administration in low esteem. The public was pleased by the violence of the opposition press campaign, and enjoyed the fiery debates in the Chamber of Deputies, especially during the agitated period when newly elected or reelected representatives were seated, but its enthusiasms were not aroused by the politicians' campaign, since it was accustomed to doubt their sincerity anyway. The conservative lower-middle classes would not forgive the high taxes, but mostly they wanted the administration's term of office to end peaceably, in the hopes that the new President, Rodrigues Alves, would initiate a less drastic policy. The Republic had already suffered much at the hands of its saviors.

On November 15, 1902, when he stepped down from the presidency, Campos Sales experienced a final outburst of popular antipathy for his government, cleverly fostered by the opposition newspapers. His passage from the presidential palace to the railway station, where he was to embark for São Paulo, was accompanied by prolonged jeering and booing from the crowds that lined the streets. His pride must have suffered greatly from the public hostility, which contrasted so greatly with the acclamations Prudente de Morais had received four years earlier. But Campos Sales's conscience as an administrator must have been clear. After the sacrifice demanded of him by the Brazilian people, he was leaving his successor a house in order, its accounts in balance.

Republican politics had been degraded more than ever by his system of control through the governors. The democratic significance of Congress had been debased. The last hopes of free play between representative institutions were fading. His admitted buying of newspaper influence had officialized journalistic corruption.

His extreme monetary deflation had provided a screen behind which bankers and speculators, both foreign and domestic, reaped excellent profits. Nevertheless, Campos Sales had to his credit his perfect personal uprightness, his tolerance, and the firmness with which he met his government's commitments. Without his four years of strong fiscal rule, it would have been very hard for Rodrigues Alves to embark on his large program of public works.

To the further credit of Campos Sales's administration were the first decisive steps taken to develop the Civil Code, submitted to Congress as a draft bill by Clóvis Bevilaqua. In foreign policy he had tried to bring about closer continental relations, which had so greatly concerned the first republican rulers. The arbitration of the old Misiones conflict had not hurt the friendship between Brazil and Argentina. In August 1899 Argentine President Júlio Roca made an official visit to the capital of Brazil, a visit Campos Sales returned in the following year. The Baron of Rio Branco had scored another diplomatic victory in the dispute over Amapá. Joaquim Nabuco, despite his enormous efforts, had not been as successful in the contention with England about British Guiana. But the essential fact in 1902 was that the Republic could look back on its past internal disorders and financial ventures as a closed chapter, and was ready for a new time of order and constructive work.

6

In a number of significant ways, modern Brazil dates from 1930. As Thomas E. Skidmore of the University of Wisconsin points out, the *Estado Nôvo* of Getulio Vargas encouraged a profound transformation of the nation. Politically, Vargas' regime repudiated the decentralized formula of government of the First Republic, curtailed many of the powers and prerogatives of the states, and thereby undermined the role of the old landed interests, the "colonels." Whether by accident or by design, the *Estado Nôvo* favored the industrialization of Brazil. While the emphasis on coffee survived, the government's stress of industrialization decreased coffee's importance within the national economy. A charismatic figure, Vargas spoke for a country in a state of change, especially for the new urban masses whose support he courted with a populist program of social benefits and labor legislation.

Thomas E. Skidmore:
Politics in Brazil*

The Estado Nôvo brought irreversible changes in the institutions of political life and public administration. Most important, Vargas transformed the relationship between federal authority and state authority, and thereby moved Brazil much closer to a truly national government.

In 1945, Brazil inherited a federal executive which was immeasurably stronger than the one the revolutionaries had seized in 1930. The process by which the federal government was steadily strengthened at the expense of state and local government began in November 1930 and was accelerated after 1937. There was a political and an administrative aspect to the process, although the two were closely related.

The federal government increased its powers in the administrative sphere in two different ways. First, many functions previously exercised by state and local government were shifted into the area of federal competence. Before 1930 many of the most important functions of government had been exercised by the states, which enjoyed wide autonomy. States such as São Paulo, for example, were in the habit of directly negotiating foreign loans to be used for facilities such as railroads and docks, or for the financing of the coffee support program. In the fundamental areas of education and labor, responsibility under the Old Republic had been left almost entirely to the states. Immediately after the revolution of 1930, the situation began to change. For many years critics of the old order had been arguing that Brazil's enormous social needs demanded a national effort by a strong federal government. Even before the Constitution of 1934 had codified this new role, the Vargas government, in its provisional status, gained by decree of November 11, 1930, broader powers than any previous government had ever enjoyed. A new Ministry of Labor, Industry, and Commerce was created in December 1930, and supervision over the production and marketing of coffee was transferred from state to federal auspices, in return for a higher level of support. New federal institutes of pine, tea, salt, and sugar and alcohol were set up after 1937; these government-sponsored cartels represented the assumption of federal responsibility in areas in which no government had previously claimed authority.

This leads to the second method by which federal administrative predominance grew: federal activity in new areas. The Vargas years saw a repudiation in Brazil of the "gendarme" theory, which held that the state should be a policeman, not a participant. Increasing federal intervention in the economy required new federal agencies which, in turn, further weakened the relative power of the states and municipalities. Federal ownership in industries such as railways and shipping, and mixed public-private corporations—a favored technique for stimulating investment in basic industries after 1938—responded to the policy direction of Rio de Janeiro. In this system, regional influences could be brought to bear only through the channels of national government.

New federal responsibility in two other areas—social welfare and labor union organization—further increased federal power. Although federal activity in these areas accelerated under the Estado Nôvo, and was considered by Vargas to be the cornerstone of his new political style after 1943, it had been initiated even before the Constitution of 1934. Income-flows channeled through the social welfare institutes and labor syndicates, although not part of federal revenues, were nonetheless transfer payments supervised by federal and not state or municipal authorities. The effect was to increase direct federal contact at the local level, thereby undermining the foundation of the *política dos governadores* ("politics of the governors") which had prevailed before 1930.

The power of state and municipal government was also eroded by the restricting of traditional sources of tax revenue. Tax jurisdictions were revised by the constitutions of 1934 and 1937, in the latter case eliminating what had been a major source of state revenue—interstate (called "export") taxes. This was an important step in creating a national market.

Along with the overall growth of federal responsibility went a growth in federal bureaucracy. The latter was institutionalized under Vargas with the creation of DASP (*Departamento Administrativo do Serviço Público*), the federal agency set up in 1938 with functions roughly equal to the combined roles of the Bureau of the Budget and the Civil Service Commission in the United States. DASP became an important instrument for raising administrative standards, but it was also a means by which Vargas could increase his personal control (and, for his successors, the powers of the President) over federal administration.

All of these additions to federal administrative authority and competence had great political repercussions. The federal executive gained enormous patronage power, both in the sense of federally controlled jobs and in the sense of the favoritism or discrimination inherent in the exercising of the growing administrative powers. It included, for example, control over low-interest loans from the Bank of Brazil, public works projects, differential exchange rates, and import controls. This increase in the political leverage of the presidency was felt most strongly in those parts of the country which were most dynamic politically—the urbanizing areas. Thus Vargas was able to use the greatly strengthened federal executive to forge what Brazil had failed to achieve before 1930: a more truly national polity.

The growth of new political institutions on the federal level therefore served two purposes: it was part of the process of unifying the sprawling country administratively; and it helped enable the President to articulate a national network of political alliances.

The increased centralization under Vargas was a reaction to the decentralization imposed by the Republican constitution-writers of 1889–91, who had wished to undo what they regarded as the harmful overcentralization of the Empire (1822–89). Except for the Paulistas, who still treasured their uniquely efficient regionalism, the majority of those who welcomed the end of the Old Republic in 1930 hoped for a more centralized Brazil. This was especially true of the urban classes, who had failed to win what they considered their rightful political representation from the agrarian-dominated political elite. Both the liberal constitutionalists and the tenentes knew that their goals had greatest prospects for success under a strong federal regime. If it came to a choice between anarchy and authoritarianism, a surprisingly large number of the revolutionaries of 1930 were willing to opt for the latter, if only implicitly.

In effect, they were unwilling to fight the dictatorship without first seeing what it might accomplish. Indeed, many of the institutional innovations of the Estado Nôvo were merely logical extensions in the growth of the federal executive which had begun in Vargas' first phase. With the exception of a few institutions, such as the propaganda and press censorship agency (*Departamento de Imprensa e Propaganda* or DIP) and the secret police, the administrative structure of the Estado Nôvo was as much a response to the challenge of effectively governing and rapidly transforming the country as it was a set of devices to facilitate Vargas' personal rule. This fact helps explain why the Estado Nôvo began and ended with relatively little social tension.

In addition to the administrative changes, what were the political techniques which Vargas used to increase his own power and that of the federal government? Once installed in the presidency in 1930, he had been faced with the immediate problem of consolidating the new regime's power. Since 1889 national politics had been the prerogative of the leaders of the most powerful states. Minas Gerais and São Paulo had been the leaders in this system, with Rio Grande do Sul and Rio de Janeiro growing in importance, and Bahia and Pernambuco declining in relative power. From 1930 until 1945 Vargas strove to replace this quasi-confederation with a strong federal executive (redounding to Vargas' greater personal power, of course) at the expense of the state political machines. By the midpoint of the period, 1937, Vargas had succeeded to a remarkable extent in neutralizing the local political oligarchs who previously had been the key to national politics.

It was this outmaneuvering of the opposition in the principal states which enabled Vargas to capitalize upon the division, demoralization, and ineptitude of the political forces generated by the Revolution of 1930. Even before the coup of 1937, Vargas had amply demonstrated his extraordinary talents of political persuasion. He seldom failed to cultivate a minority faction in a state where the leadership was hostile. By assiduously maintaining intimate political contacts with the "opposition," Vargas was able to hold out the promise of federal endorsement if the pro-Vargas faction should reach power. Since the patronage powers of the federal government were growing enormously, federal favor could be of great value to a local politician. It could mean influence over the growing operations of the federal authorities in his locality. Without Vargas' support, such influence was far more difficult. After the coup of 1937, it was impossible. But even before the Estado Nôvo, Vargas demonstrated how effectively he could use persuasion, cajolery, and the promise of spoils to exploit for his own benefit the traditional power struggles within the political leadership of the major states.

There were other assets which Vargas enjoyed in his dealings with state politicians. For those who harbored national ambitions, Vargas' blessing was almost indispensable after 1935, and a *sine qua non* after 1937. With the rapidly growing federal responsibility in so many fields, as staked out by the actions of the provisional government of 1930–34 and by the Constitution of 1934, any Brazilian politician who wished to help direct his country's destiny had to contemplate national politics or federal administration. The leverage which Vargas thereby gained is obvious.

One of Vargas' constant targets was the extreme regionalism

of some states, of which the São Paulo revolt of 1932 was the leading example. Vargas appealed to the higher sentiment of nationalism and was thus able to cut across conflicting regional sympathies. After the coup of 1937, Vargas adopted a more direct approach: in late November 1937, the dictator held a public ceremony at which he burned the traditional state flags.

Both before and after 1937, Vargas made frequent use of "Interventors." This was the title, as noted earlier, given to the federally appointed Governor who was also invested with legislative powers. Where states were rebellious, Vargas resorted to using military officers as Interventors. Although their power was limited by their own ability to gain the cooperation of local power centers, some Interventors proved highly successful deputies of federal authority. By using a bevy of such devices, Vargas was able, in the major states, to undermine the traditional political clans and to create in their place a network of nationally oriented local alliances. In the Vargas era, these alliances were designed to be loyal to the President himself. Perhaps the most successful case of Vargas' cultivation of a state leadership was Minas Gerais, where his Interventor, Benedito Valladares, was a valuable ally in the preparations for the coup of 1937. After Vargas' fall in 1945, these pro-Vargas state leaderships proved to be responsive to orders from other holders of national power, demonstrating that Vargas had fashioned a system of national government which would outlast him.

In explaining Vargas' political success after 1930, one should also note that he managed to make himself the symbol, in the eyes of many of the younger generation, of a sense of national purpose. From 1930 to 1932 he had been able to exploit the ideas, enthusiasm, and administrative ability of the small group of younger military, known as the tenentes, and their civilian allies, such as Oswaldo Aranha. Even after most of their number had become disillusioned or had been discarded by Vargas, there were other idealists who identified their hopes with the revolutionary President. Francisco Campos, a young lawyer from Minas Gerais and author of the Constitution of 1937, is the most famous example. There were many others, like José Américo de Almeida. Some were to desert Vargas before the coup of 1937. The reasoned support of younger intellectuals, usually of middle-class background, helped to furnish at each stage an aura of legitimacy for a leader who was not given to ideological self-justification. Such intellectual legitimacy was important for many Brazilians who quietly approved Vargas' policies but wished to be given some rationale for the President's actions.

Although Vargas himself was not given to nourishing a "cult of personality," he allowed his propaganda agency (DIP), through both its national and its state offices, to chant his praises in publications such as the monthly *O Brasil de Hoje, de Ontem e de Amanhã* (first published in 1939). Yet Getúlio undoubtedly looked on such adulation skeptically. He approved it as long as it continued to absorb the energy of some otherwise restless intellectuals and filled a vacuum left by the suppression of democratic politics. But Vargas' reliance on these instruments borrowed from European fascism was in no sense irreversible. He was well aware of the irreverent humor that his countrymen, especially the Cariocas (residents of the city of Rio de Janeiro), aimed at the would-be dictator. Vargas later explained that during the years from 1930 to 1945 "popular jokes were my guide, indicating a safe path in the midst of the pleasant smile and the delicate venom distilled from the good humor of the Carioca." He concluded that it was "this profound respect for the popular intelligence" that "created the identity of minds and the communion between the actions of the government and the will of the people."

Despite his immodesty, Vargas was justified in pointing to his masterful knowledge of Brazilian psychology as one of his greatest political assets. Visitors to Brazil during the Estado Nôvo, such as journalist John Gunther and constitutional lawyer Karl Loewenstein, were fascinated by the way in which Vargas' political dominance was in part based on his chameleon-like ability to embody the national character. His exasperated enemies invariably labeled him "Machiavellian." This description was accurate; Getúlio would also have found it flattering.

But what about the role of political parties? As noted in the analysis of new political forces, the Estado Nôvo was an authoritarian, non-party way out of Brazil's political inexperience and the resulting political deadlock of the mid-1930's. A genuine innovation on the level of political parties would have been the creation of truly national organizations. Neither the liberal constitutionalists nor the tenentes had been able to accomplish this before the first national parties—the Integralistas and the Communists—unwittingly abetted Vargas' plan to impose his authoritarian rule. Since Vargas took great care not to create any government party, the Estado Nôvo produced no new parties. The brief operation of the Electoral Code of 1932 had, however, demonstrated how important party organization would be under free elections. The lesson was not lost on Vargas, who nevertheless postponed as long as possible any thought of organizing his own political movement. The "non-political" system of the Estado Nôvo offered the perfect medium for his great talents of conciliation and manipulation which in turn depended upon highly personal contact with opponents and allies.

During the last two years of the Estado Nôvo (1943 to 1945), Vargas was farsighted enough to realize that his dictatorship could not survive the war. His fascism, although second-hand, was bound to be shaken by the coming demise of fascism in Europe, toward whose defeat the Brazilian Army was contributing an expeditionary force. In 1943 Vargas therefore endorsed the efforts of one of his most trusted political lieutenants, Labor Minister Marcondes Filho, who began propounding the rationale for a new political movement. Vargas was anticipating the moment when the political system would be reopened, and power would rest on the electoral process.

This attempt to build a new political base was part of a three-pronged effort by Vargas to preempt the left of the political spectrum. First came the extensive social welfare legislation (such as medical and pension benefits), designed to gain worker loyalty for the paternalistic government which had implemented these programs. The doctrine to justify this system was *trabalhismo,* which Marcondes Filho spelled out in his famous radio broadcasts, "A Hora do Brasil," starting in 1942. Furthermore, the new union structure was administered under close control from the Ministry of Labor, thus giving the government an important source of influence within the urban economy, as well as a vast patronage instrument for converting potential opponents into political clients. Government control over the unions (*Sindicatos*) took several forms. First, only those unions recognized by the Ministry of Labor were legal. As the union organization increased after 1941 under government pressure, the Labor Ministry was able to place its agents (later termed *pelegos* or "political henchmen") in positions of leadership, thus excluding the independent labor militants (including especially anarcho-syndicalists and Communists) who had been active in the fledgling labor movement before 1937. The "bureaucratization" of the union structure was given a further institutional basis with the introduction of the compulsory labor union membership dues (*impôsto sindical*) in the amount of one day's wages per year deducted from the worker's pay-check. The funds were then distributed to the government-recognized unions by the Ministry of Labor. This paternalistic organization imposed upon the labor sector by Vargas was part of the overall corporatist economic structure that the Estado Nôvo government laid out for the entire urban society.

Vargas' third tactic was to be a Labor Party based on a coalition of the government-dominated labor unions and the "progressive" forces that Vargas hoped to lead by embracing programs of industrialization, economic nationalism, and social welfarism. In a speech in 1943 discussing his postwar political plans, Vargas promised that workers would have a prominent role among the "new groups that are full of energy and enthusiasm, capable of faith and of carrying out the tasks of our development." In 1944 he called on the workers of São Paulo to join the government-supervised unions and thus participate in the necessary "change of mentality" required by the "rapidity of the transformations in economic life."

The last two years of the Estado Nôvo therefore foreshadowed the beginning of a new ("third") phase in Vargas' political career. During his first phase (1930 to 1937), he played the role of the political arbiter and conspirator for dictatorial powers. The second covered the dictatorship of the Estado Nôvo. Now, after 1943, Vargas was in effect laying the groundwork for his later emergence as a "democratic" leader who would rely on support from a new popular movement as well as from more established groups such as rural landowners, São Paulo industrialists, and the bureaucracy. Before we can understand how the "third" Vargas was able to return to power in 1950 after having been forced from office in 1945, we must first examine those innovations in the area of economic policy, which, along with the changes in political institutions, were to make the era from 1930 to 1945 a watershed in modern Brazilian history.

7

The *Estado Nôvo* introduced and coincided with a radical transformation of the national economy, but in both a political and an economic sense the changes did not proceed far enough. Much of the old structure survived and created a conflict between the present and future needs of Brazil and the pre-1930 establishment. Celso Furtado, a Brazilian economist, believes that the basic problems stem from the attempt to impose industrialization which, he says, came as a byproduct "of policies aimed at other objectives," on the "substructure of an economy based on the export of primary products." Many of the new industrialists, particularly in São Paulo, had a vested stake in the coffee economy. Thus no completely autonomous class of industrialists won control of national policies. Industrial Brazil, therefore, lacks a political voice commensurate with the necessity to reorient policy if the nation is to enter the modern industrial stage. This weakness, writes Furtado, underlies recent political difficulties.

Celso Furtado: Diagnosis of the Brazilian Crisis*

Brazilian economic development over the last three decades has been a typical case of industrialization directed toward substitution for imports. The expansion of coffee plantations that took place under the stimulus of the high prices prevailing in the late 'twenties led the country into an overproduction crisis at the very moment when the world market was becoming disorganized. Thus the country had simultaneously to face both the external crisis that obliged it to cut imports by half and an internal crisis provoked by the need to finance large surpluses of coffee production. In effect, there were years when the amount of coffee purchased for accumulation or destruction represented as much as 10 percent of the Gross Internal Product. The immediate aim of this policy was, of course, the defense of the coffee-growing interests.

Purchase of surplus coffee financed by expanding the means of payment tended to inflate the money income and to depreciate Brazilian currency abroad, which also favored the coffee growers and coffee merchants, since the price of this product went up in local currency although its international exchange rate was declining. This policy, however, had far wider consequences than were foreseen at the time. In effect, the rapid and persistent depreciation of the currency constituted a powerful protectionist barrier for domestic industry, which began to operate two or three shifts daily with the aid of small additional investments. The profits of

* From Celso Furtado, DIAGNOSIS OF THE BRAZILIAN CRISIS, trans. by Suzette Macedo (Berkeley and Los Angeles: University of California Press, 1965), pp. xiv–xxiv.

the external sector declined, since official backing could only partially compensate for the drop in the real value of exports. Manufacturing production began to attract entrepreneurial capacity and financial resources on a growing scale. In this way, at the same time that the volume of foreign trade was reduced, productive capacity became more diversified. Between 1929 and 1937, while imports declined by 23 percent, industrial output rose by 50 percent.

The most recent phase of Brazilian industrialization is equally illustrative of the disparity between the political objectives aimed at and the results achieved. With a view to defending the international price of coffee, which was threatened by the large stocks still held in Brazil, the Brazilian government, immediately after World War II, followed a policy of external over-valuation of national currency. Experience had demonstrated that devaluation of the cruzeiro would have adverse repercussions on the international price of coffee, leading to a deterioration in the country's terms of trade. This policy, however, had the same effect as a lowering of the customs tariff, leaving national industry unprotected in the face of external competition. The strong protests of industrial interests were ignored, and the more powerful interests associated with foreign trade prevailed.

Once again, however, it was the indirect consequences, unforeseen by the policy-makers, that, in the long run, proved to be of the greatest significance. Exports rose rapidly while over-valuation of the currency was maintained, exhausting the reserves accumulated during the war and initiating the process of piling up external debt. Since coffee was the over-riding consideration, and since a fall in coffee prices would have proved even more serious in view of the external debt, the government chose to introduce a system of controlling imports rather than devaluate the cruzeiro. This import control necessarily tended to favor the purchase of capital goods and other inputs in order to defend the level of existing industrial activity. Immediately below, in the scale of priorities, came the machinery destined to expand the capacity of existing industries. Thus, under the aegis of the defense of the external price of coffee, a twofold protection of industry was created: for all practical purposes, importing of "similar" products was prohibited, and exchange coverage was guaranteed for primary products, intermediary goods, and machinery at a subsidized rate. The government's firmness in maintaining this policy when the small coffee harvest of 1949 was announced was the cause of the sharp rise in the price of this product that took place in that year. On the other hand, the rise in coffee prices created the conditions that led the government to persist in its policy. In brief, as an indirect consequence of the policy of defending coffee prices, a substantial portion of the income created between 1949 and 1954 by the improvement in the terms of trade was transferred to the industrial sector by means of exchange subsidies.

The above observations make it clear that Brazilian industrialization was less the result of deliberate policy than the indirect consequence of measures taken to favor the interests of the traditional export economy. Unlike the classical type of industrialization, which got under way by creating its own market through the relative drop in prices which it promoted in markets previously supplied by craft industries, industrialization of a "substitution" type, like that which occurred in Brazil, takes place during a phase of rising prices of manufactured products, the result of a steep decline in the importation of these products.

The fact that industrialization occurred as a by-product of policies aimed at other objectives had various consequences. Thus, the effort to convert the substructure of an economy based on the export of primary products into an industrial system was not undertaken at the right time. The size of the country led to the creation of a constellation of regional economies linked to the foreign markets, but between the members of the constellation there was a limited mobility of production and little interchange. Industrialization had to be based on the integration of these semi-autonomous economies, which called for important investments of social capital by the Public Authority. On the other hand, obstacles to the import of "non-essential" products were raised without any compensatory measures. In this way, the less "essential" a product was, the more attractive investment in its production became, since such industries were relatively more protected from external competition.

The subsidy implicit in imports of machinery provoked further distortions, with even graver consequences to the process of capital formation. Thus, excessive imports of equipment, with an eye to future speculation, led to the formation of idle capacity in certain industries, reducing the efficiency of the economic system as a whole. On the other hand, a rise in the capital coefficient per worker was favored, a situation which tended to aggravate the crucial problem of any underdeveloped country, which is the existence of a structural surplus of manpower.

Whatever may have been the characteristics of the industrialization process, there is no doubt that it entailed consequences for the country's social structure, with important repercussions on the institutions supporting the traditional power system. It would not be out of place to recall that the economic system and social structure of Brazil in 1930 had changed little from the century before. The country's economy continued to be based on the export of a number of tropical products, chiefly coffee, produced on the great estates, and the State continued to finance itself chiefly on the basis of taxes imposed on foreign trade. About four-fifths of the country's population lived on the large estates or was in one way or another subject to the direct authority of the great landowners. Only a small fraction of the population, about 1 percent, participated in the political process. The national state was vaguely identified by the mass of the population through some of its principal symbols. Local offices, even when these were integrated into the federal bureaucracy, were in the hands of the landowners, who held control of the municipal and state governments. In short, those who were in power possessed all the means to keep themselves in power.

Stagnation in the export agricultural sector, concentration of investments in manufacturing activities, and finally the growth of state activities have brought about important changes in the country's social structure over the last three decades. The principal manifestation of change was a process of rapid urbanization. In effect, the Brazilian population, which in 1920 was about 30 million, with about 7 million living in the cities, is today more than 80 million, of whom more than 35 million are concentrated in urban areas, with a much greater proportional growth in medium and large cities. As the urban population represents a much higher coefficient of literacy than the rural, it is natural that political activity should have undergone an important shift in its center of gravity, at least insofar as the electoral process is concerned.

These changes in the social structure did not, however, find any adequate correspondence in the framework of political institutions. The lack of an industrial class, whose position had been defined in terms of a conflict of interests with the basic interests of the former ruling groups, hindered the emergence of a new leadership who could promote the modernization of the institutional framework. Many causes can be found to which to attribute this lack of renewal in Brazilian political leadership, during a period when such important changes were taking place in the country's social structure. I shall draw attention only to the fact that industrialization which begins late in the present century has to create a considerable geographical concentration, in view of the importance of external economies, the need to operate on a basis of large units, the concentration of supplementary services, such as power supply and transport facilities, and so on. Thus, the São Paulo region came to represent an increasing proportion of Brazilian industrial output, and at present contributes approximately 40 percent of this output. This geographical concentration of industrial activity, in a country with a power structure organized on a federal basis, necessarily tends to reduce the political importance of the industrial sector. This circumstance, coupled with the fact that many industrialists also had agricultural interests, contributed toward continuing control of the principal centers of political decision by the leadership connected with the traditional economy.

To the lack of influence on political leadership by the industrial class must be attributed, to a large extent, the slow modernization of the political institutional framework in Brazil. Political constitutions, including the latest (established in 1946), have been a powerful instrument in the hands of the traditionalist oligarchy for preserving its position as the principal political force. The present federal system, in providing considerable power for the Senate, in which the small agricultural states of the most backward areas have a decisive influence, places the legislative power under the control of a minority of the population living in areas where the interests of the great estates hold undisputed sway. On the other hand, as representation of the individual states in the Chamber is proportional to population, illiterates are represented by literate fellow-citizens. Thus, the vote of a citizen living in a State where 80 percent of the population is illiterate is worth five times as much as the vote of a citizen living in a state with one hundred percent literacy. Since the traditional oligarchy is most powerful in the most illiterate areas, the electoral system contributes toward the maintenance of this oligarchy, which finds in illiteracy one of its props. This fact is not without bearing on the strong reaction shown by many local authorities in the more backward regions against the introduction of techniques for simplifying the spread of literacy.

Control of the principal centers of a power system is not a sufficient reason, however, for the majority of the population to accept as legitimate the authority emanating from this control. And it is because this legitimacy has been increasingly lacking in Brazil that the exercise of power by the ruling class has become increasingly difficult. In effect, the relative growth of the urban electorate has offered a permanent challenge to the control of the electoral system by the parties based on the oligarchy. Experience has already shown that, if the creation of new parties is possible, a movement based on the urban centers can decide the results of a major election. In fact, elections of the President of the Republic and State Governors in the more urbanized states have been increasingly influenced by forces that evade control by the oligarchy. Thus conditions had arisen in which the Executive Power represented emergent political forces that defied the control of the Establishment, which concentrates its forces in Congress. Tensions between the two power centers had increased over the last fifteen years, and had on occasion even led to hindrance of government action.

Changes in the Brazilian political process must be analyzed in the light of the modifications that have taken place in the country's social structure and particularly in the characteristics of its urbanization process. Unlike the classical case observable in Europe during the last century, in which urbanization expressed a rapid change in the occupational structure, for most of the industrial working class in Brazil urbanization has been much more complex. Brazilian industrialization was not accompanied by disorganization of the craft industries, and consequently the first-generation industrial worker was not conscious of having suffered any social degradation. On the contrary, having emerged from conditions similar to those of a rural serf, the worker was aware of having risen in the social scale. However, industrialization was only one of the factors responsible for urbanization. In actual fact, during the decade between 1950 and 1960, while industrial output grew at an annual rate close to 10 percent, employment in industry increased at a rate of 2.8 percent, or approximately half the rate of urban population growth. Increased public expenditure, with a heavy concentration of income creating an expanding market for services, is another factor responsible for the creation of urban employment.

The urbanization process does not constitute, however, a simple reflection of the changes in the country's occupational structure. The underemployed population living in urban areas has actually increased at an even greater speed than the number of people effectively employed in industries and services. This is a phenomenon that is not easy to explain if the country's present agricultural structure is not taken into account. The agricultural pattern that predominates throughout the country, based on rudimentary techniques, has been increasing its costs as a result of the natural exhaustion of soils and the moving of farms further inland from the principal consumption centers along the coast. According to the 1960 census, more than 90 percent of Brazilian agricultural land was situated on medium and large estates utilizing no more than 8 percent of this land for crops. While extreme underutilization of land continues, as a result of the way in which agriculture is organized, the expansion of the land under cultivation has been dependent to a large extent on multiplying the small estates, whose average size has decreased between 1950 and 1960, according to agricultural census figures for these years. Bearing in mind that this decrease in the average area of the small holding is coupled with soil exhaustion and increased distances from consumption centers, it is not surprising that the standard of living for a great part of the rural population has decreased. This population tends to move to another agricultural region to try to find some form of occupation. From this inter-rural migratory process a growing proportion of the population tends to filter into the urban areas, where even the most precarious livelihood seems attractive compared to the insecurity and extreme poverty of life on the land. In this way, in all Brazilian cities, medium and large, great masses of the underemployed begin to congregate, occasionally being employed in public works, building sites, and unstable jobs in services.

Together with the working class, who are of declining relative numerical importance, and the mass of the underemployed, who are of growing relative importance, the urban population is made up of a substantial and growing contingent of the "middle classes." Here, too, the simple transposition of concepts derived from different historical experiences must be avoided. The middle classes of the classical European model were marked by the presence of the "petit bourgeoisie," who were self-employed and motivated by a strong individualistic spirit, the basis of the Liberal ideology. The present Brazilian middle class is basically made up of white-collar workers, earning medium and high salaries, who work in the numerous government organizations, private banks, offices of industrial and commercial firms, and the various forms of services concentrated in big cities. This middle class is the backbone of the organs of state at their administrative level, the organs of communication, and the cultural institutions. Because they influence movements of opinion and interfere in the organs of decision, these middle-class groups have managed to acquire a series of privileges that range from control of agricultural prices to free higher education for their children. Although intellectually inclined toward the idea of development, and often adopting Leftist positions, the middle classes undoubtedly constitute a privileged group within the present system of income distribution.

This heterogeneous urban population, in which a privileged middle class exists side by side with a growing mass of the underemployed, had become the new decisive factor in Brazilian political struggles. Unlike the happenings in Europe in the last century, where social struggles assumed an increasingly defined form as a conflict between groups with growing class consciousness, which permitted the expression of these conflicts in terms of a political dialogue based on the confrontation of economic interests, in Brazil social tensions express states of dissatisfaction among a growing urban mass difficult to characterize. This amorphous mass is what constitutes the basis for the Populist movements that characterize Brazilian political struggles in recent decades.

In view of this rupture in the basis of the power system, the very principle of legitimacy has been seriously compromised. In order to make itself legitimate, the government must act within the framework of constitutional principles and at the same time fulfill the expectations of the majority responsible for its election. However, in attempting to carry out the substantive mandate of the masses who elected him, the President of the Republic necessarily came into conflict with Congress, and was faced with the alternative of betraying his program or forcing an unconventional way out. In ten years this unconventional way out has included one suicide, one resignation, and one violent deposition. It could be argued that the Presidential candidate could offer a realistic program, taking into account the power of those who control both Congress and a considerable part of the state apparatus. But this moderate candidate would find it difficult to get himself elected, since another candidate would readily be forthcoming who was prepared to come to terms with the demands of the masses.

The emergence of a mass society, paving the way for Populism, without the formation of new ruling groups able to work out a plan for national development as an alternative to the traditionalist ideology, has been the chief characteristic of the Brazilian historical process in its most recent phase. The Populist leaders, conscious of the psychological state of the masses, called for the country's rapid modernization through "basic reforms" and "structural changes." Control of the principal political power centers, however, continued to be in the hands of the traditional class, who have known how to use Populist pressure as a bogey for bringing to heel the new emergent forces connected with industry and foreign capital. These circumstances, responsible for the growing political instability, favored military intervention and indeed this did in effect take place in March, 1964. The intervention, however, did not eliminate the roots of conflict but only fostered in the old ruling class the illusion of an entrenched security. Now, unless development as a basic aspiration for the Brazilian community is successfully suppressed, social pressures will continue to grow if changes are not introduced into the social structure, and the profundity of these changes will have to increase with the passage of time. A society that shows itself incapable of creating a ruling class equipped to guide its process of change is not necessarily a society that tends to remain stagnant. Nevertheless, there is a high probability that the social cost of such change will increase, if particular historical conditions permit a strengthening of the forces opposed to social change.

Suggestions for Further Reading

Rollie Poppino has written the most comprehensive one-volume survey of Brazilian history, *Brazil: Land and People* (New York, 1968). A standard but uncritical version of the rule of Dom Pedro II is Mary W. Williams, *Dom Pedro the Magnanimous, Second Emperor of Brazil* (Chapel Hill, 1937); a more balanced account was written by Clarence H. Haring, *Empire in Brazil, a New World Experiment in Democracy* (Cambridge, 1958). In *The Life of Joaquim Nabuco*, translated and edited by Roland Hilton, *et al.* (Stanford, 1950), Carolina Nabuco discusses the career of her father, one of Brazil's leading figures in the nineteenth century, and examines the diplomacy, politics, and society of the empire and early republic. For an intellectual history of nineteenth-century Brazil, read the work of Joao Cruz Costa, *A History of Ideas in Brazil*, translated by Suzette Macedo (Berkeley and Los Angeles, 1964). The race issue, which looms large in Brazilian history, attracts the interest of a growing list of scholars. The first to call attention to the uniqueness of Brazilian race relations, and in the process to establish the standard interpretation, was Gilberto Freyre in his famous *The Masters and the Slaves; a Study in the Development of Brazilian Civilization*, translated by Samuel Putnam (New York, 1946). Frank Tannenbaum followed Freyre's interpretation with his continent-wide view of slavery in *Slave and Citizen, the Negro in the Americas* (New York, 1947) which, in endorsing the Brazilian's thesis, stresses the moral, legal, and institutional superiority of race relations in the Iberian systems. Marvin Harris, *Patterns of Race in the Americas* (New York, 1964) is a hard-hitting attack on the Tannenbaum-Freyre view. In *Brazil and Africa*, translated by Richard A. Mazzara and Sam Hileman, with an introduction by Alan K. Manchester (Berkeley and Los Angeles, 1965), José Honorio Rodrígues, a Brazilian scholar, also breaks with Freyre. The politics of the revolution of 1930 can be studied in Jordan M. Young, *The Brazilian Revolution of 1930 and the Aftermath* (New Brunswick, 1967), while the personal career of its leader is covered by John S. W. Dulles, *Vargas of Brazil* (Austin, 1967). An excellent analysis of the political difficulties of contemporary Brazil is Juarez R. B. Lopes, "Some Basic Developments in Brazilian Politics and Society," Eric N. Baklanoff, ed., *New Perspectives of Brazil* (Nashville, 1966), pp. 59–77.

III

Cuba: A Sugar Economy in a Capitalist and Communist World

Before the Revolution of 1959, few historians in the United States gave much thought to Cuba. Most of the writings of Cuban scholars were virtually neglected or known only to a handful of experts at leading universities. Since the Revolution of 1959 and especially since Fidel Castro's adoption of a Marxist-Leninist blueprint for his island, Cuban history has received the attention of numerous students of history and economics.

Cuban history falls into three main periods. From the early sixteenth century until 1898, the island was a Spanish colony. Spain generally favored its more prosperous mainland colonies over Cuba during the first two centuries. Late in the eighteenth century, the collapse of the neighboring Haitian sugar economy offered the Spaniards in Cuba a golden opportunity to cultivate and export sugar to the European market; this export trade began the transformation of the formerly sleepy island into an appendage of Western capitalism. Spaniards and Cubans reaped the benefits. Meanwhile, American capital began to play a principal role in the sugar economy. Hoping to hold on to its colony, Spain tightened its grip on Cuba. Led by José Martí, the patriot thinker and leader, and frequently supported by American interests, the Cubans ultimately revolted in 1895 and won their independence with military assistance from the United States.

In the era that followed, American interests established a virtual protectorate in Cuba and drew the island into the capitalist vortex. The more obvious political controls, such as the Platt Amendment, were abolished in 1934 after the Cubans revolted against the dictator Gerardo Machado, a spokesman for powerful American financial groups. The economic controls survived, however. The Revolution of 1933, an effort to modify the more blatant shortcomings of the dependent capitalist economy, ended with the failure of the administration of Ramón Grau San Martín to win recognition from the United States.

The failure of the Revolution, which voiced the aspirations of youthful reformers, left the political and economic picture substantially undisturbed and permitted Fulgencio Batista, an army sergeant, to dominate local politics until the mid-1940s. Unfortunately for the future of Cuba, Grau and his Auténtico politicians, who defeated Batista's candidate in the election of 1944, offered only a paper alternative to Batista's program. They left the old economy intact and discredited middle-sector government. Grau's successor, Carlos Prío Socarrás, proved particularly venal and weak. Favored by the indifference of the population to the Auténticos, Batista staged a coup in 1952 that toppled Prío's regime. He governed until deposed by Castro in 1959.

Most of the early studies of Cuba focused on the years before 1933. Leland Jenks wrote his controversial book, *Our Cuban Colony* (New York, 1928), which analyzed the sugar economy of the island and the part played by American capital. Three significant studies appeared in the Batista era. Lowry Nelson, a sociologist at the University of Minnesota, published his *Rural Cuba* (Minneapolis, 1950), which is a careful field study of society and the sugar economy. The Commission on Cuban Affairs published its *Problems of the New Cuba* (New York, 1935), which explored the domestic ills of the island and the consequences of the failure of the Revolution of 1933. It warned that political and economic difficulties would continue unless Cuban leaders responded to demands for reform. The *Report on Cuba* (Baltimore, 1951) of the International Bank for Reconstruction and Development repeated many of the opinions of the Commission on Cuban Affairs and observed that most of the earlier recommendations had gone unheeded.

The readings in Part III explore various aspects of the first half century of Cuban independence: the meaning of the sugar economy, the collapse of the Revolution of 1933, and the kind of society that existed in 1958 which, in the opinion of some, made possible the rapidity and success of Castro's Revolution.

Castro's regime adopted Marxism and Leninism as the law of

the land and introduced major economic and political changes. However, none of the changes altered the island's almost total dependence on sugar. The planters lost control of their vast estates and American capital and markets no longer perform a role in the production and consumption of sugar. Sugar export remains the backbone of the economy; Communist-bloc nations purchase the bulk of the sugar. Further, Cuba has severed traditional diplomatic ties with the United States and joined the Communist-bloc nations.

The study of the Revolution offers a host of unanswered problems for scholars to analyze: What was the nature of the upheaval? Was it, as the United States Department of State has argued, a middle-class movement? Did Fidel Castro betray the Revolution by abandoning his supporters and espousing radical reforms that curtailed opportunities for the middle class? Obviously, the betrayal thesis rests on the assumption that Cuba had a middle class. But did it? If not, could Castro have betrayed the Revolution?

1

By the 1920s the jobs of a majority of Cubans depended on the cultivation, harvest and export of sugar cane, an activity geared to foreign demand and largely controlled by foreigners. Cubans both profitted and suffered from their reliance on sugar. However, intellectuals came to mistrust the industry, and in the 1920s spokesmen for the first generation of Cubans born after independence from Spain increasingly challenged the assumption of their elders that their well-being stemmed from the prosperity of sugar. This interpretation gained adherents in the 1930s and encouraged the publication of a major work by Fernando Ortiz, a sociologist-historian. In his *Contrapunto Cubano del Tabaco y el Azúcar*, he describes the impact that the sugar industry exercised on Cuba, explaining that, in displacing tobacco, which he calls the plant of free men, sugar enslaved the Cubans. This excerpt deals only with the sugar industry because it has a greater impact on the present economy.

Fernando Ortiz:
Cuban Counterpoint*

There can be no manufacture of sugar without machinery, without milling apparatus to grind the cane and get out its sweet juice, from which saccharose is obtained. The mill may be an Indian *cunyaya*—a pump-handle device resting against the branch of a tree, which as it moves up and down presses the cane against the trunk—or a simple two-cylinder roller moved by animal or human power, or a titanic system of mills, wheels, cogs, pumps, evaporating-pans, boilers, and ovens, powered by water, steam, or electricity; but it is always a machine, fundamentally a lever that squeezes. Sugar is made by man and power.

It is possible for the *guajiro* living on his small farm to make a little sugar squeezing the juice out of the cane by the pressure of the *cunyaya,* that simple device with its single lever which the Indians used, simpler even than the *cibucán* with which they pressed the yucca. Probably it was with the Indian *cunyaya* that the first juice was squeezed out in America, from the cane planted in Hispaniola by Christopher Columbus. But it was impossible to develop production on a commercial scale with so rudimentary an instrument. The first settlers in Hispaniola devised and set up grinding mills operated by water or horse power.

To be sure, these mills which were known in Europe before the discovery of America were all of wood, including the rollers. The maximum of juice that could be extracted from the cane was thirty-five per cent, and the sugar yield was only six per cent. But in the manufacture of sugar the grinder was always as essential as the evaporating-dishes and the other vessels for the filtration of the settlings and the clarification of the syrup.

For centuries sugar was manufactured in these *cachimbos.* . . . In the year 1827 Cuba had over one thousand centrals. The limited capacity of the mills was the cause of the small scale of their operations. At this time the average size of the numerous plantations in Matanzas, for example, was only about 167 acres of cane, and some

* Composite of excerpts from CUBAN COUNTERPOINT: TOBACCO AND SUGAR, by Fernando Ortiz, trans. by Harriet de Onis. Copyright 1947 by Alfred A. Knopf, Inc. Reprinted by permission of the publisher.

750 in wood and pasture land. For a good central 1,000 acres was enough.

In 1820 the steam engine was introduced into Cuba and marked the beginning of an industrial revolution. The steam engine changed everything on the central. The process of the penetration of the steam engine into the sugar industry was slow; half a century went by from the time it was first employed in the grinding mill in 1820 until 1878, when it was applied to the last step of the process—that is, in the separation centrifugals. By the end of the nineteenth century everything about the central was mechanical, nothing was done by hand. Everything about the organism was new. The framework continued the same, but the organs, the joints, the viscera had been adapted to new functions and new dimensions. For as a result of the introduction of steam not only was completely new machinery installed, but everything grew in size. The increased potential of energy called for enlarged grinding capacity of the mills, and this, in turn, made it necessary for all the other apparatus in the sugar-milling process to expand. But only in the last third of the nineteenth century did the Cuban sugar central begin that intense growth which has brought it to its present-day dimensions.

The Cuban sugar mill, despite the complete transformation of its machinery brought about by the steam engine, grew slowly in productive capacity, both in machinery and in acreage. As late as 1880 the size of the centrals was not extremely large. At that time the centrals of Matanzas Province, for example, averaged some 1,650 acres all together, of which only about 770 were planted to cane. This delay in the growth in size of the centrals, despite the possibilities afforded by the introduction of steam-powered machinery, was not due so much to the revolutions and wars that harassed the colony and laid much of its land waste for years as to the economic difficulties that impeded the development of transportation by steam—that is, the railroads. Railways were first introduced into Cuba in the year 1837, before Spain had them, by a company of wealthy Creoles. But it was after the ten-year revolution that steel rails were invented and that they became cheap enough so they could be used on a large scale on the centrals, not only on lines from the mill yard to the canefields, but to link up the mills and the cane-growing zones with each other and with the ports where sugar was stored and shipped. From this time on, the railway lines reached out steadily toward the sugar cane and wrapped themselves about it like the tentacles of a great iron spider. The centrals began to grow in size, giving way to the great latifundium. By 1890 there was a central in Cuba, the Constancia, that produced a yield as high as 135,000 sacks of sugar, at that time the largest in the world.

The machine won a complete victory in the sugar-manufacturing process. Hand labor has almost completely disappeared. The mechanization has been so thorough that it has brought about a transformation in the industrial, territorial, judicial, political, and social structure of the sugar economy of Cuba through an interlinked chain of phenomena which have not been fully appreciated by Cuban sociologists.

In the twentieth century the sugar production of Cuba reached the peak of its historical process of industrialization, even though it has not yet passed through all the phases necessary for its perfect evolutionary integration. Mechanization, which reached Cuba in the nineteenth century with the steam engine, began to triumph in that century and created the central; but it is in this twentieth century that the machine has given rise to the typical present-day organization, the *super-central*. This type of mill has been the logical outgrowth of mechanization, and from it have streamed a whole series of derivations that because of their complicated interlocking structure and the relation of cause and effect have not been clearly understood or properly analyzed. It is sufficient to point out here that the principal characteristics typical of the Cuban sugar industry today, and the same holds true in a greater or lesser degree of the other islands of the Antilles, and happens to a certain extent in other similar industries, are the following: mechanization, latifundism, sharecropping, wage-fixing, supercapitalism, absentee landlordism, foreign ownership, corporate control, and imperialism.

Mechanization is the factor that has made possible and necessary the increased size of the centrals. Prior to this the central's radius of activity was the distance suitable for animal-drawn haulage. Now, with railroads, the limits of extension of a central are measured by the cost of transportation. It is a known fact that cane cut in Santo Domingo is milled in Puerto Rico and transported to the mill in ships. The mill and the railroad have developed simultaneously and their growth has made necessary planting on a larger scale, which explains the need for vast areas for cane plantations. This phenomenon also gave rise to the occupation of virgin lands in the provinces of Camagüey and Oriente and the consequent shifting of the agricultural center of Cuba. These Cyclopean machines and those great tentacles of railways that have turned the centrals into monstrous iron octopuses have created the demand for more and more land to feed the insatiable voracity of the mills with canefields, pasture land, and woodland.

On the heels of the mechanization came the great latifundism

—that is, the use of a great extension of land by a single private owner. Latifundism was the economic basis of feudalism, and it has often reproduced this state. The struggle of the modern age has always been, particularly since the eighteenth century, to give man freedom and sever him from his bondage to the land, and for the freedom of the land, liberating it from the monopolistic tyranny of man. Today this process is on the way to being repeated in the Antilles, and one day we shall see agrarian laws enacted to disentail the lands held in the grasp of mortmain. The agrarian latifundism today is a fatal consequence of the present universal system of the concentration of capital. Every day industry needs more and more means of production, and the land is the most important of them all.

The central is now more than a mere plantation; there are no longer any real planters in Cuba. The modern central is not a simple agricultural enterprise, nor even a factory whose production is based on the raw materials at hand. Today it is a complicated "system of land, machinery, transportation, technicians, workers, capital, and people to produce sugar." It is a complete social organism, as live and complex as a city or municipality, or a baronial keep with its surrounding fief of vassals, tenants, and serfs. The latifundium is only the territorial base, the visible expression of this. The central is vertebrated by an economic and legal structure that combines masses of land, masses of machinery, masses of men, and masses of money, all in proportion to the integral scope of the huge organism for sugar production.

Today the sugar latifundium is so constituted that it is not necessary for the tracts of land or farms that constitute it to be contiguous. It is generally made up of a nuclear center around the mill yard, a sort of town, and of outlying lands, adjacent or distant, linked by railroads and under the same general control, all forming a complete empire with subject colonies covered with canefields and forests, with houses and villages. And all this huge feudal territory is practically outside the jurisdiction of public law; the norms of private property hold sway there. The owner's power is as complete over this immense estate as though it were just a small plantation or farm. Everything there is private—ownership, industry, mill, houses, stores, police, railroad, port. Until the year 1886 the workers, too, were chattels like other property.

The sugar latifundium was the cause of important agro-social developments, such as the monopolizing of land that is not cultivated but lies fallow; the scarcity of garden produce or fruits that would complement the basic crop, which is sugar—the reason for the latifundium's existence—because the effort required for this can be turned to more profitable use from the economic standpoint;

the depreciation in value of land that it does not need within the zone monopolized by the central, and so on.

Within the territorial scope of the central, economic liberty suffers serious restrictions. There is not a small holding of land nor a dwelling that does not belong to the owner of the central, nor a fruit orchard or vegetable patch or store or shop that does not form part of the owner's domain. The small Cuban landowner, independent and prosperous, the backbone of a strong rural middle class, is gradually disappearing. The farmer is becoming a member of the proletariat, just another laborer, without roots in the soil, shifted from one district to another. The whole life of the central is permeated by this provisional quality of dependence, which is a characteristic of colonial populations whose members have lost their stake in their country.

The economic organization of the latifundium in Cuba has been blamed for consequences that are not properly attributable to it, such as the importation of cheap labor, especially colored. First Negro slaves were brought into the country, then laborers from Haiti and Jamaica. But this immigration, which lowers the wage level of the whole Cuban proletariat and the living standard of Cuban society and upsets its racial balance, thus retarding the fusion of its component elements into a national whole, is not the result of the latifundium system. The use of colored slaves or laborers has never been nor is it a social phenomenon due to latifundism or to the monopolizing of the land. Both these economic developments are essentially identical: with the concentration of the ownership of land comes the concentration of laborers, and both depend directly upon the concentration of capital resulting from industry, especially when the process of mechanization demands more land for the plantations upon whose crop it depends, more labor to harvest it, and, in an endless progression, more machines and more and more money. The land and the laborer, like the machine itself, are only means of production, which, as a rule, are simultaneously augmented, but often the increment of one is followed by that of the others. When there was an abundance of land and before the machines had reached their full development, sugar-planting used large numbers of Negro slaves brought in from Africa; at this time the latifundium had not yet come into being. Later, as the machines grew in power, they demanded more and more cane plantations, and these, in turn, more and more labor, which was supplied by white immigration and the natural growth of population. But as the speed of the development of the sugar industry outpaced that of the population, and great centrals were established on vast tracts of virgin land, everything had to be brought in: machines, plantations, and—population. It was the swift occupation of large and new sections of Camagüey and Oriente that, aside from other secondary economic considerations such as the scale of wages, brought about a revival of "traffic in Negroes," who were now hired on terms of miserable peonage instead of being bought outright, as under the earlier system of slavery. In Puerto Rico the latifundium developed after its great demographic expansion, and as it has a dense and poverty-stricken white population, it has not been necessary to bring in cheap labor from the other islands. . . .

Sugar was mulatto from the start, for the energies of black men and white always went into its production. Even though it was Columbus who brought the first sugar cane into the Antilles from the Canary Islands, sugar was not a Spanish plant, nor even European. It was native to Asia, and from there it was carried along the Mediterranean by the Arabs and Moors. For the cultivation of the cane and the extraction of its juice the help of stout slaves and serfs was required, and in Portugal, as in Spain and Sicily in Europe, in Mauritania and Egypt in Africa, in Arabia, Mesopotamia, Persia, and India in Asia, these workers were as a rule of Negroid stock, those dark people who from prehistoric times had penetrated into that long strip of supertropical areas and gave them their permanent dark coloring, the same stock that in the Middle Ages invaded it anew with the waves of Moslems, who never felt any hostile racial prejudice toward the Negro. Sugar cane and Negro slaves arrived together in the island of Cuba, and possibly in Hispaniola, from across the sea. And since then Negro labor and sugar cane have been two factors in the same economic binomial of the social equation of our country.

For centuries the workers in the centrals were exclusively Negroes; often even the overseers were colored. This was true of the mill workers as well as of the field workers, with the exception of the technicians and the management. It was not until the abolishment of slavery, the influx of Spanish immigrants after the Ten Years' War, and the introduction of the sharecropping system that white farmers were to be found on the Cuban sugar plantations.

The nineteenth century in Cuba was marked by the change in the labor system brought about by the prohibition of the slave trade and, much later, by the abolition of slavery and the substitution for it of hired workers. The abolition was proclaimed by the Cubans fighting a war of secession against the mother country, and later by Spain in 1880–6. The cessation of the slave trade coincided with the introduction of the steam engine, which increased the productive capacity of the mills, and the abolition of slavery (1886) was simultaneous with the use of steel rails and the development of the railroads, which increased the radius of activity of the centrals. Cheap labor was an imperative need, so Spain, no longer able to smuggle in slaves or bring in more Chinese coolies or peons from Yucatán, began to export her own white laborers. As a result the proportion of Negroes in the Cuban population began to diminish. In the distribution of colored population in Cuba today the greatest density is to be found in the old sugar-growing sections, not in the tobacco-raising areas, which were settled in the main by white immigrants from the Canary Islands and peasants of old Cuban stock. Tobacco drew upon the free white population, whereas for sugar cane black slaves were imported. This also explains why there are no invasions of migrant seasonal workers in the tobacco industry, and still less of Haitians and Jamaicans, who were brought in to make the harvesting of cane cheaper. . . .

It must also be set down that the union between sugar and the Negro had nothing to do with the latter's race or pigmentation; it was due solely to the fact that for centuries Negroes were the most numerous, available, and strongest slaves, and cane was cultivated by them throughout America. When there were no Negroes, or even together with them, slaves of other races were to be found on the plantations—Berbers, Moors, mulattoes. The alliance was not between the canefield and the Negro, but between the canefield and the slave. Sugar spelled slavery; tobacco, liberty. And if on the tobacco plantations of Virginia along with the black slaves there were white ones, purchased in England with bales of tobacco, on the sugar plantations of the British West Indies there were also black and white slaves, Irish condemned to slavery by Cromwell, and even Englishmen who had been sold for 1,550 pounds of sugar a head; or, as we would put it today, the price of an Englishman was five sacks of sugar. This did not happen in Cuba. There may have been an occasional white slave there, more probably a white female slave, in the early days of the colony, but not afterwards; and although it is true that there were near-white mulattoes who were still slaves, the whiteness of the skin was always the sign of emancipation in Cuba.

The seasonal nature of the work involved in sugar, in both the fields and the mill, is likewise very characteristic and of great social consequence. The cutting is not continuous, and whereas it used to last almost half a year, it is now almost never longer than a hundred days, and even less since legal restrictions have been placed upon it. All the rest of the year is "dead time." When it is finished, the workers who came to Cuba for the harvest in swallow-like migrations leave the country, taking their savings with them, and the native proletariat goes through a long stretch of unemployment and constant insecurity. A large part of the working class of Cuba has to live all year on the wages earned during two or three months, and the whole lower class suffers from this seasonal work system, being reduced to a state of poverty, with an inadequate, vitamin-deficient diet consisting principally of rice, beans, and tubers, which leave it undernourished and the ready prey of hook-worm, tuberculosis, anemia, malaria, and other diseases. . . .

Foreign predominance in the sugar industry was always great, and now it is almost exclusive. Tobacco has always been more Cuban because of its origin, its character, and its economy. The reason is obvious. Sugar has always required a large capital investment; today it amounts to a veritable fortune. A century ago a well-balanced central could be set up with a hundred thousand pesos; today the industrial plant alone is worth a million. Moreover, ever since the centrals were first established in America, all their equipment, with the exception of the land, has had to be brought in from abroad. Machinery, workers, capital, all have to be imported, and this makes necessary an even larger outlay. If the sugar industry was capitalistic in its beginnings, with the improvement in mechanical techniques and the introduction of the steam engine more elaborate mills were required, more canefields, more land, more slaves, greater investments and reserves—in a word, more and more capital. The entire history of sugar in Cuba, from the first day, has been the struggle originated by the introduction of foreign capital and its overwhelming influence on the island's economy. And it was not Spanish capital, but foreign: that of the Genoese, the Germans, the Flemings, the English, the Yankees, from the days of the Emperor Charles V and his bankers, the Fuggers, to our own "good-neighbor" days and the Wall Street financiers.

Even in the palmy days of the Cuban landowning aristocracy, which sometimes unexpectedly acquired fabulous fortunes and titles of nobility through their centrals, the sugar-planters always suffered a certain amount of foreign overlordship. The sugar they produced was not consumed in our country and had to be shipped raw to foreign markets, where it became the booty of the refiners, without whose intervention it could not enter the world market. The sugar-planter needed the underwriter, and he, in turn, the rich banker. As early as the middle of the sixteenth century the sugar-planters were requesting loans of the brokers of Seville and of the kings, not only to continue with their enterprises, but even to set them up. This was another factor that contributed to sugar's foreignness. Its capitalistic character obliged it to seek abroad the creditors and bankers not to be found here or who, when they existed, were merly agents of the brokers of Cádiz or the English refiners, who supplied machinery and financial support but who through their loans at usurious rates could dictate their own terms and prices from London and Liverpool, and later from New York. When María de las Mercedes, the Countess of Merlin, wrote her *Viaje a la Habana,* well along in the nineteenth century, she was amazed at the fact that the rate of interest charged the Cuban planters by foreign loan-brokers was thirty per cent a year, or two and a half per cent a month.

By the end of the Ten Years' War, when through the progress in metallurgical techniques the great mills and the networks of railways were introduced in the centrals, the capital required for a venture of this sort was enormous, beyond the possibilities of any one person. This brought about three economic-social developments: the revival of the sharecropping system of cultivation, the anonymous stockholders' corporations, and the direct control of foreign capital over the management and ordering of the centrals. And finally, as a result of the financial depression after the first World War, industrial and mercantile capitalism was replaced by the supercapitalism of banks and financial companies, which today constitute the foreign plutocracy that controls the economic life of Cuba. One of the effects of this has been the greater dependence of the tenant farmer, who, according to Maxwell, received his fairest share of returns in Cuba, his gradual disappearance, and, finally, the complete proletarianization of the workers in the central, from the fields to the mill, where an executive proconsul holds sway as the representative of a distant and imperial power. The "foreignness" of the sugar industry in Cuba is even greater than that of Puerto Rico, which is actually under the sovereignty of the United States.

The foreign control of the central is not only external but internal as well. To use the language in vogue today, it has a vertical structure. There are not merely the decisions of policy taken by the sugar companies in the United States, from that radiating center of moneyed power known as Wall Street, but the legal ownership of the central is also foreign. The bank that underwrites the cutting of the cane is foreign, the consumers' market is foreign, the administrative staff set up in Cuba, the machinery that is installed, the capital that is invested, the very land of Cuba held by foreign ownership and enfeoffed to the central, all are foreign, as are, logically enough, the profits that flow out of the country to enrich others. The process does not end here; in some of the supercentrals even the workers are foreigners, who have been brought into Cuba, under a new form of slavery, from Haiti and Jamaica, or by immigration, from Spanish villages.

This foreignness is further aggravated by absentee landlordism. There were already absentee owners a century ago, who lived at ease in Havana, leaving the mill in the hands of a manager. But since 1882, when a North American, Atkins, bought the Soledad central, becoming the first Yankee planter of Cuba, absentee landlordism has been on the increase and has become more permanent, more distant, more foreign, and, in consequence, more deleterious in its social effects on the country.

Before, this absentee landlordism was periodically attenuated by inheritance, through which, upon the death of the planter, this accumulated wealth returned to society through his children and heirs. This is not so any longer, for the planter, if this name can be given to the organization that in the eyes of the law is the owner of the central, is born outside the country and dies a foreigner, and even has no heirs if it is a corporation. The great wealth of capital needed for these supercentrals could not be raised in Cuba, and the tendency toward productive capitalism could not be held in check from within. And so the sugar industry became increasingly denaturalized and passed into anonymous, corporative, distant, dehumanized, all-powerful hands, with little or no sense of responsibility.

By 1850 the trade of Cuba with the United States was greater than that with the mother country, Spain, and the United States assumed for all time its natural place, given geographical conditions, as the principal consumer of Cuba's production as well as its economic center. In 1851 the Consul General of Cuba in the United States wrote officially that Cuba was an economic colony of the United States, even though politically it was still governed by Spain. From then on sugar for North American consumption was king in Cuba, and its tariffs played a greater part in our political life than all the constitutions, as though the whole country were one huge mill, and Cuba merely the symbolic name of a great central controlled by a foreign stockholders' corporation.

Even today the most pressing problem confronting the Cuban Treasury Department is that of being able to collect its revenues by levying them directly against the sources of wealth and their earnings, making no exception of foreign holdings, instead of continuing the indirect taxes that fall so burdensomely upon the Cuban people and fleece it. Cuba will never be really independent until it can free itself from the coils of the serpent of colonial economy that fattens on its soil but strangles its inhabitants and winds itself about the palm tree of our republican coat of arms, converting it into the sign of the Yankee dollar.

This has not been so with tobacco, either in the field or in the workroom. The tobacco-grower was a simple countryman who required no machinery beyond a few tools and who could supply his own needs from the limited resources of the local general store. Whereas the sugar-planter acquired wealth, titles of nobility, government posts, refinement, and, at times, a desire for progress, the *veguero* was always a small, rustic, rule-of-thumb farmer. While the planter gave Cuba railroads before they were introduced into Spain, and Havana had its flourishing theater presenting plays and operas as good as those of Madrid, the *veguero* still rode his horse through the woods and found his entertainment in cock-fights, songs, and country dancing. . . .

Sugar was an anonymous industry, the mass labor of slaves or gangs of hired workmen, under the supervision of capital's overseers. Tobacco has created a middle class, a free bourgeoisie; sugar has created two extremes, slaves and masters, the proletariat and the rich. "There is no middle class in Havana, only masters and slaves," the Countess of Merlin wrote about her own country a century ago. Then she goes on to say: "The *guajiro* prefers to live on little for the sake of having his freedom." On the sugar plantations there existed the overlordship and the serfdom of underling and master; on the vegas there was the free industry of the humble peasant. The old colonial aristocracy of Cuba was almost always made up of rich planters on whom a title had been conferred because of their wealth in mills and slaves. Sugar titles rested on black foundations. The sprightly archpriest long ago observed (op. cit., stanza 491):

> *Suppose a man's an utter fool, a farmer or a boor,*
> *With money he becomes a sage, a knight with prestige sure;*
> *In fact, the greater grows his wealth the greater his allure,*
> *While he not even owns himself who is in money poor.*

It is easy to see how the social organization involved in sugar production (mill and plantation) had, in addition to its capitalistic character, certain feudal and baronial features. Another clergyman, Juan de Castellanos, who was also a poet, put it very well in one of the thousands of verses that make up his famous *Elegías:* "A plantation is a great estate." But he also said, referring to the plantations: "Each of these is a domain."

The tenant farmer, who made his appearance in the sugar set-up in the role of an intermediate class, never had anything but a walk-on part, important only for what he stood for and said as he entered and left the stage. . . .

With sugar . . . everything was favor and privilege. The sixteenth century was not yet half run and Cuba was already receiving money from the royal coffers to assist in the establishment of cane plantations, without any strings attached and with free grants of land, which then abounded and which the crown wished to see settled. In 1517, barely five years after the conquest of the island, the planters of Cuba obtained from the King the first moratorium for their debts. In 1518, under a royal edict of December 9, the royal exchequer undertook to act as land bank for all who wanted to start a sugar plantation in Hispaniola, offering them "aid from the royal treasury" and canceling their debts. And the privileges did not end here. . . .

All the colonial governments favored the sugar-planters. They received loans of money, grants of land; the forests were cleared for them, experts in the manufacture of sugar brought in, duties were suspended, sales tax forgotten, smuggling winked at, a moratorium declared on debts, railroads built, loans made, treaties drawn up, monopolies ignored, religion weakened, heretics tolerated, civil liberties curtailed, the people tyrannized, and independence delayed. And to work the mills and plantations thousands and thousands of miserable wretches were killed or enslaved: Negroes from Africa, Indians from Yucatán, Mongolians from China. For the profit of the sugar plantation whole communities were dragged from their homes, blood flowed like the syrup from the cane, and all races suffered the lash, the stocks, and the prison cell.

Even today Cuba's national economy is governed by the sugar industry, which enjoys constant protection, even though the centrals are no longer Cuban, in exchange for special tariffs on imports, which are not Cuban either. . . .

The sugar industry . . . because of its exotic origin, its European antecedents, and the foreign capital invested in it, is economically centrifugal. It came to the country from abroad; it is the trader in it for foreign consumption who attempts to establish himself in Cuba and encourage its cheap production here; but those in control are not Cubans and the profits are reaped far from here. And for this sugar has exercised an almost tyrannical pressure throughout our history, introducing a constant note of oppression and force, without contributing toward the creation of robust institutions such as education, government, and civic responsibility. It was sugar that gave us slavery, that was responsible for the conquest of Havana by the English in 1762, that dictated their leaving in 1763, that caused the slave trade to flourish, that evaded the restrictions laid upon it, that robbed Cuba of its liberties throughout the nineteenth century, that brought about and maintains its colonial status and economic backwardness. As far as its primary dirigents are concerned, sugar in Cuba has always been an exogenous force, from without to within, to get what it could from the country, an oppressive, weakening force. . . .

Sugar . . . has been under foreign control superimposed on the island's government. The history of Cuba, from the days of the conquest to the present moment, has been essentially dominated by foreign controls over sugar, and the greater the value of our production, the greater the domination. During the centuries of the colonial period this power which was and is the controlling force in the economy of the Antilles was not, properly speaking, located in Madrid, inasmuch as ever since the sixteenth century the Spanish crown was only the legal machinery that, in exchange for the comfortable, well-paid, parasitical upkeep of its dynastic, aristocratic, military, clerical, and administrative bureaucracies maintained order among the peoples of the Peninsula and America and exploited their inhabitants under systems of feudal absolutism, leaving the economic initiative and control in the hands of the commercial, industrial, and financial capitalism of the more astute centers of Europe—Genoa, Augsburg, Flanders, London, and, in the nineteenth century, New York. By the same token we sons of free Cuba have sometimes asked ourselves whether our officials and politicians are serving the interests of our people or those of some anonymous sugar corporation, playing the part of deputized guards of the great Cuban sugar mill at the orders of foreign owners.

2

The protest of the 1920s, which resulted from the disastrous consequences of the Great Depression, culminated in the Revolution of 1933, which toppled the regime of Gerardo Machado. Its successor, the reform administration of Ramón Grau San Martín, spoke not only for the middle sectors, but embodied the dreams of the discontented young. Unfortunately for his backers, Grau's government survived just four months. Although the conservative administration that followed was based on a strange alliance of the old elite and a sergeant-led army, it left many of Grau's reforms on the statute books but did little to implement them. The Revolution of 1933, therefore, had only a marginal effect on Cuba. Charles A. Thomson, an American scholar, placed responsibility for Grau's failure on domestic unrest and poor leadership. But he also indicted American policy and particularly the activity of Sumner Welles, the American ambassador. Thomson believed that American policy may have sabotaged "plans for social reconstruction."

Charles A. Thomson:
The Cuban Revolution*

THE REVOLT OF THE SERGEANTS

The revolution of September 4, 1933 was a unique event, not alone in the history of Cuba, but possibly in that of all Latin America. In a successful barracks revolt, which cost not a single casualty, the rank and file of the army, led by a group of sergeants, ousted the entire group of commissioned officers. This movement overthrew the Céspedes government and set up another headed by a Pentarchy, or Executive Commission of five members.

On the nights of September 3 and 4 the sergeants secured permission to meet at Camp Columbia for consideration of a proposed reduction in pay and a new order restricting their promotion. Discussion at the first meeting resulted in an agreement that the officers should be removed from power until these questions were settled. On the following night a group of student leaders, hearing rumors of the insurrection, arrived at Camp Columbia before 10 p.m. to find Fulgencio Batista, a sergeant-stenographer, acting as head of the movement. It is apparently doubtful that the chiefs of this revolt had foreseen that their coup might involve a change in the civil government. Some of the first members of the Student Directorate to arrive at Camp Columbia report finding the sergeants were still undecided on this point. These civilians were soon joined by other members of the Directorate, together with a few professors and intellectual leaders who specially enjoyed their con-

* From Charles A. Thomson, THE CUBAN REVOLUTION: REFORM AND RE-ACTION, *Foreign Policy Reports*, XI (January 1, 1936), pp. 262–270, 276.

fidence. The students finally persuaded Batista and the other sergeants to accept as the political platform of their movement the program for a provisional government promulgated by the University Student Directorate on August 22. With the support of the sergeants, the Student Directorate proceeded to name five members of an Executive Commission to serve as heads of the new government. The following four were unanimously nominated: Dr. Ramón Grau San Martín and Dr. Guillermo Portela, professors in the University; Sergio Carbó, a journalist; and Dr. J. M. Irisarri, a leading lawyer and intellectual, the author in part of the student program. Batista was at first suggested for the fifth member but he declined, and the choice finally fell on Porfirio Franca, a retired banker, whose standing in financial and commercial circles, it was hoped, might strengthen the new régime with conservatives.

The coup of September 4 was received with amazement in both Cuba and the United States. The army, the bulwark of law and order, had fallen into the hands of an unknown group of sergeants. The civil government was controlled by a group of "revolutionary" intellectuals, backed principally by university students. An adventitious feature, "the government of five Presidents," intensified the general bewilderment and concern. Labor unrest and Communist agitation, which had spread widely throughout the interior under the Céspedes régime, threatened a devastating social revolution. The various political factions adopted differing attitudes toward the new government: some were friendly, some hostile, some "expectant." The United States was unfriendly and warships were being rushed to Cuban waters.

The army provided the most urgent problem for the Pentarchy. The sergeant leaders of the revolt at first announced that they would return control to the commissioned officers as soon as the new government was consolidated. Batista declared: "There will be no promotions, nor any increases in pay, as a result of this movement . . . I would resign rather than accept any promotion." The officers were summoned to the Presidential Palace and invited to name five of their number who, together with Sergeant Batista, would form a Military Junta. The offer, however, was rejected; the officers refused to recognize in any way the validity of the September 4 revolution, which to them signified complete subversion of army discipline. On September 7 Sergio Carbó, acting independently of other members of the Pentarchy, signed a decree making Batista a colonel and chief of staff.

On September 8 the ousted army officers, who numbered approximately 500, began gathering at the National Hotel, an 8-story steel and concrete structure situated on a hill overlooking the

Malecón, Havana's ocean shore drive. That evening the enlisted men stationed machine guns around the hotel and attempted to search it, but the arrival of Ambassador Welles, who was then making his residence there, led to the retirement of the soldiers, and the officers remained in the hostelry.

Meanwhile, members of the government were conferring with representatives of various factions—Nationalists, *Menocalistas, Marianistas,* the ABC and OCRR—in an endeavor to secure their cooperation. When these negotiations failed, it was announced on September 9 that the Pentarchy would resign, and on the following day Dr. Ramón Grau San Martín became the new Provisional President.

The attitude of the United States was an important factor in the fall of the government of five. Although the coup had been bloodless and order was maintained both in Havana and the interior, serious alarm was expressed by officials in touch with Ambassador Welles. Amid haste and confusion a sweeping precautionary program was initiated by the United States. The entire Atlantic fleet was marshaled for quick action, 30 naval vessels were rushed toward Cuban waters, a thousand marines were concentrated at Quantico, and it was announced that Secretary Swanson was en route to Havana. These measures, which—according to the State Department—were designed solely to protect the 5,500 Americans resident in Cuba, provoked strong resentment in Cuban government circles and widespread concern throughout Latin America.

In an attempt to allay these apprehensions, President Roosevelt induced Secretary Swanson not to land at Havana but to proceed to Panama in accord with the original plans for his trip. The White House also hastened to declare that the United States did not want armed intervention in Cuba. Washington's chief concern was for the protection of American citizens and the prevention of anarchy. On September 6 President Roosevelt called to the White House the diplomatic representatives of Argentina, Brazil, Chile and Mexico, informed them of his desire to share with them full information on the Cuban situation, and assured them that his government was seeking by all possible means to avoid intervention. This step, which recognized the interest of other American countries in the Cuban situation, had a distinctly favorable effect on Latin American opinion. A note of September 8 from Argentina to Washington, however, expressed the hope that intervention in Cuba would be avoided under all circumstances and urged the granting of full self-determination to "youthful nations" as the "only method which will assure on this continent the stability of political institutions."

THE GRAU REGIME

On September 10, 1933, Dr. Ramón Grau San Martín became Provisional President. The new executive pledged himself "before the people of Cuba, in whose hands the sovereignty of the nation rests, to carry out the entire revolutionary program," at the same time promising respect for all interests in the island and regard for cordial relations with foreign nations. Dr. Grau, a distinguished physician and a professor in the National University, had been a prominent opponent of the Machado dictatorship, but before becoming a member of the Executive Commission had never participated actively in politics.

The new régime, which found its chief support in the surging nationalist enthusiasm aroused by the accession of the Pentarchy, faced a difficult problem in charting its future course. While it could not for one moment forget the preponderant influence of the United States, it could by no means ignore the angry rumblings of discontent among the island's masses, reduced by the depression and the Machado tyranny to unprecedented depths of hunger and misery.

Not only the varying pressure of circumstances, but inner conflicts made the government's course a shifting one. While Secretary of the Interior Guiteras demanded radical social reform, Batista and the army—which had carried through its revolution—desired a conservative program, which might bring United States recognition and a period of tranquillity favorable to the consolidation of the military's new position. President Grau stood between these two tendencies. Throughout his rule, nationalist sentiment rather than radical doctrines dominated the consideration of economic questions. The government was pro-labor and anti-capital to a considerable degree because, in Cuba as in Mexico, capital is predominantly foreign.

On September 14 the Grau government promulgated statutes under which Cuba would be provisionally governed. These pledged the maintenance of "absolute national independence and sovereignty," respect for all treaties, and the prompt calling of a constitutional convention, elections for which were subsequently set for April 1, 1934. Meanwhile, the administration would have power "temporarily to submit individual rights to a régime of governmental fiscalization" or control, a phrase which was interpreted as implying dictatorial powers. "Tribunals of sanctions" were to be set up to judge former *Machadistas* and political offenders.

The government's difficulties were complicated by the political inexperience of President Grau and that of his cabinet. Public order was threatened by the anomalous position of the army, whose commissioned officers were in open revolt against the main body. Politically the régime could not claim to represent even a majority of revolutionary factions. It was opposed by the ABC and the OCRR secret societies, as well as by such parties as Mendieta's Nationalists and Menocal's Conservatives, all of which, except the last named, had been represented in the ill-fated Céspedes cabinet. Moreover, it was attacked from one side by business and commercial interests, and from the other by left-wing labor and Communist groups. Its principal civilian support came from the University Student Directorate.

The first weeks of the new government were a time of bewilderment, confusion, wild rumors, continuous political negotiations in the capital, and widespread unrest throughout the interior. Government in the provinces had degenerated to large degree into a mass of conflicting local autonomies. Havana appointees often were not recognized and at times forcibly prevented from exercising jurisdiction.

On September 15, under the auspices of the Havana Rotary Club, negotiations were opened between the government and the Opposition, looking toward the possible formation of a coalition régime. The Opposition delegates demanded that Dr. Grau place his resignation in the hands of a Junta including all the anti-Machado factions. The students regarded Dr. Grau as a symbol of the nationalist program to which they were committed; they opposed sharing power in a coalition government with the old-school politicians, fearing that such a step would lead to sabotaging of their revolutionary aims.

The lack of United States recognition complicated the problems facing the government. Immediately following the inauguration of President Grau, Havana dispatches reported the "official American viewpoint" as prescribing four conditions which the new régime must fulfill in order to win recognition: it would be required to show capacity to govern, maintain order, receive distinct popular support and comply with all its obligations. These conditions were based, it was alleged, on the responsibility of the United States under the Platt Amendment to assure the maintenance of a government "adequate for the protection of life, property and individual liberty." Since recognition by Washington was considered almost a *sine qua non* for the continued existence of any Caribbean government, such a policy practically condemned the Grau régime to struggle within a vicious circle. For without recognition it could not fulfill the conditions of recognition. The hostility of Washington encouraged Opposition elements and the rebellious army officers, thus increasing the government's difficulties in demonstrating its capacity to maintain order and consolidate its political position.

Refusal of United States recognition, together with the presence of the cordon of war vessels around the island, had the paradoxical effect of strengthening the government by arousing a wave of anti-American feeling. In an effort to allay this sentiment and refute the charge that the United States was insisting on the organization of a pro-American régime, Secretary Hull issued a statement on September 11 in which he asserted that Washington was willing to let Cuba solve its own political problems. He declared that the administration was "prepared to welcome any government representing the will of the people of the Republic and capable of maintaining law and order throughout the island."

Relations between the government and Mr. Welles were apparently improved by a conference which the Ambassador held with the Student Directorate on September 15. He was reported to have assured the students that a Cuban government would not be barred from recognition, either because of its revolutionary origin or its radical program. He further denied any hostile bias to the Grau régime. On September 20 Secretary Hull clarified Washington's future course of action by declaring that in case of danger Americans would be asked to come to port towns for protection under the shelter of United States warships, thus intimating that a policy of evacuation rather than intervention would be followed. Five days later he announced that landing parties would be used only for the protection of lives, not of property.

Desire for United States recognition was in part responsible, it is alleged, for an offensive against Communists and other radicals in the labor movement which the government initiated late in September. On September 29 a demonstration in Havana honoring the ashes of Julio Antonio Mella—youthful Communist leader assassinated in Mexico by Machado agents—led to a clash with the army in which six were killed and 27 wounded. The headquarters of the Communist-led National Confederation of Labor and the Anti-Imperialist League were raided, and furniture and literature piled in the street and burned.

The government's offensive against its opponents on the left was soon matched by a decisive victory against the former army officers who had taken refuge in the National Hotel. On October 2 at 6 a.m. the army opened fire on the hotel. The bombardment continued—save for a 3-hour armistice to permit the evacuation of foreigners—until four in the afternoon, when the officers ran up a white flag. While they were being marched from the hotel in some confusion, an unexpected shot precipitated panic among the soldiers; bullets flew again, resulting in the slaughter of 10 persons, almost all of them officers. One American was killed by a stray shot during the battle, and damage to the hotel was placed at $100,000. The failure of the United States to land marines, even in the case of open conflict, evidenced Washington's determination to avoid intervention.

On November 8 the Grau-Batista régime was faced by another armed threat. Rebel forces, backed by the ABC and recruited from the army, police and civilians, seized Atarés Fortress, various police stations and other strongholds in Havana. The movement was crushed after a 2-day battle, inept leadership being a primary factor in the defeat of the rebels. The repression of the revolt further fortified the position of the Grau government and strengthened particularly the influence of Batista and the military.

THE GOVERNMENT'S NATIONALIST PROGRAM

The Grau régime termed itself the representative of the authentic revolutionary impulses of the Cuban people, and because of this claim its supporters came to be known as *auténticos*. Its motto was "Cuba for the Cubans," and a spirit of frank and aggressive nationalism dominated its activities and policies. The régime took early action to eliminate Machado influences from political and governmental organization, and named commissions to "purge" public offices. On September 19 the Grau cabinet approved a decree dissolving all old political parties, since the former dictatorship had captured the organization of these groups. On October 6 the National University was conceded complete autonomy from governmental control.

The mounting wave of strikes and the social unrest rife among the masses were primary factors in shaping the government's program. While frequently resorting to repression, the authorities sought through social and labor legislation to remedy the conditions responsible for the discontent. On September 19 Grau signed a decree establishing a maximum working day of 8 hours. On January 9, 1934 the government fixed a minimum wage for the 1934 sugar crop of 50 cents for cutting, gathering and hauling each 100 *arrobas* of cane. This meant, at the official estimate, a daily wage of 75 cents in contrast to less than 20 cents received in 1933. A decree on Labor Organization of November 7, 1933 sought to

Cubanize the labor movement and restrict Communist influence by limiting the rôle of foreign leaders. It required that all union officials be Cuban citizens, and all labor organizations were ordered to register in the Department of Labor; those failing to do so faced the penalty of dissolution. Strikes were prohibited unless demands had previously been submitted to government arbitral boards, whose decisions were compulsory in character.

On the following day, November 8, President Grau signed the decree on Nationalization of Labor, popularly known as the "50 per cent Law." This required all industrial, commercial and agricultural enterprises to employ native Cubans for at least half their total working force (excepting only managers and technicians who could not be replaced), and to pay half the total payroll to Cubans. These last two laws served to mobilize nationalism in the struggle against communism and proved markedly effective in checking the radical drive.

By the 50-per-cent law the government attracted the support of the Negro and unemployed masses. But this measure served also to excite the active opposition of the 600,000 Spaniards in Cuba. Spanish antagonism was further stirred by a Grau decree which obliged the large mutual benefit societies to employ in their hospitals and clinics only members of the National Medical College. On December 21, 1933 it was reported that the Spanish government was considering an appeal to the United States to intervene under the Platt Amendment for the protection of Spanish life and property. Washington lost no time, however, in indicating unofficially that such a request would be refused.

Although United States interests had been active in opposing practically all the labor legislation of the Grau régime, American hostility was particularly aroused by action affecting three large corporations: the Chase National Bank, the Cuban-American Sugar Company, and the Cuban Electric Company, a subsidiary of the Electric Bond and Share Company. The Chase National Bank had provided $80,000,000 to the Machado régime for financing a public works program which included the construction of a costly central highway for the island and an elaborate Capitol building in Havana. These loans had become extremely unpopular in Cuba, not only because of the close association of the Chase Bank with the dictator, but because of certain questionable practices connected with their negotiation. In response to this popular feeling the Grau government, when it came to power, promptly suspended deposits of public works revenues with the Chase Bank, giving no reasons for the act. A later decree of January 12, 1934 ordered cessation of all payments on the public works debt.

The Delicias and Chaparra sugar mills in Oriente province,

the $10,000,000-property of the Cuban-American Sugar Company, were seized by government authorities on December 20, 1933. The mills had been shut down because of labor troubles, but it was hoped that governmental action might avoid continuance of a stoppage which would mean increased poverty and possible lawlessness among the surrounding population.

The Cuban Electric Company clashed with the Grau government on two fronts: a dispute on rates, and a labor conflict which led to the temporary seizure of its properties. Its rates in Havana for the individual consumer were 15 cents per kilowatt, a figure approximately twice that currently charged in the larger cities of the United States. After the accession of President Grau, the company offered to make a flat 20 per cent reduction in all rates for residential and commercial service. But this concession proved insufficient, and on December 6 the President issued a decree lowering provisionally by approximately 45 per cent the maximum rates for gas and electricity established in 1902. Despite strong protests from the company, the new rates went into effect on February 8, 1934.

Meanwhile, the corporation had become engaged in a long-drawn-out conflict with its employees. Following the company's refusal to accept certain demands, the workers went on strike on January 13, 1934. The movement paralyzed the activities of the capital, which was left without light, power or street-car service. Its water supply, pumped by electricity, was also endangered. On the following day the government issued Decree No. 172, which authorized "provisional intervention" on the part of the authorities in the administration of the company. The strikers at once returned to work, and for three weeks the concern was under government management.

During the Grau period, government revenues were at a low figure, due to various fiscal amnesties which had previously been decreed, to payments of advance taxes secured by preceding governments from petroleum companies, as well as to the opposition of conservative economic interests. None the less, service was maintained on all of the island's external obligations—except the Chase loan—without recourse to a moratorium, such as was later declared by the Mendieta government.

GRAU LOSES SUPPORT

Following the crushing of the Atarés revolt on November 9, the Grau-Batista régime stood probably at the peak of its strength. Its success against that insurrection challenged anew the expediency of Washington's non-recognition policy. This policy had been widely attacked in the United States, and its wisdom was questioned by important figures in the Washington administration. Ambassador Welles consequently returned to the United States for a conference with President Roosevelt on November 19 at Warm Springs, Georgia. Following that meeting, the President issued a statement on November 23 declaring that the United States felt "neither partiality for nor prejudice against any faction or individual in Cuba." United States recognition of a government in Cuba afforded "in more than ordinary measure both material and moral support to that government," due to the historically close relationship and the treaty ties existing between the two countries. Washington consequently held that it would not be "a policy of friendship and justice to the Cuban people as a whole to accord recognition to any provisional government in Cuba unless such government clearly possessed the support and approval of the people of that Republic." Although the statement represented a decisive victory for the Cuban policies advocated by Mr. Welles, it was announced that following a brief return visit to Cuba he would be recalled to Washington to resume his position as Assistant Secretary of State and would be replaced by Mr. Jefferson Caffery.

By this time Mr. Welles had become completely *persona non grata* to the Cuban government. On November 15 President Grau had addressed a personal letter to President Roosevelt, in which he requested the recall of the envoy. After reviewing the success of the government in quelling the Atarés revolt, he declared:

> I am led to request in my own name, as well as in that of my government, that you kindly put an end to the perturbing action of Ambassador Sumner Welles, for the maintenance of the high regard and traditional friendship which exists between our respective countries.
>
> He has repeatedly disclosed his partiality by holding communication and dealings with the enemies of the Government, and very particularly with those implicated in the uprising which we have just put down with energy mingled with generosity.
>
> We shall welcome in Cuba any representative of your Excellency imbued with the good neighbor policy which you have outlined with the hearty approval of all the American nations.

Throughout the Grau régime Mr. Welles had firmly resisted strong pressure for intervention on the part of business groups— American, Spanish and Cuban—as well as from other conservative interests. But ill-will prevailed against him in government circles, founded not only on the policy of non-recognition, for which he was held chiefly responsible, and the continued presence of United States war vessels in Cuban waters, but also on his attitude and activities with relation to internal political questions. In the first place, he was believed to be personally hostile to President Grau, to members of the Student Directorate and to other individuals in the government. This hostility contrasted sharply with his high admiration for various leaders in the ABC Opposition group. In the second place, his residence for several days in the National Hotel, after the ousted army officers had begun to gather there, had handicapped the government in taking aggressive action against this center of counter-revolution and led to numerous charges, including some from officers in the hotel, that the Ambassador had encouraged the rebellion. Third, repeated visits to the Embassy by leading Opposition figures for conference with Mr. Welles accentuated the government's resentment and fostered suspicions that he was actively meddling in island politics.

But while foreign opposition was undeniably a factor of first importance in undermining the strength of the Grau government, the régime was forced to wage a constant battle against the antagonism of Cuban groups. Its domestic opponents resorted to a campaign of bombing, roof sniping and terrorism. In addition, tax dodging was encouraged among the wealthy, and strikes among labor. As the autumn wore on, business men were increasingly apprehensive about the sugar grinding season, scheduled to begin in January. Many companies announced that, owing to excessive labor demands and unrest, their mills would be unable to operate. Growing tension between blacks and whites—the former strongly pro-Grau, the latter often anti-government—appeared to threaten racial conflict.

The government suffered, moreover, from progressive attrition among its supporters. As early as October 19 the A.B.C. *Radical*, whose leader had been a member of the Revolutionary Junta of Camp Columbia, issued a manifesto bitterly criticizing the Grau administration, charging that it had failed to establish peace, order, justice and liberty. On October 30 a temporary vote of confidence in the Student Directorate was secured from a large university assembly only after hours of wrangling. On November 6 the Directorate—feeling that its mandate had expired—declared itself dissolved, announcing, however, that its members would continue to support President Grau as individuals. On January 6 an assembly of University students, angered at apparent predominance of military influence in the government, voted definite opposition to the Grau administration.

The lack of discipline prevailing in the army during the first two months of the administration and the arbitrary acts of numerous officers had seriously embarrassed the government. In many cases army leaders, acting solely under the orders of Colonel Batista, appointed local civil officials in the provinces with complete disregard of the Secretary of the Interior, who normally held jurisdiction over such posts. In other cases the efforts of the Minister of Labor to achieve peaceful solutions for sugar mill strikes were balked by the arrest of strike leaders on the part of the military and violent actions against the workers. Grau supporters believed Batista, now supported by the conservatives, ready to sacrifice the President, if that were necessary, to win recognition.

By the middle of December public opinion in Havana had become almost unanimously hostile to the Grau-Batista régime. To cap the hostility of Welles and Washington, the opposition of the Spanish colony, the enmity on one hand of industrial and commercial leaders and on the other of Communist-led labor, and finally the loss of student support, the government was faced by divisions within the cabinet. Opposed to a left-wing faction, in which Dr. Antonio Guiteras, Minister of Interior, represented the most important figure, was a group of more conservative tendencies. It was reported on December 22 that four of these Ministers had presented their resignations.

THE HEVIA INTERREGNUM

On the afternoon of January 14, 1934, a conference was held by Grau, Batista and Mendieta. The President was informed by Batista, according to reports, that unless he resigned United States intervention was probable. Grau replied that for some time his resignation had been in the hands of the Revolutionary Junta, and that he was willing to withdraw if a successor could be found who would merit the confidence of all factions. Batista declared that Mendieta was such a candidate and Grau, realizing that the proposed candidate had probably been assured both army and United States support, congratulated Mendieta and left the meeting. At a cabinet session that evening Grau authorized two members of the cabinet to present his resignation to the Revolutionary Junta of Camp Columbia, which had been called into session.

The meeting of the Junta, over which Batista presided, was long and stormy. The attempt to secure approval for the election of Mendieta met with strong opposition. He was attacked as the representative of reaction and of the old politicians. As a compromise, certain leaders—including Batista and Sergio Carbó—accepted Carlos Hevia, Secretary of Agriculture in the Grau cabinet. Mendieta was then consulted and signed a statement pledging his support to Hevia. The latter, however, refused to accept office in the absence of definite action by the Revolutionary Junta. To meet this situation, Dr. Grau assembled in the Palace members of the Junta, together with his cabinet, who finally took action in designating Hevia as Grau's successor.

President Grau left the Palace on the afternoon of January 15, at which time Hevia became President *de facto*, although he did not take the oath of office until noon of the next day. The new régime, however, was denied effective support and Hevia presented his resignation to the Revolutionary Junta, sending it early on January 18 to Batista as the presiding officer of that body.

THE MENDIETA GOVERNMENT

At a meeting on January 18, 1934 leaders of the most important anti-Grau factions voted united support of Colonel Carlos Mendieta as Provisional President, and the new executive took the oath of office that afternoon. His accession represented the victory of Cuban conservatives, Colonel Batista, and Washington over the nationalist, left-wing and pro-labor forces which had been prominent during the Grau régime. His inauguration, attended by widespread rejoicing, was hailed as presaging the end of the political turmoil which had so long gripped the island. In the new cabinet, or "government of concentration," the *Unión Nacionalista* received the greater number of posts, but portfolios were also held by the ABC, the *Menocalistas* and the *Marianistas*.

The new administration proved itself speedily able to satisfy Washington's definition of a stable and representative régime. Following a conference at the White House with the diplomats representing the Latin American countries, President Roosevelt on January 23 announced recognition of the Mendieta government. This support was extended within five days of Mendieta's accession to power, in contrast to the 4-month refusal to recognize the Grau government. Moreover, Secretary Hull proclaimed the withdrawal of 10 of the 16 United States naval vessels then in Cuban waters.

Immediate action was demanded from the new government in the economic field to assure the success of the sugar grinding season, which had been scheduled to begin on January 15. In the political field, its principal task was restoration of a sufficient degree of political tranquility to permit the holding of elections for re-establishment of constitutional government. United States assistance was considered indispensable for the attainment of both economic and political goals. President Mendieta announced that he was counting on Washington's cooperation in abrogating the Platt Amendment and securing a "reasonable" sugar quota, a new reciprocity agreement, reorganization of the external debt, and American "monetary assistance."

On February 3, 1934 the government promulgated a Constitutional Law which superseded the Constitutional Statutes of the Grau régime and revoked both the 1901 constitution and the Machado amendments of 1928. Authority was concentrated in the person of the Provisional President. The cabinet, appointed by him, was accorded powers to legislate by decree-laws; Cuba had been without a congress since the fall of Machado. The President also was to name an advisory Council of State. Elections were to be held before December 31, 1934 to choose delegates to a constitutional convention. To check the revolutionary drive for reprisals against former Machado supporters, the new document prohibited confiscation of property and suspended the death penalty until the constitutional convention could reach a definite decision on capital punishment. . . .

CONCLUSION

The fall of Machado initiated two revolutions in Cuba—one political, the other social. The first sought to supplant dictatorship and return to constitutional democracy. The second envisaged such social reconstruction as would restore control of land and economic life to the Cuban people. To date both revolutions have failed of their objectives. The Machado régime has been eliminated, but behind the present administration looms the Batista dictatorship, less "constitutional" and more military than its predecessor. Although some degree of prosperity has returned to the island, economic recovery has not brought political tranquillity. Unrest is still widespread and revolutionary groups constantly plot armed insurrection. As in 1933, the University and secondary schools are closed to Cuban youth.

Defeat has also attended plans for social reconstruction. Attempts at reform under Grau were succeeded by reaction under Mendieta. Some excellent labor legislation found a place on the statute books, but workers' organizations were shorn of effective power. The return of prosperity strengthened conservative interests, and thus helped to block projected change. Moreover, left-wing groups lacked cohesion, discipline and a common working program. The labor movement, largely under Communist direction, fought those political factions—the ABC, the *auténticos* and Young Cuba—which were pledged to economic and social change. These parties, in turn, not only waged war on each other, but were torn by internal differences arising from personal ambition, doctrinaire attitudes and other factors.

During the period under discussion, the United States played a peculiarly decisive rôle in Cuban affairs. The Roosevelt administration sought to remedy the island's economic malaise by a program of active cooperation. Whatever prosperity Cuba today enjoys is largely the result of United States policy on sugar and trade. The very success of this program, however, reveals the degree to which Cuban independence is limited by the American tariff.

The Washington government won praise by its refusal to exercise open political control in Cuba. It rejected insistent demands for the landing of marines. The Platt Amendment, with its right of intervention, was abrogated. Such evidences of self-restraint did not mean, however, that the United States had ceased to exert marked influence over Cuban developments. In addition to the economic policies already mentioned, recognition proved a powerful instrument in the hands of the Roosevelt administration. It was extended promptly to Céspedes and Mendieta, but denied to Grau. Refusal to recognize this latter régime helped to doom, as it now appears, the most promising opportunity for a constructive solution of the Cuban problem. Less patent, but not less important, than recognition was diplomatic pressure. This proved an essential factor in Machado's fall; it seriously weakened Grau and correspondingly strengthened Mendieta; it contributed to the ascendency of Batista. But with all the undeniable power of this weapon, its limitations are worthy of note. Mr. Welles failed under Céspedes in his endeavor to keep the revolution within constitutional channels; he failed under Mendieta to assure island stability through a "representative," middle-of-the-road coalition. Similarly, prospects that Mr. Caffery's insistence on elections will remedy Cuban unrest are not, at this writing, particularly hopeful.

If the fundamental purpose of the Welles-Caffery policy was to avoid prolonged civil warfare and danger to American enterprises, it may claim some success. The forces of protest have been driven underground—but whether to disappear or to reappear in more aggressive form, the future alone will decide.

3

Compared with the Mexican and Bolivian revolutions, the only other socio-economic reform upheavals in the history of Spanish America, the Cuban Revolution of 1959 moved with astonishing speed and success. In less than a year Castro and his supporters had vanquished their opposition, consolidated their military victory, and destroyed the foundations of the old regime. The Mexicans required more than three decades to accomplish it, and the Bolivians never completely implanted their revolution. In the opinion of Ramón Eduardo Ruiz, one answer lies in the nature of Cuban society—in the absence of the traditional Spanish American elite, in the existence of a splintered middle sector, and in the weakness of institutions.

Ramón Eduardo Ruiz:
Cuba*

Cuba has dictatorships and constitutional masquerades simply because that is the way that the majority of the Cuban people want it.
HERMINIO PORTELL-VILA

I

To the surprise of scholars who, on the basis of their knowledge of Cuban history, predicted minimal socio-economic change on the Cuban scene despite Castro's victory, the Revolution moved with astonishing speed and spectacular political success. In a matter of months an agrarian reform law was not merely promulgated but carried out—over the strong protests of traditional interests with an unbeaten record of opposition to socio-economic reform. By the end of the first year of revolution the old rulers of Cuba had lost virtually all political authority, while professionals and other mem-

* From Ramón Eduardo Ruiz, CUBA: THE MAKING OF A REVOLUTION (Amherst: University of Massachusetts Press, 1968), pp. 141–163.

bers of the supposedly growing "middle class" were beginning their exodus from the island.

In the light of past failures to carry out reform in Cuba, what accounts for Castro's accomplishments? Obviously no single explanation provides a full and satisfactory answer, but every attempt to explain the success of the Revolution must take into account the peculiar character of Cuba in 1958.

II

No coherent society existed in Cuba in 1958, no stable or well-knit structure but simply, as the sociologist Lowry Nelson noted, "a society in a state of emergence." The individual components of Cuban life did not constitute a nation. While Cubans were profoundly nationalist, their society—a collection of pieces held together by circumstance and historical accident—encompassed economic conflicts, ethnic rivalries, and rural-urban differences that mocked the myth of nationhood.

A number of factors determined the island's fragmented society. No permanent, homogeneous ruling class had evolved on the island. The local ruling group, continually in the process of transformation, established no true hegemony. Because Spanish feudalism never had taken root on the island, no traditional landed élite existed. The large sugar plantations dated back only to the waning days of the colonial period. For more than three centuries the land had been widely distributed; thus the relative insignificance of latifundia checked the rise of the Spanish feudal system.

Sugar and the influx of American capital further disrupted growth of the plantation common to the Spanish mainland colonies. Even the large estates left behind by Spain largely disappeared; therefore, no class of landed patricians in the pattern of Mexico or Peru, or serfs tied to the land and bound by law to the *hacendado*, characterized Cuba. An American-owned, agro-industrial unit substituted for them, fostering an entirely different relationship between management and labor and, in the process, eliminating the existence and need for an élite in the Spanish-American sense.

Recently Cuba had acquired a pseudo-aristocracy of bourgeois background whose wealth had been won by participation in the economic life of the Republic—a plutocracy, maintained the scholar J. F. Carvajal, which stepped into the breach when the Spaniards departed. This new group merged with the remnants of the old colonial élite, and both eventually joined hands with American investors who poured capital into the sugar industry after the Platt

Amendment provided the necessary guarantees. On the basis of antecedents and values—a concoction of Spanish, Cuban, and American ingredients—the new plutocracy had little in common with an agrarian élite. Except for a high per capita income which distinguished it from less affluent groups, its ties were with the bourgeoisie. A neo-entrepreneurial clan lacking the élite's consciousness of unity and class and exercising only a limited leadership, this plutocracy in no sense controlled society in the manner of the élite of Peru or Colombia, which dictated not merely the economic, but the social and political system. Edmundo Desnoes, a contemporary Cuban novelist and writer who resigned as editor of *Vision* in order to return to Cuba in 1960, makes this point bluntly in his *Inconsolable Memories*. "That's the only thing for which I have to thank the revolution . . ." which, he writes, "really fucked up all the damned half-wits who hoarded everything here! I can't say 'governed' because they didn't have the foggiest idea of what a ruling class is all about."

The problem of defining and understanding the middle class raises nearly insurmountable difficulties. The lateness of independence, the monocultural system, the preponderant role of foreign capital, the sugar latifundia, and the absence of small industries—all these questions, as Carvajal indicates, markedly influenced the class structure of Cuba.

In his study, Lowry Nelson points out that outside observers might conclude that the Cuban social structure consisted simply of upper, middle, and lower classes. Such a definition, he warns, oversimplifies "a complex situation." If wealth and income are the criteria, Cuba undoubtedly possessed an upper and lower class. But, he emphasizes, a sixth sense advises him that Cuban society had not "set" or "jelled." The class variations between extremes of wealth and poverty make any attempt to generalize dangerous.

Instead of three groups, Nelson divides Cuban society into two major categories. In the top echelon he includes upper-upper, middle-upper, and lower-upper groups; at the bottom, he lists upper-lower, middle-lower, and lower-lower groups. The upper class embraces managerial people as well as office workers, and those "descended from upper-class families regardless of their present state of wealth and income." In the lower class, he places manual laborers and those "descended from families of this class." Cubans, according to Nelson's thesis, could not be classified solely on the basis of income—since income is of secondary importance in the subtle socio-psychological distinctions that make class identification difficult.

The problem of defining middle class involves, in essence, a question of attitudes. Was there a Cuban middle class with its own set of values? Because the middle groups identified themselves with the plutocracy and its values, Nelson concludes there was not. Rather, the middle groups wanted to resemble the upper class, to live in similar style, in luxury if possible. The distinction between rich and middle class was a difference in standard of living and not one of attitudes: the rich simply had more than the less affluent.

In addition, it is imprecise to speak of a national bourgeoisie, for the middle groups were almost totally identified with United States interests, corporations, and finance. It had few holdings of its own and few exclusively native interests to protect. As Boris Goldenberg argues, the spirit of anti-imperialism, a feature of any native entrepreneurial class, found no spokesmen among the Cuban bourgeoisie—especially after 1933, when United States trade and economic concessions drew American businessmen and the Cuban bourgeoisie closer together. Students and the intelligentsia even accused Cuban entrepreneurs of being pro-American.

Although it is an axiom of politics that an independent middle class is the product of native interests, the bourgeoisie, dependent on the foreigner, had virtually ignored the need to build native industry. Not until 1927 were fledgling industries even protected by legislation. Moreover, immigrants, particularly Spaniards who seldom accepted the island as their permanent home, weakened considerably the nationalist sentiment of the middle groups. True, the tide was beginning to turn; native Cubans were entering business for themselves, establishing a small but growing number of light industries and winning a larger share of the sugar industry. Domestic shoe production, for example, supplied more than 90 per cent of domestic demand, while textiles represented only 2.7 per cent of Cuban imports. Despite this belated trend, however, no basic shift occurred in the economy: imports of fixed capital goods, to use one illustration, had not declined but grown from 52.6 per cent in 1949 to 60.9 in 1958. Private enterprise was still largely foreign; educated Cubans, schooled mainly as doctors or lawyers, turned to public office for a livelihood, converting the national treasury into their chief employer. At the bottom of this nebulous class, an army of petty traders, entertainers, guides, and procurers—"bourgeois" in outlook and aspirations—exacted a living from the tourist industry and the tastes of the luxury-minded. Many had jobs only during the tourist season.

Nowhere was the weakness or nonexistence of the middle class more evident than in rural Cuba. With 40 per cent of the population labeled rural and a far greater percentage dependent directly or indirectly on agriculture, the island should have possessed a rural middle class. It did not. Apparently, the *colonos*, renters, and sub-renters, as well as the foremen, superintendents, and mill-managers engaged in the sugar, tobacco, and coffee industries, which made up a sizeable population, formed a middle class. Close inspection, however, revealed that in practice these groups lacked an independent role of their own; they were at the mercy of the entrenched interests and, as such, resembled their urban counterparts.

In summary, the middle class did not exist as a class. It was a collection of groups, none with a clear concept of its place in society, but each imbued with a set of petit ideals, the sum of which did not add up to an ideal of class. Passive in its political attitudes, each group had involved itself in national issues only when threatened directly. No unanimity of opinion on national questions bound them together, especially on matters relating to the political and moral health of the country. In 1952 each group accepted passively Batista's coup, as each had bowed before the political chicanery of the past.

The lower classes were equally fragmented, united only loosely by the common bonds of poverty and want. A small, urban proletariat lived in the slums and shanty towns of Havana and other cities, their numbers swollen periodically by hordes of unemployed workers from the country in sugar's dead season. The jobs of the urban proletariat were mainly in construction, the making of tobacco products, public utilities, shipping, and those service industries closely tied to the influx of tourists. The field hands and men permanently employed in the sugar mills, tobacco *vegas*, and cattle ranches were their allies in the countryside. A minifundist group of 250,000 small farmers and their families, who eked out a precarious existence by cultivating an average of fifteen acres of land, nearly half as sharecroppers or squatters, lived on the fringe of the workers' world.

A labor force of 700,000 without jobs or only seasonally employed—almost double that of men with full-time jobs—colored markedly the structure of the bottom order. Approximately half had jobs during the *zafra*, or for a few months of the year in the construction business. To cite Robin Blackburn's perceptive analysis, this labor section "was not even exploited in the relationship of production; it was simply excluded altogether," it had no stake in society. All told, out of an employable work force of approximately 2.7 million, more than one out of four had no jobs, either for the entire year or a major part of it.

The index distinguishing upper-income from lower-income

groups, the affluent from the poor and exploited, ran along rural-urban lines. Nearly everyone in the countryside was in the lower class, while virtually all upper-income individuals lived in cities and towns, in a land preponderantly agricultural in its economy, where three-fourths of the population depended on agriculture.

Rural residence and poverty distinguished a majority of the populace. An impoverished mass of unemployed or under-employed, a rural population identified with the cultivation of one crop, and a small urban proletariat—these were the major components of Cuba's lower class. Though laborers had banded together in labor syndicates, the harsh economic reality of the seasonable and unpredictable sugar economy undermined much of their organizational strength, in particular that of the sugar workers' union, the largest in Cuba. No social or ideological bonds held the workers together or integrated the majority of them into the structure of society. In this sense, the lower class had fewer loyalties to Cuban institutions than the amorphous middle groups. Embittered and frustrated, many workers had readily lent themselves to the machinations of agitators and reformers, whose main goal was drastic transformation of the society. Labor had even accepted workers' soviets for the sugar industry in 1933, while individual members of the lower class shared a widespread cynicism about each other, their government, their laws, and their country's future.

Nowhere was this distrust more glaring than in organized labor's relations with management. No mutual trust, no willingness to cooperate existed between the two, according to the World Bank's *Report on Cuba*. Labor and management blamed each other for the various ills that afflicted them. Though organized labor had made sizeable gains since the 1930's, the sentiment of its members was one of "revenge"—a response, concluded the Bank, conditioned by past abuses of management. Distrustful of their employers, workers ruthlessly exploited all advantages at the bargaining table, while their leaders rose to prominence "by displaying a maximum of aggressiveness."

In the Bank's analysis, the workers and their leaders were the victims of anxieties born of a stagnant economy, of the chronic unemployment that haunted their lives. An army of ill-housed and hungry men and their families were always there to remind the employed of the pitfalls that befell the victim who lost his job. Having suffered previously, the workers had little faith in the ability or will of investor and government to build new industries or provide additional jobs. Management-labor relations, meanwhile, were conducted on an impersonal basis. A legalistic approach, in which the human factor was usually absent, conditioned management's view of labor. Few of management's experts, lawyers in the main, had first-hand knowledge of labor conditions, either in their own industries or on a national level. The extent of unemployment, the cost of living in a given area, housing and health conditions—these considerations, all of supreme importance to the worker and his family—were seldom weighed carefully by the experts and their employers. In the opinion of the Bank, labor-management-government relations had reached an impasse in 1950. Without marked improvement, Cuba could expect "progressive deterioration" of its economic picture. It would find its ability to compete in the world market dramatically curtailed while at home production, employment, and income would decline. As social tensions grew, rich and poor alike might easily turn to a dictatorship to "solve" their problems.

Questions of color and race split society in other ways. One out of four Cubans claimed Negro ancestors, either from Africa or the West Indies. The census of 1953 acknowledged that 27.2 per cent of the population was colored; the correct figure may have been higher. Furthermore, despite apologists for Spanish colonization who vehemently deny its existence in the Spanish American empire, race prejudice—the Spanish brand mixed liberally with ingredients imported from the United States—divided the nation along color lines.

In general, upper-income groups were white: color darkened at the bottom of the social scale. Manual laborers were frequently of Afro-Cuban background, and nearly all men of black skin were poor. The rural work force had a pronounced African tinge, especially the cane-cutters and the unskilled in the tobacco and coffee industries. Although it would be a mistake to interpret Cuban society in the context of North American racial attitudes, darkness of skin in Cuba as in the United States tended to identify low social position.

The race question has enjoyed a prominent historical role. It strongly influenced the movement for independence, delaying its coming. While Simón Bolívar and José de San Martín were winning independence on the mainland, Cubans remained loyal to Spain in the face of efforts by Mexico and Colombia to liberate them. The Cuban census of 1817 tells a good part of that story: blacks outnumbered whites, while on the mainland only 2 per cent of the population was of African stock. Cuba had more Negroes than the continental colonies of Spain, and until 1850 the growth of the Cuban population responded largely to the importation of Negroes. Alexander von Humboldt, the renowned German scientist who visited Cuba near the turn of the century, estimated that more than

90,000 Negroes were imported between 1521 and 1791. In the opinion of others, Cubans had smuggled more than half a million Negroes onto the island after Spain formally abolished the slave trade in 1820, nearly all with the connivance of the local Spanish captain-generals. According to some figures, approximately 650,000 blacks, all told, were landed on Cuban soil by the mid-nineteenth century. From that time on, the relative number of Negroes in the local population declined, until in 1899 the census reported fewer Negroes than in 1837. The movement for independence appeared only after the whites gained numerical ascendency.

As historians point out, distrust of the Negro frequently kept many would-be liberators loyal to Spain. Fearful of the role that "liberated" Negroes might have in a republic, local Spaniards and Creoles opposed independence or favored annexation to the United States before the Civil War. With the defeat of the Confederacy, the Cuban slavocracy turned its back on union, preferring to remain under Spain, as the events of the Ten Years' War testify. When Cuba finally won its independence, there were twice as many whites as blacks. In brief, color often divided patriots from loyalists.

Directly or indirectly, the Negro frequently supported the cause of reform. As the exploited laborer on the sugar plantations, he had persistently opposed the system, first pleading for his emancipation and then demanding higher wages and better working conditions. In the beginning the enemy was the white landlord, Spaniard or Creole, and later the foreign-owned corporation. When his master identified with Spain, the Negro accepted the cause of independence, fighting and dying for it, and providing a number of patriot leaders, among them the legendary mulatto Antonio Maceo. In the course of his history as a slave and later as a poorly paid cane-cutter, the Afro-Cuban frequently rebelled. In the nineteenth century, slave revolts broke out in 1812, 1827, 1843, and 1879, and in 1912, under the Republic, a Negro revolt erupted, led by Evaristo Estenoz, who claimed that his people had been denied equality. In the midst of Estenoz' efforts to organize a Negro political party in Oriente, the Independent Party of Color, fighting broke out between Afro-Cubans and government troops sent to suppress the movement. Some 3,000 blacks died in this race war, stirring animosities which did not subside for decades.

In the twentieth century, Negro protest, with the exception of the ill-fated revolt of 1912, merged with that of labor. Much of the labor trouble of the twenties and thirties had roots in "colored" Oriente, which suffered every affliction of the sugar industry. As cane-cutters, mill-hands, marginal farmers, or manual laborers, Afro-Cubans were the first to feel the pinch of hard times. A majority of the permanently unemployed or underemployed was undoubtedly of Afro-Cuban stock. The North American brand of race prejudice, which entered Cuba with United States capital and tourism, tended to aggravate the pattern of racial discrimination. At the social level, meanwhile, Afro-Cubans with distinctly Negroid features had little access to the best hotels and bars in Havana or the social clubs of whites.

Discriminated against in jobs and snubbed by the social élite, the Negro was, nevertheless, courted assiduously by politicians, particularly those out of office. From the time of Estrada Palma, first President of the Republic, whose Moderate party had the backing of the wealthy and of professional people, the Negro identified with the opposition. Hence, Afro-Cubans initially sided with the Liberals who promised them political and economic equality in return for their support. In practice, Liberals as well as Moderates and Conservatives feared the black multitude and kept it from winning political power, while they exploited the Negro's political naïvete for narrow and selfish ends. In 1920, to cite one notorious case, Menocal and the Conservatives wooed the Negro vote in order to elect Alfredo Zayas and thwart the Liberals, but to accomplish this end, they had to split the overwhelmingly Liberal Negro vote by reviving a feud between secret Negro religious sects. On their promise to espouse the Conservative cause, the ñáñigos (a voodoo clan) were permitted to parade publicly and perform their ceremonies without interference from local authorities. During the 1933 Revolution, student leaders of the Directorio Estudiantil, many of whom accepted neo-Darwinist racial concepts, tried to rally Negroes behind Grau's regime. Grau's social legislation won over many Negroes and mulattoes, but frightened whites who earlier had resisted their demands. For his part, Batista employed his own multiracial background to appeal for Negro support.

In 1958, nonetheless, it would have been an error to speak of a Negro population entirely outside the mainstream of the island's life. The Negro had enmeshed himself, racially and culturally, in Cuba. Nicolás Guillén, the noted Afro-Cuban poet, pointed out that the Negro had contributed immeasurably to the island's development. Economically, the Negro had been the backbone of Cuban life for centuries. Without him the great sugar plantations, which had rewarded their owners handsomely, could not have thrived. The entire background of the nineteenth century would have been very different had Africans not made the island their home. In Guillén's opinion, the African had created in Cuba a true mulatto psychology, an intermediate culture, the Negri-blanca, which formed the fun-

damental character of the Cuban people and which, in the mind of
the poet, was neither black nor white but mixed and totally fused.

Yet the colored population, paradoxically, was too often an
unassimilated element in society. Though racial discrimination in
Cuba was less intense than in the American South, the Afro-Cuban
had tasted the bitter fruit of inequality and had behind him a long
history of protest, insurrection, and native leadership. An exploited
minority, the colored population had few loyalties to the system,
and little preparation for changing it by democratic or peaceful
means.

III

A society split by wide income differences, in which rich and poor
lived in separate worlds, where a pervasive spirit of mistrust set
individuals and groups against each other, provided shaky foundations for its institutions. In reality, the infant Republic never developed institutions of its own. The laws, the courts, and the
government rested on a colonial experience that left the Cubans
unprepared to rule themselves, and on foreign models ill-suited to
domestic conditions. The institutions were victimized by public
apathy, corruption, and self-interest.

No institution mirrored more accurately the native scene than
the political parties. In the beginning, three factions battled for
supremacy on the local political scene: the Conservative, Moderate,
and Liberal parties. Until the late twenties, they divided the public
coffers among themselves and joined forces to prevent a successful
attack on their monopoly. In the 1930's the Conservatives renamed
themselves the Democratic party; the more status-quo minded
among them formed the Republican party in the forties. In the
meantime, the Liberals became allies of Gerardo Machado, a stigma
that virtually destroyed them as a potent political force after his
downfall. All were conservative parties of wealthy Cubans with
little mass support. Their program eulogized private enterprise,
"democratic and honest" government, and opposed Communism.
Their platforms expressed regret for the passing of the "good old
days," and when the chips were down, they preferred dictatorship
to "chaos and disorder."

Opposed to the Liberals and Conservatives were the reform
"parties" of the middle sectors. From the early thirties until the
late forties, Grau's Auténticos headed the list of these parties. He
and his followers challenged proponents of the status quo only

briefly, and when they fell into line after accepting an accommodation with the older parties, Grau won the presidency in 1944 with the support of reactionary Republicans. Embittered by the turn of events, reformers organized the Party of the Cuban People, the Ortodoxos, who claimed the mantle of Martí for themselves. By 1958 the Ortodoxos had split into moderates and radicals. Apparently a rule of thumb dictated the course of Cuban politics: conservatives remained faithful to their banner, but reformers, both individuals and parties, eventually joined the enemy camp.

The protest of the fifties was against all parties for, as Leslie Dewart states, all parties were totally discredited. When Batista seized power in 1952, middle-sector government was in a state of virtual political bankruptcy. Party goals were the spoils of office and the public treasury, for distribution among party hacks and leaders. The parties functioned in a world of their own, independent of public demands and aspirations, where loyalty to the party, its members and its leadership dictated decisions and the outline of political philosophy. No one, explained J. González Lanuza, more resembled a Conservative than a Liberal. Party leaders with whom members identified, and who had welded them together, enjoyed immense stature, for the parties were personalist organizations, directed and controlled by one man: if successful at the polls, by the president of the Republic; if not, by the man who aspired to succeed him. At the local level, the boss on his way up the political ladder or the *jefe político* dispensed favors granted him by his superiors in return for his support. Cuba's political history had been the story of such men: the Menocals, Machados, Batistas, and Graus. The *caudillo* ruled, the chieftain who put personal and party needs above political principles and ideology, who served the foreign investor and the affluent. In the history of the island, wrote Carlos Márquez Sterling, "the point that stood out was the reliance on the *caudillo* as an expression of the Cuban intellect." Not surprisingly, therefore, Cuba, with the exception of the Auténticos in the 1930's, had no party of truly national or popular scope. Fidel Castro stepped out of that setting.

On the political front, violence characterized almost a third of the Republic's history: the first decade of the twentieth century, the late twenties until 1936 and, again, after 1953. In the countryside the Cuban had turned to the guerrilla warfare he had utilized against the Spaniards in the Ten Years' War, in the period from 1895 to 1898, and against Machado and Batista. Rich and poor alike indulged themselves in the national pastime of terror.

The ABC, one of the island's legendary protest groups, was a case in point. Organized in December 1931 to battle the Machado tyranny, it employed terror to combat terror. Composed mainly of young men from intellectual and professional ranks, the ABC won national acclaim for its ability to intimidate Machado and his gang of hired thugs. All members belonged to one of three alphabetical cells, from which the society took its name. During its heyday, the ABC had 2,000 members who, in the words of Ruby Hart Phillips, Havana correspondent of the New York *Times*, were "pleasant-mannered, well-educated youths, despite the fact they were certainly murderers." Sick of the cynical generation of 1895 veterans who had run Cuba since independence, the ABC resorted to violence to combat political ills, meanwhile urging abrogation of the Platt Amendment and a gradual break-up of the extensive American-owned plantations. On the fall of Machado, the ABC dominated the short-lived Céspedes administration and, after Grau toppled Céspedes, focused its terror tactics on Grau and his allies, openly supporting the unsuccessful revolt against them in November 1933. The ABC, however, was not alone in its use of violence. After Batista's thugs shot Antonio Guiteras in May 1935, members of "Young Cuba," which had been headed by Guiteras, sought revenge by killing every man who had participated in the murder of their leader. Eddie Chibás, idol of Cuban idealists in the late forties, won his spurs as a young man by throwing a bomb at a streetcar in the days of Machado. Mobs in Havana looted stores and wantonly killed Machado's backers after the dictator abandoned the city.

Without an effective political apparatus, Cuba was left at the mercy of the army; its two national chieftains, Machado and Batista, had controlled more than half the Republic's history. Unlike the military in other Spanish American countries, where the army's ties with the élite often fostered an "unholy trinity" with church and landlord, the Cuban army had an unconventional background. It was of recent origin—a twentieth-century phenomenon dating back less than five decades—the progeny of American policy architects who, having watched a motley band of malcontents oust Cuba's first president in 1906, decided to build an army to prevent a similar occurrence in the future. In one of his last acts, therefore, Charles E. Magoon had provided for a permanent army. However, the rebels of 1906 had been veterans of the struggle for independence and members of the Liberal party which had popular sympathy. Thus, from the beginning, the army was a foreign institution and, in the eyes of countless citizens of the island, an enemy of true patriots as well as the tool of vested interests.

Magoon further muddied the situation by appointing as the army's commander-in-chief "Pino" Guerra, the very man who had captained the organized revolt against Estrada Palma. When Estrada Palma announced his reelection, so legend has it, Guerra, then a Liberal representative in congress, walked out, threatening to "seek justice somewhere else." To train him and to build a modern army, Magoon dispatched Guerra to France and the United States to study military organization and tactics, to make impossible a repetition of the kind of revolt Guerra had engineered.

Although a foreign institution, the military took on local characteristics. As the servant of successive administrations from 1909 to 1933, the army had cloaked itself in the mantle of its sister institutions from Mexico to Argentina. The "Hispanization" of the army began with Guerra. In 1912 President José Miguel Gómez had decided that his reelection alone could save Cuba from chaos, but he feared the army, for Guerra was a vocal supporter of Gómez' rival, Alfredo Zayas. To rid himself of Guerra, Gómez offered him a special mission to Europe and a lucrative reward. When Guerra adamantly declined, Gómez had him shot. Fortunately for Guerra, the would-be assassins proved inept and he escaped with a wounded leg. Not one to repeat a mistake, Guerra resigned, leaving his post in the hands of Gómez' closest friend. Later, Guerra embraced Gómez, and the two helped to thwart Zayas' presidential ambitions. Yet not until the advent of Machado did the army become the personalist body native to Spanish American politics. A military man himself, Machado transformed the army into his personal tool and, in the process, into the spokesman for the rich and well-born. Ironically, it was this pampered military that overthrew him in 1933.

When Batista and his sergeants, men of humble antecedents, ousted a clique of officers from control of the army, they created a wholly new military situation. As army boss, Batista granted commissions to 527 enlisted men; only 116 of the former 500 officers, those willing to accept a mulatto commander, kept their commissions. By deposing the officer clique whose background identified it with ruling groups, Batista divorced the military from the traditional power structure; by race and social position, Batista and his men belonged to the lower classes. Yet Batista's betrayal of the revolutionaries in 1934, who undoubtedly had majority sentiment behind them, destroyed what mass popularity the army had won in its earlier coup. Born of mutiny and betrayal, the post-Machado army became the puppet of Batista, a military establishment shorn of traditional ties with the élite, an opportunist, predatory army of professional soldiers of the lower class but devoid of any class loyalties, distrusted alike by the populace and the affluent.

Thus Batista's army found itself in an anomalous situation. It was not popular, yet its personnel by race and class had close ties with the poor. The army had a high percentage of Afro-Cuban officers, approximately one out of three. General Querejeta, a Negro, commanded the army in 1949. Such a military had few staunch defenders in the ruling cliques; nonetheless, the army had consolidated its position by siding with the vested interests, the enemies of reform. The plebeian army, therefore, was caught between spokesmen for the status quo who decried change in any form, and the populace, with which the army had bonds and which demanded change.

To keep his hard-won victory, Batista walked a tightrope: to placate his men, he increased the size of the army, raised the pay of its officers, and allotted to it a larger share of the national budget. He limited opportunities for graft but never cut them off entirely, gave the army a more active role in political affairs, and employed soldiers to carry out social reforms, even asking them to build schools. In this manner, Batista's army achieved a new image by the late thirties. But the *caudillo* never strayed far from the premise that led him to betray Grau. His army maintained the status quo, which placated native and foreign interests, and, in return, the plutocracy learned to live with the mulatto sergeant turned officer-politician.

After 1944 the Auténticos attempted to purge the army of Batista's cronies, but ultimately failed. Grau began the shake up, replacing Batista's chief-of-staff with an officer of his own choosing and shifting or retiring the military commanders of the six provinces. When Grau and Prío Socarrás quarreled, Prío launched his house-cleaning of the armed forces, ousting Grau's men and substituting his own. Prío had doubtful success, for army officers twice plotted his overthrow before 1952. The Auténtico purge of the military, obviously, had not paid dividends, for the coup that returned Batista to power was the work of the army. Yet the coup alienated the army even more from responsible public opinion. Hence, in 1958, its position remained unchanged; it was a personalist military force lacking close links with either the wealthy or the poor, without strong roots in the socio-economic structure of the island or in the life of the people. The strength of the army rested on arms supplied by the United States, which stamped the military as an alien force in the minds of nationalists.

The Catholic Church occupied an analogous position, because it had failed to act as a cohesive element, or to unite, as it so often did on the SpanishAmerican mainland, the conservative, traditional forces in society. In Cuba it was merely another feeble institution with only superficial strength. True, the Church enjoyed a wide popular base in the 80 per cent of the people who were nominally Catholic. Approximately a tenth of them practiced their religion, however. Compared to Peruvians, Colombians, or even Mexicans, Cubans were not a religious people. Thousands of them—including women, who tended to be more "Catholic" than their menfolk—had embraced the materialistic doctrine of Communism. In his study of the churches in the island, J. Merle Davis claimed that the Cuban, though raised in the Roman Catholic fold, was "outwardly an agnostic"; and according to Leslie Dewart, a Catholic philosopher who spent long years on the island, "The Church and any organized, institutional practices are to most Cubans . . . ridiculous and beneath contempt." Of the Spanish American people, then, the Cuban was the least Catholic in his practices and attitudes, in terms of his devotion to the Church, his support of it, and his aesthetic and social life.

Institutionally, the Church was especially weak in rural areas. The Spanish colonial clergy had never built a large number of churches in the villages and towns, and nothing was done to shift the emphasis after independence. Without churches, there was no substantial rural clergy, which left contact between priest, cane-cutter, and farmer to happenstance. Even on a national level, Cuba had just 725 priests for a population of six million, one for every 7850 inhabitants. In the end, observed Lowry Nelson, as an established, functioning institution the Church was "virtually nonexistent" in rural Cuba. In large measure, therefore, the farmer, colono, and field-worker had no major stake in the fortunes of the Church.

Racial questions helped isolate the Church even more from rural people. Much of the countryside, and certainly heavily populated Oriente, was of Afro-Cuban stock, but more than three-fourths of the clergy was Spanish, including nearly all of the hierarchy. The alien priests, therefore, failed to establish much contact with the Afro-Cuban population or to minister to its spiritual needs. Davis reported "no religious life" among Afro-Cubans. The inability of the Church to respond or communicate helped to explain, at least in part, the survival of crude forms of African spiritualism in small Afro-Cuban communities. Thus the Church could not claim a rural army of the faithful, nor call upon the rural people either to defend the Church's institutional position or that of society as a whole.

Nor was the Church a national pillar of strength. Except for a small, loyal band of largely urban and upper-income faithful, the Church had no mass following. Unlike the Church in other Spanish American republics, where it successfully resisted lay criticism, the Cuban Church had lost its special standing. Church and state were separated in 1900 and, less than two decades afterward, divorce was legalized. Nor had the divorce law simply languished on the statute books. Thousands of Cubans had taken advantage of it. In the twenties Machado signed a decree liberalizing the divorce law on the pattern of Nevada legislation, hoping in this manner to attract business to the island. Batista's own divorce in 1944 touched off a wave of divorces among army officers and politicians. A law enacted in 1900 had made marriage a civil contract, though the Cuban clergy had eventually prevailed on American occupation authorities to permit marriage in either the Church or civil courts. However, of the 107 municipalities polled on this change, 80 opposed it, as did three of the six provincial governors and all but one of the magistrates in courts of first instance. In relation to other Latin American countries, a surprisingly large number of Cubans belonged to Protestant congregations. The Masonic lodges in Cuba were the largest in all of Latin America; every major town had its lodge, while their membership, which included such famous names as José Martí and Antonio Maceo, invariably played leading roles in the political and economic life of their communities.

Historical factors underlay this picture. The quality of the colonial clergy had been poor; too often the hierarchy had staffed Cuban churches with ecclesiastical offenders from the mainland colonies. Since Church and state were united under Spain, the clergy had opposed independence, incurring the wrath of the patriot fathers and alienating majority sentiment on the island. Nor had the Church indicated any deep concern for the plight of the poor. As a Spanish institution, the Church was a bond between colony and mother country, a bond that must be severed if Cuba was to be free. No wonder, then, that debates over the Church question were among the most acrimonious at the 1901 Constitutional Convention, which abolished the state-supported Church and decreed freedom for all religious sects and, in so doing, liberated the island from the clerical issue that haunts much of Spanish America.

In summary, the Church, loosely allied with upper-income groups, its national position weak and virtually absent in rural Cuba, particularly among Afro-Cubans, was an institution with little vitality or inclination to support reformers. Only a minority of lay Catholics opposed Batista; while one of the cardinals of the Church, Manuel Arteaga, traveled to the National Palace to congratulate the *caudillo* on his coup. The Church could not hold society together or rally public opinion, either in self-interest or on behalf of the status quo.

Despite the splintered nature of society, unity existed, a unity reflecting growing awareness of what it meant to be Cuban, and of Cuba's destiny as a people. In the 1920's a wave of nationalism engulfed the island; subdued in the forties, nationalism was on the move again by 1958, with a militancy of its own among the intelligentsia and the youth of Cuba. The result of years of frustration, of hopes dashed before they were reality, the new nationalism voiced popular aspirations for a society free of the old evils and the foreigner. The new nationalism advocated the return of the land to its native owners, diversification of agriculture, and industrialization. Believers dreamt of liberating the people from the foreign yoke, on which they placed the burden of responsibility for past failures. And the yoke, in their minds, was the United States.

IV

This, then, was the structure of Cuban society in 1958. Cuba was a country with an affluent layer closely identified with American capital at the top and, at the bottom of the social scale, a large working mass, often exploited but better off than its counterparts in Spanish America. In between, amorphous middle groups existed, all striving to keep up appearances with the rich and equally dependent on foreign markets and imports. Neither the army nor the Church played its accustomed Spanish American role, though both were loosely tied to the status quo. Of the political parties none, with the exception of the Communists, had managed to build a tough, disciplined organization; none had survived the rigors of the Batista dictatorship of the fifties. Organized labor, in the interim, had succumbed to the venality of the times, which were increasingly difficult for hundreds of thousands of workers whose livelihood depended on the fickle sugar industry.

4

In the past many scholars have assumed that the Catholic Church represents a formidable barrier to the spread of Communism in Spanish America. However, in Cuba the Church offered token resistance to Marxism and quickly succumbed. Leslie Dewart offers his explanation for the downfall of the Church in the next reading.

A Canadian Catholic scholar from the University of Toronto whose concern is the survival of Catholicism in the revolutionary world, he believes that the Church exercised only a tenuous hold on the Cubans. Sympathetic to the broad social objectives of the Revolution, he is critical of the Church for its failure to offer a meaningful program and enlightened leadership.

Leslie Dewart:
Christianity and Revolution*

Much of the world's understanding of the Cuban revolution has suffered from a general absence of historical perspective and from insufficient knowledge of Cuba's historical background. This is especially true with regard to the conditions of the Church in Cuba before the revolution. Though many have recently discovered that indifference to the institutions of religion is the norm among Cubans who are Catholic by inertia and custom, deeply devout in an instinctive way, and in communion with the Church only through the desiccated umbilical cord of cultural tradition, we are not as likely to know that the profound alienation between the people and the clergy, (hence between the people and the sacraments and the liturgy), began well over a century ago. As Cuba began to acquire a national consciousness and stir from her long colonial lethargy, the Cuban hierarchy and clergy, who had always remained more closely identified with the mother country than with the masses, chose to remain faithful to Spain. This, of course, does not differentiate Cuba from dozens of other colonies, Spanish and otherwise. The process is well known and one need only mention it in order to mark the origin of the cleavage between the people and their pastors, who in Cuba as elsewhere since early modern times had increasingly thought of themselves alone as "the Church." The peculiar effect that this had for the Spanish colonial Church, and nowhere more markedly than in Cuba where the independence movement was more protracted, was that it tended to preserve the clergy and hierarchy in an outlook characteristic of Spanish Catholicism: The breath of modern times, thus, had vivified Cuba no more than it had Spain.

To say that the outlook of the Cuban Church had remained

* From Leslie Dewart, CHRISTIANITY AND REVOLUTION: THE LESSON OF CUBA (New York: Herder and Herder, 1963), pp. 92–101.

Spanish is no more than to say that it had remained medieval. Medieval is not of itself a pejorative term. There was a time when to be medieval was to be progressive and abreast of the times. But that was seven centuries ago, and time has since gone on. If an institution is medieval today then it is by definition anachronic, and perhaps it should be otherwise. The Spanishness of the Cuban clergy and hierarchy is one of the factors that must be understood if one is to appreciate the concept of State-Church relations that the Cuban Church tended to regard as an ideal.

The wars of Independence saw the Church lined up solidly and militantly, though not very effectively, against the Cuban patriots. In 1898, on the eve of the defeat of Spain, the Bishop of Havana wrote a pastoral letter "for civilization, against barbarism," that is, for colonial rule rather than independence. The effects of such a teaching may be easily deduced. Protestantism, however, was too foreign to Cuba, and so the advantage fell to freemasonry as it chose to identify itself with the cause of independence. Some historians have argued, indeed, that freemasonry's co-operation made Cuban independence from Spain possible. It is unimportant whether the claim is correct: It is widely believed. What is certain is that many events of French history were repeated in Cuba before the end of the 19th century. By 1898, when Spain was vanquished, the Catholic Church was discredited; it was also so powerless that active anticlericalism was not, and has never been until very recent times, a problem.

The Church and the clergy became figures of fun. If one thought of them at all, they were to be ridiculed, but to be neither feared nor hated: the feeling remains in Cuba to this day that organized religion is a matter for women and young children. The same Cuban who would as likely as not openly wear a medal around his neck (Castro wore one as late as 1960), would not wish to be seen speaking civilly to a priest or entering a Church on Sunday, so heavily taxed might he be with the charge of effeminacy and unvirility. The depth of this feeling can perhaps best be gauged from the fact that clerical concubinage (which is probably not as frequent as elsewhere in Latin America) is frowned upon by Catholics, but is one of the few ways in which Cuban priests can hope to earn a modicum of respect from other Cuban men.

Since the turn of the century the Church seemed gradually to have become uneasily and unstably acquiescent in conditions it could not change. Its isolation brought about its involution, partly checked only by a religious revival of ambitious proportions among the urban middle classes beginning in the late 30's and continuing into the 40's. But the complexion of the clerical face of the Church did not appreciably change. The Spanish clergy still predominated in proportions of about four or five to one. Most of these belonged to religious orders, relatively few of which were engaged in pastoral work. The majority of the Cubans among the clergy were secular. A small number of Canadians and a very few American priests had arrived since the end of World War II.

As an illustration, one can note the national composition of the Cuban hierarchy. As late as March 1960, out of six Cuban dioces one was vacant, two were headed by Spaniards, and three by Cubans. Since then the vacant diocese has been filled by a Cuban, and a number of Cubans have been appointed auxiliary bishops. However, when another diocese fell vacant through death in November, 1960, it was filled, even at this late date, by a Spaniard. As of this writing, then, out of Cuba's nine bishops only three are Spanish but these three head half the Cuban dioceses. It goes without saying that only the suspicious could see in this traditional sort of national configuration anything sinister. But perhaps only the imprudent could rejoice in it, and one imagines that only the unsophisticated could think that it is irrelevant to an understanding of Cuban events.

Immemorially, then, the Church in Cuba thought of itself, correctly, as impotent, as barely surviving under duress, as threatened by secularism, indifference, freemasonry and, in the last twenty years or so by Protestantism as well. To the Cuban high and low clergy this was especially humiliating in view of the privileged position of the Church in Spain. They knew that Cuba would never realize the Spanish ideal, yet this ideal, being a matter of Christian principle, as they thought, was never to be given up in intention. The Church, thus, was caught in a vicious circle: it was discontent with the here and now, but it saw no other solution than trying to hold on to the past. This was the sort of posture that, by its own implications, could not but confirm the stagnation from which the Church suffered.

The problem of the shortage of priests may provide an enlightening instance of how the vicious circle went. For two generations the shortage was made up, as far as it was ever made up, by the massive importation of Spanish regulars. It is relatively unimportant that the heavy dependence upon regular clergy appears to have reduced appreciably the influence of the dioceses, though this condition may have tended further to increase the reaction of involution of the hierarchy. It is more important that the Spanish as a whole have not yet become quite reconciled to the reality of having lost their Empire, and most especially Cuba. Many still entertain, and voice, thoughts of a possible reversal of history. The

Spanish clergy's militant Spanishness toward the former colony, no less than their conception of what the relations between clergy and people should be, operated generally only to the disadvantage of the Church and tended to diminish the appeal that the priestly ministry might have had for Cuban Catholics.

Naturally, with few native vocations the congregations could not very well maintain seminaries and houses of study in Cuba, so Cuban candidates were sent abroad. Until recently that meant, of course, Spain: Thus, even the native clergy became hispanicized. One should not misconstrue this disadvantage of a Spanish clergy as due to xenophobia, from which Cuba is fortunately almost totally free. The difficulty was specifically Spanish. For example, Canadian priests were sufficiently liberal, and up-to-date to earn respect and admiration. And what was probably the most powerful single agency in the Catholic revival of Cuba's middle classes, namely, the Christian Brothers—who established their first Cuban foundation at the turn of the century—was until very recent times almost entirely French in composition. It should be added that, unlike the Spanish clergy, the Christian Brothers usually became Cuban nationals. In time they attracted native vocations in great numbers. They were also unique in having had a native Cuban provincial. Their contribution to the modernization of the Church in Cuba was as magnificent as it was unemulated.

Further to compound the sinuosity of the circle, since early Republican times the Church had concentrated its resources in education work for the upper-middle and upper classes, a condition that prevailed without exception until after World War II, when a few schools for the poor began to appear. The hierarchy seem to have reasoned logically, but not necessarily perspicaciously, that the faith of these classes could be built up most easily and quickly, and that once this was accomplished the middle classes would constitute a sort of élite that would help carry the Gospel to the humble and the poor. The plan was successful enough in the first respect, but certain side effects were not foreseen. They may well have been unforeseeable. For instance, the Church lay itself open to the charge that it was neglecting the poor and courting the rich. Worse, it also lay itself open to the temptation of actually doing so. It seems, indeed, that to some extent it did so: And, upon occasion it did so extravagantly and even unnecessarily. For instance, despite the traditional policy of the Cuban Church to avoid taking sides in temporal matters, "in view," as the formula went, "of the spiritual mission of the Church," Batista's last regime, after his *coup d'état* in 1952, enjoyed an unprecedented degree of episcopal benison during six and a half of its not quite seven years. Some

Cubans thought that this departure from custom was not totally unrelated to the justly famous largess of Batista's second wife— a largess which was itself a departure from Cuban type. Since Batista's first wife was still living, Marta Fernández de Batista's generosity was, justly or unjustly, suspect and was widely commented upon unfavorably.

However, the Cuban Church's consortium with the rich was never so much a compromising reality as a tempting thought to be delighted in morosely. But the Church by its own choice did depend especially upon certain classes for whatever native clergy could be recruited. Would vocations come out of this middle- and upper-class elite? This was, of course, the objective of the policy: Otherwise, the problem could not be solved.

The answer, as it turned out, was disappointing. There were many vocations, of course, but in general the distance between the Spanish clergy and the Cuban people proved too much, even under these conditions, to be bridged very rapidly. The hope of a native clergy simply did not materialize. Moreover, what vocations there were went largely to the religious orders. Two reasons can be given for this: First, the Catholic schools were owned, directed, and staffed without exception by regulars and, consequently, vocations normally went to them; second, only the religious orders could offer the opportunities for work and advancement (e.g., positions in Spanish seminaries, education abroad, advanced training, employment in Cuban schools) that would attract the elite. Relatively few city dwellers in Cuba had as much as seen the Cuban countryside—and to be well educated in Cuba was to belong to a certain class. The possibility of living away from the city did not easily and naturally occur to what was, literally, the Cuban bourgeoisie. Thus, because pastoral work was being neglected, even in the city, vocations from the sort of people who would ordinarily have considered going to remote and backward country parishes simply were not forthcoming in sufficient numbers.

It can be said in all sincerity that this reluctance was more than understandable. Only those who have actually chosen to go to the most inhospitable lands could possibly cast the first stone of criticism in their direction. For if the Cuban Church as a whole was poor, the country parishes were indigent. A country pastor would have starved if he had had to depend upon the parishoners' support. The peasants themselves were not only so needy, but generally so indifferent that only a few would have given even if they had been able. Since the end of World War II the situation was alleviated in part when a few sugar mills began to relieve the diocesan burden by paying pastors' salaries and ordinary parochial expenses. On occasion they built little chapels. The hierarchy appears to have thought that if the Church in Spain was justified in receiving a subsidy from the State, how much more justified was the Cuban Church in accepting the benefaction of private enterprise.

Recently, since the break between Castro and the Church, the Cuban hierarchy has maintained that to make too much of such arrangements was an unfair attack upon the prestige of the Church, and it has defended its action on the grounds that the clergy was entitled to take such salaries, and that no conflict of interests influenced the priests unduly. "We do not know . . . of a single case of a priest in a sugar cane plantation or refinery who acted as an instrument of exploitation . . . [whereas we know of] many cases in which the priests defended the rights of the workers, putting themselves on their side in cases of strikes." It is quite unnecessary to stipulate that the clergy were, indeed, entitled to take such salaries, and that Castro's criticism of the Church in this particular respect was grossly unfair. As to the question of the interests thus vested, there is not the slightest reason to believe that the Cuban bishops deviated in the least from the truth in the foregoing declaration. Compromising situations, however, can be entered into in the best as in the worst of faith, and wittingly as well as not. The dependence of the rural Cuban Church upon the fringe benefits of the companies owned by American and Cuban millionaires was, however unavoidable, only an immediate palliative and an eventual millstone. It did not really bring the Church close to the people. Native vocations did not thereby increase, though no one can say of course what might have been the case if the system had endured ten decades instead of only one. But, as with other measures, the chasm between the Church and the destitute masses, far from being bridged, was ultimately deepened by this.

It is easy to be wise after the event. Perhaps none of the consequences of these palpable realities were actually foreseeable. In any event, they went unchecked. The point is not that the hierarchy did anything wrong, but that it operated exclusively within the set of assumptions defined by the almost total *acceptance* of the social and political conditions of Cuba, not as desirable, but as irremediable. The Church did not plan for change, but for stability; when revolution finally came, it was the last thing the hierarchy was prepared for.

5

One phase of Cuban history ended in 1961 and another began. In December of that year Fidel Castro publicly embraced "Marxism-Leninism" and committed Cuba to a Socialist revolution. The reaction both inside and outside of Cuba to Castro's epoch-making speech ranged from the cries of "I told you so" by conservative critics who had always suspected the bearded leader of being a "Communist" to the simplistic theories of American liberals who placed the entire responsibility for Castro's socialistic course on policy-makers in Washington. In the following essay, James O'Connor, a political economist, offers another interpretation of Cuba's socialism. He writes that economic, not ideological, reasons explain the shift to socialism, and that socialism was a logical extension of the island's economic and social development and was not the product of "conspiracy," either in Washington or in Havana.

James O'Connor:
Cuban Political Economy*

The thesis of this paper is that the social revolution in Cuba (1959–61) was inevitable in the sense that it was necessary for the island's further economic and social development. The nationalization and consolidation of industry, the collectivization of more than one third of Cuba's farm land, the complete reorganization of the labor unions and the banking and commercial systems, and thoroughgoing economic planning, rescued the island from permanent economic stagnation. For this reason, Cuban socialism can be explained and understood in the context of the social structure of the old society—not as the sour fruit of some "abnormality" or "conspiracy."

A corollary of this thesis is that any ruling group which failed fundamentally to modify or replace Cuba's old economic institutions could not count on a long and stable tenure. It also follows

* From James O'Connor, ON CUBAN POLITICAL ECONOMY. Reprinted with permission from the *Political Science Quarterly*, Vol. LXXIX, No. 2.

that the political orientation of any political leader of "liberal" or conservative persuasion who wished to retain power would have to shift more or less rapidly to the Left to correspond with social reality.

The argument may be summarized as follows:

> *1.* From a very early date the Cuban economy developed along capitalist lines. Pre-capitalist forms of economic organization—traditional, feudal, or mercantile—were in no way important features of the old society. During the twentieth century, the island's economy acquired the significant characteristics of monopoly capitalism, chief among which was the cartelization of markets. Monopoly controls blanketed Cuba's social economy and blocked the fulfillment of the island's true economic potential by wasting land, labor, and capital, and other economic resources.

> *2.* Throughout the political revolution which triumphed in January 1959, a small group of men acquired and retained the initiative. These men were non-Communists, and, while forming an alliance with the Cuban Communist party in late 1958 or early 1959, consistently kept the initiative during the social revolution of 1959–61. What is more, this social revolution was rapid, relatively peaceful, and defended by the vast majority of the Cuban people. These observations suggest that a social revolution of a specifically socialist character was not merely an ideological product, but a realistic and authentic response to social reality.

> *3.* The political revolution was not marked by sharp class conflicts, and revolutionary programs drawn up before 1959 had appeal for nearly every Cuban social and economic class. Class conflicts developed out of the economic and political measures of the Revolutionary government which destroyed revolutionary unity by systematically discriminating against some classes and in favor of others and by polarizing political attitudes on the questions of elections, political parties, and relations with the United States. It is said that these measures provide prima-facie evidence that Fidel Castro betrayed the original spirit and aims of the revolution (the betterment of the economic, social, and political condition of the Cuban people) when in fact they may have been the logical outcome of an attempt to realize these very aims.

I

From a very early date Cuba exhibited the main features of modern capital economy. Unlike most Latin American economies, Cuba lacked an important subsistence sector and nearly all segments of the population were integrated into the market economy. As early as 1899 over two thirds of the rural labor force were engaged in the cultivation of cash crops, while subsistence farming employed probably less than one quarter of the work force.

By mid-century the subsistence sector had been nearly totally submerged by specialized agricultural production for export and home consumption. Throughout the countryside the propertied rural middle class gave way to foreign capital, which exploited opportunities for large-scale production, and corporate and absentee ownership. Following the sugar crises of the nineteen-twenties a fine web of relationships began to bind together agriculture and high finance; the bankers also had a finger in commerce and, to a lesser degree, manufacturing.

The great part of the island's agricultural production was organized along monopolistic lines. Output restrictions, pegged prices, and other forms of monopolistic control blanketed sugar, tobacco, rice, potato, and coffee farming. In the key sugar sector, mill owners, growers, and wage workers all had powerful organizations. Outputs, wages, prices, and the distribution of sugar earnings were determined by the mill owners or growers cartels, or by a three-cornered bargaining relationship on the level of national politics.

In industry there were 150 employers' associations of one kind or another, many of them with wide powers over their members. Compulsory "producers' associations" dominated sugar and tobacco manufacture, and the great public utilities each had clear monopolies in their fields. As for the labor movement, it was, compared with the island's labor force, one of the largest in the world, and the central federation enjoyed unusual power over its affiliates. There was, besides, an extremely well developed "labor aristocracy" which had sealed off a number of important labor markets from outside competition, and which was mainly responsible for the extraordinarily low relationship between labor productivity and wages.

In short, the economic institutions which we are accustomed to associate with the high income capitalist nations overlaid the island's market system. It should be stressed that monopoly practices in Cuba's product and labor markets sprang up in the soil of a market economy. Restrictions in the rural economy were not of the type ordinarily associated with a system of traditional agriculture, and controls in the labor market were not those customary in mercantile or neomercantile systems. Cuba's economic institutions were capitalist institutions, historically specific to Cuba. These institutions had, by and large, a monopolistic character, as well. For this reason, they placed limits on the pace of Cuba's economic development by inhibiting the improvement of agricultural yields, wasting land, barring the wide introduction of a mixed, scientific agriculture, placing ceilings on labor productivity, and, in general, on the ability of the economy to mobilize and utilize domestic and foreign capital efficiently.

In an economy which had been stagnating since World War

II (ignoring temporary ups and downs in the sugar market), it should be unnecessary to emphasize the implication of these limits on economic growth for the nature and scope of the Cuban Revolution.

II

Against this background, the character of the political and social revolutions in Cuba is more comprehensible. In the *political* struggle against President Fulgencio Batista the decisive influence was apparently the dedication of a small band of young men. From the attack by Fidel Castro on the Moncada Barracks in July 1953, throughout the guerrilla war of 1957–58, until late 1959, when the Castro group firmly consolidated political power, not a single peasant revolt ignited the Cuban countryside. Passive resistance, surreptitious aid to Castro's forces, there were, to be sure; unlike a dozen other political revolutions, however, the peasant classes failed to grasp the initiative at any point in the struggle. Early in 1959 Comandante Ernesto (Che) Guevara, Castro's closest associate, appropriately described the Cuban peasants as the revolution's "invisible collaborators." The labor movement, in which over one half of Cuba's labor force was enrolled, figured even less prominently in the rebellion. It was in January 1959, after the regular army had received Castro's final blows, that the working classes shut down Havana's industry and commerce. Earlier, a general strike in April 1959 had been a total failure. The new Revolutionary government consistently retained the political initiative; the general strike in late January in the port city of Manzanillo protesting the leniency shown by the revolutionary tribunals toward war criminals was apparently the only major reversal of roles.

In the *social* revolution of 1959–61, the liquidation of Cuba's private property system was invariably initiated by the ruling group. The peasantry did not spontaneously seize and cultivate idle lands; with a handful of exceptions, they failed to claim even the small fields in which they labored until the new government formally turned these tracts over to them. To be sure, a decree published in February denied rights to land under the coming Agrarian Reform Law to any peasant who without authorization occupied properties belonging to someone else. More significant than the existence of the law is the fact that it did not have to be enforced. Nor did the urban workers and sugar mill laborers independently occupy the factories (this was a sharp departure from the abortive social revolution of 1933) ; rebel army or militia units at the direction of the central government took possession of Cuba's farm land and industry.

These two sets of events—the exclusive and individualistic flavor of the political revolution and the almost bloodless social revolution—are intimately connected. The social revolution was more or less orderly because the political revolution transferred power from one relatively small group of men to another, and because the masses of Cubans at the very least passively supported the social revolution.

In this context, it is significant that Cuba's is the only specifically socialist social revolution in history which was not authored by local Communist parties with or without the backing of the Red Army. Not until 1959, when the actual fighting had ceased, did Castro's 26th of July Movement win the open backing of the Cuban party (the Partido Socialista Popular, or PSP), although this is not true of some individual Communists who sided with Castro somewhat earlier, and, as might be expected, survived the 1962 spring and summer purges of old-line Communists almost to a man. The political careers of many of the old-line Communists were painfully brief. Subject to bitter public and private attacks by the 26th of July Movement's organ, *Revolución*, during most of 1959, the party members gained footholds in the new revolutionary organizations in 1960 *after* the major expropriations (with a few exceptions, most notably the trade unions in which they had always figured strongly and in two or three important offices in the National Agrarian Reform Institute [INRA]), helped shape the mass organizations and the new party, the ORI (Integrated Revolutionary Organizations), into their image of revolutionary associations in 1961 and early 1962, only to be deprived of many of their positions in the spring and summer of that year and replaced by non-Communist revolutionary personnel.

In connection with the question of the source of political initiative, it is important to point out that in the history of modern revolutions the Cuban experience was unique in another respect, and departed especially sharply from the October Revolution. Irresistibly drawn to the peasantry in order to consolidate power, Lenin paved the way for the seizure of the estates. By this very measure, though, the central authority deprived itself of effective control of the land. Fifteen years passed before the rural economy was collectivized and integrated into the structure of the planned economy. The Cuban Revolution spared Fidel Castro an analogous problem, since the seeds of a planned rural economy were planted *simultaneously* with the transformation of land ownership. The fact that the Cuban farm worker and peasant never had the political initiative made possible the immediate collectivization of the cattle, rice, and sugar sectors of the rural economy. The fact that the better part of these sectors was already organized into large-scale producing units which had long utilized land, labor, and capital inefficiently made collectivization practical, feasible, and rational.

This development distinguishes the Cuban Revolution not only from the Russian Revolution, but sets it apart from the Chinese, the Mexican, and even the Bolivian experiences, as well. In Mexico the peasants at times had absolute initiative; until 1952 the Chinese leadership by force of circumstances emphasized individual ownership of the land; so did the Bolivian revolutionary group, and so it does today. The anti-feudal character of all these upheavals, though, was mirrored very faintly in Cuba, for reasons we have already discussed.

A summary of our argument to this point discloses that: non-Communist revolutionaries made a socialist revolution on an island where feudalism (or the neo-feudalism of pre-revolutionary Soviet Union, China, Mexico, and Bolivia) was largely absent, but where capitalistic, monopolistic controls were prominently featured. The PSP never had the political initiative either before or during the key stages of the social revolution; the party, in fact, at first even opposed those sections of the May 1959 Agrarian Reform Law which encouraged collective production of agricultural commodities. The aim of the revolutonary leadership was to get the stagnating Cuban economy off dead center to improve the social and material conditions of the Cuban people. When they turned to socialistic forms of economic organizations to realize this aim, they were supported by the majority of Cubans. From all of this evidence, one can clearly make a case that socialist economic planning in Cuba was less an ideological product than an expression of hard economic necessity.

III

Socialism—public ownership of the means of production—sometimes emerges from class conflict, and is invariably accompanied by more or less severe political warfare between classes. Cuba was no exception. The political revolution had a distinct classless character (at least no single class had the initiative during this phase of the struggle), but sharp class conflicts developed in the course of the social revolution. The emergence of these conflicts was accompanied by dramatic changes in the Revolutionary government's political line.

Beginning in mid-1959, after the Agrarian Reform Law put Cuba and the world on notice that a thoroughgoing social revolution was in the making, a Revolutionary government began to mark off sharply the "revolution" from the "counterrevolution." Departing from his previous position, Castro was the first to insist on the black and white nature of the struggle, an attitude that was quickly adopted by other government officials. Divisions and differences of opinion over revolutionary policy existed within the governing group—the struggle between the Castro group and the "old" communists is one instance—but the main lines of both domestic and foreign policy were (and are) seldom questioned, or in doubt. The extreme polarization of Cuban politics after mid-1959 is well exemplified in speech after speech delivered by Cuban government leaders. In this theme, the revolution and the Cuban nation are made one and the same, as indicated by Castro in early 1960: "To be a traitor to the Revolution is to be a traitor to the country. The destiny of our sovereignty is at stake. . . . We have decided that either we are or we are not a free country. And we are and want to be a free country."

From mid-1959 to the present, however, *genuine* cleavages in Cuban politics have been sharp and opposing opinions have been fiercely held, defining a political mood which corresponds in many ways to social and economic reality. From January 1959 on, a series of profound economic and social changes accompanied these inimical attitudes, and to a large degree were responsible for them. There were no less than *fifteen hundred* decrees, laws, and resolutions during the first nine months of 1959. Unquestionably, nearly every new measure—especially those affecting the property system —drew some Cubans closer to the Revolutionary government and repelled others, leaving few indifferent. At the very least, each major law (the rent reduction and price control laws, agrarian reform, and the "intervention" of the utilities are some examples) compelled the ordinary Cuban to question his own political orientation; the most sweeping of these occasioned cabinet crises, resignations, flights abroad, and their cumulative effect led to the short war at Playa Giron in April 1961. The basis for the demand to choose sides —for or against the Revolutionary government—was therefore laid by the government's early economic and political measures. To make such a demand required some confidence that a sizeable body of opinion would confirm the government's position. This suggests that the original revolutionary legislation might be likened to a whirlpool expelling odd debris, yet sucking in the hull of the ship. Be that as it may, it is certainly likely that the slogan itself, together with the heady spirit in which it was launched, contributed to a political atmosphere in which a middle position became increasingly unrealistic and untenable. Castro's personality, after all, confers on the revolution a very special flavor. When he told an audience in the summer of 1960, at the time the United States acted to bar Cuban sugar from the mainland market, "In each cooperative we are going to build a town . . . with or without the quota. Each little town will have a school for the children of the members of the cooperative, with or without the quota . . . ," he conveyed a sense of boundless optimism apparent as early as the famous "History Will Absolve Me" speech in 1953 and by which his associates were invariably impressed. Reading through his speeches and declarations one is struck by the fact that the image of defeat, or even retreat, rarely, and then only reluctantly, appears. This nearly limitless confidence undoubtedly has affected Cuban politics and the island's economic development.

IV

That the new government chose to polarize opinion around the fundamental issue of its own support cannot be fully explained by Castro's optimism, however. It had the alternative—in place of isolating, indeed outlawing, any opposition, the logical climax of the government's actual policy—that of allowing his opposition to form into functioning interest groups. From there, employing the tactics of divide and conquer, he might have thwarted any potential majority coalition. These groups or parties would probably have ranged from the "left-opposition" of the small Cuban Trotskyite movement all the way to the moderate right of the large sugar and commercial interests (supposing that they had purged their numbers of pro-Batista elements). The leadership of the revolution, by playing one group against another, ceaselessly probing the weaknesses of each, might have retained power indefinitely.

Yet this policy seemed to have little relevance to the Cuban scene of 1959–60. Its usefulness is evident if in a crisis the ruling group cannot count on clear majority support; an example that springs to mind is British rule in India. Had the British rulers been foolish enough to imitate Castro's policy, they would have driven the opposition together, in the process probably creating a majority capable of threatening their own rule. Only a ruling group which anticipates majority support can for very long afford to alienate opposition elements so thoroughly that they are compelled to form strong working alliances. The Castro government appeared to be well along this path in the summer and fall of 1960 at the height of the first crisis with the United States.

Finally, the only dialogue between the "revolutionary party" and the "counterrevolutionary party" was literally at gun point. The social revolution had been consummated. Relations with the United States had totally deteriorated. And Castro, together with thousands of 26th of July Movement "liberals" and "reformers" had been radicalized and labelled "betrayers." Why did events follow this course?

V

Early in 1959, Castro was in every sense a popular hero whom many did not hesitate to compare with Martí. Among the island's nearly seven million people, few concealed their esteem, fewer still their respect. Even for the business community the future seemed promising. A leading business and financial organ reported that "American concerns with Cuban interests generally did not expect the change in Cuba's government to hamper their operations." In Cuba itself, the United States embassy took an optimistic view of the long-term investment possibilities. Some firms pre-paid taxes to help Castro consolidate his new government and others planned to accelerate investment programs temporarily postponed during the fighting. Business leaders in Cuba who "as recently as one month ago were gravely concerned about the revolution" apparently had undergone a radical shift in temper. Their doubts would soon return, however, for a rather elementary reason.

On the one hand, a wide range of pressing social, economic, and political problems, some of which had lingered on for years and others of which were fresh, containing unknown implications, confronted the triumphant rebels. In a hundred arenas, the new government struggled to make, implement, and enforce measures demanded by these problems. On the other hand, before assuming power, the Castro group had published or broadcast certain policy statements and decreed certain laws, enforced in those territories seized and occupied by the Rebel Army. Castro, the guerrilla leader, however, had embraced policies of a vague and ambiguous character; ideas were endorsed which Castro, the national politician, would later discard. The original (October 10, 1958) decree taking up the agrarian problem will do as an illustration. Article 2 promised all farm operators cultivating fewer than 27.2 hectares a plot of land of at least that size free of charge. This provision was directly incorporated into the major May 1959 Agrarian Reform Law. Where contiguous land was available this policy was carried out in practice. Article 6 of the October decree, which provided expropriated landowners with compensation, was also contained in the law of May 1959, although, with a handful of exceptions, it was not complied with. However, nowhere does the early law touch on the related problems of foreign properties or the *latifundium,* obviously political questions of a profound character. The vague reference to these problems in the introduction of the October decree could only raise more questions than it could answer. This is but one instance of the vagueness which seems to have characterized Castro's early outlook, and not a very conspicuous one at that. One authority has compiled a whole catalogue of other of the revolutionary's "broken promises."

A great many people were therefore understandably uncertain about the concrete steps the new government would take in the areas of economic development and domestic politics. The regime began to show its hand almost at once (by "intervening" the Cuban Electric Company, for instance), but the anti-Batista moderates whom Castro placed in the first cabinet made it a point to reassure the business community. President Urrutia himself proclaimed that Cuba needed and wanted foreign investments.

VI

With the benefit of hindsight it is tempting to conclude that Castro's group deliberately concealed their true designs from the Cuban population and opinion abroad as a tactical move to win all the support they could possibly get. It is not intended definitively to defend or refute this view here. It will be useful, though, to suggest that this hypothesis fails to exhaust the possibilities. Castro, for example, might very well have been confused or uncertain over the concrete problems—the agrarian problem, the question of economic development, and pressing political problems such as widespread government corruption, the fragile Cuban party system, and elections—which for years had been prominent features of the Cuban scene. The rebel leader, after all, surrounded himself with as varied a group of advisers as any national politician in memory: centrist careerist politicians, Keynesian economists, ex-and-would-be-bureaucrats, sincere liberals, professional revolutionaries, and amateur Marxist tacticians—there was very little advice Castro could not get if he wanted it. No less important, his own knowledge of Cuban economic and social life was apparently confined to three or four major areas. About the large class of small tenants and squatters in Oriente Province, the sugar industry, and the condition of the very poor throughout the island, he certainly knew a great deal. He had never been, however, in close touch with the problems of the tobacco farmers and other more or less well-to-do Cuban rural workers (apart from the sugar growers). And on the subjects of urban industry and trade and the city working class, he had much—as it turned out—to learn. In this connection, it is interesting to point out that in his first essay on the Cuban Revolution, Theodore Draper, who was later to develop the "revolution betrayed" thesis, wrote: "When Fidel Castro entered Havana . . . no one knew what he was going to do. It is doubtful whether he himself knew, except in the most general terms." As a matter of fact, this actively squares with Castro's own self-evaluation, expressed on numerous occasions, but never so frankly as in the famous "Marxist-Leninist" speech of December 1, 1961. Two months later he characterized the revolutionary leadership in these terms: "We were like a man with a vocation for music. But a man's vocation for music does not grant him a right to call himself a musician if he has not studied musical theory. When we started our revolutionary struggle, we already had some knowledge of Marxism-Leninism and we were in sympathy with it. But, by virtue of this, we could not call ourselves Marxists-Leninists. . . . We were apprentice revolutionaries."

There is also the possibility that both opinions, the one favorable to Castro, the other, because he is made out to be a deliberate liar, very unflattering, are partially true. In this event, the "conspirator" theory loses much of its bite; it is not hard to understand why a politician would hesitate to reveal plans which he knows may be unrealistic and never be put into action.

VII

Whatever the case, the fact is that his early support was extremely heterogeneous, and, for this reason, any policy would be bound to appear as a kind of betrayal to someone. No policy, though, would likely be considered a betrayal by everyone. To put it differently, few measures, and no really important ones, could possibly be universally popular; at the same time, every measure would heighten the loyalties of some of his followers. It was certain, therefore, that his universal popularity in January 1959 would be transitory. The struggle between the Association of Sugar Cane Planters and the Sugar Workers Federation over the issue of cane cutters' wages is a good example of the many class conflicts which would eventually spoil revolutionary harmony. On April 15, 1959, the new government decreed a fifteen per cent rise in the wage rates of the cane cutters. The cane planters (*colonos*) were ordered to pay the wage increases in full; they were to be reimbursed, however, by the mill owners, to the extent of one third of the extra wage costs. The *colonos* quickly voted among themselves to repeal the decree, arguing that the wage advance would make their farms "non-operational." Their protest was without effect. It goes without saying that the disputes which raged over the May Agrarian Reform Law and the Urban Reform Law a little later were argued strictly in class terms. And over the issues of elections and reconstruction of the Cuban political party system, and relations with the United States, it was the professional and middle classes which turned against the Revolutionary government. In the ranks of the poorer rural and urban workers and the marginal peasants there was little or no agitation for the reintroduction of the political forms and institutions dominating the Cuban scene prior to Batista's coup in 1952, nor was there great fear of the island's powerful northern neighbor.

While the economic and social measures divided the island along class lines to produce a kind of "reactive" class conflict, there was no mass agitation for the reorganization of the Cuban economy. The interventions and expropriations of 1959–60 clearly had the support of the majority of Cubans (even the relatively conservative sugar growers supported the seizure of the estates) ; but the poorer, underprivileged classes failed to *initiate* these actions. For this reason, an explanation of Cuban socialism which runs along the lines of pure "class struggle" doctrine is obviously forced and overly abstract.

This admission, however, does not rule out the possibility that Castroism and Cuban socialism were built on economic—not ideological—foundations. First, one cannot characterize the Cuban Revolution as primarily anti-feudal; quite the contrary, the Cuban economy exhibited all the main features of well developed (one is tempted to say, over developed) capitalism. What is more, Cuban capitalism was monopoly capitalism; *for this reason, the Cuban economy failed to grow as rapidly as existing technology, savings, and the supplies of labor and land permitted.* What inhibited the island's economic growth was not the absolute supplies of factors of production, but the way in which they were *organized.* Viewed in this context, it is highly suggestive that the "ideologists" apparently failed to have the political initiative at any time; we know that the Cuban Communist party did not make the revolution, and it remains to be proved that Fidel Castro was inevitably to term himself a "Marxist-Leninist." Finally, we know that it was possible more or less peacefully to forge socialism in Cuba, implying

that most Cubans were ready (or at least willing) to accept a socialist economy, in marked contrast to the Russian experience.

6

Despite Marxism much of the old economic framework survives in
Cuba. The early attempt to industrialize at the expense of agriculture has been abandoned, sugar is still the mainstay of the economy.
However, the new ideology has wrought profound changes: the
state owns and controls the sugar industry, private enterprise has
virtually disappeared, and the demands of national development
dictate the patterns of production and consumption. One of the
best indicators of the extent of the transformation is the attempt
of the Cuban government to eliminate "material incentives," that
is, to circumvent the wage system of the capitalist economies. The
goal, as Castro says, is to remove Cuba from a money economy. In
the next reading, Adolfo Gilly, an Uruguayan supporter of Castro's
experiment, discusses the problems confronted in the effort to substitute material incentives. His essay first appeared in the Uruguayan journal, *Marcha*, in 1963.

Adolfo Gilly:
Inside the Cuban Revolution*

Enormous forces are stirring inside the Cuban Revolution.
During this whole year [1963], under tightening pressure, a leap
has taken place which was in part stimulated, and in part limited,
by the turns of the Sino-Soviet dispute. The factors in this change
are both national and international. Its ultimate source must be

* From Adolfo Gilly, INSIDE THE CUBAN REVOLUTION, translated by Félix
Gutiérrez (New York: Monthly Review Press, 1964), pp. 1-12. Reprinted by
permission of Monthly Review Press. Copyright © 1964 by Monthly Review
Press.

sought in the gigantic transformation which the revolutionary forces and movements are undergoing in the whole world during these years, and in the growing strength of the Cuban people who, far from feeling intimidated, are inflamed by continued foreign provocations and aggressions. Although to the superficial observer Cuba's internal development appears uniform, rectilinear, and unbroken, these profound processes are reflected in one way or another in the leadership of the Revolution, the team around Fidel Castro, its policies, actions, and recent stands. They will be reflected much more directly, in the not too distant future, in new measures and initiatives which are sure to arise in revolutionary Cuba. In this work, we shall try to lay bare the domestic and international forces which are determining both the immediate problems of the Revolution and its future course of development.

INDUSTRY OR AGRICULTURE?

"Industry is the moving force of development and agriculture its base," say the Chinese. But is it necessary to give priority to agriculture to gain the means for developing industry, or to industry to push the development of a modern and productive agriculture? This is one of the many dilemmas being raised in Cuba now, dilemmas in both domestic and international policies. These dilemmas always present themselves in interrelated clusters, so that to solve one in a certain way strongly influences the manner of tackling the others.

It is not enough to say that a "just proportion" and a "harmonious relation" should be established between the two sectors. How define this proportion? And where locate this harmony? The answers bring us right into the field of politics and into the midst of the polemics going on among the leaders and the technical, economic, and political cadres of the Cuban Revolution.

In the first years of the Revolution, until almost 1962, the leadership thought it could industrialize Cuba quickly even to the point of manufacturing producer goods. This idea was unrealistic and had to be abandoned by the Cuban leaders: Che Guevara has acknowledged the error more than once, most recently in the course of his participation in Algerian discussions on planning in the summer of 1963.

But this does not mean that the idea of industrialization has been abandoned, industry being the basis of progress and of raising the standard of living of the population. Well then, where will the funds for industrialization come from?

Cuba is a country which depends in great measure on foreign

trade. With what it gets for sugar, tobacco, and other agricultural exports it acquires the industrial products it needs. This structure, inherited from the capitalist and semi-colonial past, cannot be changed by an act of will, but only by the planning of future development. For this change, capital is needed. And during the entire initial stage, it can only come from two sources: international financing or income earned from foreign trade.

Although Cuba's access to financing from capitalist countries has been closed off, there are now in its stead the credits extended by the socialist countries, primarily the Soviet Union. But these credits are not limitless, and they must also be used to cover the enormous costs involved in replacing all of Cuba's industrial equipment and all of its technology, inherited from North America, with that of the socialist camp. There is, at least for the present, no other choice: the blockade is very tight, and North American machinery which comes to a stop for lack of replacement parts is very difficult to start up again. When this happens, new machinery must be imported from the socialist countries. Think of what this means to an underdeveloped country without great financial resources. It is not surprising that the blockade causes destruction which costs Cuba the equivalent of a small war. In the light of this reality, it is easy to understand that talk in the abstract about the difficulties of the Cuban economy, supposedly attributable to nationalization and planning, makes no sense.

The credits mentioned above have placed Cuba in an unbalanced commercial position, particularly with the Soviet Union, and this introduces a new element of pressure on all the policies of the Cuban Revolution. Cuba is a debtor of the Soviet Union, and this debt has been increasing, not diminishing, a situation not entirely displeasing to the United States government which understandably trusts Khrushchev more than Fidel Castro.

For the rest, the resources provided by foreign commerce derive primarily from sugar. The production of sugar fell until it reached its lowest point during the last harvest, and the destruction of the 1963 hurricane promises an even smaller harvest in 1964.

On his return from the Soviet Union in 1963, Fidel Castro placed even greater emphasis on the need to expand cultivation of sugar cane and production of sugar, and to concentrate all energies on agriculture as the basis for the development of the country. The assured market for sugar in the socialist countries, he said, should provide the resources for economic development. He emphasized not only sugar cane but also dairy cattle, a branch of agriculture in which he said Cuba could, provided it made the necessary effort, attain yields comparable to those of a country like Holland.

This means, according to Castro, devoting more resources to

the countryside, resources which can be obtained only by reducing investments in early industrial development. In a later speech, for example, he questioned a project for an iron mill in Santiago de Cuba which had previously been approved.

Cuba needs to increase its agricultural production; everyone in the island knows this. On the state farms, production costs are considerably higher than on private farms; and it would be very difficult to convince private farmers of the advantages of joining a collective if in practice they do not see the nationalized farms producing greater yields.

Even among private farmers there has been a sector uninterested in increasing yields. This is due partly to political reasons, an attitude of passive and sometimes active resistance on the part of the well-to-do farmers against the revolutionary government. The so-called "second agrarian reform" was a blow directed at this sector: this decree recently nationalized all farms between five *caballerias* and thirty *caballerias,* of which there were more than six thousand on the whole island.

But the problems do not end here. The small farmer also has reasons for not increasing production too much. He measures his results and his gains not by the amount of money the state pays him but, primarily, by what he can buy in the market with this money. And in the market at the present time he cannot buy many of the industrial products previously imported because they are simply not there.

To spur the small farmer to produce more, the state stores, the *Tiendas del Pueblo* of the countryside, must offer him a greater variety and quantity of goods. Although the stores are well-stocked by present Cuban rationing standards, there is no doubt that here too the effects of the blockade are felt.

For this reason, the advocates of priority for industrial development maintain that, to encourage an increase in agricultural production, the production of industrial goods must be given an immediate push. They add, on the other hand, that increasing the state farms' productivity does not depend so much on larger investments —which would have to be taken from industry and would, after a certain point, not yield a proportionately higher return—as on better organized work and production in general, on improved organization which is also needed in the development of industry. There is no reason, according to Cuban technicians, why each dollar's worth of product on the state farms should cost approximately a dollar and twenty cents, nor why the private farmer should continue to get a substantially better yield with inferior technical resources.

There is no solution through large-scale importation of consumer goods from the socialist countries. For one thing, foreign exchange is lacking and the balance of trade is becoming increasingly unfavorable. And for another, such goods are already in short supply in the socialist countries themselves.

Moreover, equalling Holland's dairy production seems as adventurous a hope as building a self-sufficient industry in a few years. It is not the underdeveloped countries but the industrialized ones, with all the technical and social advantages they possess, which are capable of achieving this kind of productivity.

Given this point of view, priority always goes to industry no matter where you start from.

In recent speeches, Fidel Castro has left the dilemma still unresolved. Meanwhile the national polemic continues between the "industrializing" sector, headed by the Minister of Industry, Comandante Che Guevara, and the "agricultural" sector represented by Carlos Rafael Rodriguez, president of INRA (the National Institute of Agrarian Reform), who comes from the old leadership of the *Partido Socialista Popular* (Communist Party).

The controversy takes in other problems, principally international policy and the policy of organizing the national economy. There, as we shall see, the alignments are repeated.

MONEY OR REVOLUTION?

Increasing production is one of the major concerns of the Cuban economy. In the present situation, it is not only a problem of investment but also of the productivity of labor in existing enterprises, agricultural as well as industrial.

The slow increase in productivity per worker—in some areas it is at a standstill, in others it is actually decreasing—creates various problems. On the one hand, there is an excess of labor in many industries. Nobody has been laid off and, owing to a lack of important raw materials or breakage of machinery, production has had to be cut back. When small nationalized shops have been merged or closed down as obsolete, all of their workers have been found other jobs, or have been sent to technical schools at their old pay, or have been continued in jobs in the main superfluous. What the Cuban state has avoided in all cases is that nationalization should mean layoffs and unemployment. But productivity has suffered.

On the other hand, new administrative personnel in the nationalized enterprises, quickly mobilized to replace the old directors and administrators, lacked experience, and this led to a deterioration in the internal organization of these companies. This has not always happened, but the Revolution has only recently begun to establish its own administrative continuity at this level and to train new administrators in special schools.

There has also appeared, under different guises, a relative relaxation of work discipline. For a long time the government has been fighting that early tendency to suspend work for political meetings and rallies, insisting that all such activities should take place outside working hours. (It was very easy in the past for the administration of an enterprise "to politicize itself" and disorganize production with the best political intentions in the world.)

But work discipline is not worth anything if the worker does not have a direct interest in what he is doing, whether the interest derives from his support of the Revolution, from personal enthusiasm for his particular job, or from desire to earn more money. This is particularly true of the kind of discipline which exists in Cuba, voluntary for the most part and free from political and economic methods of coercion.

What incentive impels a worker to produce more? In a capitalist country, it is clearly a combination of money rewards and a system of punishments; the latter may take the form of layoffs or external pressures of one kind or another on his conscience.

In Cuba, the system of punishments practically does not exist, except in extreme cases of proven production sabotage or complete non-performance of work. Until very lately, no system of rewards existed either. This is the starting point of the controversy about whether material incentives (money rewards) or moral incentives (socialist ideals) are most effective in moving the worker to increase his production and take an interest in his work.

The school of thought which in socialist countries could be defined as conservative or rightist maintains that only material incentives (a system of rewards so closely differentiated as to amount to piece work) can increase production. The defenders of this view present various arguments about the "socialist" character of material incentives, despite the fact that since Marx's time socialist theorists have recognized that such a system is essentially capitalist and should be resorted to under socialism only as a temporary and transitional measure to be gradually abandoned as the economy approaches closer to the socialist ideal.

The school of thought which, in contrast, can be defined as left-wing maintains that material incentives, though one may have to make use of them in certain cases, must be completely relegated to second place. In this view, the principal incentives for a worker under a regime of transition to socialism should be revolutionary enthusiasm, the understanding that he is working to build socialism, and the stimulus provided by the example set by consciously socialist vanguard workers. This view asserts that a system of material incentives, if widely used, undermines the foundations of socialist development, obliquely reintroduces the seeds of capitalism, and gravely underestimates the importance of the workers' revolutionary enthusiasm.

In Cuba, Carlos Rafael Rodriguez is one of the advocates of the first school, Ernesto Che Guevara of the second. Blas Roca has come out more or less openly for material incentives, and Osvaldo Dorticos for priority to moral incentives. Given the veiled or indirect form which controversies take in Cuba, none of the statements of these men has been completely clear, the differences being rather matters of shading and emphasis. Nevertheless, an emphasis here and an emphasis there do signify the existence of a profound and real controversy.

The technicians from the European socialist countries—primarily from the USSR and secondarily from Czechoslovakia—have strongly urged upon the Cuban leaders the need to give priority to material incentives. In their countries, the need for such incentives has been raised to the level of a theory; and what their economic leaders offer to the workers is not simply the vision of a socialist future or of the development of the revolution in other countries, but above all the prospect of buying a television set or better clothes or even a motorcycle or automobile. This, in its way, serves to depoliticize work and encourages a tendency for everyone to devote himself to his individual future: the workers to busy themselves with producing and the leaders with leading, that is, with politics.

In Cuba, it is a cult to depoliticize nothing. Politics—that is, the Revolution—is the daily bread of every Cuban. And if a whole sector of the Cuban leadership, including its most important figures, insist on moral incentives, it is because they want to stimulate production by consciously basing their decisions on politics.

But the very character of moral incentives is under discussion in Cuba.

For example, one of the ways of raising enthusiasm for work is the emulation campaign. Emulation is measured by a point system for punctuality, attendance, quantity and quality of production, and other similar indices. In each factory, workers who want to participate sign up for the campaign. Those who win—that is, those who each month make the highest points in their category— are given honorific distinctions as "vanguard workers." At the regional and national levels, other prizes are given, such as a week's paid vacation at some tourist center or a trip to a socialist country. But the real point of the emulation campaign is the moral satisfaction of being recognized as a vanguard worker.

All this is inconceivable in a capitalist regime, where the enterprise is private and is operated for profit and where the worker is not interested in production, which is the owner's concern, but in his wages. In a regime where private property has been nationalized, on the other hand, there are neither bosses nor private profits, and the workers do take an interest in production and themselves carry it forward.

Nevertheless, emulation often has a formal character. Norms are fulfilled because they have been established, and routine takes over the whole system. Emulation for emulation's sake, without other outside inducements, runs the permanent risk of becoming one more bureaucratic institution, something which leaves the worker quite indifferent.

Another form of moral incentive is the example set by volunteer workers. On Saturday afternoons and Sundays, "red battalions" of volunteer workers undertake to perform special tasks, such as cutting cane, or working in a factory or office different from those in which they are regularly employed. These volunteer workers are a minority, but they are a big minority and they have inexhaustible enthusiasm. During the sugar cane harvest, caravans of trucks leave the cities at dawn with volunteer cane cutters for nearby fields.

There is another type of more sustained volunteer work: the worker or office employee who puts in as many hours as needed at his own regular place of work to complete some urgent job or to solve some problem which the lack of replacement parts, raw materials, or technicians has created.

In all this money plays no part. The driving force is enthusiasm for the Revolution, the conviction that the job is for the good of all and for oneself too. It is, above all, the worker's discovery of a meaning in his daily work: he does it no longer just to make a living, but to build something which he sees and feels as his own.

This is not, however, all there is to it. The big problem is not to mobilize a minority, given this environment, but to attract and arouse the majority. And it is at this point that one school says it is possible to succeed and the other maintains that there is no incentive as effective as money rewards to induce the great majority to raise their productivity.

At present Cuba is establishing a system of work norms (norms which exist in all organized capitalist businesses) to fix the quantity and quality of production for each operative. For performance above the norm, a premium is paid which rises to twenty percent of the total wage: this is the maximum paid, for if production is higher, it is an indication that the norm is too low and should be readjusted. It is clear that these norms, although they introduce a form of premiums, do not add up to a system of money incentives of the kind which exists in some other socialist countries.

Yugoslavia is the country which in one sense has gone furthest with this kind of incentive; there the principle of "the material interest of workers in production results" is put into operation by self-management committees. These committees run the businesses from the larger economic point of view as well, and they are interested in economic results—profits—being the highest possible, for these profits are mainly distributed in the form of bonuses among the personnel of the company.

So effective in appearance, this system in practice brings with it competition between the different companies, agreements among companies not to increase production but to increase profits, disorganization of the central economic plan, and privileges for more modern enterprises at the cost of poorer or more backward ones. That is, it attacks the very heart of the functioning of the system of transition to socialism, central planning and the subordination of individual effort to the collective objectives of society.

Without quite copying the Yugoslav system, the school represented by Carlos Rafael Rodriguez would introduce the principle of distributing the enterprise's profits to its personnel as material incentives. This method of functioning means that the management's economic performance is measured by money, by the higher or lower profits which the company makes.

Minister of Industry Che Guevara is opposed to this theory; he wants to keep the economy centralized and to measure economic performance by centrally controlled economic indices in accordance with guide lines set by each year's plan. The extent to which the enterprise over- or under-fulfills these indices will tell if it is functioning well, regularly, or badly, and what has to be corrected.

The school represented by Che Guevara shows a particular hostility to gauging performance by profits, a hostility which derives from the fact that using this criterion reintroduces a type of semi-competition among enterprises and breaks down the centralized management of the economy. Competition tends to take precedence over planning, and the individual's or the enterprise's material interest over socialist collective interest embodied in the plan. According to the Cuban Minister of Industry, the socialist economy tends, furthermore, toward centralized management, and this trend will be accentuated more and more as automation and linear production programming are introduced. Running enterprises on a profit basis introduces, on the other hand, individualistic and anti-socialist monetary incentives as the driving force of production; socialist consciousness is thus reserved for holidays and revolutionary celebrations.

Che Guevara in one of his speeches said that while capitalist competition is "a struggle among beasts," the system of self-management aiming at maximum profits is "a struggle among caged beasts."

Since the controversy is unresolved, both systems exist in Cuba today: in INRA enterprises, financial self-management; in those of the Ministry of Industry, control by budget.

Externally, this whole question is linked to the discussion going on now in socialist countries on the functioning of the law of value during the transition to socialism. Articles on this very question have been published which take issue with each other: one by the Minister of Industry in the magazine published by his Ministry, and the other by the Minister of Foreign Commerce, Comandante Alberto Mora, in the magazine Comercio Exterior.

Internationally, this problem arises in the system—and its working methods—of commercial relations between socialist countries (particularly in Comecon, the Council for Mutual Economic Aid); and domestically, in the criteria used in determining wage scales in Cuba. The partisans of material incentives advocate stretching the scale out, while the partisans of moral incentives want to compress it. Thus, one proposal would set a scale of one to ten, from the minimum wage of 75 pesos a month (with deductions) to the maximum salary of 700 pesos for a Minister; another, on the other hand, would hold this maximum down to 500 or 550 pesos. If you want to appeal to socialist consciousness, then the trend to greater equality is a fundamental factor.

The opponents of material incentives have another argument at this juncture: when there is a scarcity of consumer goods as in Cuba today, raising wages does not, after a certain point, mean much to the worker, for he cannot buy what he would like. Consequently, if material concerns are to be his outlook, he would rather earn less and make less effort.

On this last point the statistics look bad: in 1962 wage payments, pensions, etc., rose to approximately 2,500 million pesos, while total sales of merchandise did not exceed 1,700 million. Even discounting savings, there still remains an inflationary gap which oscillates between 500 and 600 million pesos without a counterpart in merchandise to absorb it.

Other aspects of the controversy lead directly to politics. To interest workers in production, banners and honorific mention are not enough. Appeals to socialist consciousness are not enough either. The threat of invasion in October, 1962, evoked an economic phenomenon which was later discussed and studied in Cuba: with fewer personnel—since many were mobilized—enterprises maintained and increased production. In the face of danger to the Revolution and the country, everyone started to produce. National life had a central, concrete goal: to defeat the imperialist enemy.

On the other hand, situations of political uncertainty for the Revolution—the unresolved dispute between the USSR and China, for example, a subject which vitally intercsts the whole Cuban people—have a contrary effect. Interest in production slackens. A good turn in the Latin American revolutionary movement awakens enthusiasm. If the Cuban leaders in their speeches, appeals, and policy decisions ally themselves with this turn, heightened enthusiasm is evident the very next day in the streets and centers of production. This is not an exaggeration: in any enterprise where production is intimately tied to politics and not to the enterprise's profits, political events in which the workers take part or which arouse them, call forth their support in the form of greater productive efforts. The same thing happens in the Soviet Union itself where it has been observed that productivity increases in factories filling orders for Cuba. . . .

Suggestions for Further Reading

The best survey of the history and development of Cuba is Wyatt MacGaffey and Clifford R. Barnett's *Twentieth-Century Cuba* (New York, 1965) which, though ultimately anti-Castro, strives for objectivity. Every student of Cuba should read Lowry Nelson's *Rural Cuba* (Minneapolis, 1950) ; written in the 1940s, this book offers a concise picture of the sugar economy and its impact on rural society. Two studies provide the background of United States-Cuban relations. Leland H. Jenks, *Our Cuban Colony* (New York, 1928) covers the early period; Robert F. Smith, *The United States and Cuba: Business and Diplomacy, 1917–1960* (New York, 1960), discusses the period preceding the revolution. The period between the two major revolutions in Cuban history, 1933 to 1959, is analyzed carefully in two semidocumentary studies that merit careful attention: Commission on Cuban Affairs, *Problems of the New Cuba* (New York, 1935) and International Bank for Reconstruction and Development, *Report on Cuba* (Baltimore, 1951). The prevailing interpretation in the United States of Castro's Revolution of

1959 is stated by Theodore Draper, *Castro's Revolution, Myths and Realities* (New York, 1962) ; to its author, Castro betrayed a middle-class revolution. For a study of Castro, whose remarkable character has shaped the course of the Revolution, see his *History Will Absolve Me* (New York, 1959), Herbert L. Matthews, *The Cuban Story* (New York, 1961) ; and Frank Tannenbaum, "The Political Dilemma in Latin America," *Foreign Affairs*, XXXVIII (1960), 497–515. Jorge Mañach, a Cuban intellectual, has written a sympathetic account of José Martí: *Martí: Apostle of Reform* (New York, 1950). For a discussion of revolutionary Cuba see Dudley Sears, ed., *Cuba, the Economic and Social Revolution* (Chapel Hill, 1964) and José Iglesias, *In the Fist of the Revolution: Life in a Cuban Town* (New York, 1968).

IV

Mexico: From Independence To Nation

Scholars divide the history of the Mexican Republic into four principal eras. The first is the critical period or, in the traditional version, the age of Santa Anna that begins with independence in 1821 and concludes with the *Reforma* of the 1850s, the second historical stage. Traditional histories of the critical period stress the personalistic rule of Antonio López de Santa Anna whose military ineptness cost Mexico half of her territory in the war with the United States. More recent studies focus on the era itself, examining carefully the conflict of ideas inherent in the struggle between Federalists and Centralists and the attempts of Mexican economists to find solutions to their country's financial difficulties. The new studies have altered the traditional view; Santa Anna emerges as one of many actors on the stage, rather than as the maker of history. He ruled in the absence of a consensus, which proved impossible until either the Conservatives or the Liberals controlled political policy.

Ultimately, the Liberals defeated the Conservatives but not before the Conservative disciples of Lucas Alamán launched a desperate attempt to recoup their losses by importing French troops and a foreign prince to defeat the Liberals under Benito Juárez. Surprisingly, few scholars have thoroughly explored the ideas that led to the crowning of Maximilian of Austria as Emperor of Mexico. Maximilian received support because he promised to fulfill a dream that dated back to the winning of independence. The Conservatives who sponsored independence and accepted Augustín de Iturbide as Emperor had wished to install a foreign prince as their ruler. Failing to find a foreigner, they accepted the eager Iturbide. Unhappily for the Conservatives, Iturbide proved inept and the result was political chaos and economic disintegration. In an attempt to revive the monarchical formula, the Conservatives turned to Napoleon III and Maximilian. An analysis of the monarchical program, therefore, provides an insight into the conservative view of Mexico's problems.

History demonstrates that reform movements ultimately lose their vigor and that revolutionaries and reformers become conservatives with time. The course of Mexican liberalism in the nineteenth century adds validity to that axiom, for the Liberals of the *Reforma* became the supporters of the *Porfiriato*, the thirty-year dictatorship of General Porfirio Díaz, which is the third era in Mexican history. A practical man, Díaz ignored philosophical and intellectual approaches to national questions. His program stood for peace, order and material progress. Yet his cohorts, the *científicos*, spent much time and effort attempting to explain and justify policies that exploited peasants and favored the elite. To the *científicos*, positivism justified their views and when that formula became inadequate they added elements taken from Spencer's Social Darwinism and Mill's economic interpretations. The results, at least for the majority of the Mexican people, were disastrous.

Not surprisingly, Diaz' policies eventually invited protest. In an attempt to end the dictatorship, Francisco I. Madero, the son of a wealthy landowning family from Coahuila, opposed Díaz in the election of 1910. Díaz jailed Madero and easily won re-election. Undaunted, Madero fled to the United States and from there organized a revolt that toppled the dictatorship early in 1911. Madero, a political reformer willing to accept many features of the old regime including the collaboration of the ruling families, proved weak. His policies alienated him from his followers, but failed to win the backing of his critics. The military with the encouragement of the elite deposed and murdered Madero in February, 1913. The architect of Madero's death, General Victoriano Huerta, declared himself President of Mexico. However, the enemies of the old regime refused to accept Huerta and a new wave of fighting engulfed Mexico. The military phase of the Revolution did not subside until 1917 and the drafting of the Constitution of that year.

The Revolution, the fourth period in Mexican history, has attracted the attention of every Mexican scholar. To a majority of them, the reasons for the upheaval originate in the agrarian program of the dictatorship which, they believe, deprived the peasant of his lands and concentrated land ownership in the hands of the *hacendado* class. Not all historians support this thesis, nor does the essay included in the readings.

Since 1917, Mexico has enjoyed the benefits of many reforms, but scholars differ in their interpretations of the era. Some believe that reform characterizes the entire period from 1917 until today. They talk of the "continuing" Revolution. Others believe that the Revolution ended with the conclusion of the presidential term of Lázaro Cárdenas, a reformer who broke up the great estates, befriended the Indian, and nationalized the petroleum industry. In their opinion the regimes since 1940 have forsaken the Revolution. Perhaps a majority of Mexican scholars supports this interpretation, which is the theme of a number of outstanding literary works including Carlos Fuentes' novel, *Where the Air is Clear*. It may be possible for the student to arrive at an interpretation of his own through the study of the agrarian, educational, and Indian programs implemented since the 1920s because they represent the promises of the reformers who waged the Revolution. Have these programs received identical support in the era from 1917 to the present? If not, is there a "continuing" Reovlution?

Mexico's patriot fathers, as Luis Villoro, a Mexican historian-philosopher, writes, expected miracles from independence but events quickly disillusioned them. Independence opened the way for political chaos and the economic disintegration of the new Republic. The awaited utopia did not materialize. Instead, Mexicans quarreled among themselves. The middle sectors, disciples of José María Luis Mora, proposed a federalist remedy, a formula divorced from the past, for the ills of Mexico. Their opposition, the triumphant Centralists, accepted the teachings of Lucas Alamán who linked the failures of the era with the wish to depart from successful colonial principles three centuries old. The conflict between the two groups did not end until the victory of the *Reforma* when the Liberals finally imposed their blueprint on Mexico.

Luis Villoro:
La Revolución de
la Independencia

THE GREAT DECEPTION

The first voices of discord were heard when the insurgent writers permitted their enthusiasm for the future to blur their view of reality. If in 1814 *El Pensador Mexicano* painted a gloomy picture of the character and potential of the creoles, it was not from malice. Its skepticism reflected years of futile misfortunes suffered by the country. The revolution continued to mark time; independence still remained to be won, while the Mexican seemed incapable of reaching his objectives. His only contribution was a fratricidal war. The disillusionment brought the defects of the creole to the surface and crushed his optimism. Nevertheless, not everyone shared his reaction, and the angry polemic that it produced verifies it. The time of frustration had not yet arrived.

The collective enthusiasm of 1821 caused past wrongs to be forgotten; but when independence was achieved, things did not turn out as hoped. In particular, the problems of the national treasury and the very low productivity of the mines—inundated in large part during the insurrection—began to undermine the confidence of many Mexicans in the promised prosperity. The peace was disturbed once more and discontent returned. In 1823 optimism still persists; nevertheless, predictions of failure are not absent, such as that of the *Gaceta del Gobierno:* "The Mexican nation—it says— finds itself reduced to the utmost destitution; the sources of its wealth were obstructed, the capitalists had emigrated, confidence was wanting, and waste, robbery, and dilapidation abounded. Sad is the prospect before the leaders; they are given a cadaver and it is their duty to give it life." But these are not more than passing clouds: all the wrongs are considered remediable and hope yet lives

---

* From Luis Villoro, LA REVOLUCIÓN DE LA INDEPENDENCIA, trans. by Natalia Marrujo de Ruiz (Mexico: Universidad Nacional Autónoma de Mexico, 1953), pp. 210–235.

intensely. The road to disaster begins a few years later; economic difficulties increase, political factions multiply, extremist ideas threaten to transform themselves into violent explosions, and the first signs of anarchy appear. With the imminent expulsion of the Spaniards near, [José María Luis] Mora sees a horizon full of omens. "In our judgment, this terrible wrong is now inevitable. It is the first of many others that will follow and contribute to the ruin of the country." Actually, peace and security will not exist again for this generation, whose life will pass between civil war and terrorism. The revolutions follow each other year after year; in them perish or go into exile most of the great men who forged the new nation. Periods of demagoguery and anarchy alternate with epochs of despotism. The majority lives a prisoner of fear and conspiracies; if in the government, of foreign intervention; if in the opposition, of political persecution. A state of hypersensitivity and tension grips society. The new world does not appear; the Colony persists in its essential characteristics; neither democracy nor the enlightenment is successfully established. On the contrary, the weight of oppression and of ignorance is felt as never before; misery and helplessness are general; mineral production scarcely manages to recover from the damages suffered; the measures taken to insure freedom of commerce and industry do not provide the expected results; the internal debt reaches fantastic levels under the constant menace of foreign interventions, first from the Spaniards, and later from imperialistic English, French, and German capitalism, which begins to be seen as a threat. European intervention is dreaded. In the end, the most bitter deception supplants admiration for the United States. Bustamante reflects the deep depression that the conflict with France in 1838 left in everyone. He believes that all nations, even the North-American, merely want to exploit the weak and he sees clearly the danger of imperialistic capitalism, "perhaps more fatal than . . . armed conquest." While the enemy army advances, internal division continues; for a moment the disaster seems inevitable: ". . . The nation will sink into the abyss of disorder" . . . . The peace treaty concludes the humiliation of the Republic. "It seems, my friend"—Bustamante sadly writes—"that heaven decreed that our degradation and vilification have no end." How his language has changed! Would we recognize in these phrases the insurgent who predicted with jovial enthusiasm the advent of an opulent empire, kingdom of liberty and peace? A few years have sufficed to make him a sad and humiliated man, a few years to witness the destruction of his most beloved projects and to contemplate the uselessness of a whole life of suffering and work. And the helplessness appears to have no end. After the ridiculous despotism of a Santa Anna there develops what appears to be the final blow: the nation that Mexicans considered the birthplace of liberty, "guide" and "beacon" of independence, the United States, seizes half of the territory of the Republic.

That is the world of Mexico, and not the utopia expected. It is then that Mexico's history is written. Bustamante, upon renewing his account, tells us that it will be a history of the misfortunes of his country, a study of the cause "of the errors and misconduct of our government." Two years after the war with the United States, Lucas Alamán begins his work, which the same tone of bitterness permeates from start to finish. "To witness in the space of a few years this immense loss of territory," he writes at the conclusion of his *History*, "this waste of our wealth . . . this annihilation of a select and brave army, and particularly the total extinction of the public spirit, which has destroyed all sense of national character, not finding Mexicans in Mexico and contemplating a nation that has advanced from infancy to decrepitude, without having enjoyed more than a glimpse of the vigor of youth nor given other signs of life than violent convulsions, leads one to acknowledge with the great Bolívar that independence was purchased at the expense of the benefits that Spanish America enjoyed, and to give to Mexican history the title that the venerable bishop Las Casas used for his general history of the Indies: *History of the Destruction of the Indies*." So great is the despair that overwhelms the writer, that independence itself appears to him in somber colors; then, having lost all hope, sorrow overwhelms him. . . . :

> If present evils make the present Mexican nation the victim
> of foreign ambition and internal disorder disappears, to give rise
> to another people, to other habits and customs that may even
> destroy the Castilian language in these countries, my work may
> still serve other American nations, if any of them know how to
> apply the lessons of that experience, to see by what means the
> most happy hopes vanish and how the errors of men can make
> useless the most beautiful gifts of nature.

What a different future from that, which as a young man, together with the other deputies of Cádiz, he saw for his country! It is the bitter deception of a generation that knew itself called to create an empire and lived only long enough to see its degradation and to foresee its death . . . . No wonder his language reflects the deepest melancholy. Of what value for that generation was all its enthusiasm and its efforts? Perhaps the loss of its country and the eternal oblivion of history . . . . Mexico "appears destined to have

Please let her go. It's
her own book, It's O.K.

Limited Loan
Desk

the peoples who have formed it in diverse and remote ages disappear from its surface, leaving scarcely a memory of their existence. . . ." As the Mayas, buried beneath the jungle, the Toltecs who departed slowly to the South, the Aztecs whom misfortune obliterated from the land . . .

> thus also the present inhabitants will be forgotten and, without obtaining even the compassion that they deserved, it will be possible to apply to the Mexican nation of our day what a celebrated Latin poet said to one of the most famous persons of Roman history: *Stat magni nominis umbra,* no more than the shadow remains of a name famous in another time.

The revolution continues but now bitterness colors it. The same spiritual tone stamps itself on all the concepts of the epoch, whatever may be their political tendencies. However, according to the situations which men occupy, the common disenchantment will show distinct hues. In Alamán sensitivity predominates before the brevity and mutation of the historic. In a few years, his country has been overturned: it "has changed its name, its boundaries, its people in the influential part of the population, its form of government, its habits and customs. . . ." And no longer can the mature man recognize the world of his adolescence; everything has changed in sixteen years. Will he perhaps be able to find his own past when all his human warmth has died? How can he find himself lost in a land different from that which he knew? Perhaps the same objects of yesteryear may surround him, but now nothing retains the form that he loved in them, and he feels a foreigner in his own land. Nothing is more painful than this death in life: to lose irremissibly one's own world, to see it buried in oblivion and to remain alone, shipwrecked in a land that is no longer recognizable. Alamán feels that his country has escaped from his hands as all things human escape. The sarcasm of the time, against which no refuge exists, muddles everything . . . . He cannot recognize himself in the world that surrounds him; but the need ultimately to find himself remains with him. He flees constantly in search of a vague objective . . . but the dissatisfaction endures and no change gives him what he desires. Alamán suspected that this restlessness could be one of the causes of the revolutions of his epoch, produced—he says—by "the weariness of well-being or the wish to be better, that in nations eventually produce the same effect as prolonged suffering". . . . But it is Lorenzo de Zavala who hit upon the most apt phrases: "It was, rather, a vague impulse to substitute other persons, other things, for the existing ones. It was that restlessness that everyone experiences in a newly reconstituted society, that anxiety, that wish to change the situation . . . ."

The same disposition of spirit reveals itself differently in Mora's *Discourse About the Natural Course of Revolutions*. There are happy revolutions—he observes—but also frustrated ones. The first focus against a specific obstacle; the action polarizes around it and satisfies itself fully when the obstacle is eliminated. Here the revolutionary objectives are—we would say—external. The movement does not seek a transformation of man, but the simple removal of a barrier that hinders action. But, in other occasions, the obstacle is overcome and the dissatisfaction endures. When this happens the frustration remains embedded in man; then we can believe that we are facing another phenomenon. Because *"there are revolutions that depend upon a general movement in the spirit of nations"* . . . .

THE CRITICISM OF UTOPIANISM

In December of 1823, Mier pronounced his famous "prophecy" about the Federation, which one may consider the first statement on the theme of the frustrated revolution. Denouncing the "North-american mania" and the desire to imitate foreign systems, he stressed "the enormous difference in situation and circumstances that have existed between them and ourselves." Because we "have kneeled for three centuries under the yoke of an absolute monarch, we only succeed in taking one step without stumbling in the unknown state of liberty. We are like infants whose swaddling bands have been recently removed, like slaves who have just loosened old chains." The weight of habits compels one not to anticipate too much, to progress with slow steps on the road to appropriate reform. The revolutionary concept survives; the problem is to make it effective by adopting a safe rate of progress adjusted to the situation. Between independence and the realization of the chosen society intervenes a long process; the "imitators" seem to forget it and risk falling into the "madness" of "desiring from the first attempt at liberty to reach the summit of social perfection." A "Jacobin" tendency—according to Friar Servando—pretends to put into work principles logically unassailable, "principles, if one wishes, *metaphysically true,* but inapplicable in practice, because they consider man *in the abstract* and such a man *does not exist* in society." Brilliant words! As we have said—just as the abstract election of a pure liberty manifests itself, in fact, as slavery, so also the "metaphysical" truth, incapable of acquiring *existence,* reveals itself as erroneous, because the only truth is historical and existential. Because of this a political system, logically irreproachable, can be false in a given moment. The principle of popular sovereignty that the Jacobins demagogically manipulate, although true in the abstract, becomes impossible to realize in the concrete circumstance and is, therefore, a falsehood of the epoch and a lie in the mouth of the idealogues. However, this does not invalidate the principle when it takes form in a modern society.

The criticism of "utopianism" stems as much from the "core" of the revolutionary mind as from the counterrevolution. In the two cases it will have distinct reasons and lead to different conclusions. . . .

The fundamental characteristic of the utopian attitude is its life in the imaginary, which could be summed up in Mora's criticism of the idealogues who "separate themselves from the real world in order to devote themselves to the ideal" and who try to give laws to a people who exist not in the imagination of politicians but on the surface of the land and with elements that have nothing in common with the abstractions of those who pretend to govern the people and to give them lessons. It is this characterization that we find also in Alamán when he speaks of "fantastic and ideal" or "imaginary" systems, and also in Zavala . . . . The utopian concept tends to locate itself in some foreign place that, by its distance, can assume the role of model. The model is the country that furnishes the ideal system with an appearance of existence. Zavala defends the excessive desire of the imitator on the basis of his lack of experience: "Where could we, the future deputies, have acquired those lessons of the profound art of governing, so complicated and difficult? It was necessary that they attempt to imitate what was more within reach of their acquired knowledge." The models more useful initially had to be the Constitution of Cádiz and, in its turn, the French Assembly. A little later, the Northamerican federal system would also exercise a strong fascination, principally in the elaboration of the Constitution of 1824; and England itself did not cease to be examined as an example.

What happens, in essence, is that the chosen project transcends considerably the present and aspires to attain in one stroke the distant future. Many revolutionaries suffer from haste because, impatient to attend the advent of the society which they have selected, they plan it as though it already existed. It is Alamán who finds the proper phrase to describe the development. "Never in political matters—he exclaimed referring to the Constitution of Cádiz—had *such an immense gap* been covered *in a single leap.*" "Conceded now by the decree of the Córtes," he adds, "a liberty which in fact had almost no limitation, the most distant extremes had been touched in a moment of time" . . . .

"Our generation," said Zavala, "has been transported instantly to a species of moral sphere distinct from that in which our fathers lived . . . . We have seen generations on the march that have posed before us as suddenly *changed, without being able for a long time* to realize completely the state of the society that makes possible the principles that they adopted." The separation between change and realization that Zavala stressed in the cited phrase is transformed into a contradiction when the two extremes, separated by actual time, manifest themselves in distinct and simultaneous strata in the society.

> Those powerful agents of human life [the hereditary customs of the Colony] stand in contradiction with the theoretical system of the established governments, and the fathers of republican forms cannot deny that they have only clothed ancient man with the garb of the declarations of rights and principles . . . What have they done to substitute habits and customs analogous to the new state of things?

Zavala points out the contradiction between life and thought that characterizes his epoch. But this contradiction is present— and perhaps the author does not see this—because the chosen society attempts to coexist *at the same historic time* with the ancient. Instead of submitting to the actual flow of events, man appears to want to dislocate it and to make himself its master. The elements that can be organized voluntarily, that is, the organisms of administration and government, the juridical institutions, the educational system, etc., conform to the social ideal, while the irrational economic situation continues unchanged. Society seems to split into two spheres that keep distinct provisional records. The utopian thinker finds in the bureaucratic world created by the revolutionary class, the rational remedy of a space-time that he can discern on the edge of his projects; then he attempts to identify himself with that space-time of his creation and ignores the authentic.

Mora, for his part, insists that the utopian attitude, attempting to realize a perfect good, only introduces anarchy and the "partisan spirit" that consumes and divides all . . . . If an attempt is made to achieve what is good through the use of armed force, the only result is to submerge the society in a state of perpetual commotions and disturbances, because "even in order to bring about the good—said Mora wisely—one needs opportunity." . . .

THE PRETERIST SOLUTION

In his book, Alamán's conception of history is not presented in an organized manner. We can, however, piece it together if we keep in mind the character of the historical conscience that formulates it. [Alamán followed the Preterist school which believes that the present and future needs of a society are determined by the character of its past.] The interpretation of events in the work of Alamán expresses the attitude of the euro-creole class. Our author makes clear his position during the [revolutionary] struggle, identifying himself as much with the criticism of the Hidalgo movement as with the independence efforts of the euro-creoles. Iturbide's revolt merits his approval, but he condemns Congress and the activity of the middle class. If he often bitterly criticizes Iturbide, he does so in the name of the same Plan de Iguala, undermined by the ambition *or* the stupidity of its author. In the progressive destruction of the Plan and in the abandonment of the idea of "transition" that justifies it, Alamán sees the reason for the calamities of the era. A disciple of "dynamic preterism," he proclaims himself a believer in the continuity and persistence of the past and in the gradual transformation of society. Because, he writes, "in the civil order, more than in the natural, everything is *gradual,* because civil order *is no more than natural order modified* by causes that act even more slowly such as religion, ethics and learning. We never see nature act in sudden movements. The exceptions are earthquakes and tempests, and they are not creative but destructive" . . . . Alamán defends the revolution of Iguala because "it adhered to the customs formed during 300 years, to the correct opinions, to the interests created, and to the respect that the name of the monarch inspired. Faced with a revolutionary movement, he upholds repeatedly the necessity to advance by degrees and to maintain a continuity between the future and the past. The act of calling upon the royal Spanish family "formed a continuation of reigning princes uninterrupted since the Conquest. In a land such as Spanish America, where the Conquest is everything and from it is derived the right of property, whose only source are the grants of land made in the name of the monarch, this succession legitimized and strengthened all rights, which today do not rest on any base whatsoever. . . ." We have encountered these ideas before: the Colony and, in its time the Conquest, are seen as the origin of contemporary society; the past maintains its dominance by means of the system of established *rights;* the revolutionary movement, on the other hand, by denying the colonial centuries, "does not rest on any base" . . . other than liberty. From the first pages of Alamán's work, historical development is conceived as emerging from the past in a continuous bond with it: he describes "a country where everything that exists *has its origin* in that prodigious Conquest . . . ." According to Alamán, the error of the revolution would be to break the historical continuity. Throughout his work, the inability of the author to explain any movement which falls outside of his interpretation of history is obvious. At times his perplexity is translated into exclamations of indignation, and at others into confessions of incomprehension. The creoles, he says for example, attack the Conquest *"with a kind of frenzy impossible to explain, as if they were* heirs of the conquered peoples and compelled to avenge the harm done to them." The creole *is not,* according to Alamán, the anti-hispanist that he *elects to be;* he *is* the descendant of Spaniards, and his family tree imposes upon him "obligations," duties. The revolutionary, on the contrary, would undoubtedly believe that his only duty was to be against his ancestors in order that he be free to choose his role. In that "kind of frenzy" of which he speaks, Alamán could have found the explanation he was seeking. But a preterist conception of history can admit no categories. Thus Alamán attempts to explain the "madness" of the creole as a phenomenon of psychological fascination for foreign theoretical systems, thus mistaking the effect for the cause.

The role of the historian is to illuminate the past in order to discover the laws that link events. His usefulness does not stem from the narration of events, "but in analyzing the influence that events have upon one another; in linking them together in such a manner that the first events make clear the cause of the latter, and in these the precise results of the former, with the idea in mind that past experience serves as a guide for the future." The historian, therefore, must make the event intelligible by revealing its hidden links with causality. This can be done with the past, with inalterable events that have already occurred; but the present state of things is beyond human foresight. The engine of social growth does not lend itself to rational calculation. "The great events in nations are never the results of prudent calculation, but the results of causalities or combinations outside of human foresight" . . . . Alamán observes that Mexico has continued to develop in spite of all organizational plans and on the margins of all revolutionary movements. In his diagnosis, on the one hand, the situation of the exchequer is critical, the government anarchic, the institutions unstable and the political situation distressing. On the other hand, "the well-being of the Mexican Republic is general; wealth has increased; mining and agriculture prosper; the fine arts have reached heights previously unknown; and all that implies abundance" is greater in Mexico than in any European capital. Therefore, he concludes, "everything that is the work of nature and the fruits of private effort has progressed; all that which required the action of public authority has declined." Therefore, "the political institutions of the nation are not what it requires for its prosperity." The governmental and administrative machinery, planned rationally, stand in contradiction to the infrastructure of society . . . . In the *preterista* experience, which finds the cause of historical development in social spontaneity, planning, rather than respresenting an element of progress, makes normal growth difficult . . . .

Alamán believes that he sees in the Colony an example of that slow and even evolution in which the spontaneity of society guided development. "All the immense continent of America, today a chaos of confusion, of disorder and misery, then moved with uniformity, *without violence*—it can be said *without effort*—and all of it moved in a *progressive order* towards continual and substantial improvements." The "effort," a manifestation of choice, was absent, and with it violence; a smooth order reigned in the absence of liberty. With the Colony as an example to emulate, Alamán will tend to reduce rational planning to the level of a purely administrative function. The ruler will be the man of experience who will not allow himself to be deceived by "the fantasies of theories and the nonsense of systems." The regime of Anastasio Bustamante, which our author directs in practice, is based on this idea. It avoids all social and economic reform but, in turn, "Mexico was then able to hope of becoming a nation, on the basis of the belief that, in order to do this, its own resources, administered with purity and economy, are sufficient." In the purely administrative work, Alamán attempts to restrict considerably the political role of Congress and to impose the power of the state on the different classes and castes, reducing the congressional role to that of regulator of its own spontaneous development. Naturally, that power would rest primarily on the dominant propertied class. . . .

THE FUTURIST SOLUTION

We have already seen that Mora discovers in the utopian and anarchic deviation of the revolution one of the principal reasons for its ills. But the malaise also stems from the existence of "bodies" that impede progress. Above all, the malaise is in the army, dominant since 1821, which has no productive role in society and exists and keeps intact its privileges only by maintaining the nation in a constant state of civil war. All warring factions seek the support of the military, whose preponderance takes the form of an armed domestic struggle or military despotism. In the second place, is the high clergy, in control of nearly all of the national wealth, and also economically non-productive, which monopolizes all usable capital and places serious obstacles to their investment in industry.

Even more than the army, the clergy acts as an autonomous "body" within the nation, subject only to its own laws and regulations, and defended by civil laws that shield it from the reforms of the revolution. Through its monopoly of education, its spiritual strength which stems from its prestige, and its use of religion for political ends, the clergy keeps alive the habits and the ignorance of colonial days. When these two bodies [army and clergy] form an explicit or tacit alliance, all social progress is made impossible and only one alternative remains: despotism or armed rebellion. Therefore, the cause of internal disorder is complex, and anarchy itself is the the result of the economic situation. Further, Mexico supports the onerous colonial heritage in the infrastructure of society. The revolutionary bureaucracy can only create a network of institutions and governmental formulas which are superimposed and leave intact the ancient order. But even within the conscience of men the formulas have changed, but not the men "habituated to Spanish despotism, raised and nourished on its habits and customs." Nothing is more difficult to combat than habits, against which almost always good intentions are powerless. "Nations, as well as people, are subject to certain madnesses . . . rooted so deeply in the spirit of men that their extirpation is made supremely difficult and can only be corrected with time, meditation, and the moderation of passions." The error of the "utopians" is not in their attempt to eliminate these habits, but in thinking that they are free of them and in belittling their strength in the belief that they can be extirpated easily. . . . Nations do not change their ideas by a change of government; ideas inherited from oppressive regimes survive for a long time." Political emancipation should follow, as Leopoldo Zea has emphasized, "the emancipation of the mind."

To Mora, the contradictions between the institutions of government and social-economic reality can be explained by either of two interpretations: to an excess of revolutionary zeal or to the tenacious survival of the past. If we accept the first interpretation, we would say, in accordance with the counterrevolutionary currents, that the revolution has gone too far and that we must stop its impulse. If we accept the second interpretation, we will maintain, in accordance with the "leftist" view, that the revolution has not progressed sufficiently and we must carry it out. But both perspectives are false because they pretend to give a global diagnosis on the basis of a partial view of the total picture. Mora's thought rests on the willingness to consider simultaneously both aspects.

The solution which our author proposes combines the acceptance of historical currents with a "futurist" attitude. According to Mora, the harm is not in "conversion" and in progress, but in forgetting its true historical significance. The failure of utopianism should be interpreted solely as the result of deviation from the true revolutionary line; thus, it should lead us to renounce the world we want and to the attempt to transform society. Mora remains a believer in the value of rational plans and free discussion in order to propel progressively the nation. Given the alternative of choosing between a future world or the survival of contemporary society, Mora invariably supports the former. Yet one must not forget that, even after the system is adopted, "everything still remains to be done in Mexico" . . . .

The reform required is not psychological or political, but economic; it means little to change the social superstructure if the regime of property is left intact. While Alamán saw the solution in reform of political institutions in order to adjust them to the social-economic situation, Mora believes that successful reform changes that situation, in accordance with a specific farsighted plan. It is necessary to act in such a way that the monopoly of property and power exercised by the military and ecclesiastical classes will disappear. Until this is done, all arguments over the suitability of institutions are futile, because the fundamental causes of the problems of the century will remain. The utopian as well as the concept of "retrocession" impede the transformation of society by pretending to solve problems by acting mainly on the political superstructure.

In the opinion of Mora, all political approaches essentially seek the same end: "At the extremes as well as at the center, the same thing is always sought, that is to say, liberty." In effect, liberty is sought in the attempt to erect a power with which to free oneself from anarchy. With that, Mora puts the problem in perspective: the two approaches may pursue the common welfare, but the first will not give up its search for liberty despite disorder, while the second will submit to oppression in order to achieve peace. But although both seek liberty, will they achieve it? The "leftist" path is unrealistic and can only lead to an anarchy in which the army and a swollen bureaucracy are the beneficiaries. That encourages dictatorship and reaction, even when its intention was to avoid it; all that is achieved objectively is either the stagnation or retrocession of society. The counter-revolution, on its part, seeks the continuity of order. Although it pretends to avoid despotism and the evils of previous regimes, upon attacking the revolutionary forces, it finds itself powerless before a tyranny which, without intending to, it creates. Thus, in practice the two apparently antagonistic tendencies produce a similar result. It is so, says Mora, because both derive from the same inherited habits. "We have only transferred this formidable power from one to many or, what is the same, from the king to the congresses. "Under the name of extraordinary privileges, this despotism has governed, since 1823, as much in the national government as in the states." Thus, he thinks that the similarity of results that stem from the tendencies are so obvious that they can only be explained—with a somewhat simplistic criterion—as the result of a common cause: the heritage of the colonial mentality. . . .

Mora's formula seeks progress without denying the limitations that history imposes. Reform will deal with the economic situation. By making liberty effective, it will attempt to avoid anarchy, not through a worship of the existing order, but by the slow and gradual application of reforms adapted to the circumstances; seeking order, the formula will avoid despotism, not by the sterile road of political institutions, but by transforming the economic reality which creates it . . . .

2

Few students of Mexican history, either Mexican or American, have probed with care and sympathy the conservative thesis which culminates in the invasion of Mexico by the army of Napoleon III and the Empire of Maximilian. Although Mexicans have written favorable accounts, they embody an extreme Catholic, anti-Liberal Party bias. American scholars are either uncritically pro-Juárez or strongly anti-clerical and hostile to Napoleon. It is in this context that the work of Jesús Reyes Heroles must be read. A historian and economist, the former head of the national petroleum monopoly, and therefore a member of the official family which views President Benito Juárez as the great man of Mexico, Reyes Heroles not only offers an objective account, but explains why Mexican conservatives, whom he finds no less patriotic than their Liberal foes, ultimately invited a European power and a foreign prince to rule their country.

Jesús Reyes Heroles:
El Liberalismo Mexicano*

The privileged classes have demonstrated by 1840 that they cannot stabilize society by maintaining their privileges, either with a de facto government and a liberal platform or with a constitutional oligarchical government. There appears, as we have seen, a third plan: constitutional despotism. This is generally accepted by the privileged classes. . . . But, within these classes, doubts exist as to which is the better road to follow. These divisions of opinion are solidified during the regime of the *Bases Orgánicas*. In the failure of constitutional despotism, these differences of criteria and the incompatibility of interests among the privileged play a role comparable to the liberal opposition.

The government of the traditionally privileged classes sought a broader base for itself when [Lucas] Alamán attempts to create a privileged industrial class. But despite Alamán, the prevailing conservative current, without totally rejecting his proposal, favors a government of the traditionally privileged classes. A few years are enough to prove that the alliance advocated by Alamán cannot be formed. If economically the attempt to industrialize fails, politically it is self defeating. However, before that occurs, the conservatives modify their thesis. The goal is no longer a government of the privileged classes, but of the rich and powerful classes (*clases pudientes*). That which in progressive liberalism represented a theoretical principle is converted into a program of action and regimentation once the failure of constitutional despotism is evident. More than an evolution of conservative ideas, there is an overlapping of ideas, or a coexistence of different ideas within the conservative sector. Before constitutional despotism is implanted, [José Miguel] Gutiérrez Estrada arrives at the idea of monarchy by a route very different from that which leads Alamán, approximately six years later, to an identical goal. A knowledge of conservative thought is indispensable if one is to understand the method and liberal strategy that ultimately triumphs, as well as the successive tendencies that confront liberalism and the contra-

* From Jesús Reyes Heroles, EL LIBERALISMO MEXICANO; LA SOCIEDAD FLUCTUANTE, trans. by Natalia Marrujo de Ruiz (Mexico: Universidad Nacional Autónoma de Mexico, 1958), II, pp. 331–344, 347–353.

dictions which become the antagonistic or, at least discordant, ideas of its enemies. The internal logic of the political struggle transformed democratic liberalism into the majority current, and thus made it possible to obtain a certain degree of unity of doctrine. The same conflict, the contradictions in the colonial classes, which became more apparent as the colonial social and economic structure suffered modifications, encouraged the coexistence of antithetical ideas or the rapid outdating of conservative programs of government.

PEACE WITH A MONARCHY

The story of Gutiérrez Estrada is dramatic. He is a disciple of progressive liberalism, and a friend of [José María Luis] Mora, who holds him in high esteem. A Scottish-Rite Mason, he suffers personally from the attack on the oligarchy: he is among those exiled. Under these conditions he quickly despairs of the Republic, of his generation and, out of desperation, fatigue and a lack of consistency and firmness of character, he gives up a struggle which he feels is sterile and interminable. He knows too well the privileged classes to believe in 1840 that they can succeed by themselves. Also, he knows well the fickleness of the military. Only a monarchy can provide peace and stability. In his search for peace, he becomes an advocate of monarchy: with this idea he anticipates by six years a strong conservative faction and in the end he identifies with it. The repercussions that Gutiérrez Estrada's ideas had on our political life, the popularity which they attained among the rank and file of conservatives, makes it possible for these ideas, at the same time that they anticipate subsequent ideas that led to the intervention, to help us to know, along with later concepts, the other face of Mexican political evolution.

Gutiérrez Estrada fears for Mexican society. He knows that it will be destroyed unless the factional struggle is halted. In 1840, he believes that he stands between the belligerent parties. Consequently, because of his neutral position, he expects that they will listen to him. He makes his views known during the regime of the *Siete Leyes,* which he judges inoperable. He desires peace at any price and he foresees no end to the present conflict if the charters of 1824 and 1836 are not excelled. He does not defend the institutions of 1836: the *Siete Leyes* were "the product of circumstance and for the benefit of certain people." Nor does he think it advisable to restore the Constitution of 1824. Among the terrible results of constitutional oligarchism was "to erect one altar in front of another." Frightened by Urrea's coup of July 15, 1840, he prays for peace, recalling the old cliché that "if peace is not established on a solid basis, it matters little whether one is the conqueror or the vanquished." The political laws in dispute cannot govern the country. The conflict between the two constitutions, "in addition to being insoluble," will produce, along with the alternating triumphs of one or the other, grave convulsions within society. Besides being incapable of providing a basis for peace, the two constitutions suffer from other major faults. The *Siete Leyes* inspire distrust in a large sector of the population. Furthermore, many of "their supporters believe that the *Leyes* cannot prevail for long, either because of the unpopularity of some of their stipulations or because no public authority exists sufficiently strong to overcome the inevitable and powerful resistance which they provoke." Even less can an opposition be overcome that wraps itself in the banner of the Constitution of 1824. Conversely, "in the midst of the weakness or moral insensitivity into which our society appears to have fallen," due to the exaggerated importance attributed to democratic principles, the Constitution of 1824 weakens "the ties which bind with a common core the diverse parts of the national political body" and leads us to destruction "in the most complete state of social disintegration." It is necessary, above all, to dispense with both charters because both represent "special interests" in society, a society that remains unstable, oscillating, and without peace. Therefore, Gutiérrez Estrada proposes the convocation of a convention "so that once the general unrest is over" a remedy be found for the ills of Mexico. The convention or constitutional assembly would attend to the "necessity of rebuilding the social structure."

Gutiérrez Estrada has no faith in his generation. Are there among us, he asks, men like Lafayette or Casimiro Perrier? "Because unfortunately we do not have that type of man, true and living products of a society more advanced than ours in every sense, and because of what the experience of twenty years has taught us, that is why I look with horror and dread at all that smacks of revolution, whatever may be its nature or justification." His lack of faith in his generation is total: "For this reason, and because one cannot hope for wisdom except from the coming generation, if by chance it has the schools in which to learn, I have no faith in what exists or in what the present generation may be able to accomplish." Yet "regardless of how harmful this confession may be to our self esteem," he says, it is nevertheless the truth: there can be no peace in Mexico while the present men govern. To this conviction he adds another: ". . . I have had many opportunities to convince myself in a practical manner that liberty can exist under all forms

of government, and that a monarchy can provide much more freedom and happiness than a republic." In addition, to quote Gutiérrez
Estrada,

> We have experimented with a Republic in all forms: democratic,
> oligarchical, military, demagogical, and anarchical. Thus all the
> parties in their turn, and always with detriment to the happiness
> and honor of the nation, have tried every possible republican
> system.

If after sixteen years "of free and unencumbered activity" the
Liberals have not been able to make "a reality" of the republican
system, "it certainly means that the system does not suit us." Obviously, "there still remained entire classes of society, the products
of Spanish colonial domination, and of customs produced by the
education of the era and perpetuated by the habits of three centuries," which must be eliminated "in order to establish republican
principles on their ruins." But the attempt to destroy did not fail
for lack of effort "by the most enthusiastic supporters of the Republic" who have employed all the means available to them in order
to achieve this destruction, but who failed because the job proved
superior in its magnitude to their effort. If "they proved unable
to complete the task of destruction, an undertaking proverbially
less difficult than that of creating and rebuilding, what hope could
the nation have in the physical and moral power of these men?"

Given these conditions, Gutiérrez Estrada proposes that the
constituent assembly or convention decide "with proper impartiality whether a monarchical form of government (with a sovereign
of royal lineage) might not be more suitable to the character, customs, and traditions of a country which since its founding was governed by monarchy." At that moment Gutiérrez Estrada discovers
the parable which the monarchists of 1846 adopted later and which
is employed to justify Maximilian. "As a colony of a weak and unfortunate monarchy, Mexico reaches a high level of prosperity,
splendor and fame"; with the Republic, "all is ruins, desolation,
poverty, killings because of civil strife and, in summary, disgrace-
ful discredit." In order to put an end to those ills, we must return
to that in which we originate; monarchy. The Republic is not for
our people.

> Say what you wish about the advantages of a republic wherever
> it can be established, and no one will proclaim with more en-
> thusiasm those advantages than I; nor will anyone lament more
> sincerely than I that Mexico cannot now be that privileged coun-
> try. But the sad experience of what that system has meant to
> us seems to authorize us to attempt in our country an experi-

ment with a genuine monarchy in the person of a *foreign prince*.

Foreign royalty is indispensable if we want to overcome our problems. A form of government "cannot be good or bad, convenient or inconvenient, except in as much as it is either good or bad for the people for whom it is intended." To endow a people with a form of government opposed to that in which they have lived, is a grave error; history offers many examples of that. Gutiérrez Estrada fears that some may believe that he is a partisan of despotism: "On the contrary, I can assure you that even the most liberal governments still seem tyrannical to me; but precisely, because I love liberty, I want for my country that liberty which will benefit it." Not all people can enjoy the same degree of liberty. Peace cannot be born again in Mexico if we continue with the same system and the same men . . . .

There will be no peace so long as we remain a Republic. The conflict will persist because "the strongest partisans of a Republican system are the first to acknowledge that it has not been possible to consolidate the Republic among us because everything in Mexico is monarchical." It is useless to want forcibly to make ourselves into something that we are not. We cannot compare ourselves with the United States: democracy works for them, but not for us. The monarchical system signifies peace for Mexico: "For that reason, I repeat, it seems to me that the moment has arrived in which the nation should direct its sights toward the principle of a democratic monarchy, as the only means of achieving the peace we so ardently desire. With it we can save our nationality:

> I cannot discover any other way to preserve our nationality, now imminently threatened by the Anglo-Saxons who, having settled on this continent, prepare to invade everything in behalf of democratic principles, an element of life and strength for them but of weakness and death for us. In the shadow of democratic principles, it is clear, our neighbors have prospered, while we have retrogressed in every way, morally as well as materially.

So disillusioned is Gutiérrez Estrada with the republican system that he believes that the gains of Mexico in "certain branches of industry" and perhaps "in luxuries"—which, in its present condition, are ruinous to the nation—should not be attributed to the system, but viewed as the result of our independence and as the "natural benefits of the century." . . . His disappointment or pessimism extends further: "Perhaps we should put the entire blame on the republican system, origin and source of our perpetual troubles, for the tardy arrival of these natural benefits." In the opinion of Gutiérrez Estrada, we have not even known how to replace the Spaniards with our own people. The state of the nation is physically and morally deplorable and obviously it is going to worsen day by day. The existence of this state of affairs leads Gutiérrez Estrada to his second argument: the defense of the integrity of our territory. If we continue as we are, we will not be able to resist the "advancing tide from the North, which has already invaded our territory and which will inundate everything, using democratic principles for justification" . . . . Therefore:

> If we do not change our behavior, we will probably see within twenty years the stars and stripes of the North American flag flying over our National Palace . . . .

Later Gutiérrez Estrada will stress the defense of the integrity and the independence of Mexico. Conceived as a justification for the monarchy which he supports, the idea is to equalize North American power by seeking aid from a foreign nation through a monarch. To obtain this equilibrium, he is ready to offer inducements to European powers to intervene in the affairs of Mexico: the interests of England, France, Spain and Prussia "in the preservation of a market which, in addition to strongly stimulating the mercantile and industrial sectors of those nations, contributes annually 20 or 25 million pesos to the development of European factories, should merit the attention of statesmen." He makes his argument even more clear:

> Because if Mexico stopped being an independent state; if Mexico did not evolve a stable government free of revolution; if, in summary, the mines suspended their activity because of anarchy, or if those mines fell into the hands of the United States, Europe would no longer receive their products and the loss each year of such a large sum would cause havoc in the industrial relations of the European continent.

He writes this in 1847. But in the thinking of Gutiérrez Estrada, disappointment in the democratic system and desire for peace take precedent over the survival of the country. His idea of equalizing the strength of the United States by installing in Mexico a power with European roots was anachronous. But, just as he was prophetic in regard to our relations with the United States, he was also prophetic in demonstrating that the vestiges of the colonial order could only maintain themselves with outside aid.

A GOVERNMENT OF THE WEALTHY
AND POWERFUL CLASSES

The cold reception given the proposals of Gutiérrez Estrada convinces even those who secretly agree with him that the time is not ripe to make public such a project. Still, the collapse of the regime of the *Siete Leyes,* the momentary liberal surge of 1841–1842, the destruction of the constitutional Congress, and the approval by "notables" of the *Bases Orgánicas,* do not resolve the national problems. Constitutional despotism lacked the public support necessary to govern. Even the privileged classes are aware of this. Before the *Bases Orgánicas* are formulated, Paredes Arrillaga proposed another solution. By intuition or on the advice of others, he comes to understand that in order to maintain some of the privileges, fundamentally those of the military to which he belongs, that it is necessary to reorganize the country politically and socially, to dispense with political parties and to govern with the support of the "productive and wealthy classes." It is necessary to control the parties and to reduce them to impotency.

Besides evil, Paredes Arrillaga sees stupidity in the liberal projects of the men of 1828 and 1833. It is not enough to sit in the Chamber of Deputies to get "as if by magic, power" sufficient to do what the army does not want done. The government can make its own the interests of the landowning and wealthy classes. The interests of these classes is the national interest and the government can win their support by opposing doctrinaire liberals. The idea is to govern with the wealthy classes, uniting them to the army:

> The government is, I believe, approaching this desired unit by
> calling together the representatives of the wealthy and powerful
> classes and working out with them the basis of the accord, in
> which they will have the guarantees which they want and
> which they will support as their own work. Later the govern-
> ment can function on the basis of this principle and thus give all
> acts of government a more solid foundation than possible with
> the accords of ordinary and extraordinary assemblies.

Paredes Arrillaga recognizes that instability stems from the weakness of the traditionally privileged classes. Conversely, national evils stem from "calling, without any distinction being made, upon the proletariat, the laborer, the ignorant, and the property owner, the businessman and the sage to decide what is most convenient for the country." The result is comparable to that of a council of war in which the troops, the officers, and the generals discuss and vote and reach a decision on the basis of a majority of votes. The solution is obvious: "Let us seek out the well-to-do classes, which in politics are what generals are in war; let us work in accord with them and the problem is resolved." Subsequently, Paredes Arrillaga returns to his idea that the government must rest "on the opinion of the well-to-do classes which, because they have much to lose, have no choice but to favor order." However, he is not so naive as to want to relinquish the supreme authority to these classes; the idea is to offer them a "certain political role, although purely passive," through the corporations that speak for them. "Such are, in my judgement, the municipal councils, for matters concerning the Church; the Commission on Development, for matters pertaining to commerce; the mining deputations, once they are reestablished; the Boards of Industry. Others could be organized among property owners who encourage agriculture; also tribunals and medical associations; and perhaps something could be done to give representation to persons in the literary professions." We are speaking of two chambers integrated by these corporations. The high military and ecclesiastical functionaries would compose the upper chamber and represent the interests of their classes. "The rest of the people would be represented by another chamber to which no member of the proletariat could belong." In this, a dozen years later, Paredes Arrillaga is in accord with Mora. In the election of the Lower Chamber, no right to vote would be given to anyone with less capital than 3,000 pesos or an income of 1,000. Only in this way, according to the caudillo, could one count on "a true and solid constitution based on real interests and not in theories that our politicians and our rebels attempt to transplant, though in our land these theories degenerate into principles that foster anarchy."

The idea does not jell. The military faction headed by Santa Anna, far from wishing to share its power, wants to act independently. Its fundamental motive was to free itself of the controls imposed by the oligarchy. It operates as a reaction to constitutional oligarchism. The result is a constitutional despotism imposed not by the military, but by a faction within it, and not as the desire of the other privileged class, the clergy, but accepted by it, to be sure, as a desperate measure in order to permit the military to find a way out of the problem. The situation proved impossible and thus Santa Anna, governing with the *Bases Orgánicas,* is compelled to relinquish his authority by forces that constitute part of the state machinery: an opposition Congress that is dissolved; a Council of State which is constitutionally subordinate but which rebels; a faction of the army, which under Paredes Arrillaga, has revolted in Guadalajara. José Joaquín Herrera, with less than a year of office under the *Bases Orgánicas,* is deposed by Paredes Arrillaga who champions the Plan de San Luis Potosí of December 14, 1845, which promises a new constitutional assembly. The idea of a government of the wealthy and powerful classes, which will embody the monarchist ideal, will be put into effect during the ephemeral regime of Paredes Arillaga. Alamán is the genius behind this new intent, no longer to halt the political evolution of the country, but to invert it. The government of Paredes Arrillaga, blind to the course of history, acquires importance for its reformulation of the conservative program which will argue: 1) that the conservative classes cannot be unified; 2) that it is doubtful that the wealthy and powerful classes can agree on a conservative program; 3) that the liberal forces have created such a state of animation and opinion that the country will not accept a return to the past—which would satisfy the needs of the conservatives.

On January 24, 1846 the first issue of *El Tiempo* appears. Edited largely by Alamán, it provides the means for the reformulation of the conservative program. In that first issue the general outline of conservative thought is made clear: the laws should be adapted to realities and not attempt to modify them. The state of permanent revolution in which the country has lived stems from the fact that the laws do not mirror reality. The rules should recognize and direct that which exists and not try to change it. Legislation should be in accord with the state of things. The name of the newspaper embodies the recognition that "we look to the past for the lessons and experiences which will direct us in the present. We believe that the present contains and nurtures the germ of progress of the future." Although conservative in principle, the newspaper will not attempt to "close the door to progressive advancement."

Undoubtedly, the political plans of Alamán and Paredes Arrillaga, based on the asumption that sufficient time was available to them, were to be made known gradually as public opinion was made receptive. But sufficient time was denied to them because, with the publication of the first ideas, the liberal press put together the jigsaw puzzle and precipitated the events, because the monarchical idea engendered a general repudiation. Further, the ideas of the groups in that episode were already public knowledge.

It is obvious that *El Tiempo* wanted to sow its neo-conservative ideas in homeopathic doses. But the liberal press capitalized on a number of careless slips. A mental lapse in the second issue of *El Tiempo* offers a golden opportunity. *El Tiempo* wants to know why it is possible that a country "governed by a monarchy, from which it is separated by an ocean, was able to live in peace and progress for a period of 300 years"; and how is it that when the country becomes independent "it has not enjoyed a single day of peace." "Is it possible that the destiny of this country was to live under foreign tutelage, and that by breaking its foreign bonds, it fell out of its natural orbit?" The answer is still negative: ". . . its separation from the metropolis was a benefit that should never produce ill effects." The problems stem from laws unadapted to realities. "But to change that which exists, to destroy the mechanism that kept in check the movements of society, and to substitute complicated and impractical systems, was the worst of all errors."

The idea of a government by the wealthy and powerful classes appears in the third issue. *El Tiempo* publishes José María Luis Mora's *Discourse On the Necessity to Define the Right of Citizenship in the Republic in Terms of Property*. The maneuver is skillful: It relies on a liberal to justify an electoral law that is about to appear . . . .

We, says *El Tiempo*, "who do not believe firmly either in monarchy or in the Republic," who "only believe in independence and liberty, defend the bold view that the new Congress has the authority to organize the country once and for all, with only the happiness of the people in mind." And *El Tiempo* proceeds even further. It will uphold, it says, a number of heresies:

> We are quite capable of believing that liberty can exist as much
> in a representative monarchy as in a Republic. We much prefer
> the monarchical institutions of England or France to the re-
> publican institutions of Venice.

All republics, large or small, have succumbed to tyranny and have eventually been conquered. It adds that Hidalgo and Morelos "did not speak one word about a federal or central Republic," and that they shed their blood for a greater and nobler cause: ". . . only for the independence of the country." To Hidalgo and Morelos, *El Tiempo* adds Iturbide: ". . . three champions of our fatherland" . . . .

The project for a government of the wealthy and powerful classes emerges three days later: a decree to convoke an assembly which, according to the Plan de San Luis Potosí, will organize the nation, "without any limits being placed on its freedom of decision." *El Tiempo* publishes and endorses the Plan. Even when *El Tiempo* acknowledges that it has not studied the Plan with the required care—a strange confession since the decree was largely the result of Alamán's work—it confidently declares "that the proposed electoral system is the most reasonable that we have seen applied in the Republic." Because:

> For the first time property, industry and commerce are represented; for the first time the magistracy are summoned, all of the legitimate and truly representative classes and professions, to ponder the future of the country.

The decree states that the Congress will be composed of 160 deputies elected by nine classes in the following proportion:

Rural and urban property and agriculture	38
Commerce	20
Mining	14
Manufacturing	14
Literary professions	14
Magistracy	10
Public administration	10
Clergy	20
Army	20

Certain classes are given the right of direct election. In no case are there more than two steps involved in indirect elections. Within the criteria of election by classes, every effort will be made to give representation on the basis of distribution of population by Departments by giving a variable number of representatives to each class within them. The clergy would not be permitted to attend the Congress as proprietors of property in mortmain. Citizens who belonged to two or more classes would have an active and passive vote in each and could be elected by the various Departments in which they had their property or business although neither residents nor natives of them.

The key to conservative thought was the idea of class solidarity of interests. In its first issue, *El Tiempo*, after describing the horror with which clergy and property owners viewed federalism and popular assemblies, acknowledged that these classes had given a leading role to the military. That "role would have less importance if the military had not been seen as the natural ally of the proprietary class and the clergy." And it adds: "The interests of these two groups are, on the other hand, intimately tied together". . . .

THE POLEMIC OVER MONARCHY

The project for a government of the powerful and wealthy classes did not evolve beyond an idea, in part because of the imprudence of the monarchists and partly because of the interpretation that Alamán makes of Mexican history. *El Tiempo* carries on a polemic on monarchy with *El Memorial Histórico, Le Reforma, El Monitor Republicano* and *El Republicano.*

The liberal thesis proclaims the inadmissibility of monarchy as antiquated and oligarchical in character. The principal historical polemic is waged with *El Memorial. El Tiempo* defends Iturbide and condemns twenty-five years of history. Essentially, its arguments in support of monarchy stress: 1) The loss of Texas, "the threat to the Californias," and "the secession of Yucatán" stem from the form of government adopted; 2) The federal system has encouraged the intervention of the United States, because the latter, since our first Congress, "have made themselves the arbiters of our affairs. Taking advantage of our inexperience, the United States gave us forms of government contrary to our needs." 3) Since our needs are not those of the United States, their form of government is not applicable to Mexico. 4) Monarchy is not anachronous. 5) The republican form of government destroys the unity of countries and the proof lies in what is taking place in Spanish America. "The Monarchical principle, on the contrary, has the great virtue of conserving nations." 6) Monarchy would make it possible to acquire an ally with which to defend ourselves against the United States.

La Reforma, El Republicano, El Monitor, and *El Memorial* refute the historical interpretation of *El Tiempo.* On February 3, 1846, *La Reforma* attributes our ills not to the Republic, but to its lack of "purity," engendered at certain moments by conservative forces, which encourages *El Tiempo* to accuse its adversary of supporting federalism. La Reforma initiates an important argument: Mexico cannot have monarchy. Monarchy would lack "a solid foundation" because no aristocracy exists. *El Tiempo* now argues that a constitutional monarchy does not require an aristocracy of birth. On February 4, *La Reforma* recalls Gutiérrez Estrada and the repudiation of his letter. *El Tiempo* challenges this point, stating that the letter, "the product of disinterested conviction, but highly inopportune and imprudent, surprised equally friends and adversaries of the author."

Given the unpopularity of its orientation, *El Tiempo* moves skillfully. It attempts to play off the army against the Republic. If army and Republic "do not mutually exclude one another, at least it is difficult to unite them." In this manner, *El Tiempo* answers *La Reforma* which argues that army and monarchy could not be cast in the same mold in Mexico. *El Tiempo* revives [Lorenzo de] Zavala's criticism of democracy in a memorial which as governor of the State of Mexico he presented in 1833. The newspaper, in the end, seeks refuge in the freedom of the press. Before doing that, however, it had acknowledged that its adversaries were numerous "and, because of it, represented the popular party, that of the majority in the nation," a confession that the conservatives will soon forget.

The truth is that Paredes Arrillaga went far in his monarchist adventure. Gutiérrez Estrada discerned the intent from the first statement of Paredes Arrillaga:

> The manifesto that the new chief of the Republic published left no doubt about his intentions. Although leaving to a constituent assembly the authority to determine the form of government which should rule the country in the years ahead, the manifesto indicated clearly that only a monarchical form could liberate the government of anarchy . . . and provide . . . the peace it badly needs . . .

Paredes Arrillaga began his monarchical adventure without either the support of the social forces or even conservative unity. In regard to the latter, Antonio de Haro y Tamariz, a cabinet minister under Santa Anna, strongly criticizes Paredes Arrillaga and Alamán. In his opinion, the "sad politics of the belfries" have returned with them. He thinks of Alamán as a man of "ominous fame" and, not without irony, he observes that the country lacks an aristocracy to support monarchy. "The only way to improvise a powerful nobility would be to convert the generals of the Republic and other able men into dukes, barons, counts, etc. But they cannot indefinitely maintain themselves independently of the political factions and, it must be remembered, that from the moment that they no longer represent ideas and dress in the livery of courtesans, they would be without influence and power in every sense."

Therefore, monarchy could not prosper. Already by May 20 the Guadalajara garrison had rebelled. It declared that Paredes Arrillaga's decree convoking an assembly was contrary to the sovereignty of the nation and in pursuit of monarchy. On the 4th of August General Mariano Salas revolted in the capital with the Plan de la Ciudadela and federalism was quickly reinstated . . .

THE CONSERVATIVE HISTORICAL INTERPRETATION

The monarchical principles of the conservatives remain substantially unaltered in the coming years. *El Heraldo* and *El Universal* repeat basically the same arguments. The latter, nevertheless, places greater emphasis on the idea of an equilibrium of powers, on the need to introduce a force to check the powerful influence of the United States, an argument that took root after the war [of 1846–1848]. *El Universal,* which first appears on November 16, 1848, sustains a polemic with *El Siglo Diecinueve* and *El Monitor Republicano* and makes impossible the coexistence of conservative and liberal ideas with the charter of 1824 and the reform of 1847. This is apparent in the government of Herrera. But in its political ideas, *El Universal* adopts a refrain: our conflicts and problems have made Mexico "the toy of the *sister* Republic." It repeats the phrase again and again.

El Universal, however, learns from the experience of *El Tiempo,* and is much more cautious in the presentation of its monarchist plans. Actually, the liberal newspapers, such as *El Monitor,* are the ones that call the conservatives monarchists. Still, the monarchist leanings of *El Universal* emerge clearly. Its anti-federalism is obvious. Far from denying it, *El Monitor* reiterates it systematically.

Alamán is the soul of *El Universal.* He recognizes the need to give the conservative party a body of doctrine and a special interpretation of Mexican history. In terms of the former, the conservative party is described as "the party of order," the antithesis of the oscillations of Mexico; furthermore, a flexible definition of the conservative party is adopted. ". . . The conservative party is that body which wants to preserve as sacred tradition: religion, property, the family, authority, rational liberty, in summary, the essential fundamentals of any well-organised society." Of course, the definition also includes antifederalism and the negation of the liberalism of the charter of 1824 and the amendment of 1847. *El Universal* is bold in regard to the second point, that of giving the history of Mexico a conservative interpretation. On September 16, 1849, *El Universal* makes two basic interpretations of the history of Mexico. First, the 16th of September of 1810 "was not the first day of our political existence nor was the Grito de Dolores the origin of independence." Secondly, Iturbide, "the enemy of insurgents but a friend of independence, completed the huge task—with the support of the true principles. . . ." Consequently, Mexico owes its independence to "the men of the conservative party." Further: "The cause of independence prevailed because it was necessary that it triumph." Its result: the tragedy of Mexico . . . .

Shortly thereafter *El Universal* . . . publishes, apropos the Grito de Dolores, a series of articles to clarify what it meant to say on September 16, entitled "The Vindication of History and of the Independence of Mexico." The argument is crudely and impolitically presented:

> Our article published on the last 16th day of September had no
> other project than to remove from our interpretation of history a
> wrong that, in our opinion, has been done to it, and to credit to
> it among its most glorious accomplishments the Grito de Dolores
> and the insurrection that followed. It was also our intention to
> remove from the independence of Mexico the stain of having had
> a cradle unworthy of its name and its glory.

The impolitical historical thesis completes the parable: the
conservatives made independence a reality in order that the liberalism of the mother country not enter the colony. At the time of
independence the conservatives were not able to find a foreign
monarch, and the course of succeeding events led them to one conclusion. In the days of the colony, its component parts, with the
mother country's help, remained strong. If in independence the
colonial forces cannot maintain and impose themselves, then help
for them must be found abroad. The defense of Iturbide and, consequently, of a conservative independence under a monarch, offers
historical roots to the political program—if the antecedents that
led to the War of Independence are denied.

3

The lengthy dictatorship of Porfirio Díaz spans the period between
1876 and 1911. Unique in the history of nineteenth-century Mexico
for its ability to provide peace and order, the dictatorship confronted the Liberal politicians of the time and particularly the
científicos, Díaz' inner circle of advisers, with the need to justify
a national program that neglected the poor on behalf of national
development. Their justification or rationale, a concoction of Auguste Comte's positivism mixed freely with ideas taken from Spencer and Mill, is the subject of the next essay. Leopoldo Zea is a
distinguished Mexican historian and an authority on positivism.
Zea explains why the Liberals in the days of Juárez accepted the
doctrine and what eventually corrupted, to the detriment of the
majority, not merely the theory but its disciples.

Leopoldo Zea:
Positivism*

THE POSITIVIST GENERATION

The fruits of positivist education directed to the political order made themselves felt immediately. Porfirio Díaz had risen to power after a revolution which unseated the heir of the exalted Benito Juárez, President Sebastián Lerdo de Tejada. By 1878 there arose in the capital of Mexico a new political group which made its voice and its ideas heard in a periodical entitled *La Libertad* and which carried the Comtean banner "Order and Progress." A number of its editors had been students under Gabino Barreda or had been formed in the system of education which he had established under the reforms introduced by President Benito Juárez in 1867.

This new group began to stir up public opinion about one idea, that of *order*. However, theirs was a new type of order which resembled in no feature the colonial order which had been broken by the liberal triumph, a new kind of order which was not the order upheld by the conservativism which had been annihilated on the hill of the Campanas. The new group called itself conservative; however, a liberal conservatism. Our purpose, it declared, is liberty; however, our methods of achieving liberty are conservative. We are before all else conservators of order as an instrument for the achievement of authentic liberty, which is not, cannot be, the anarchy which weighed upon the country for half a century. They called themselves conservatives because their methods were contrary to all other methods for attaining liberty. Liberty, they held, is achieved by way of the free natural development of which [Gabino] Barreda spoke and which his disciples called evolution. Not revolution, but evolution. This is change in accordance with laws within a determined order.

What is urgent for the achievement of an authentic liberty is the establishment of an order which makes that liberty possible. This is what Mexican liberals had not been able to understand and still did not understand. They had tried to give the people liberties

* From Leopoldo Zea, POSITIVISM, A. Robert Caponigri, ed., *Major Trends in Mexican Philosophy* (Notre Dame and London: University of Notre Dame Press, 1966), pp. 231–245.

for which they were not ready; the result had been anarchy. The
first thing was to educate, to create in the mind a knowledge of liberty and of the obligations which liberty implies. So long as Mexicans did not have this knowledge, all utopian laws and constitutions would be useless, alien to the reality of the situation. The
liberal constitutions and laws these must be, were not capable of
creating the liberty of which they spoke; theirs was a simple-minded
utopianism, proper to minds without a sense of reality, without a
practical direction of spirit.

Finally, however, thanks to the educational reforms of positivism, there had arisen a generation capable of directing the nation along the best roads, a practical generation, positive, realistic.
The generation about to come to power would establish the social
order from which would arise the liberties which the liberals had
ineffectively pretended to establish. This was a generation capable
of creating the bases of a democratic government resting upon authentic social freedom. Meanwhile, as this generation was creating
those bases, the important thing was *order*, the political and social
order which would make possible, in the near future, the dreamed-
of liberal government. It was necessary to put an end to widespread
anarchy, which continued despite the triumph of liberalism over
colonial conservatism. There stood as the principal obstacle to the
abolishment of anarchy the liberal Constitution of 1857. The ideal
liberty advocated by that Constitution could be reached only after
the creation of the habits and customs which would give it life
within each Mexican. Before that it was impossible of fulfillment.

What most makes one indignant, wrote Francisco G. Cosmes,
one of the editors of *La Libertad,* is that there still exist men of
such retarded mentality that they still believe in the ideas maintained by the legislators of 1857:

> after half a century of constant struggle for an ideal which,
> once attained, had produced only lamentable results for the
> country, it is a cause of great sadness, in truth, to see that while
> the atrocious wounds which the revolutions and the civil war
> have inflicted upon the Republic are still bleeding, the revolution-
> ary ideal still finds among us those who defend it.

And Justo Sierra, director of the same journal, wrote in criticism of the constitution-makers of 1857:

> Our fundamental law, made by men of the Latin race who be-
> lieve that a thing is certain and realizable since it is logical;
> who try to make human, brusquely and by violence, any ideal
> whatsoever; who pass in one day from the domain of the abso-
> lute to that of the relative, without transitions and without

shadings of color, and seek to force people to practice what is
true only in the domain of pure reason—these men (perhaps we
are of their number) who confuse heaven and earth, made for
us a noble and elevated code of alliance, but one in which everything tends to diffusion, to the autonomy of the individual raised
to the highest degree, that is to say, to the stage at which it
would seem that the force of social duties ceases and everything
is converted into rights of individuals.

Utopia must come to an end. A new period of history was approaching, a realistic period directed toward an order whose final
term would be the realization of that which had only been a mere
utopia. Toward this end would march the forces of the new generation, a generation conscious of its historical mission. No longer
following Comte, but rather Darwin and Spencer, this generation
would maintain the necessity of strengthening Mexicans for the
struggle for life and for passing from the military era, the era of
order, to the industrial era, the era of work and of the triumph of
the individual.

To utopian and anarchistic liberalism there had to be opposed
a realistic liberalism, a liberalism of order, a conservative liberalism. We desire, said Justo Sierra,

the formation of a great conservative party, composed of all the
elements of order that in our country possess the capacity of
rising to public life. We do not carry as our banner a person,
but an idea. We plan to gather about it all those who think that
in our country the period of seeking to realize its aspirations by
revolutionary violence is over, all those who think that the
definitive moment has now arrived for organizing a party more
devoted to *practical* than to *declamatory* liberty, and are profoundly convinced that progress resides in the normal development of a society, that is to say, in order. . . .

"We do not carry as our banner a person, but an idea"; in
these words was enclosed the ideal of the new order, an order
whose force did not depend upon the will of a "caudillo," but an
impersonal order derived from the very minds of Mexicans. However, this order remained, for the moment at least, one more utopia.
Above all it was necessary to educate the people for such an order.
In the meantime any kind of order would be good. The problem
seemed insoluble: one sought to abandon an order which depended
on the will of a "caudillo"; nevertheless, someone of sufficient personal prestige was needed to lay the bases of the new order. This
"someone," of course, would be nothing else but a simple instrument, something transitory until Mexicans could acquire the mental

habits necesary for an autonomous order, that is an order free from any force external to it.

For the moment it was necessary to limit liberties which were manifestly utopian. It was necessary to create confidence in the country, the only path along which it might initiate a process of regeneration:

> Rights! [exclaimed Francisco G. Cosmes] Society already has rejected them; what is necessary is bread. In place of these constitutions filled with sublime ideas, not one of which have we seen realized in practice . . . I would prefer peace, in whose shade or shelter it would be possible to work tranquilly, with some security for its interests and to know that, instead of launching themselves into the hunt, the flight, of the ideal, the authorities would hang the exploiters, the thieves, and the revolutionaries. Fewer rights and fewer liberties, in exchange for greater order and peace. No more utopias. I want order and peace, even at the price of all the rights which have cost me so dearly. And more, [he went on] the day is not distant when the country will say, I want order and peace even at the price of my independence.

How to achieve this order and peace for which they called out in such urgent need? Not by means of arbitrariness, they said; not by way of the governments of persons which have been so harmful to the country.

> There is nothing more odious [said an editorial in *La Libertad*] or more contrary to progress among us than the dominion of one, or several, men without "regla fija." That is what we think about dictatorship.

Nevertheless, the Mexican reality, the state of affairs, had given rise to dictatorships, to tyrannies. To have done with them, it is necessary to transform that reality. Meanwhile, however, one has to put up with it. In order "to have done with dictatorship in fact . . . we must establish a practicable constitution"; however, since that is impractical in the prevailing circumstances, "we are content to seek extraordinary authorizations for these extraordinary circumstances." And Francisco G. Cosmes said in another of his articles:

> We have already realized an infinity of rights which produce only misery and distress in society. Now we are going to try a bit of honorable tyranny to see what effect it might produce.

This "honorable" tyranny would prove to be that of General Porfirio Díaz.

FROM COMTE TO SPENCER

The generation educated by Gabino Barreda, that of men who were going to lead the destinies of the nation along the road of progress, would find itself too confined within the limits of Comtian positivism. This doctrine, no matter how hard Barreda had tried, could not justify the kind of liberty which might have the greatest interest for the future Mexican bourgeoisie, the liberty to enrich itself, with no limits save those of the capacity of each individual. Comtianism, in the strict sense, subordinated the individual to society in all the fields of material good. This was the meaning of the "sociocracy" of Comte; such is what his positive politics would establish. Comte's politics, like the religion of humanity, had not been accepted by the Mexican positivists because they considered them contrary to the interests for which positivism itself had been accepted. The important thing was to form the directing class of the Mexican bourgeoisie, which was more and more powerful as time passed. The model to which this class should conform was offered by the Anglo-Saxon countries.

The theoreticians of the Mexican bourgeoisie very soon found a theory which might justify their interests. This was offered by the English positivists John Stuart Mill and Herbert Spencer, especially the latter, and, with them, by the evolutionism of Charles Darwin. This doctrine seemed most completely to coincide with the interests which needed to be justified. These men were, moreover, the highest expression of that practical spirit which the Mexicans so much admired. According to these doctrines it was necessary to educate the Mexican people. English positivism, far from opposing the idea of individual freedom in the greatest number of its expressions, justified it. The great examples of this fact were the liberal regimes in England and in the United States: Spencer opposed the coercive state, and Mill defended individual liberty. In the theory of both the state proved to be nothing else than what [José María Luis] Mora desired: an instrument of protection for all and each of the individuals who made up the society. Even more, the Spencerian idea of progress would make it possible to offer, at least for the future, an ideal of liberty, that for which the people had struggled on different occasions. To establish this promise it was necessary only to make a determined degree of progress.

And here we return to make connection with the group of young positivists who, from the pages of the periodical *La Libertad*, demanded a new order and aspired to establish an honorable dictatorship. This group no longer followed Comte, but rather Mill and Spencer. How then could they justify ideas which seemed to be contradictory? They would find this justification in Spencer's idea of evolution. The fact would seem to him beyond doubt, Sierra would say, that society is an organism which, though different from others (the reason why Spencer called it a superorganism), has undeniable analogies with living organisms. Equally with animal organisms, society is subject to laws of evolution. In accordance with these laws, all organisms realize a movement toward integration and differentiation in a process which goes from the homogeneous to the heterogeneous, from the indefinite to the definite. In the social organisms the movement is from social homogeneity to individual differentiation, from complete order to complete liberty.

In this form the idea which the older liberals had held about liberty was not denied; what was denied on the basis of the *Principles of Sociology* of Spencer was that Mexican society had reached the high level of progress which was necessary to obtain that freedom. These men did not think, as had the Comtians, that this freedom belonged to a stage of metaphysical transition; rather, they were convinced that it was a goal to be achieved. It is not something *past*, but something in the *future*. In order, however, that such a condition might come about, it is necessary first that society should *evolve* in that direction. For this reason the new conservatives opposed the Constitution of 1857, considering it utopian, that is, outside its proper place in time. Such constitutions can be good only for countries like the United States, given the high degree of progress they had achieved, not in countries like Mexico, which found themselves at an inferior stage of development. "Is it not against good sense," they asked, "to raise a mighty edifice upon muddy ground without first casting solid foundations?"

The first thing to be done was to look to the material future of the country. Liberties are useless in a materially depressed country. When that future is reached, liberty in its many forms will come about by addition, by natural evolution.

> The day when we are able to say that the basic charter has procured us a million freeholders, we will have found the constitution which is suitable for us; then it will no longer be a word on our lips, but a plough in our hands: the locomotive on the track and money in everyone's pocket. Freedom of ideas will come. We prefer normal and slow progress to precipitating matters by violence.

These men stood for progress by way of evolution, not revolution. The urgent, the immediate thing to be done is to strengthen society, to integrate and to homogenize it. To the degree that society becomes integrated, becomes homogeneous, the more will it become differentiated and defined. To the degree that social order becomes more permanent, the more will individual liberty take form. Up to this time, the positivists thought, Mexico had been a land without order and, therefore, a land which had not complied with the laws of progress as revealed by Spencer. For this reason it is necessary, before all else, to establish order. It is not possible to go from anarchy to true freedom.

Now the demand for a strong state becomes natural and justified, a state which would assume the task of setting up the order so necessary for the progress of Mexico. Now it becomes natural, as Justo Sierra says, "for a people . . . who exist in the most miserable conditions of life, to seek the invigorating force of a center which would serve to increase the power of cohesion." Otherwise, "to the contrary, incoherence will become every day more pronounced, the organism will not integrate, and the nation will be aborted." It is disorder, Sierra goes on, which makes of the Mexican nation one of the most feeble and most defenseless social organisms within the orbit of civilization. While Mexico goes on destroying itself, "there lives alongside us a marvelous collective animal, for whose enormous intestine there does not exist alimentation enough and which is armed and ready to devour us." Before this colossus we are exposed "to being a proof of Darwin's theory, and in the struggle for existence we will find all possibilities against us."

POSITIVISM AND THE REGIME OF PORFIRIO DÍAZ

"Political evolution," the evolution of liberty in the field of politics, was to be sacrificed on the altar of what Sierra used to call "social evolution." That is, on the altar of the social evolution of the Mexicans, indispensable in order to arrive at that supposed political liberty, all this liberty was to be limited. To uproot the habits of disorder from the mind of the Mexican was a very difficult task.

> Unfortunately, [Sierra said] these congenital habits of the
> Mexican have come to be a thousand times more difficult to up-
> root than the domination and the privileged classes it es-
> tablished. Only the progress in the conditions of work and of
> thought in Mexico would be able to bring about so great a
> transformation.

Only a strong state would be able to bring about such a change.

On the day a group or party succeeded in maintaining itself as an organized body political evolution would continue on its march.

> And the man, more necessary in democracies than in aristocracies, would emerge; the function would create the organ.

All political power, and with it the freedom of Mexicans, would be turned over to a strong man, to General Porfirio Díaz.

> In order that the President [Sierra continues] might be able to bring to completion the great task which he has taken on his shoulders, he needs the very greatest concentration of power in his hands, not only legal authority but *political authority* as well, which would permit him to assume the effective direction of the political bodies, legislative bodies, and governments of the states; of *social* authority, constituting himself supreme judge of peace in Mexican society by general assent! . . . and of *moral authority*.

However, all of these delegations and abdications of power to one man had to be compensated by the action of the state in the field so important to the leaders of mental emancipation: education. The honored tyranny was an educative form by means of which the Mexicans were going to learn the meaning of freedom.

On November 26, 1876, General Porfirio Díaz, who had risen in arms against the government of Sebastián Lerdo de Tejada under the cry of "no re-election," made himself interim president after the triumph of his troops. On December 5 of the same year he ceded power to General Méndez, but reassumed it, provisionally, on February 16, 1877. On September 25, 1880, with his consent, General Manuel González was elected; however, in 1884 Díaz returned definitively to the Presidency in which office he was to remain until May 25, 1911, on the triumph of the Mexican Revolution. About General Díaz were grouped all of the political forces of the country. His figure came to symbolize that peace and order for which the men brought up in positivism had clamored so loudly. Materialism and dehumanization were converted into models of life by the generation which was formed during his regime: industry, money, railroads—and always more money. Progress seemed to triumph definitively. Social evolution seemed to march forward with giant steps; however, in this euphoria there was forgotten that for the achievement of which, so it was claimed, order had been established: freedom. They conformed to a very special kind of freedom: the freedom of enrichment. It was a freedom in which not all classes could participate.

The absence of authentic liberty, Sierra was to protest, had necessarily brought about the abortion of everything that had been gained in the field of evolution.

A new type of Mexican arose with "porfirism," who, by comparison with the liberal generation which had preceded, described themselves in the following manner:

> We are charged [they said] with our lack of beliefs, with our positivism, our poorly hidden disdain for the institutions of the past. All that is true; however, it is due to the different education which we have received. You [they went on with reference to the liberals] nourished yourselves in philosophical matters on Voltaire and Rousseau, on the Encyclopedists, on the "Choix de Rapports" of the French Revolution, and the most advanced among you, in the lofty metaphysics of the German school, while we study logic in Mill and Bain, philosophy in Comte and Spencer, science with Huxley and Tyndall, Virchow and Helmholtz.

A different education would produce men equally different.

> You [they continued] came out of the lecture rooms drunk with enthusiasm for the great ideas of 1789 and, citing Danton and the Girondonists, hurled yourselves at the mountains in order to combat the clergy, consolidate reforms, demolish the reactionaries, and outline our laws upon the beautiful utopias which were then current in philosophical transactions. We, by contrast, less enthusiastic, more skeptical, maybe more egotistical, seek a new explication of the binomial theorem, dedicate ourselves to natural selection, study sociology with enthusiasm, concern ourselves little with the celestial spaces, but a great deal about our earthly destiny. We concern ourselves with questions which cannot be submitted to the slide rule of observation and experience. The part of the world which interests us is that part which we must study by means of the telescope and other instruments of scientific investigation. We do not know the truth, needless to say, at first sight. In order to come to it we must make long voyages to the regions of *science;* we must give ourselves to arduous and constant labors, to laborious and patient investigation.

The new generation considered itself destined, by reason of its capacity, to guide and direct the country. Its methods were sure, perfect, and precise. They were the methods of science, those they learned in the schools as Gabino Barreda had reformed them. Those methods, they said, would be applied to the solution of all the problems of Mexico, including its political problems. In 1881 they were already speaking in Mexico of the "scientific school of politics." In 1886 a number of its members entered the Chamber of Deputies. Some of them were to become outstanding figures in the regime of Porfirio Díaz: Justo Sierra, Pablo Macedo, Rosendo Pineda, Francisco Bulnes, and others. All of them, together, would impress their mark on the period which is known by the name of "porfirism." There began the era of the "scientists."

POLITICAL ORDER AND ECONOMIC FREEDOM

In 1892 the political party called "Union Liberal" issued a manifesto in support of the fourth re-election of Porfirio Díaz. In it was formulated a program intended to satisfy the interests of the ever-more powerful Mexican bourgeoisie. It spoke of analyzing the Mexican social situation, its problems, and their solutions from a scientific point of view. For this reason the opposition and the mass of the people in general, whose political rights had been trodden underfoot for all practical purposes, began to call that party by the disrespectful and ironic title "Party of the Scientists."

The manifesto also spoke, among other things, about the necessity of conceding greater liberties to Mexican society, since Mexico seemed to have reached a higher level of progress. It seemed that at last the promised freedoms were to be granted. Earlier it had been necessary to grant a greater power to the executive; at this moment, however, it seemed that the hour had come to grant greater liberties to the people. . . .

Recalling the slogans of the old liberal party, this new union believed that liberty is not possible until a certain level of order has been attained. Now, however, this order seemed to be an achieved fact, thanks to the government of Porfirio Díaz. With order established it would be possible to take a further step in the achievement of liberty. What would this step be?

> We believe the moment has arrived to begin a new era in the
> historical life of our party [says the Union]; we believe that
> the transformation of its directive organs into organs of govern-
> ment has already been achieved; we believe that just as peace
> and material progress have achieved this end, it's now the task
> of political action, in turn, to consolidate order, it behooves it to
> demonstrate that from this day forward revolt and civil war can
> only be an accident and that peace, based on the interests of the
> will of a people, is the normal state. For that reason it is nec-
> essary to establish peace as the cornerstone of liberty.

With this increase of liberties it would become possible to decide whether or not Mexican society had attained that level of order necessary to obtain still greater liberties. The new political party proposed a series of liberties for which it thought the Mexican people had now become ready; however, among them electoral liberty is not to be found because it was thought neither important nor opportune. The people could have other liberties more important than that.

> The nation [the manifesto adds] would desire that its government might find itself in a position to demonstrate that it considers the present peace as a definitive state of affairs by the economic reorganization of certain branches of the Administration. . . . It would desire that national *freedom of commerce* might, through the suppression of internal tariffs, be established as fact and no longer be but an aspiration periodically renewed. . . . Only in this way will peace be assured to future generations of Mexicans, whose resources have been tapped to create our credit and our progress, the means of continuing that progress and even of *accumulating a reserve of capital* which might be transformed into greater well-being and vigor. In such conditions peace would never appear costly.

What does all this mean? It is asserted that greater liberties must be granted, but immediately it is said that electoral or political liberty is the least important among them. What is immediately sought is freedom of trade and, more inclusively, an economic liberty which would permit the accumulation and formation of capital. What is sought is the reduction of the interventions of the state in the economic field, not in the political area. Political liberty is betrayed or sacrificed in exchange for liberty of enrichment, a liberty, obviously, which could only benefit those who possessed resources capable of being incremented. It can be seen, consequently, that there was no question of granting the kind of liberty which had been of interest to the older Mexican liberals.

Political order and economic freedom: such is the ideal of the Mexican bourgeoisie. Political order, maintained by General Díaz, was to be placed at the service of the economic freedom of the bourgeoisie. As far as political rights were concerned, the bourgeoisie would reserve its power to demand them only for the occasion on which an attempt might be made against the freedom of enrichment. Political freedom, the right to the election of the governors, could be limited for the good of an order which satisfied the interests of the Mexican bourgeoisie, and since the government of General Díaz insured peace, its re-election was necessary.

In this way the bourgeois order identified itself with national order, and the bourgeois party with the people. With national order achieved, it would be necessary to ensure the liberty which served its interests. Díaz was the man called upon to concede this liberty and to see that it was not obstructed.

> The Republic [the manifesto says] is aware that it is the efficient
> cause of its progress and tranquillity; however, it also knows
> that a certain man has collaborated in the first stage in giving
> practical form to general tendencies, and he is the citizen whom
> the convention has elected to occupy the Presidency again.

The authors of the manifesto affirm that if he is being re-elected for the fourth time, it is not because he is considered an indispensable man, but rather because in his previous three terms he had given proof of his capacity to govern in accordance with the interests of the nation. In this manner the bourgeoisie had succeeded in making of Porfirio Díaz the "honored tyrant" who would satisfy its interests. For this reason it had supported him and would continue to support him so long as he remained so. From the beginning the theoreticians of the bourgeoisie had distinguished between what they called "personal dictatorship" and "social dictatorship." The first was of the type of dictatorships of which Mora had spoken, that type which serves the interests of a determined group or social body, such as the clergy or the military. The second was, simply, the dictatorship established to protect what the bourgeoisie called the interests of society, that is, its own interests.

For his part, Porfirio Díaz, a power-oriented man with a mentality similar to the kind which the educators of the bourgeoisie had sought to extirpate, was not satisfied to be a mere instrument of the bourgeoisie. He rejected the limits which it sought to impose on him, so far as his political power was concerned. He was not disposed, consequently, to maintain the order which suited the Mexican bourgeoisie, but rather demanded the total transfer of that power to himself.

Justo Sierra, with the genial intuition which made him outstanding among the members of his generation, understood that this delegation of political liberties to the person of the dictator was dangerous, "terribly dangerous for the future because it *imposes* habits contrary to those of self-government, without which one may have great men, but not great peoples." And he vowed that at this crossroad of its historical life the Mexican people would not err.

4

Most historians believe that the Revolution of 1910 stemmed from rural unrest. In their opinion the Revolution represents an agrarian movement. Among the minority that dissents from this view is Francisco Bulnes, a *científico* of the Díaz era who was also a scholar-intellectual known for his unorthodox interpretations. Bulnes wrote prolifically on the old regime and on the Revolution. He rejected the opinion that the agrarian policies of Díaz led to the upheaval of 1911. In his version an ambitious and growing urban middle class, the product of the *Porfiriato*, ignited the flames of the holocaust. He denied that Díaz had deliberately robbed the poor of their lands. The problem of Mexico, he insisted, lay not in the agrarian program of the dictatorship but in the scarcity of arable land. Does contemporary Mexico's continuing "agrarian problem" support the validity of at least a part of Bulnes' theory?

Francisco Bulnes:
The Whole Truth About
Mexico*

MARVELLOUS LANDS AND GRASPING LANDHOLDERS

Don Luis Cabrera has rightly said: *"La Revolución es la Revolución"* (A revolution is a revolution), which is only another way of saying what has been said before: *"Pour faire une omelette il faut casser les œufs"*; and what has been shattered beyond the power of belief is the unfortunate Mexican people. But apparently this tremendous work of destruction, carried on with the aid of crime, war, dementia, the spirit of vengeance, the appetite for pillage and all the repugnant, antisocial traits of prehistoric sav-

* From Francisco Bulnes, THE WHOLE TRUTH ABOUT MEXICO; PRESIDENT WILSON'S RESPONSIBILITY (New York, 1916), pp. 36–41, 43–45, 48, 51–54, 76–81, 96–99.

agery, seems to be of little consequence if in the end the indigenous race be raised—even over the terror-stricken, bleeding and agonizing remnants of the nation—to a height capable of conferring upon its country an enviable renown, the race itself flourishing in the maternal bosom of the "Republic of Solidarity."

The revolutionists have defined the agrarian question in the following terms. . . .

First—That Mexico possesses in great abundance marvellous agricultural lands capable of feeding, even to excess, an enormous population of one hundred million, according to some; of two hundred millions, according to others, and of even more, according to those who more closely approximate in intelligence the inferior vertebrates.

Second—That these mavellous lands are not actively cultivated, owing to the fact that they are monopolized by a handful of cruel landowners who hold them undeveloped, in order to keep up the price of necessary commodities and enjoy the enormous gains obtained through the monopoly of the land, which once belonged to the Indians and which was stolen from them by the Spanish conquerors.

Such is the fundamental basis of the social upheaval which has submerged Mexico and brought it into such unenviable prominence before the nations of the world.

Before discussing the important and far-reaching problems emanating from the revolutionary proposition, it is necessary to examine it calmly and dispassionately, and subject it to an intelligent analysis.

THE FIRST LIE

A formidable fact exists in our economic life which destroys the spectacular foundation of the Mexican Revolution. For more than twenty years past the fiscal statistics, published monthly and annually by the Mexican Treasury Department, show a yearly increase in the importation of corn and wheat from the United States or the Argentine. These importations are greater when more or less serious failures in the corn and wheat crops occur in Mexico. . . .

This proves that not even in the years when the yield of corn and wheat has been greatest in Mexico has the output been sufficient for the needs of its inhabitants, from which fact it may be deduced that Mexico has had more than twenty years' experience of the impotency of her lands to contribute enough for the support of her population.

In order to bolster up the lie of the great richness of Mexico's corn-raising lands, the revolutionists assert that this impotence is intentional, brought about by the avariciousness of the landholders, who, wishing to keep up the prices, cultivate only a limited area, insufficient to meet the national demands.

Such an accusation is absurd, as will presently be seen. According to the agricultural statistics published by the Department of Fomento, the annual production of corn varies in the best seasons from 50,000,000 to 60,000,000 hectolitres, and if the lands which produce these had the wonderful fertility attributed to them in 1803 by Baron Humboldt (75 hectolitres per hectare) it would be necessary to cultivate only 800,000 hectares to produce 60,000,000 kilograms of corn; and as in Mexico one man is required for the cultivation of every 5 hectares of land, it follows that if the marvellously fertile lands of 1803 existed at present, the grasping landholders would employ only 160,000 day laborers. By what means have the remaining 1,800,000 lived, who make up the sum total of our day laborers and who are accounted for in the agricultural statistics issued by the Department of Fomento?

Is the official figure of the number of day laborers engaged in the cultivation of corn and wheat given by the Department incorrect, or are there actually only 160,000? If two-thirds of these laborers are heads of families, and each family consists on an average of five persons, and if there are only 160,000 day laborers engaged in the cultivation of corn, it follows that Mexico does not possess 12,000,000 poor inhabitants, but merely a laboring population of 4,000,000.

In order that 2,000,000 families may live from the product of the land set aside for corn-raising, it is indispensable that the yield be very small in order to afford an opportunity to employ 2,000,000 men in the maximum production of 60,000,000 hectolitres.

THE RÉGIME OF MISERY IN MEXICO

In Mexico there are three distinct divisions of land: the hot lands; the temperate lands and the cold lands of the central plateau, and the semi-arid lands of the northern plateau. The majority of the Mexican population is found grouped upon the central plateau, for reasons which will later be explained. Agriculture will not flourish where water is not available, and nations, which do not command large capital for the construction of the necessary irrigation plants in the arid regions, are driven to depend in their agricultural work upon the more or less uncertain rainfall.

In Mexico this factor plays an important part, and may be considered the key to the nation's problem of poverty and misery.

Unfortunately, physical conditions in Mexico are such as to present grave obstacles to the progress of civilization and the improvement of the people's condition, along lines possible in other countries.

THE HIGH-WATER MARK OF THE RÉGIME OF MISERY. . . .

In short, deducting from the Mexican territory the sections occupied by the great mountain chains and their branch ranges (which are considerable), the gorges, the ravines, the sloping lands, the immense desert tracts (which have no, or scarcely no, rainfall), the extensive grazing lands and the summer stubble pasture lands of the central plateau, there remain available for the cultivation of cereal or leguminous products the 10,000,000 hectares of land, designated by the report of the Department of Fomento, and further confirmed by data furnished by agricultural corporations and political and administrative associations.

A country whose entire area consists of 200,000,000 hectares, of which only 10,000,000 can be claimed for the cultivation of products suitable for human consumption, cannot be considered an overwhelmingly rich country, scarcely even moderately rich. A country which can count only upon five per cent of its lands to produce the elements from which its population must directly draw its life, cannot be considered otherwise than distinctly poor in this respect.

THE DEATH AGONY OF THE MEXICAN PEOPLE

A people situated as is the Mexican people, with only 10,000,-000 hectares of lands capable of producing cereal or leguminous products, will be prosperous or wretched according to the efforts expended upon its arable section. In France the production is under intensive cultivation 45 hectolitres per hectare of corn, and 10,-000,000 hectares of productive land would under intensive cultivation produce 450,000,000 hectolitres of corn annually, besides at least one-fourth as much in beans, which can be raised in the same furrow with corn. Corn, combined with beans, constitutes for a people depending upon it for their sustenance, an absolutely healthy, hygienic and highly nutritious food. Consequently, the people possessing 10,000,000 hectares of arable land suitable for the production of cereal and leguminous products, can maintain a population of 90,000,000 in a region where propitious conditions exist. The Mexican people, on the other hand, numbering only 15,000,000 and possessing 10,000,000 hectares of arable land, in great part almost exhausted and, consequently, meagre in its yield, is nothing more than a people in the last stages of dissolution.

Baron Humboldt, in his *Ensayo Político sobre la Nueva España*, based upon careful and conscientious computation, assures us that in 1803 the average yield of the arable lands was 150 grains of corn for every grain sown, which represents 75 hectolitres of corn harvested per hectare.

In the *Boletín Mensual de la Secretaría de Fomento*, for February, 1912, published by the Mexican Government, there appears the report of the *Cámara Nacional Agrícola de León* (state of Guanajuato), rendered to the Department of Fomento, in which it is stated that the average production of the famous lands of the Bajio has fallen to 8 hectolitres per hectare. I cannot at this moment recall whether it is in No. 3 or No. 4 of the said bulletin that the average of these corn lands for the year 1910 is given, showing a fluctuation of from 8 to 10 hectolitres per hectare.

From these figures, which are not those of the Mexican demagogues, the subsidized newspapers, the mediocre statesmen or the lay apostle devoid of learning, some idea may be formed of the miserable plight of the Mexican people in 1915. If the lands set aside for the cultivation of corn in 1803 yielded, on account of their remarkable fertility, 75 hectolitres per hectare, and if these same lands yielded only 8 to 10 hectolitres per hectare in 1910, it is evident that if the Mexican people continue to depend upon extensive agriculture for their maintenance, their total annihilation by starvation is near at hand. This is all the more certain if we take into consideration that in 1803 the Mexican population was only 5,000,000, whereas now it is 15,000,000, three times more, indicating a serious situation for the people if the decrease in the productiveness of the land continues at the present alarming rate.

It will not be necessary for this decrease in productiveness to reach its lowest limit to accomplish the complete annihilation of the Mexican people. It will suffice for the production to be reduced to 3 hectolitres per hectare to deprive the laborer's family of the means of subsistence; and it will surely incapacitate the laborer for his work, because of the lack of proper nourishment, if the production be reduced to 2 hectolitres per hectare.

The salvation of the Mexican people is easy in theory. It will suffice to have them pass from extensive to intensive agricultural methods, not an easy or practical achievement, and virtually an impossible one in the limited time that the alarming decrease in the productiveness of the land makes imperative.

From the foregoing data it will be seen that the Mexican agrarian problem cannot be solved by the mere distribution of lands which in a very short time will be practically worthless. The agrarian problem consists in something far more difficult—the creation of lands for the people. The distribution of the lands for the continuance of extensive agriculture would be more harmful for the Mexican people than if they were retained by the landholders, as I shall presently show. . . .

MEXICO ALWAYS A FAMINE-STRICKEN NATION

The irregular rainfall has been the cause of Mexico's almost chronic state of starvation, even in the days when its wonderfully fertile lands could have sustained a population fifty times greater than that which Mexico had after the Conquest, when the Colonial Government had established a civilizing tranquillity.

All honest persons who plead for pity for the Mexican Indian, who applaud the immolation of two or three millions of Mexico's inhabitants on the altar dedicated to the uplift of the indigenous race, all foreign and national statesmen who consider it their duty to intervene in "the Mexican question," are in honor bound to read the following lines, relative to Mexico, written by Baron Humboldt: "We have yet to examine the physical causes which almost periodically check the natural increase of the Mexican population. These are smallpox, that dread disease called *matlazahuatl* by the natives, and *above all famine,* the effects of which are felt for a long time afterwards." . . .

By the reading of Baron Humboldt's book (the only student who ever wrote realities about Mexico), the statesman, even though he be mediocre—and for him the reading becomes a duty—will reach the conclusion that the Mexican people in 1803 were already a people long used to the ravages of famine, presenting the truly sad spectacle of a nation which in three centuries had barely doubled its meager population of 2,000,000 existing at the time that the stable Colonial Government replaced the period of Conquest. And these conditions existed notwithstanding its immense territory (New Spain comprised also the states of Texas, New Mexico, Arizona and California), which afforded ample lands for cultivation and for the maintenance of more than 100,000,000 human beings.

As it is manifestly impossible for a constitutionally starved people to be a rich people, the oft-reiterated statement of Mexico's great natural agricultural wealth, outside the warm zone, has been a lie fabricated by Mexicans, not by Baron Humboldt.

The joint action of three leading factors, the irregularity of the rains, the frosts and the impoverishment of the arable lands by centuries of extensive agriculture, has brought about an intolerable condition.

By way of illustration, let us take 1,000 hectares of land as good as some that is to be found in the Valle del Suchil and that of las Poanas in Durango, which in a good year are capable of yielding as much as 200 hectolitres of corn per hectare. The cost of working a hectare of Mexican land by the extensive method of cultivation is scarcely 20 pesos, including such items as rent, general expenses, taxes, interest on capital invested, and a good profit for the planter. This, however, is the cost of cultivation of one hectare of non-yielding crop, not including, therefore, the cost of harvesting, transportation, storage and thrashing. If a planter cultivates 1,000 hectares and has a total loss of crops for a period of ten years, he has lost 200,000 pesos. But if in the eleventh he happens to reap an excellent crop, he gets 200,000 hectolitres of corn, which, sold at 3 pesos a hectolitre, would bring him 600,000 pesos, balancing the loss of the poor years and giving him a large profit. This example proves that the planter may prosper notwithstanding the irregularity of the rains.

But when the lands are exhausted, as is the case in the district of Bajio, and the yield in favorable seasons has fallen as low as 8 hectolitres per hectare, it requires only one bad year for every two good ones to ruin the planter. This is precisely what has happened in Mexico. The constant decrease in the productiveness of the arable lands has created an intolerable situation for the planter and, consequently, also for the Indian. And if the planter, who can counterbalance these losses by reducing his expenses, by taking his family to live at the plantation in order to economize, by mortgaging his property, by big loans from banks and money-lenders, finally ends in bankruptcy, how could the Indian meet the situation as an independent planter, having none of the resources of the landed proprietor? It is certain that the great majority of the eighty-five per cent of the Mexican population . . . was horribly destitute prior to the revolution of 1910. The chief cause of its misery, however, is not to be found in its want of liberty, its lack of universal suffrage, in the Cientificos, in dictatorships, landowners, plutocrats, individuals or corporations, but in its climate. If, as Baron Humboldt has said and facts have proven, the Mexican nation was famine-stricken when it had at its disposal the most fertile lands in the world, capable of feeding a population fifty times greater than that which it had in 1600, it is offensive for men of supposed learning and culture to attribute the misery of the Mexican people exclusively to a handful of individuals who have put in an appearance only within the last generation.

The solution of the Mexican problem and the salvation of its people is to be found, as I have previously said, in the substitution of the intensive method of cultivation for the extensive. But this cannot be accomplished by the simple recommendations of the peevish professors of the School of Agriculture in the City of Mexico and the clamors of the self-appointed sages who are constantly doling out advice upon subjects that are quite beyond the reach of their intellectual equipment.

The cost of harrowing and sowing one hectare of land in Mexico, destined for corn dry farming, does not exceed 12 pesos; and if the crop is lost there is no further expense to be incurred. A planter who owns 1,000 hectares of arable land, estimated at about 300 pesos each, would have a capital of 3,000 pesos, and the loss of his crop would mean the loss of 12,000 pesos. But if he undertakes the intensive method, the cost of cultivation per hectare in Mexico for a non-yielding crop cannot be less than 80 pesos, and the loss of the planter who cultivated 1,000 hectares would be in a single year 80,000 pesos; and in three bad seasons out of ten, or perhaps out of five, or out of three, he would be totally ruined. Intensive agriculture, in order to be a success and to safeguard the interests of the planter, must be able to depend upon assured crops; and as in Mexico, on account of the irregularity of the rains and the frosts, such a guarantee cannot be given, it is impossible, in the face of scientific evidence and in the interests of the planter and of the Mexican people themselves, to introduce the intensive method of cultivation, unless the security of the crops has first been guaranteed by the installation of adequate irrigation facilities.

Irrigation alone, however, will not enable the Indian to establish intensive cultivation in Mexico. Other conditions must prevail, which I shall endeavor to make clear as we progress with this necessarily cursory review of our interesting but somewhat somber social problem. . . .

THE REVOLUTIONARY LEGEND
OF THE LANDHOLDERS

Various elements have contributed to the growth in the Mexican public mind of the fable of a luxurious landholding class, gross oppressors of the rural people, or, more correctly, of what has lately become the fad—the indigenous race. Among these may be counted, the voraciousness of the bureaucracy, the ignorance of the newcomers, the chagrin of the defeated, the visions of patriots and the illusions of students.

Landholders of this type existed in the early Colonial period —landholders such as the Conde del Valle de Orizaba, who owned seventy-seven plantations in the central plateau, and the Marques de San Miguel de Aguayo, who owned 1,000,000 hectares in the section which is now comprised by the states of Durango and Coahuila. But the concentration of arable lands into great plantations has almost entirely disappeared. The present planter's land is made up of from second- to fourth-rate grazing ground, bare mountains and stretches of arid desert. One of the Mexican planters of this latter type is the famous Don Luis Terrazas. He undoubtedly possessed 6,000,000 hectares of land in the state of Chihuahua, but only 4,000 hectares of this was arable land.

A Mexican planter, as a rule, possesses a minimum of arable land, a considerable tract of summer stubble grazing ground, some woodlands, a goodly collection of barren mountains and a great stretch of unimproved land, utterly worthless because of its inferior quality. This statement can be proved by absolutely indisputable facts. Not even ten per cent of the mountains are timbered, and the balance are either huge, naked rocks or are covered with a lifeless kind of growth that depresses rather than raises the spirits of the enterprising worker.

Those 70,000,000 hectares of worthless lands, comprising a territory greater than the whole of France, have owners, and there are consequently in Mexico landholders whose assets equal naught. Proprietors of this description cannot be said to be a hindrance to the indigenous, or any other race, their only office being apparently to serve as targets for the shots of the agitators who constantly point them out as the rapacious plunderers of the marvellous lands belonging to the Mexican people.

Don Jose Lorenzo Cossio, a sincere and self-denying friend of the indigenous race, and a professed partisan of the division of land, in his treatise on rural lands in Mexico, published in 1911, says: "It is true that the people lack land, but it is false to say that it is due to the great concessions of the Colonial period. . . .

After enumerating the causes that influenced the subdivision of the lands that were possessed by individuals, Señor Cossio declares that the monopoly of property was reestablished by the dictatorship of General Diaz. He says: "But more especially the monopolistic and property-rights-destroying policy of the Government has made pass into the hands of the few what was once enjoyed by the many."

According to the data presented by Señor Cossio, whose treatise is entirely favorable to the revolutionary thesis, the Mexican Government from 1857 to 1906 came into possession of 72,335,907 hectares. Of this 13,764,607 hectares were adjudicated according to the laws promulgated by President Benito Juarez and former administrations. Señor Cossio has nothing to say about these as they were adjudicated to more than ten thousand claimants. He reserves his censure for the alienation by the Porfirio Diaz Government of more than 58,000,000 hectares which were distributed almost gratuitously among twenty-eight of the President's friends. With regard to this Señor Cossio has written: "It is for this reason that this law has been the one that has most profoundly affected the land problem; and it may be said that in great part it served to prepare the present revolt, because it has once more monopolized the national territory, despoiling the many to enrich the few."

Señor Cossio submits the following official data concerning the survey of unclaimed lands made during the dictatorship of General Diaz.

STATES AND TERRITORIES WHICH WERE SURVEYED	HECTARES
Chihuahua	14,612,366
Baja California	11,604,584
Sonora	3,216,394
Durango	789,009
Coahuila, Chihuahua, Sonora, Durango and Tamaulipas	5,214,306
Chihuahua and Durango	1,043,099
Chiapas	328,016
Yucatan	251,878
Tabasco	780,176
Vera Cruz	45,856
Sinaloa	45,981
Puebla	73,173
Oaxaca	60,701
San Luis Potosi	12,543
Guanajuato	5,166
Islas del Golfo de Cortes	164,098
Total:	38,247,346

RÉSUMÉ

Unclaimed lands surveyed in the northern states occupied by extensive mountain chains, immense deserts and from second- to fourth-rate summer stubble grazing ground, and scarcely any arable land	36,689,837
In the warm zone	1,539,800
In the temperate and cold zones	17,709
Total:	38,247,346

The remainder of the lands surveyed up to the 58,000,000 hectares present the same desolate appearance. The work was suspended in 1891, and the lands surveyed later were surveyed under concessions, with the results given in the foregoing table.

Almost all the surveying has been done in the arid zone, comprising immense deserts, salt plains and gigantic mountains, where an insignificant minimum of workable land exists. Deducting from these surveyed lands some of the good territory of the temperate zone of the state of Chiapas, and those of the Yaquis in the state of Sonora, which occupy a small area of that state, there are not to be found in the much-talked-of 58,000,000 hectares of land snatched from the Mexican people by the covetousness of the mighty, even 15,000 hectares of lands suitable for the cultivation of cereal and leguminous products. From the year 1840 all the arable lands in the northern states had passed into the hands of the inhabitants of these states, who held them by legal titles or by that of prescription. It is true that General Diaz by his law of unclaimed lands, promulgated in favor of his friends, constituted great landholdings which were afterwards transferred by them to foreign enterprises. But these were composed of those lands which did not produce food for the people and which could not be constituted into small holdings; neither could they be distributed among poor ranchers, because the summer stubble grazing ground of this section, smaller by far than the absolutely desert land, is under the ban of frequent and tremendous droughts which kill the cattle. To derive any profit from these, the investment of great capital would have been necessary in order to install hydraulic plants to overcome entirely, or at least in a measure, the natural deficiencies.

THE TRUTH ABOUT THE LANDHOLDERS

In the central plateau, where almost all the lands adapted to the cultivation and cereal and leguminous products are to be found, there are no landholders who could, to any great extent, injure the interests of the poor class, because the plantation that exceeds 1,000 hectares of arable land is the exception. The following facts will amply bear this out.

According to the carefully prepared statistics of the Department of Fomento, forty per cent of the total corn production is grown in Guanajuato, Jalisco and Michoacan, the joint area of which is 173,810 square kilometers, and deducting from these the mountains, ravines, the precipitous plains, the great lakes of Chapala, Patzcuaro and Cuitzeo, there remain 50,000 square kilometers for agriculture and cattle-raising. These three states, which produce forty per cent of all the corn available for the maintenance of the Mexican nation, comprise 1,114 plantations and 9,515 ranches, according to Vol. IX, p. 495, of the General Statistics of the Mexican Republic.

The area of land suitable for cultivation or cattle raising represents sixty per cent of the available 50,000 square kilometers of the states we have under consideration; consequently, each of the 1,114 plantations has an average area of 18 square kilometers or 1,800 hectares. And it must also be borne in mind that the summer stubble grazing ground predominates over the arable land, bearing out what I have said that it is an exception in the most fertile states of the Republic, which enjoy the most favorable rainfall conditions, to find plantations of more than 1,000 hectares. An average area of 320 hectares may be approximately assigned to the 9,515 ranches located in these states. It cannot be said, then, that the situation in that part of the Republic which produces forty per cent of the corn consumed by the Mexican people is such as to inspire rage and to call forth anathemas against the landholders. What has been said of the plantations of this section is true of all those to be found south of the 22d parallel of north latitude. . . .

INEVITABLE CONCLUSIONS

The problem of feeding the people in Mexico and of neutralizing the terrible ravages of hunger had, up to 1910, only one rational solution—irrigation. It was the only means of saving and enriching the people, as irrigation would have considerably increased the extent of the arable lands. It would have given security to the crops raised in those sections where the fertility of the land permits of extensive agriculture, and, above all, reclaimed that great portion of the arable land which is almost depleted, by permitting the introduction of the intensive method of agriculture.

Unfortunately for Mexico, Señor Limantour, noted for his undoubtedly upright, well-balanced financial negotiations, failed to recognize Mexico's need in this respect. The situation had been well known to men of science since 1899, when the national credit reached a height indicating the possibility of undertaking irrigation of the country on a large scale. The Department of Fomento, which is responsible for the economic progress of the country, was directed from 1880 to 1907 by deluded persons—honest and otherwise—or by very honorable persons without initiative or a real understanding of the vital needs of the country.

Don Olegario Molina assumed control of the Department of Fomento in 1908, and was thoroughly alive to the stupendous obligations which his position imposed upon him, and set about energetically to try to carry them out. He began by removing certain abuses which laws regarding unclaimed lands had produced, and by taking up the study of the national lands which were under the control of his department, and which were destined for national and foreign colonization. He understood that the salvation of the nation depended upon not losing a single drop of available water, obtained either through precipitation or from rivers, lakes, ponds or wells to be found on Government lands. He worked until he obtained constitutional reform which centralized, under Federal control, all the water rights which were not held under incontestable titles. He initiated and by means of previous free discussion obtained the approbation by the Federal Congress of the water laws which would enable the Government to undertake without delay the irrigation of the country. He obtained an appropriation of 600,000 pesos to defray the cost of engaging a commission of engineers who were to select the sections to which preference should be given in the irrigation plan, and to point out the best means of carrying it out. In 1908 Secretary of the Treasury, Limantour, founded the financial institution known as *Caja de Préstamos para la Agricultura y Fomento de la Irrigación* (Loan Fund for Agricultural Work and the Development of Irrigation), with a Mexican capital of 10,000,000 pesos silver, and obtained, besides, a loan of 50,000,000 pesos silver with Government guarantees. The firm of Pearson & Son was engaged by the Department of Fomento to study the conditions in the vicinity of the river Nazas, which is the source of the fertility of the "Laguna" district, and which has made possible the cotton growing of this region. A loan was granted to the Sauteña Company for the irrigation of 40,000 hectares of good land, on condition, however, that not less than 15,000 hectares, equipped with good irrigation facilities, were to be turned over to the Federal Government for the formation of small agricultural land holdings. The Department of Fomento granted Señor Cuesta Gallardo a concession to drain part of Lake Chapala, which would make possible the cultivation of a great area of notably fertile lands. Under the dictatorship of General Diaz, 3,000,000 pesos in cash was loaned to Don Lorenzo Gonzalez Treviño, uncle of ex-President Francisco Madero, to enable him to complete the extensive irrigation plants he had under construction on his properties in the state of Coahuila.

I give these facts to prove that in the two years previous to the revolution, from 1908 to 1910, the dictatorship authorized the appropriation of the large sum of 90,000,000 pesos silver, or $45,000,000, to further irrigating enterprises. This amply proves that the irrigation work contemplated by Don Olegario Molina, the Secretary of Fomento, was serious, well planned, definitely decided and energetically launched.

This proves that the dictatorship of Diaz, notwithstanding its great deficiencies, had taken up in behalf of the nation the work that a scientific study of the Mexican economical problem pointed out to be necessary. This problem is unknown to the revolutionary men of the old régime who now want to pass for men of the new era, and to the really new men who look with ambitious eyes to the supreme power without first having proved themselves capable of wielding it.

In 1910 the revolution for "the redemption of the people" had not seen the light of day, but the revolution to rebuild the shattered ambitions of the younger generation and those of the older generation, anxious to pose as belonging to the former, was then put into operation. This era of political personalism gave rise to the great social revolution which is tearing Mexico to shreds. . . .

5

The Revolution encouraged an intellectual reappraisal of what it meant to be Mexican. Refuting the positivist tenet that only productive segments of the population more white and Spanish than brown and Indian benefitted Mexico, the new intellectuals believed that all groups contributed to Mexico's strength. If the rural poor, specifically the Indian, had made a negligible cultural and economic contribution in the past, it was because their needs had been ignored by the old regime. The Indian possessed cultural, economic, and political attributes of value to modern Mexico. Intellectuals recognized that before the Indian could make his contribution he must improve his standard of living. In their opinion the key to that improvement lay not merely in socio-economic reforms, but in education. In the next essay Ramón Eduardo Ruiz, a professor of Latin American history, examines the attempts of intellectuals and educators to develop an educational program to fit the needs of the Indian peasants.

Ramón Eduardo Ruiz:
Mexico, the Challenge of
Poverty and Illiteracy*

I

During "the last ten years [the 1910's] . . . not . . . fighting but thinking has been our occupation. Violent deeds are only the signs of our mental effort to fathom the truth of our reality and of our ideals," wrote Moisés Sáenz. An era of national introspection emerged with the Revolution, as Mexicans began to analyze themselves and their society. "What are we? What would we like to be?" asked Sáenz. "What is the right of the white man, of the mestizo . . . of the Indian in the new scheme of life?" Specifically, there were two questions: what was the Mexican nationality, and what was the place of the Indian in society. Both confronted the rural school.

For the artists the answers were simple. The masses, Indian by "race," brown by color, peasant by class, were the essence of revolutionary Mexico. So Rivera, Orozco, and Siqueiros turned for inspiration to the peasant, depicting on canvas and wall his struggle for justice and equality. What the artist painted, the writer put into words. The literature of Mariano Azuela and his friends spoke of villages and peasants, of battles waged by cotton-clad warriors against the forces of city and greed. The brown peasant exemplified strength and virtue; city, landlord, and foreigner were his enemies. The lawmakers of 1917, too, recognized the Indian by giving a place in the national Constitution to the *ejido,* a village land system dating back to the pre-Conquest.

The issue, however, was not as simple for the architects of the national program of education, for the answers given would determine the orientation of the program, a matter of public concern. Public opinion, furthermore, was divided on this question, for the character of their nationality was a sensitive issue among Mexicans, hybrids of Indian and Spanish stock. Some thought them-

* From Ramón Eduardo Ruiz, MEXICO, THE CHALLENGE OF POVERTY AND ILLITERACY (San Marino, California: The Huntington Library, 1963), pp. 123–141.

selves Spaniards, or basically European; others boasted that they were "pure" Indian. And after all, what were Mexicans by race, ideals, and culture? Fundamentally, the question was whether the relationship established by the Conquest—equality of races in theory but with the Spaniard superior in practice—still existed, or whether in four centuries one group had risen at the expense of the other. Had the Indian by sheer weight of numbers and loyalty to tradition overcome the Spaniard, or had the European triumphed over the Indian? The answer to this question would determine the nationality of Mexico, which the reformers sought zealously to define. On this issue of nationality, subject to diverse interpretations, the reformers split into two general groups: the Europeanists (for want of a better term) and the Nationalists, or *indianistas*, as they were popularly called.

Equally important was the place of the Indian in society—second of the two questions. The 1921 census counted 4,179,449 Indians in Mexico. There were more than eighty groups, some small and relatively unimportant, others—like the Aztecs—numerous and significant. They were distinct in language, folklore, and culture. A few remained in the nomadic stage; some were barbarous and war-loving; the great majority farmed for a living. With some exceptions, the Indians lived in poverty, the victims of disease, malnutrition, and superstition.

Urban society, the aristocracy, and the majority of reformers looked upon the Indian as a problem. Materially he lived on the margin of the national economy, a status detrimental to his welfare and to that of the Republic. Ways had to be found to raise his living standard and to encourage his aspirations. On this point reformers were in substantial agreement; but they split over how to carry out this rehabilitation.

II

The attitude of the Europeanists on the issue of nationality and the Indian was clear; the character of Mexico had been shaped by the Conquest. "The Indian's door to the future," wrote José Vasconcelos, "was that of modern culture; there was no other door open to him but that already trod by Latin civilization." All originality began with the Conquest; only events after this "act of salvation," Octavio Véjar Vásquez added, had something to contribute to the natural perfection of the Mexican. If the ancient land of Mexico had given birth to indigenous civilizations, independent of the Old World, they had fallen before the stronger, more virile culture of the conquerors and were now merely of historical interest.

While this view had points in common with the ideology of the prerevolutionary regime, there were fundamental differences between them. As reformers the Europeanists were dedicated to the welfare of the masses; the old regime was not. Although rejecting the indigenous contribution, the Europeanists accepted the Indian as a human being. To quote Vasconcelos, "I do not believe that there is any difference between the ignorant Indian and the ignorant French or English peasant; as soon as one or the other is educated he becomes a useful addition to the civilized life of his country and in so doing contributes to the betterment of the world in general." Or as Fernando González Roa put it: "We do not deny the . . . despondency of the indigenous race, but such can surely be removed since the race is capable of enjoying the benefits of civilization." What reformers of this group believed was that with their help the Indian would become an asset to society. This was a rejection of all that "Indian" implied except the Indian himself.

There was a further difference between the Europeanists and the rulers of the past. Díaz and his followers had made a sharp distinction between the downtrodden Indian masses and the urban elite of whites and mestizos. Not only did a majority of Europeanists reject the Díaz myth of the Indian's racial inferiority, but some even denied his existence. All Mexicans were alike. There were no Indians, said a distinguished educator of the twenties: "I deny the existence of the Indian in Mexico. . . . We have only one group and one class of people—the Mexicans." Despite "ethnic groups that must still be considered as apart from us . . . for all purposes— political and cultural, in fact and in intention—we are only one people. We are all Mexicans." Why employ valuable time making ethnic studies of the population? "We gain nothing and by thinking in that way we may be damaging our sense of a coherent and homogeneous nationality."

As a group the Europeans favored Western civilization in general; as individuals many had a more specific ideology. Spain, not merely Europe, was the essence of Mexico. The mother country had forged the cultural patterns and the social institutions of state and faith; these were the bulwarks of society. "We shall not be great," announced Vasconcelos, "until the Spaniard of America feels as Spanish as the sons of Spain." The formula lay in rejecting the empirical philosophy and the utilitarian morality of the Western world, in reviving the Catholic tradition, and in resurrecting the colonial heritage. For the Conquest had brought a "clash between the democracy of the time—one of the most genuine . . . of Europe —and despotism—one of the crudest . . . of history—the despotism of Montezuma." What was fine in Mexican life rose from the Spain of the sixteenth century. Weakness had come with the disappearance of Spanish ways. "I recognized this," said Vasconcelos, "as I stood admiring one day . . . the fine old homes . . . in the ancient city of Oaxaca. As I looked around me I saw that something had happened to mar the traditional beauty of the scene." Over the years "the Whites had disappeared and the Indians from the mountains, silent and impassive in their blankets, had enveloped the streets and squares. Then I knew," he concluded, "that the tragedy of Mexico lay in this displacement and exhaustion of the conquering and civilizing blood of Spain."

Despite their deprecation of the native background, the Europeanists had an ambivalent attitude. Their ideology was the product of two worlds, nurtured on the nationalism of the Revolution. Many of them accepted the superiority of the Western world with reservations; they were too Mexican for anything else. When American dignitaries asked Vasconcelos where he got his ideas on education, he replied: "Not in Boston, but in Xochimilco. Watch the Indian there . . . see how he cultivates his tiny plot of ground to grow the finest vegetables in the world. Would it not be foolish to send him to study agriculture in Maine[?]" In his controversial *La raza cósmico* he asserted (p. 25) that the reign of the whites was destined to collapse. Their mission was to mechanize the world and to lay the foundations for the era of the mestizo.

Nature had bestowed its blessings on the mestizo—the cosmic race—offspring of "two aristocracies, both products of nature's severe selective process." Here was a race free of the defects of other races. Since individual differences stemmed more from the ability to do certain things to the exclusion of others than from the degree of total development, the mestizo surmounted these defects by complementing the weaknesses of a particular stock through interchange and assimilation. "The great periods of history," meditated Vasconcelos, were the products of hybrids, "of peoples and cultures, rather than the contribution of any privileged pure-blood nation." The myth of racial purity was the propaganda of rulers. Miscegenation, not purity, was the ideal, for "hybridism in man, as well as in plants, tends to produce finer types and tends to rejuvenate those . . . that have become static." Bridging the gap between the past and future, between Spain and the pre-Columbian world, was the mestizo. He was a Spaniard at heart even when fighting Spain, an Indian in spite of a skin turned white through fusion with the blood of the Iberian Peninsula. Resembling neither of his parents, he could not turn back; he was "always directed to the future."

As to what should be done about the Indian, the Europeanists felt that since after four centuries of interbreeding the Indian was a dying segment of the population, he was a subject for redemption and nothing more. He had nothing to offer society except himself. It was sheer intellectual snobbery to talk of reviving such things as native languages, exclaimed Luis Cabrera. Or, to paraphrase the famous pedagogue Gregorio Torres Quintero, there was no reason why the Indian should be given preferential treatment. Of course the Indian needed schools but not at the expense of the mestizo. For Mexico was no longer a colony governed by laws making the Indian a ward of the crown. The way out was through the "incorporation of the Indian into society," a society in the European mold. If the Indian could be made in the image of his mestizo neighbor, Western in thought, the problem would be solved. With this in mind Vasconcelos cast an educational plan of universal outlook. In the name of unity, schools were built to root out cultural deviations from the national scene. The school, to quote Cabrera, had "to make the race a homogeneous one, fusing its inferior elements— the Indians—and its superior ones—the whites—in the mestizo race." Like the conquerors the Europeanists accepted the equality of the Indian before God, but like Cortés and his monks they strove to make the Indian into their own image.

Supporters of these views represented a heterogeneous lot. There were intellectuals, particularly philosophers and historians— Vasconcelos was one of them—politicians, military men, and professional educators—Rafael Ramírez, for example; all served the school movement. In general, they were urban- rather than rural-minded, more linked with commerce and business—and later industry—than with agriculture. Loosely speaking, they were heirs of the doctrines of *La Reforma*. Still they had no sympathy for the Comte and Spencer of the old regime, and some of their leading spokesmen rejected empiricism in favor of Bergsonism and a *rapprochement* with the church.

Patterned after that of the Northern Dynasty, their program was conceived in terms of recovery rather than radical social change. Their reforms accepted the capitalism of the Díaz days, modified here, strengthened there; evolution was the key, not revolution. Not the destruction of the economic system, but the protection of private property, animated them. Their crusade stressed the rights of the individual and the virtues of Western democracy, which were alien to the Indian, who spoke for communal property concepts foreign to the individualistic character of Western society, as Robert Redfield pointed out in his study of Tepoztlán. Economics, too, hovered behind some of the Europeanist denial of ethnic differences in the population. There was mirrored the traditional refusal of the conservative—and the Europeanists were conservatives—to admit to the existence of class distinctions in a society of his own making.

This view, paradoxically, received strong support from some radicals, who found the stress on economics convenient. The Marxists, in particular, condemned as "bourgeois . . . think[ing] of the . . . Indian problem in juridical, pedagogic, moral or racial terms." The question was economic. How logical this union of conservative and radical thought was, the case of Rafael Ramírez illustrates superbly. A middle-of-the-road thinker in the beginning, he veered left under the tutelage of Narciso Bassols. Yet this ideological shift did not alter his views on the question of nationality and the Indian. Both as a supporter of the middle-class state and as the champion of collectivism, he never wavered from what was essentially the position of the Europeanists.

Decrying violent change, the Europeanists dictated a conservative program of rural education. For the wrong type of learning would upset the equilibrium between the mental and economic levels of individuals and groups and lead to chronic discontent by awakening desires beyond reach. This discontent was fertile soil for the seeds of demagogues interested in such radical measures as agrarian socialism. The wrong school would fan the flames of Zapatismo and lead to the destruction of the sacred principles of private property, observed Alberto J. Pani. If there was danger in mass education, however, greater peril lay in ignorance. Ignorance held the masses in check, conceded Jorge Vera Estañol, minister of education under Victoriano Huerta, but it also rendered them easy prey to agitators. The road to unity and peace lay in a moderate program of education that erased concepts of class, party, and race and left undisturbed the foundations of society.

III

These views received little support from *indianistas*. To them the nationality was Indian. Since three out of four Mexicans still lived in rural villages, the traditional home of the Indian, the great Mexican majority was Indian, wrote Manuel Gamio. Though the Spaniard had triumphed militarily and as an individual, his civilization was not transmitted to the Indian. The Spaniard was always a minority, and even the mestizo was more Indian than European. So why not accept reality—intellectually, artistically, and otherwise—and build around it? If the nationality was Indian, the Indian had a vital role to play, declared the *indianistas*. As heir to the pre-Columbian past, he had much to give the present; for, as Sáenz eulogized in one of his sentimental moments, the Indian represented "a civilization so high and delicate that at times . . . one wonders if . . . the coming of the white man . . . was not a pity rather than a blessing." There was, moreover, no reason to deny the continuing existence of the Indian, as some did. "We gain nothing and lose much by trying to reason the Indian out of our reality," announced Sáenz. "Indeed . . . this attitude is responsible for the neglect in which . . . [the] Indians . . . have been left."

The *indianistas* were a mixed lot, bound together by a common interest in rural life, a Jeffersonian faith in agriculture, and a belief in the masses. Their ranks included rural educators, anthropologists, farm experts, here and there a renegade historian, and a strange collection of artists and writers, antiquarians, and romanticists. When the political climate favored *indianismo*, which happened rarely, politician, general, and businessman echoed its sentiments. But the businessman was hardly a friend, for he had cast his lot with commerce and later with industry, traditional rivals of agriculture. At the head of the *indianista* movement was the rural expert, usually the anthropologist or the specialist on rural education, who came to know and admire the qualities of the peasants. Intellectuals with an intimate sense of rural life, they were the links between the reality of the countryside and the *indianismo* of the printed page.

Ironically, what was lacking in the leadership was the Indian himself. With few exceptions, the Indianist movement, never an organized affair, was the child of intellectuals interested in rural problems, but intellectuals who were certainly not Indian. Even at the grass roots the Indian seldom joined the crusade. Once educated, however, and therefore no longer an Indian in the Mexican sense, he often returned as a teacher or rural expert, having learned and adopted the doctrines of *indianismo*. But this was acquired or imposed doctrine, not something indigenous. While the Indian of the village usually joined in the folk festivals sponsored by a cultural mission and supported the native language program, this was not always the case. The village was often indifferent, as Ralph L. Beals pointed out in *Cherán*. Yet the symbol of *indianismo*, if it had one, was Zapata, the Indian agrarian chieftain, whose struggle for land and schools was an important phase of the Revolution.

Usually out of power and therefore free of any responsibility, the *indianistas* frequently allowed sentiment to get the better of reason. Still they were an influential and vocal minority. Their writings left a mark on social and economic theory, and their activities colored the agrarian era of the twenties and thirties.

Historically speaking, *indianismo* came into its own with the Revolution; but its roots were old. The beginnings were laid in the pre-Columbian era; the seeds of *indianismo* are also found in the scores of Indian uprisings of the colonial period and in the activity of Las Casas and his priestly cohorts, whose defense of the Indian was a cult. Certainly, the Hidalgo and Morelos uprisings had characteristics later associated with *indianismo*. Throughout the nineteenth century—especially in the early 1830's, later during *La Reforma,* and even under the Díaz regime—there were vocal individuals of *indianista* leanings. Still the movement was a more recent phenomenon.

IV

There were many factors behind the *indianista* concept of nationality. Foremost was a rising group spirit, an impulse for nationalism emerging after centuries of neglect and exploitation. In a symbolic sense, the rediscovery of the Indian gave substance to the desire to stand alone, to be free of Europe and independent of the United States, as Redfield asserted. The new nationalism was a revolt against Spain the colonizer and master, four centuries after the Conquest. It was an emotional repudiation of centuries of imitation, a reaction against Comte and Spencer, against the prejudices of Western society categorizing the Indian, and Mexicans generally, as inferior people. Viewed from this angle, *indianismo* was pride of race—racial chauvinism in some cases. For as Antonio Díaz Soto y Gama boasted to a group of visiting students from the United States: "We prefer the Indian blood that runs in our veins to the small amount of white blood from European extraction."

With *indianismo* there came an awakened interest in folk language, folk customs, and folk personality. The new interest stressed things native, using the Indian as a symbol of individual honor and pride, ideals sought by that generation. "We must take advantage of what the country gives us: men of dark skin . . . to govern us, *tequila, charanda,* and *aguardiente* . . . the beverages of plants as noble as the grape," José Rubén Romero had his Pito Pérez say. "Were the clerics to use *aguardiente* in place of wine for mass, they would be humble and kind to their flocks."

Basically, *indianismo* was a belief in the simple agrarian

economy of the peasant, long forgoten by an industrialized world. The Indian's communal system offered a way out of the dilemma posed by a lingering quasi-medieval colonial system on one side and capitalism on the other. By fusing the communal village with collectivism, the peasant would get the benefits of Western technology and avoid the dangers of capitalism or the limitations of an antiquated colonial system. Perhaps, in the final analysis, behind the cotton *calzones,* the *huaraches,* and the *ejido* lay an attack—Marxian or otherwise—on capitalism or what passed for it in Mexico. The *ejido*—and the rural school—represented *indianismo* in the countryside.

It was no surprise, therefore, to find Ramón Beteta, still the idealistic schoolteacher, suggesting in 1935 that Mexico revise her land system in order to substitute the small communal holding for private property. He saw no reason why land reform should be used to create an agrarian *bourgeoisie,* which, though new to Mexico, was antiquated elsewhere. To redistribute the land and not to go ahead with its socialization, he considered a dangerous step. Unless carried to its logical conclusions, declared Beteta, the Revolution had won a Pyrrhic victory.

Conservative hostility to Indianism was born of this attempt to meddle with the economic *status quo.* The conservative reformer had no quarrel with a weak and numerically insignificant group that suggested a return to a nebulous and ill-defined "Indian culture" and raised no protest when the Ministry of Education subsidized mural art critical of the middle class. But here was an attack on private property in the guise of a cultural crusade, and conservatives rallied to protect the old order.

In the light of this picture, the school-church issue of the twenties and thirties, which divided reformers, takes on new meaning. In general the conservatives remained loyal Catholics or at least gave lukewarm support to the church. With some exceptions, they were ready to accept the church as vital to the future of Mexico, and some were willing to accept modification of Article 3 of the Constitution, which dealt with education. After all, the church gave tacit approval to the *status quo* and, since the days of Juárez, had posed no threat to the middle class. So long as the church refrained from political intrigue harmful to the social order, which it was willing to do if its own position was not threatened, the conservatives were ready to share education with the church.

On the other hand, the *indianistas* considered the church a vested partner of the *status quo,* thus a logical target. If the school was to achieve its purpose—the transformation of society—the church, as constituted, had to go. As Sáenz wrote, "If religion is to function in a constructive way in the life of our people, the church-to-be must be willing to deal with the realities of the present life in accordance with the *social* and *political* ideals [italics mine] for which we are striving." There could be no enduring harmony while there existed an ambivalence between present and future life, between material and spiritual values. Viewed from this perspective, *indianismo* was an extension, often with collectivist undertones, of the anticlericalism of the nineteenth century, which was rooted in the struggle for power between church and state.

Further, unlike traditional anticlericalism, which was neither anti-Catholic nor anti-Christian, *inidanismo* denied both the faith and the church. The village—so ran the argument—while deeply religious, was neither Christian nor Catholic; its faith was a strange mixture of pagan rite and Catholic worship, both degenerate and misunderstood. Christianity, instead of replacing the ancient cults, had merged with them. Why not accept this fact and blend the two, asked Sáenz, for "out of pagan feeling and Christian conception and practice, a new manner of religion may come about where a complete synthesis of life will be realized." Or, as Gamio asserted, the destruction of many aspects of pre-Conquest worship was regrettable, not especially because of their religious character, "but . . . because of the originality, the significance, and the rare beauty in the work of art which pre-Columbian mythology [had] created." Nothing since the Conquest had aristically equaled or surpassed "the decoration of the Maya temples, the bas-reliefs of Palenque, the plumed serpents of Teotihuacán, [and] a thousand other marvels." Since the mixture of Catholic dogma and pre-Hispanic pantheism had not produced anything equal to that art born of the union of aesthetics and mythology in the ancient world, why not replace "classic occidental mythology" with courses in school on the mythology of the New World?

What these *indianistas* asked was that the church support their social order and accept the school's right to blend pagan worship with Catholicism. While the conservative reformer was familiar with the paganism of the village and with anticlericalism, this was asking too much of him. He balked and gave his support to the church.

V

On the question of nationality, there was general agreement among the *indianistas*. But when the immediate problems of the Indian population faced them, they drifted into three ill-defined groups or wings: romanticists, radicals, and moderates.

For the romanticists—the antiquarians, folklorists, artists, and poets—*indianismo* was, in practice, the cult of the lyrical and little else. Having accepted *indianismo* in theory, the romanticists had nothing to offer. Their idealized Indian had scant relation to the flesh-and-blood Indian in the countryside. Their Indian inspired the artist, was eulogized as quaint, furnished material for "scientific investigation," or was displayed in museum cases. Because their interest was sentimental, the romanticists played a theoretical and minor role.

Though the radicals were often equally guilty of stressing the lyrical, their weakness was the impracticality of their social and economic proposals. They called for total reform: confiscation of haciendas, collectivization of land, socialized education. They dealt in wholesale condemnations and categorical imperatives, leaving no room for compromise. With little actual experience in rural affairs, with no clear understanding of the cultural factors involved, they, like the romanticists, had little to offer beyond doctrine. For the radical was an agitator, a dreamer with only a sketch of a program vast and intricate, which would require the careful planning of every detail.

The practical reformers—the Sáenzes and Gamios—were in the moderate wing. They forsook the city to work with Indian groups in the village, saw that the nationality issue was meaningless unless there were tangible benefits for the Indian, and envisaged an agrarian nation with a place for the Indian as well as for the machine. They gradually came to be known as *indigenistas,* and the philosophical, often lyrical, *indianismo* of earlier years gave way to their "scientific" *indigenismo,* a movement concerned primarily with alleviating the socioeconomic plight of the Indian. It was the *indigenistas* who laid out the educational program for the Indian, partly on the basis of Gamio's experiments at San Juan de Teotihuacán.

VI

The task of the practical *indigenistas* was to help the Indian raise his living standard, to make him a part of the national stream of life. Of primary importance was the matter of approach or method, which in turn called for intimate knowledge of Indian characteristics. From this problem arose the question of what are Indian characteristics, or, more succinctly, "What is an Indian?" The racial classification—which, in the census of 1921, defined an Indian as one of "more or less pure" blood—proved inadequate: how could one decide who was "pure blooded" after four hundred years of racial intermixing? Further, the Indian question was not one of blood but of the plight of a group or segment of society, declared the *indigenistas*. So the census of 1930—while still taking race into account—adopted the new socioeconomic definition put forth by the *indigenistas*. For the Indian, life revolved around Indian things: the planting stick instead of the plow, corn in place of wheat, the *rebozo* or *serape* for the coat, and usually a native language spoken in preference to Spanish. Racially, he was more "Indian" than Spaniard. In a psychological sense, he was conscious of being Indian, a feeling that had not diminished over the centuries, as Robert Redfield reported in *A Village That Chose Progress: Chan Kom Revisited*. By this classification an Indian, merely by a change in economic and intellectual status, became a mestizo.

Reform had to take the characteristics of the Indian into account, insisted the *indigenistas*. A meaningful education had to serve each Indian group according to its needs and thus would effect, paradoxically, a real national unity, by lifting all groups to one plane of civilization. The policy of "incorporation" ignored group differences. As the agrarian and political programs had demonstrated, there was little logic in "incorporation." If the rural majority demanded an agrarian program that would break up large landholdings and divide them among the people, many of the Indians did not need such a program. Unlike his neighbors, the Indian had held on to his tiny plot of land. To benefit him, the agrarian program had to increase the size of his land, improve his agricultural techniques, and encourage cooperative farming. Where matters of political organization were involved, the Indian, unlike his apolitical neighbor, had an organization of his own, worthy of respect and consideration, which dated back to the pre-Columbian era, wrote Luis Chávez Orozco. The Indian considered the politician from outside an invader of the worst sort. Gamio argued that the Inidan had been corrupted politically by Western society; and, in fact, the closer he lived to centers of Occidental culture, the more corrupt he was.

According to the *indigenistas*, the formula of the Europeanists not only ignored the characteristics of the Indian but rejected what Gamio called "static and dynamic" values. The "static" values were the long-forgotten higher arts and social practices of the pre-Columbian age, which were once of great significance and could be again. The "dynamic" values were the pre-Columbian practices, tools, and beliefs that still persisted in the modern era.

Among the chief "static" values of the Indian were architecture, sculpture, work in precious metals, his mythology, and an innate sense of democracy. These, in the opinion of Gamio, might be revived because the "mental processes of the Indian" resembled those of his ancestors. By being adapted to modern conditions, these "static" values could be restored to the life of today. The "dynamic" values were found in housing, food, clothing, agriculture, tools, domestic equipment, and, generally speaking, in the material things of indigenous life. There were survivals also in the intellectual concepts of the Indian, in his ethics, his aesthetics, and his religious ideas, and in his interpretations of cosmic phenomena and sickness. Some survivals were of intrinsic worth, even though they might appear degenerate. The useful ones were to be cultivated. Folk arts, now corrupted by the tourist trade, could be restored to their original authentic character. Villages and towns could be laid out as they were before the Conquest, with houses placed on small plots of land surrounded by orchards and cultivated fields—a more hygienic and picturesque plan than the compact block of buildings that the Spaniards introduced.

The *indigenistas* denied, however, that they wanted to return to the planting stick, the medicine man, and the mud hut. As they said, they did not want to "Indianize" Mexico; there was no project to restore pre-Columbian life, for if such an absurd scheme could be carried out, the Indian would be exterminated. But certainly this was not a program to "Europeanize" the Indian, to uproot him from his traditions and his environment. The goal was "Mexicanization"—the catchword—the blending of all strains into a Mexican society enriched by the contribution of the Indian. *Indigenistas*, said Gamio, "wish to . . . offer him [the Indian] an harmonious combination of the best . . . of his pre-Hispanic and colonial legacy . . . and the best elements in western culture which may be adaptable to the nature of his particular needs and aspirations." Incorporation was a false god. It not only threatened to change the way of life of the Indian, his tools and techniques, but it ignored all that he stood for. If the Indian was to have status in society, "incorporation" had to be a mutual process. The Indian had to play an important role in the social and economic life of the Republic, for if not, reform was nothing but the plan of the conqueror for a vanquished people whose spirit and way of life he had sworn to destroy. This was the warning of the anthropologist Daniel F. Rubín de la Borbolla.

No matter what the goal was, reconstruction had to start with the reality of the Indian world, declared the *indigenistas*. Should the nation later decide upon industrialization, great care would have to be taken lest the factory system be imposed artificially upon native agrarianism. It would be a national calamity to reject the farm for the factory before either the Indian or the rest of the country was prepared for it. "Production for production's sake . . . [and] a Ford every few seconds had not saved the world." The question, said Celerino Cano, an educator of note, was not how to impose an alien system upon the wreckage of the old but how to integrate the new with the old. Reform, President Cárdenas declared, had to respect the Indian as an individual and to recognize his traditions and sentiments.

The function of the school was to make the modern world intelligible to the Indian—to link the primitive with the modern. For unless this were done, declared the *indigenistas,* the tools of Western civilization could have little impact upon the village. Thus, the curriculum emphasized subjects of immediate value to the community: agriculture, animal husbandry, craftsmanship, rural hygiene, native languages, and academic disciplines geared to local utilitarian needs. But according to the *indigenistas,* the purpose was not to perpetuate peasant status; it was to help the Indian to improve his social and economic position. In the teaching of language, the objective was not to keep the Indian ignorant of Spanish but to teach him Spanish through his own language. The *indigenistas* believed that one learned a second language with more facility after having mastered his own. Above all else, the goals of education were to give the individual a sense of his own value, to justify his world to him, and ultimately to erase the myth of inferiority from the national conscience. With these aims in mind, the curriculum stressed the study of the pre-Hispanic heritage, so that the Indian might find inspiration for greatness in the record of his own past.

Unlike the conservative reformers, the *indigenistas* did not look upon education as an answer to all problems. They thought it senseless to hope to build a nation through education. That was for populations united by historic, racial, cultural, and economic bonds, where education bound existing ties more closely. But the Mexicans were not a united people; their differences were too fundamental for education to harmonize. For the *indigenistas,* then, education was only one aspect of a reform program that was entirely social.

Nor would it have been logical otherwise. The *indigenistas* had in mind a larger reform than did the conservatives. To them the school was a political organism, an instrument to use against the *status quo.* The school could never be neutral; it had to take a stand, and, by the reasoning of *indigenismo,* on all issues, particularly socioeconomic ones. It was no accident that the collectivist-minded *indigenistas* found their bible in John Dewey.

VII

Theory was one thing and practice something else, for the *indigenistas* seldom wielded political power. Yet their infrequent moments of glory came at crucial times in the history of rural education: at the start of the national movement in 1921, again in the mid-twenties, and during the reform administration of President Cárdenas.

Their initial opportunity came with Gamio's activity at San Juan de Teotihuacán. There, in one of the exciting experiments in the history of rural education, the anthropologist-educator developed and tested theories that became the guiding principles of *indigenismo*. Gamio's project, begun under President Carranza, received strong support from President Obregón but was discarded by Calles after Gamio's dismissal from the Ministry of Education in 1925.

Another limited opportunity followed almost immediately, when Sáenz replaced Gamio as Calles' undersecretary of education. Sáenz labored valiantly to implement *indigenista* doctrines. Perhaps the salient experiment of the time was the founding of a school for Indians in Mexico City: *La Casa del Estudiante Indígena*. This school had two purposes: to train leaders for Indian communities and to demonstrate to the doubting people of the capital that Indians were human beings with an intellectual capacity equal to their own. But while the students proved their ability easily—much to the astonishment of some residents of the capital—they refused to return home upon graduation. So in the end the parents lost their children to urban centers, and the rural communities did not profit from the experiment. To remedy this failing, *La Casa del Estudiante Indígena* was replaced by a number of similar schools built in rural areas where students could remain in contact with the village. Unfortunately, President Calles and his successors had little sympathy for this idea, and these schools got only what was left of funds and personnel after the needs of other institutions were met. By 1936 they were on the verge of collapse.

There was a final opportunity under President Cárdenas after 1935. His administration—firmly supporting *indigenismo*—improved the quality of Indian schools, multiplied their number, placed neighborhood primary schools under their direction, and organized a Department of Indian Education to supervise them. Then, in a bold departure from past practice, the president organized the autonomous Department of Indian Affairs to handle all Indian problems. Both the Department of Indian Education and the Department of Cultural Missions—the latter a pet of the Ministry of Education—were placed under it. Finally, in another precedent-shattering step, the administration recognized both the Spanish and Indian languages as official for rural schools.

The Cardenista period was the epoch of *indigenismo*. Although the Department of Indian Affairs and some of the policies lived on through the administration of President Avila Camacho, they were never the same again. In 1946 President Alemán, who dissented from the *indigenista* approach, disbanded the department and filled the gap with the *Instituto Nacional Indigenista,* the National Indianist Institute. Shorn of the department's cabinet rank, an orphan at birth, the *Instituto's* program reached only a tiny fraction of the Indian population. To quote the chief of the *Time* news bureau in Mexico, the *Instituto* had less money for its four centers "than the government spends maintaining the capital's fountains."

Indigenismo and *indianismo* were products of their times, the postrevolutionary decade and the world depression of the twenties and thirties. So long as nineteenth-century Europe was strong and prosperous, Mexicans imitated Europe; when World War I and depression destroyed the model and brought chaos to Mexico, Mexicans rejected the outside world. The United States experienced a similar, if somewhat more limited, reaction in the depression years of the New Deal. The WPA artist and writer took inspiration from "American" ways. Both *indigenismo* and *indianismo* were products of an era that believed in government planning, of an era that saw the Soviet experiment accorded world recognition and a planned New Deal launched in the United States.

A swing to conservatism came during the forties and grew strong after 1943. World War II created new problems and made Mexican industrialization almost inevitable. By 1949, when Jesús Silva Herzog was writing that the Revolution was only a matter of historical interest, the *indianismo* of yesterday was a forgotten phenomenon, and *indigenismo* no longer a movement of national significance. Industrialization and conservatism were the keynotes of this age; the agricultural objectives of the Revolution were in disrepute. With industrialization there was no time to worry about the Indian and his special characteristics; the Republic of the future needed technicians and mechanics, not artisans or small farmers. Nor was there much sympathy for the social welfare planning of the depression years. The reforms of the postwar years aimed to create a country able to support industry. All else was secondary.

Both *indianismo* and *indigenismo* had lost their force. Their followers no longer had their revolutionary fervor, and many of their reforms had failed when put to a practical test. The school of the *indigenistas* had faced a dilemma. As designed for life in the village, it was accused of preparing the children of the peasant for the life of the peasant; if its program sought to avoid this charge, it was said to have no practical meaning for the people of the village. In 1940, the last year of the *indigenista* experiment, the problem had been "solved" by making urban and rural curricula fundamentally the same, with some concessions to environment. But according to Ralph Beals the school, having lost contact with rural reality, made no impact on the village. There were other weaknesses. As an ideology, *indianismo* ignored the diversity of the Indian groups. While the *indigenistas* avoided this error, their movement touched only a narrow segment of the rural population: the Indian as defined by the anthropologist. Neither *indianismo* nor *indigenismo* had provided a well-rounded, practical solution to the problems of the typical mid-twentieth-century Mexican.

Yet both made significant contributions. By furnishing a platform for political debate, by raising issues' for public airing, they strengthened the cause of reform. They upheld the dignity of the Indian and the value of the village, thus giving recognition to both. The problems of the countryside were brought into national focus. Whatever its failures, the school the *indigenistas* built was closer to reality than any that had ever been designed in Mexico.

6

Mexico has moved forward on many fronts in the mid-twentieth century, but Mexicans offer conflicting interpretations of the meaning of this progress. Ruling politicians insist that their policies benefit all Mexicans; critics charge that progress is the prerogative of a minority. Unlike the Priistas who talk in terms of a "continuing" Revolution, opposition intellectuals refer to the "betrayal" of revolutionary goals. Among the latter is Carlos Fuentes, a distinguished intellectual and novelist. In his novel, *Where the Air Is Clear*, he paints a somber picture of contemporary rulers whom he finds devoid of ideals and dedicated to the pursuit of personal wealth. In the following passage, the banker Federico Robles represents the power elite. He has won his laurels with personal ability but with methods that are hardly praiseworthy; he justifies his record on the basis that it contributed to the development of Mexico.

Carlos Fuentes:
Where the Air is Clear*

"We [said the banker, Federico Robles] may be criticized on many counts, Cienfuegos, and critics say that we of the old guard, a handful of millionaires, have gathered our wealth from the sweat of the nation itself. But when you remember what Mexico was before, things take a different light. Gangs of bandits who never stopped shooting, the economy paralyzed, generals with private armies. No prestige abroad. No faith in industry. The countryside full of fear. Public institutions gone. And it was our lot to try to defend the principles of the Revolution and at the same time make them work toward progress and order and the national good. It was no easy task to reconcile those purposes. To proclaim revolutionary ideals is easy: land reform, labor laws, whatever you please. But we had to face reality and accept the only political truth, compromise. That was the moment of crisis for the Revolution. The moment of decision to build even if it meant staining conscience. To sacrifice ideals for the sake of tangible achievement. And we did it, and well. We had the right to take what we wanted, because of what we had suffered, gone through, to earn it. One man had been forced into the army, another's mother had been raped, another had had his land stolen. Don Porfirio had given none of us any way up, the door had been closed on all our ambitions. Now our ambition could grab what it cared to. Yes, but always working for the good of the nation, always taking only what was ours and taking it not for ourselves but for the nation."

On his feet in front of the window, Robles spread his hand across the anarchic expanse of Mexico City. "Look outside. There are still millions of illiterates, barefoot Indians, poor people starving to death, farmers who don't have even one miserable acre of their own, factories with no machinery, nor parts, unemployed workers who have to flee to the United States. But there are also millions who can go to schools that we of the Revolution built, millions for whom company stores and hacienda stores are gone forever, and there are some factories in the cities. Millions who, if this were nineteen hundred ten, would be peons are now skilled workers, girls, who would be cooks and maids are now typists, there are millions who in only thirty years have moved into the middle class, who own cars and use toothpaste and spend five days a year at Tecalutla or Acapulco. Our plants have given those workers jobs, our commerce has given them time-payment plans and savings accounts. For the first time in Mexican history a stable middle class exists, the surest protection against tyranny and unrest. Men and women who do not want to lose their jobs, their installment-plan furniture, their little cars, for anything in the world. Those people are the one concrete result of the Revolution, Cienfuegos, and we made them. We laid the foundation for Mexican capitalism. Calles laid it. He did away with generals, built highways and dams, organized banking. What if we did get our percentage from every highway contract? What if the collective farm directors do steal half the appropriations they are given? Would you prefer that in order to avoid these evils, we had done nothing at all? You want us to have the honesty of angels? I repeat, because of what we went through, we are entitled to everything. Because we were born in dirt-floor shacks, we have the right now to live in mansions with high ceilings and stone walls, with a Rolls-Royce at the door. Only we know what a revolution is. A revolution is fought by flesh and blood men, not by saints, and every revolution ends with the creation of a new privileged class. I assure you that if I had not been a man able to take advantage of his breaks, I would still be scratching corn-rows in Michoacán, and just as my father was, I would be satisfied. But the fact is that I got my breaks and I am here, and I am more useful to Mexico as a businessman than as a farmer. And if I hadn't, someone else would have seized what I have seized, stand where I stand now, do what I do. We, too, were of the common people, and our homes and gardens and automobiles are, in a way, the people's triumph. Moreover, this is a land that falls asleep quickly and can wake unexpectedly, and who knows what will happen tomorrow? We have to protect ourselves. To get what we have, we had to gamble. None of today's easy politics. You had to have, first of all, balls, in the second place, balls, and in the third place, balls. To do business, you had to wade into politics up to your neck and to change when the wind changed. There were no North American partners to protect against any eventuality. You gambled everything, and every day. And so we grew powerful with the true Mexican power which does not consist of a show of strength. Today no one tyrannizes Mexicans. They don't need to. Mexicans are tyrannized by what they are. And for thirty years there has been no other tyranny. What we have to do is very different, to kick the country in the ass and keep kicking it, not give in, never let it go back to sleep. Which has produced, far from upheaval and protest, admiration. In Mexico no one is more admired than a perfect son of a bitch, you know."

Robles's arms fell. Exaltation had darkened his skin, Indian color, the Indian so carefully disguised by cashmere and cologne.

"We know what the country needs, what its problems are. There is nothing the country can do except put up with us, or fall back into anarchy, which the middle class won't permit. You know, Cienfuegos, you're very sly, you just listen. Don't think I've told you any real secrets, or that I've been talking just to hear my own voice. You know more than you pretend to, maybe some day you'll want to try to scare me. Well, don't . . . that is why I've been talking. So you'll know just what you're up against. That's all."

Cienfuegos smiled, friendly and open, and in spite of himself Robles felt his hard face soften. Cienfuegos silently recalled the words of another man who had also created great power, another great and well-admired son of a bitch: "Mexico now has a middle class. The middle class is the active part of society, here and everywhere. Men of means are too worried about their wealth and their place to be of use to the well-being of the nation, and on the other hand, the lower classes are, for the most part, too uneducated to develop strength. Democratic growth rests upon the strength of an active middle class, hardworking, determined to rise." Still smiling, Cienfuegos reflected that with his flared nostrils, reptile eyes, and puffy, carefully shaven cheeks, Robles strongly favored His Excellency, the other great son of a bitch, Porfirio Díaz. For the last time the banker puffed on his cigar.

"Cienfuegos, what I tell you is so true, is so exactly the instinct of the country, that even our most leftist administrations have had to join the movement toward bourgeois stability. Mexican capitalism is indebted to two men: Calles and Cárdenas. Calles laid the foundation. Cárdenas brought it to life by creating the possibility of a large internal market. He raised wages, gave labor every conceivable guarantee, protected workers so there was nothing for them to agitate about; he established once and for all the policy of Federal investment in public works; he broadened credit, broke up land holdings and on all levels tried to stimulate a vast circulation of stagnant wealth. Those were permanent accomplishments, still living. If Cárdenas hadn't given the labor movement an official character, administrations since would not have been able to work peacefully and increase national production. And above all, Cárdenas ended Mexican feudalism. Mexico might become anything, but never again a kingdom of great absentee landlord estates ruled by a perfectly useless agrarian plutocracy. Plutocracy we may have, but thanks to *this* plutocracy, markets are created and jobs are provided and Mexico moves ahead. The Mexican Revolution has been wise; it understood early that to be effective, the time of militancy had to be brief, private fortunes had to be large. Not one important decision has been left to chance; all that has been done has been done after meditation. Each time the right man has become president. Can you imagine this poor country in the hands of a [José] Vasconcelos or an [Juan Andreu] Almazán or a General [Miguel] Henríquez? It would, to be blunt, be flushed down the drain by the rhetoric. Mexico's technological and administrative maps are drawn, and cannot be changed by newcomers. And here the story ends."

Federico Robles filled his chest with air, buttoned his double-breasted coat, and said, "Let's go. My wife has cocktails waiting for us."

He drew the window's gauze curtains shut.

7

An impressive number of American scholars of Mexican history accept the thesis of a "continuing" Revolution. According to them the Revolution, which began in 1910, survives today. Despite the emphasis given new national goals and the stress on industrialization rather than on agriculture, the major objectives of the Revolution still guide Mexican policy-makers. The welfare of peasant and worker is a primary concern of the government. The advocates of this interpretation support their opinions with statistics that demonstrate the survival and strength of agrarian, educational, and health programs for the general population. Yet not all scholars accept this view. In the essay that follows, Rene Dumont, a French agronomist who has traveled extensively in Mexico, offers a picture of the agrarian problem that questions the validity of the "continuing" Revolution thesis.

Rene Dumont:
Lands Alive*

There are two Spains: a damp one and a dry one. There are also two Mexicos. One is a very rainy one, mainly near the Gulf, and also along the Pacific, in the Soconusco, cacao country. The greater part of the country, however, is dry, including the whole of the central plateau and the northern coastal region, particularly in the west. It is even totally arid when it joins up with Arizona's "Living Desert", from lower California in the north to the famous Torreon *Laguna*. Note also the very marked relief, two long chains along either coast, the higher one towards the Pacific, and a very high plateau.

Very varied agriculture is called for, from equatorial production to temperate cultivation, but the possibilities are nevertheless comparatively limited for such a large country.

If we are to believe A. G. Gallardo, a quarter of the area of Mexico—slopes over 1 in 4—can only be given over to forests or pastures, and not even these in some places. Three-eighths of it is arid, and cannot be cultivated at all without irrigation; across another quarter, which is dry, some watering is indispensable to be sure of a crop. On the other hand, one-fiftieth requires some form of drainage or protection against flood before it can be used. There remains only a tenth of the country where the land could be worked without any previous improvement. Out of 197 million hectares (over $3\frac{1}{2}$ times as large as France) the only really cultivable land in Mexico is about 36 million hectares. Of these, 15·4 million are officially "open to cultivation"; only 4 million were irrigated by gravity, pumping or natural humidity in 1960; 2·5 million are irrigated by modern techniques; 0·8 million by private equipment—mostly pumping; 1·7 by older installations.

In 1950–4, the crops extended across 9 million hectares; 34 ares per inhabitant as against 36 in Italy, 18 in China; but the Mexican hectare has lesser potentialities. And though the population remained fairly static up to 1920, it more than doubled between 1921 and 1960, rising from 14·3 million to 25·8 in 1950, and 34·6 in 1960. With an increase of 31 per 1,000 per year (44 in the

* From Rene Dumont, LANDS ALIVE (TERRES VIVANTES) (London: Merlin Press, 1965), pp. 75–76, 80–94.

birthrate, less 13 for the death rate) Mexico beats most records, far ahead of China (2·3 per cent) and even Algeria (2·6 per cent). The area of arable land is insufficient to cope with such a rate; intensification, with water supply as its key, has become the major problem of Mexican agriculture. But even if the record pace of 1951–2 were kept up, a properly perfected water supply and control could not be achieved before the end of the century: regular watering would provide another 8 million hectares. By then, at the present rate of increase, the Mexican population is expected to exceed 100 million, nearly twice that of France. Once again there can be no solution without industrialization, the driving power of a national economy; Mexico has fortunately understood this: "Agriculturism" is on the wane. Likewise there will be no solution without birth control. . . .

In 1940, there were 14,680 *ejidos* containing 1,600,000 people with rights to the land. It was estimated then that 378,000 of these had received no land at all and that 461,000 did not cultivate their plots for want of capital and tools. It would seem that this proportion has not changed much since. In 1960, there were 20,000 *ejidos* and 2 million eligible people (not quite half the arable land, as against 51 per cent twenty years before). Not that their area had increased, but reclamation clearing had been far more active in the private sector. The total area thus distributed was almost 39 million hectares in 1950, 1·2 million of them irrigated, 346,000 fairly well watered, 6·9 million arable for dry crops, 330,000 under orchards, and 16 million under pasture. It must also be underlined that, although they have half the arable land, the *ejidos* have only 30 per cent of the irrigated areas.

FORCED SUGAR AND DOUBTFUL EMANCIPATION AT TEZOYUCA (STATE OF MORELOS)

In a corner of the agricultural bureau in Cuernavaca, south of Mexico, an Indian peasant is waiting, standing up very humbly, his sombrero in his hand. No one takes any notice of him, or thinks of asking him to sit down. Independence, followed by a social revolution, has not yet conferred upon him a true human dignity. He is apparently illiterate, which is incompatible with genuine emancipation. Like the ticket inspector in the Moscow Underground, who has no folding seat, if we accept that she is "in power", here too, it is "through his representatives". We shall soon see.

Awake and up at long last, the agronomist joined us at eleven o'clock. According to him, the situation for the *ejidos* peasants has hardly evolved economically at all. They have achieved a measure of dignity and freedom of work; they are no longer the slaves of the hacienda, but they have only exchanged one master for another, and still depend on the *ejidal* commissary elected for two years. Of course, by law he cannot be re-elected, but the law is not observed. As a link between the central power and community members, although he may not be entitled to share out the plots, in fact he does, and tends to give the best to his family and friends. . . . At first, the granting of the plots for cultivation was not irrevocable: so the man who improved his too well, ran the risk of not keeping it for very long. It was in order to reduce such a risk that the grants became permanent and, in principle, hereditary; but without the right to sell or mortgage, which are property rights.

Morelos state, below the 17,900 ft. summit of Popocatepetl, is already dramatically overpopulated: 325,000 peasants and 4 agronomists. The size of the plot granted to each does not allow it to be self-supporting, and it cannot be cultivated properly. All the more as everybody living in the country received a plot, whatever his craft or trade: Zapata spoke of "those who are in need"; the problem of widespread hunger has been the major factor taken into account in the sharing out and not the objective of higher and better production. Thus a social element has prevailed over the economic, which is dangerous. Depending on the *ejidos*, the portions vary from 20 *ares* to 3 hectares in irrigated land; Morelos has not much dry cultivation. Before the reform, the greater part of the land in Morelos belonged to thirty-four owners. Many *ejidos* people, under-provided with land, leave and go to work as peons in factories, or on what is left of the haciendas; these are now officially called "small estates", which is the name of their Union, since by law no "large" ones are allowed. The *ejidos* dweller who no longer cultivates his own plot, lets it (although this is forbidden by law) at 500 to 1,000 pesos per hectare.

Fifty-five miles south of Mexico City, at an altitude of 4,000 feet lies the village of Tezoyuca, which in 1924 received an *ejidal* grant of land (from two haciendas which belonged to the same owner) from the very hands of Zapata. It supports 90 *ejidatarios*, among them Angel Peralta who received us in his fine brick house. It is tile-roofed, and has four tiled rooms, two bedrooms with two and four beds, one kitchen, and one reception room with a linen press and two sewing-machines. This is above the average living standard of housing in Mexican villages, for the *ejido* is rich. In the big yard stood two orange-trees, an oleander, a heap of maize stalks, a thatched-roof washhouse; and another luxury, a saddle-horse, tethered to a post.

On his plot, Peralta told us, he cultivated 33 *tareras* (10 *ares* each) of rice, and 15 (irrigated) of sugar cane, plus 10 (non-irrigated) of maize. His ejidal grant of 5·8 hectares, 4·8 of them irrigated, is not far from the maximum permissible (6 irrigated hectares; or 12 arable in dry land). In 1945, the average *ejidatario* in Mexico enjoyed the use of 17·6 hectares in all, out of which 4·6 were arable, three "open to cultivation" were subject to drought, with only 0·6 irrigated.

Rotation on irrigated land starts with industrial cane for three years (first cut fifteen months after planting; then two more crops each cut after one year). It is cultivated directly by the sugar factory (rebuilt since it was burnt down during the revolutionary period), which supplies tractors for the purpose, and arranges for all the work to be done. Only the sinking of deep wells and the installation of powerful pumps by the factory have made possible such extensive cultivation of cane; his own irrigation would cost him 1,300 pesos per hectare per year. The drop in sugar price coupled with heavy taxes gives him a maximum price of 375 pesos per ton, for a yield of 60 to 80 tons per hectare (average in Mexico 51 tons). Such crops are of no interest to the peasant who finishes up with about 78 pesos per hectare per crop (even if it is an eighteen-month one) ; that is one-tenth of the average rent of 800 pesos which he can obtain for the same hectare. Besides, he has to keep up watering and stop animal depredations. So cane production, which would otherwise not be kept up, has been made compulsory, to a set pattern of alternation with rice, for private owners as well as for the *ejidos* within a certain distance from the factory. And the factory is entitled to send its tractors to plough in a crop irregularly sown!

PEASANT'S STATE, OR STATE'S PEASANTS?

Of course the peasants have their representative in the sugar factory, an *ejidal* co-operative which theoretically belongs to them as much as it does to the workers. In fact, there is no difference between this co-operative and a nationalized enterprise. If a peasant's representative were to air views different from those of the director he would soon be sent away. Should he insist on putting forward his opinion there might be an "accident". In other words the *ejidatarios* carry little weight against the power of the factory, backed by the State. Perhaps there is a political recourse, then? Did they vote in large numbers against the Government at the last election?

"Come," Peralta tells us, with the disillusioned look of an old philosopher, "who counts the votes? The Government; so what would be the use of voting against it?" Almost a quarter of the population, our *ejidatarios* make up the large mass of the electorate, the "Revolutionary Institutional Party", which has been in power for forty years now and threatens them, should the opposition ever win, that the reconfiscation of their lands would follow. So some lorries arrive in the village, and everybody climbs into them to go and demonstrate, "In whose favour?" "We shall know when we get there!"...

After the cane, alien to the peasant's economy, and reducing the area available to him for cultivation, follows rice, for several years in a row. For preparation of the ground, planting out, and harvest, Peralta has to employ part-time labourers for a fortnight or so. He pays them 10 pesos a day; twice as much as in Bajio and Tenancingo where under-employment is more prevalent. During the highest pressure of the harvest the rate may be doubled, and sometimes even trebled for a day or two, as in Chaouia.

On his dry *ejidal* hectare, ploughed with one hired team of oxen (they used a tractor for the rice-field), the *ejidatario* sows maize mixed with beans; in very wet years he may get 12 to 13 quintals. Others will try a snatch-crop of winter vegetables, tomatoes and melons after the rice harvest; our host does not because "it does not pay". He has a few fowls in his poultry yard, but no pig. All this shows that Peralta is fairly well off. Were it not for his vigorous opposition, we would have thought him a propaganda showpiece like the *ejido* where he lives. He owns privately 1·5 irrigated hectares, also given over to cane-rice rotation (in the village, the biggest owner has 9 hectares). He has four daughters, and one son at college in Palmira. With his wife and two daughters living at home, he spends about one hundred pesos (8 dollars U.S.) a week, once the rains have ensured a sufficient domestic supply of maize and beans. Besides tortillas of maize and rice, pimentos, *guaras* (leguminous pods) and eggs, he buys a few groceries. With such modest productivity, even the less poor of the *ejidatarios* do not have much buying power: how then can they play an active part in the development of national economy?

FROM THE INDIVIDUAL EJIDATARIO TO THE COLLECTIVE EJIDO: A PROGRESS

The Agrarian Code only makes it compulsory to use in common non-arable land—pastures and forests. Only 700 *ejidos*, that is 4 per cent, cultivate their arable lands collectively. They are mostly in the irrigated zones, north-west, near the Pacific, and centre north, as in the Laguna. The upkeep of a watering system strengthens communal discipline: the presence of water entails certain crops, and also dictates new techniques; it requires considerable financing, which is easier to obtain through a collective body.

In North-West Mexico, on the Pacific coast, the development of irrigation has allowed the cultivation of fertile silts which were unusable when watered by the rainfall only (10 to 12 inches). According to Infield and Freier: "It is only when Cárdenas offered them land and irrigation instead of gunfire, that he managed to pacify the most indomitable of the country's natives . . . the legendary tribes of the Yaquis, the Cossacks of North Mexico. Since then, over a dozen *ejidos* have been founded, and they are among the most prosperous in the country."

In the opinion of L. Lasny, if the collective *ejidos* of that region have done particularly well, it is largely because of the availability of land (up to 40 irrigated hectares per family) and also because of the *Banco del ejidal*. Its technicians scrutinize the cost price of each crop, and so determine the total loan required (repayable in a year at 8 per cent) based on a declaration of sowings either by the individual or by the representative of the collective *ejido*. Wisely, they make their grant progressive to correspond with each stage of a sequence of needs. Thus, one hectare of wheat near Hermosillo, in Sonora State, required 191 pesos for ground preparation, 483 during the sowing (170 for seed and 170 for nitrogen supplied as ammonia gas), 276 during the growing of the crop (170 nitrogen), 240 at harvest, and 52 for storage, losses, warrants; plus 150 for general expenses: insurance, loan interest, medical services, etc.

Thanks to the new varieties, much more immune to black blight, which have been developed by the researchers of the Rockefeller Foundation, a crop is assured. The use of fertilizers becomes a paying proposition, and Mexican yield rose from 8 quintals per hectare in 1946 to over 14 in 1957; with reasonable expectation of 23 quintals in 1966. National production rose from 3·5 to 13·2 million quintals between 1945 and 1957, completely obviating the need to import. (It must be noted that the imports had been coming from the U.S.A.) The annual increase in consumption, half a million quintals, results both from demographic expansion and from improved feeding standards: bread is steadily replacing the maize tortilla. Since 1958, in fact, Mexico has claimed an export quota, within the terms of the international wheat agreement.

CRISIS IN THE EJIDOS: MAN OR SYSTEM

But at this point the question arises: Individual *ejidal* cultivation or collective *ejido*: which is the right formula for progress? Are they to rely on institutional systems or on the purposive integrity of men? Infield and Krier stress: "The unequal development of the *ejidos* . . . startling progress next to the darkest stagnation, in the same region, under virtually identical conditions". They think that the main source of evil in the Laguna region, near Torreon, bordering the states of Durango and Coahuila, is not so much poverty as politics. Indeed, two rival organizations are to be found there: the *Confederación Nacional de Campesinos*, semi-official, and the *Central Union of Ejidatarios*, controlled by a radical left—the opposition. The latter groups the poorer of the *ejidos*, and accuses the Government of deception, underhand dealing and business operations, bad management of the banks, chiefly where the sale of the harvest is concerned, to say nothing of administrative corruption, even outright theft and fraud. . . . It demands that bank accounts be available for public investigation with an obstinacy equalled only by the lack of response. The bank which arranges the financing and sale of the crop may of course abuse its monopoly privilege, but when the *ejido* is a success, it is mainly due to the bank technicians: even if these things are *for* the people, they are not yet *by* the people.

Having mentioned that corn and cotton yields in Laguna have in fact dropped, our commentators are reluctant to blame it exclusively on shortage of water. (Overpopulation, which does not occur in Sonora where space made an economic modernization easier, is again relevant here: "Half the peasants in this region are out of work.") Yet is this the only explanation? "Why have intellectuals and peasants, who at the beginning offered their services with enthusiasm, now completely deserted the *ejidos*? Bad conditions are certainly not improved, and may even be worsened by intrigue behind the scenes, particularly in the obscure realm of politics."

Elsewhere, our authors blame indifferences and idleness. "At Nueva Italia, although anyone at all willing can earn up to 10,000 pesos per year, most labourers, in fact, earn no more than 3,000. And why? Earnings of this order are higher than those they could obtain in the hacienda system, and what is more, they can earn that much by working only half the time. Some men would sooner

increase their leisure than their income or their standard of living."
And why, pray, should the whole world abide by the law of strenuous work, originally Western European, and later propagated
throughout communist systems as far as the furthest Asiatic countries, where it was already widely current? Mexico can offer more
non-functional ostentatious showpieces, like the *ejidal* hospital of
Progresso, than initiators who do not fear a reputation for being
pernickety, like Señor Campos, who is carrying Nueva California
almost forcibly along the road to progress.

A "SMALL" PROPERTY: 240 IRRIGATED HECTARES AND 100 COWS: SETTLER AND FELLAH

Only the "small"-holders remain officially entitled to private
property. The law, which varies from state to state, limits them to
150 hectares on irrigated soil, and 200 in dry soil, for the richer
valleys. These figures were quickly reached by the spontaneous
splitting-up of haciendas seeking to avoid expropriation. Besides,
50 or even 100 hectares were soon granted as extra for each member of the family—and it is not difficult to find people prepared
to lend their names. In fact it seems since then that estates are
not subjected to the reform when owned by those who are on good
terms with the powers that be. In Sonora State, private farms can
reach 400 irrigated hectares, and elsewhere even 1,000 hectares.
And there is nothing to stop one proprietor from holding estates
in each different state.

So with Dr. Borlaugh, a geneticist from the Rockefeller foundation, we set out again on the road westwards, via Toluca, over
the Las Cruces pass (altitude 9,600 feet) in our shirt sleeves at
four o'clock in the afternoon, in mid-January, among the forests
of pine, fir and cypress. The *pulque* agaves were planted all around
the maize fields, on very steep slopes (not unlike the vine cordons
set around cultivated plots in the Basque hills). The more important farmers live in the village, to be near the school and good
drinking water. The schoolmaster, unless he be a true missionary,
does not accept a village post away from the road which will allow
him to remain in contact with civilization. Because of the north-
south mountains line, few roads go from east to west, and thus
"Mexico is full of lost villages, static ethnic groups and isolated
communities, shut away behind arid mountains, and as remote
from civilization as in Cortes' time." (T. Mende.)

Around Toluca, technical level and the overpopulation are
reminiscent of the Mediterranean and of China; although China

never reaches such high population density at an altitude of 8,500 feet. With wheat and lucerne being cultivated only by irrigation, maize is dominant. The vegetation of the countryside argues drier conditions, and at San Juan del Rio, with its high-walled lanes, we enter the Bajio. As in Spain and Portugal, theft is frequent. A long wall protects the most intensively irrigated part of Ramón Corral's hacienda, with its orchard, and its 50,000-plant vineyard, planted 8 ft. by 4 ft. apart. Expensive cars, fine gardens, opulent patio, television; nothing about Ramón Corral suggests a wretched victim of the agrarian reform and social revolution.

FOUR TO FIVE COWS PER HECTARE

Three tractors, one of them a caterpillar, 1 reaper-and-binder, 2 harvester-threshers, remind one of a modern North-American farm. The Bajio passed from the scythe to the harvester without any transitional stage. A hundred Frisian cows (and 30 for fattening), produce a daily average of 1,100 litres of milk, or a total lactation per cow per annum of about 4,000 litres. Under the tropical climate, tempered by altitude, lucerne crops, which make the basic food of the animal, merely slow down a little in winter and can be cut eight or nine times a year, with a yield each time of 1·5 to 2 tons of dry hay. With phospho-nitrogen fertilizers, it is possible to reach 3 tons per crop, and therefore to feed 4 or 5 cows per hectare. A real paradise for livestock rearing. (In the Santa Monica estate, near Mexico City, at a still higher altitude, 275 cows are fed the whole year round on 75 hectares of lucerne with a self-contained cultivation cycle—animal manure being returned to the field without any other fertilizer or rotation; lucerne crops succeed one another without interruption for over fifteen years on the same soil.) So much for the "natural superiority" of temperate countries for stock-raising.

Ramón Corral employs forty-five labourers, more or less permanently despite a certain number of individual comings and goings. "We have no labour problem here." From his point of view, all is well. He pays out one of the lowest wages in Mexico, 4·5 pesos or 36 cents for eight hours manual labour, and no food provided. The tractor-driver starts at 8, and goes up to 12, sometimes 14 pesos. The frightening unemployment in the region does not worry him; as too often happens with North African settlers, he gives his animals better living quarters than the peons.

His 240 hectares, all irrigable, are half devoted to wheat, often followed by short-cycle maize. Then 30 hectares of lentils, 30 of long-cycle maize, 15 of barley and 30 of lucerne. The cultivation trend is an alternation of lucerne with wheat and maize. Corral keeps 60 sows. He sells 300 fat pigs per year, when they are between 100 and 150 kilos (5 pesos the live kilo), and 150 piglets, for fattening to any weight between 25 and 60 kilos. They are fed on a basic diet of barley, maize, green lucerne and chick-peas; which often cost 70 per cent of the wheat price, like sorghum.

This large irrigated farm leaves the dry areas for the "real smallholders" and the *ejidos* of the neighbourhood. Their ploughs, and saddled donkeys, pass by his tractor and lorries. Their emaciated cows try to graze where grazing is dried and dead. Their livestock will be sold thin to Texas, where, within three months, the American fattener will pocket the profit. The fields have been badly distributed; the tangle of haciendas and *ejidos* is a source of wasted time and conflict, like forced cohabitation. Many *ejidatarios* still live within the hacienda limits, in their former lodgings.

There is an ugly contrast between agriculture which, because of its amputation, has been compelled to venture boldly into the pattern of modern capitalism, and adopt the latest equipment and techniques, and the small-holdings of the illiterate peasants, whether collective or private. This state of affairs is not unlike the respective positions of settlers and *fellahin* throughout North Africa, which has favoured the nationalist explosion. Here, the explosion has been, and may again become, racial and social. The economic prosperity of the United States, so close to so much poverty, enhances the explosive character. It tends to include Mexico within the bounds of its winter "kitchen garden" which as late as 1946 was limited to Florida and California. Irapuato grows—and waters—strawberries, which are dispatched in syrup, or frozen; and they plant carnations on the ridges between their furrows.

Besides, mechanization has overtaken intensification (as in North Africa), which is conducive to increasing rural unemployment. Many are the "braceros" who go over into the United States between sowing and harvesting to look for work, too rare a commodity in Mexico. There, they pick cotton, fruit, or vegetables, and perform such tasks as are difficult to mechanise, at times of pressure. Old lorries take two or three families, children and all, since they can pick french beans, peaches and tomatoes as fast as adults. Of course they cannot go to school at the same time. Nearly half these seasonal labourers are children under 14 years. One-third of them are illiterate. The *wet-backs* are those who have swum across the Rio Bravo illegally. The American farmers can then offer them very low wages, with a hint of blackmail: "If they raise hell, I only have to telephone and the police will be along immediately."

SOCIALISM AND CACIQUISM: BETRAYED OR SPED-UP REVOLUTION

Lázaro Cárdenas was right: "The *ejido* has a double responsibility: as a social system, it must release the peasant from the exploitation to which he has been subjected under feudal and individualist régimes; as an economic pattern of agricultural production, it must provide for the basic needs of the country." The social aim is partly achieved; the *ejidatario* already has more freedom and leisure. The economic aim seems at first rather less successful.

Ramón Fernández y Fernández, who directs research at the *Banco ejidal,* criticizes the system. The *ejidatarios,* who by law are his only clients, are a very peculiar type of peasant, characterized by their inability to understand bank credit. In fact, the agrarian reform has abolished an obsolete order, that of the hacienda, without any clear notion of what should follow it. It has recreated communal property, which for four centuries previously had been relentlessly harried and forced back by private property. When the ploughed area of the *ejidos* decreased from 51 per cent of the total ploughland in 1940, to 49 per cent in 1950, the percentage of their yield appears to have decreased from 36·5 to 35 per cent. So, on an almost equal area, the *ejidal* sector hardly produced half as much as its rival. Of course, the difference in their natural conditions is blatant. But the inequality of distribution of irrigated land is not enough to justify such a disparity. "The yield of *ejidal* holdings is a little below that of similar holdings privately owned, and very much below that of large estates." So said a United Nations booklet on Agrarian Reform in 1951. Since then the decline of the *ejido* seems even to have gathered speed. A study of the Cucutla region, in Morelos, shows that the proportion of ploughed land in the *ejidos* came down from 76 to 68 per cent from 1950–5. For the central part of Bajío, Dr. Carlos Manuel Castillo has shown that *ejidal* ploughing had dropped from 53 per cent in 1950 to 43 per cent in 1953. Investments in private estates are reckoned to be ten times larger there than those for the *ejidos*—the latter would not even pay for repairs to pumping equipment. "With the exception of livestock," Dr. Castillo goes on to say, "the *ejidatarios* are using up their capital resources at the rate of 3 per cent per year."

So, once more, Fernández notes, communal property is on the retreat. There is a trend, usually surreptitious, for human and natural resources to drift from the *ejido* towards private property: illegal letting of land, partial or total conversion of the *ejidatarios* into day labourers, métayers, tenants or owners of private property. Some provinces have refused to pass the laws enforcing the division of large estates. In Chihuahua, the state allows up to 40,000 hectares, claiming that for livestock-rearing only large estates are capable of modernization. The right of use of some *ejidatarios* has become no more than the charging of a rent. Such a form of tenancy shows a decadence which has accelerated during the last few years. Unless this is officially and courageously acknowledged, it is impossible to take measures to stop it.

SOCIALISM: ALL OR NOTHING

Ejidal possession is clumsy and imperfect; the land is neither socialised, nor collectivized. Only an important estate becomes the frame of a population nucleus: hence men and land are too closely bound. For the sake of a very doubtful security, freedom of choice and movement has been sacrificed. The *ejidatario* is becoming a forced labourer who, as in the *calpulli* of old, loses his rights if he ceases to cultivate his land. Besides, he finds himself incapable of developing or increasing his holding, by renting or buying a neighbouring plot. This is a complete "freeze-up" which puts a brake on free movement, always necessary for economic progress. Moreover, only one-third of the *ejidatarios* are able to make use of credit facilities. "When credit is untidily used, administrative corruption follows," Fernández concludes.

Yet this faulty framework, accentuated by lack of dynamic organizers, may not explain everything. In 1911, revolutionaries used to demand "land and books"; peasant education is the first pre-requisite to agricultural progress, and wise use of available resources. In 1910 illiteracy in rural areas was about 80 per cent and in 1940 the rate was still over 50 per cent, for children under ten. Under Cárdenas, [the] effort was intensified, and he asserted: "It is a barren, even a negative and dangerous thing to distribute only land, without also giving to those who receive it, the means of cultivating it"; and again with [Avila] Camacho and Torres-Bodet, up to 1946, improvements were carried out in that direction. It now seems to have slowed down somewhat. A "dialectical" process: after rousing the intellectual's enthusiasm for the peasant's cause, the agrarian reform has finally wakened the land-owners. Now on smaller esates, yet keen to maintain their standard of living; anxious as to the outcome of any neglect in their cultivation (or merely anxious for their very lives)—it is they who have been able to improve and intensify their methods. First discreetly, then more and more openly, since Cárdenas' departure in 1940, they have come into favour with the government—technical advice, roads, public works, irrigation.

It was certainly a difficult enterprise to set peasant agriculture on its way to progress, along a route where it could dominate its own destinies. The attempt could succeed only with the support of the most dynamic elements of the population, and total backing from the Government, who do not care to retrace their steps too openly and take the land back, because: "There would be a surplus of hats left over" (therefore a deficit of heads) as one *ejidatario* wryly commented. Therefore, the resumption of landholding is being carried out more discreetly, though no less surely. And sometimes even directly; with the *ejidal* commissary's connivance for instance.

So *caciquismo*, often associated with the name of Alemán, who retired with a fortune while Cárdenas was still working, has succeeded socialism. An evolution of the same kind is also happening in the other economic sectors. When Cárdenas—who is a byword of revolutionary integrity—nationalized petrol in 1938, his actions presupposed a long term policy of national investment. In fact, jobs are now being "found" for friends in the petrol industry; prospecting is slowed down, production remains static and scandals multiply at "Pemex". Whoever is not prepared to go the whole socialist way, would be far better not to start without assessing the consequences.

TODAY AND TOMORROW

Ramón Fernández y Fernández is certainly not lacking in courage, considering the political climate prevalent in Mexico today, when he writes in *Contemporary Agricultural Problems*: "When human qualities are lacking, and are replaced by arrogance and prevarication, a dangerous process of infiltration begins, and taints the whole of economic life. . . . Lack of honesty in our public servants is stunting our development. It is bad for the country when plunderers achieve public power, not only on ethical, but also on economic grounds. The disappearance of the concept of moral values is followed by the muddling and adulteration of concepts about all classes of values."

"The land for those that till it", is a socialist slogan from the first half of the nineteenth century in Europe, when the "man with the spade" claimed possession of land, to escape payment of excessive rents. To emancipate the "under-developed" peasant, in the true sense of the word, today requires a technical level which controls social change, assures knowledge and advisers, and through industrialization and general rebuilding of the economy, releases the capital necessary for an agrarian reform.

It is all very fine to write in front of the Agronomical Institute of Chapingo, near Mexico: *Explotar la tierra, y no al hombre* (Exploit the soil, not men), and anyway, why *exploit* the soil? It must be preserved and improved. It is not so easy to carry out this maxim in practice.

However the conclusion seems to lie within this paradox. Mexican agriculture doubled its production between 1945 and 1955, and is progressing very much faster than that of any other Latin-American country: so the agrarian reform after all can be called economic progress. But, instead of being due to the peasants who have "inherited", the success comes from the irrigation works, and from the efforts of the so-called "victims" of the reform; the agents of success are the dynamic expropriated *hacendados* cultivating smaller estates, and doing their best to recoup by higher yields what they have lost in extensive area. But without agrarian reform, without the revolution of 1910–21, things might very well have been different. While the *ejidal* movement is marking time, large estates are tending to regain power. "After thirty-five years of agrarian reform," states the Mexican Bank of External Trade in its Review, "Mexico still remains a country of large estate owners, and after a certain point, a policy of large estate economy —gain by area and not by yield—would again prevail." The inadequacies of a first experiment must therefore be forgotten and overcome: although the *ejidatario* may have lost the battle, he has not lost the whole war. He must, at the very least, keep up social and political pressure against private estates, until he is ready to become their technical competitor, and force them into economic decline.

Certainly land distribution must be completed or put right, as the same Review points out: "1·8 million peasants have not yet received any land: 0·5 million have received less than one hectare, and 200,000 have plots ranging from 1 to 5 hectares in bad, arid ground, insufficient to support a family". But, as we already know, progress in that field would be of no avail whatever, if it were not to go hand in hand with a far larger striving towards the teaching and building of technical staff and advisers, co-operative management and organized credit. The political climate prevailing at the moment in Mexico may not appear particularly promising in this respect. But excessive pessimism would amount to forgetting how far things have moved already, by comparison with other

Latin-American countries; the rich man, the exploiter who exploits both land and peasant, is no longer undisputed master, nor the only organized force. Facing him now stands—however poor—a peasant force which has at last won its social freedom, heavily clouded though this may be with delusions and deceptions. After a bad start, bristling with problems of all kinds, even "sabotaged", a bad agrarian reform is still better than no reform at all.

Suggestions for Further Reading

To fill in the background of the political events of the era of early independence, which are simply alluded to by Luis Villoro, two books should be read. Hugh Hamill, *The Hidalgo Revolt* (New York, 1933) covers the early phase of the struggle for independence; his views generally support the standard interpretation. In *Morelos: Priest, Soldier, Statesman* (El Paso, 1963), William H. Timmons concludes that Morelos proved more moderate than radical. This interpretation is shared by Villoro in his earlier study. A brief and concise essay on the nature of Mexican liberalism is Charles A. Hale's "José María Luis Mora and the Structure of Mexican Liberalism," *The Hispanic American Historical Review*, XLV (May, 1965), 196–227. Perhaps the best synthesis of the early years of independence is Charles C. Cumberland, *Mexico: The Struggle for Modernity* (New York and London, 1968) which, though a one-volume history of Mexico, examines the era carefully. On the years of Benito Juárez and the Intervention, Ralph Roeder's *Juárez and His Mexico* (2 vols., New York, 1947) provides a pro-Juárez account which, though poorly written, covers the period. No English-speaking writer has published a notable work on the *Porfiriato*. However, a number of monographs on the Revolution include material on the Díaz years. Two of them, Stanley R. Ross, *Francisco I. Madero: Apostle of Democracy* (New York, 1955) and Charles C. Cumberland, *Mexican Revolution: Genesis Under Madero* (Austin, 1952) explore the final years of the Porfirian regime and the reasons for its downfall. Both are sympathetic to Madero and credit him with having launched a socio-economic reform movement in 1910. Although published nearly four decades ago, Frank Tannenbaum's *Peace by Revolution* still stands at the head of all the interpretative literature on the Revolution; he accepts the view that the Revolution stood for agrarian reform. A combination of *Mexico and Its Heritage* (New York, 1928) by Ernest H. Gruening and the work by Tannenbaum provides a comprehensive picture of Mexico in the 1920s and the early 1930s.

Howard Cline's *The United States and Mexico* (Cambridge, 1953) and *Mexico: Revolution to Evolution* (New York, 1962) discuss the economic progress since the Alemán years. In his *The Dilemma of Mexico's Development* (Cambridge, 1963), Raymond Vernon questions, albeit cautiously, the popular conclusion that Mexico's progress is not merely spectacular, but permanent.

Chile, Peru, Bolivia, and Venezuela: The Particular Problems

V

Chile, Peru, Bolivia, and Venezuela: The Particular Problems

In no country of Latin America do political parties wield more influence than in Chile. Only in Chile have liberal and conservative groups shared political power uninterruptedly since the early nineteenth century. A popular front government, a rarity in the Spanish-speaking world, captured the presidency in the late 1930s and early 1940s. Chileans elected a Christian Democrat to their nation's highest office in the 1960s; in Latin America, Christian Democratic parties either do not exist or barely survive. Though strong believers in the ideals of the Catholic Church, the Christian Democrats of Chile demand neither blind allegiance to the faith nor adherence to the conservative stance of their Catholic neighbors. They stand for progressive reform. What explains the uniqueness of the Chileans? In their attempt to answer this question, some scholars have stressed the relatively large size of the Chilean middle class, which they believe favors change. Other scholars have noted the large number in comparison with the other Spanish colonies of land-holding peasants in the colonial period. Perhaps, in the final analysis, the stability of Chilean historical development since the 1830s underlies the peaceful and orderly political life. The question, therefore, is to explain why Chile enjoyed peace and order while its neighbors generally suffered from political chaos and turmoil.

Chileans exercise no monopoly on reform parties. Long before the Christian Democrats appeared, the Aprista party (APRA) was a major political force in Peru. Led by Raul Haya de la Torre, an intellectual who came into contact with revolutionary currents during his years in Mexico, APRA posed as the champion of the Peruvian underdog, particularly of the Indian and worker. The target of bitter and steadfast opposition from the oligarchy and the military, Haya de la Torre became a symbol of reform in countries as distant as Cuba where the ABC, a secret terrorist political band made up of the sons of respectable families, claimed to speak for the teachings of the Peruvian prophet. Despite its wide popularity in the 1930s, APRA never won political control of Peru, although the oligarchy adopted many of its programs. Formerly a quasi-Marxist organization which accepted the teachings of José Carlos Mariátegui, the famous Peruvian Communist, APRA eventually abandoned its Marxist inclinations. To critics on the political left, the party and its leader, Haya de la Torre, have betrayed their former convictions. However, APRA continues to command a leading role in Peruvian politics.

Few scholars thought Bolivia ripe for revolution in 1952. Yet, adherents of the Movimiento Nacional Revolucionario, a political club of quasi-fascist origins, toppled the old oligarchy. In less than a year Victor Paz Estenssoro and his disciples nationalized the tin mines and, prodded by the peasants, enacted a program of agrarian reform. The redemption of the Indian peasant represented a major goal for the MNR. This program was difficult to carry out successfully because the Indian-speaking population who constitute at least half of the total population are an illiterate and exploited mass of peasants and mine laborers who seldom participated in national life. By comparison with the Cuban and even the Mexican Revolutions the Bolivian Revolution appears moderate. From the beginning middle-of-the-roaders dictated its course and maintained until the end cordial relations with the United States, which Mexico and Cuba did not. Without the financial and technical assistance furnished by the United States, including gifts of surplus food, the Bolivian Revolution may not have survived as long as it did. Unfortunately for the cause of reform, the Revolution never fully accomplished its objectives. It neither markedly increased agricultural production nor solved the problem of tin, the country's major export. Rising economic and political difficulties ultimately invited a military coup that deposed the MNR in 1964. Enemies of the Revolution say it collapsed because it failed to cope with domestic needs. If this appraisal is valid, what explains its failure? Are Bolivia's problems insoluble?

Nearly every country in Latin America survives by exporting agricultural goods or raw materials. Venezuela offers a classic picture. Petroleum, Venezuela's chief product, provides 92 percent of the country's foreign exchange and 63 percent of its national revenue. Foreigners, mainly American corporations, own and control the industry. Nonetheless, Venezuela, a colonial appendage of the United States on the basis of its trade picture, enjoys the highest per capita income in Latin America and a progressive political climate. Oil revenues have made possible a start on land reform and the implementation of social welfare legislation. However, Venezuela is the target of bitter and persistent criticism by Latin American nationalists; in their opinion, a foreign petroleum cartel controls the country. However, the Venezuelan experience demonstrates that national development is possible even though foreigners own the substance of a country's economic existence. To what extent have nationalist critics, usually vociferously anti-American, been proved mistaken?

1

Few of the standard works on Chile have attempted to explain the reasons why that country has historically enjoyed political stability; the majority of them only describe the situation. Among the scholars who offer an analysis of this intriguing and complex question is Maurice Zeitlan, a professor of sociology at the University of Wisconsin. His answer comes in response to the following query: "What struggles in Chile between what interest groups . . . in what phases of the country's development, led to a legitimization and institutionalization of formal political democracy?" His analysis, which rests on seven possible hypotheses, ends with a final question: Is the historical pattern of Chile, which produced a stable political equilibrium, still viable?

Maurice Zeitlan:
Political Democracy in Chile*

Formal political democracy, "that institutional arrangement for arriving at political decisions in which individuals acquire the power to decide by means of a competitive struggle for the people's vote," is always a precarious achievement, but especially so for underdeveloped countries. In fact, "political democracy has proved so vulnerable to changes in social structure that the better understanding of these processes has become one of the major tasks of social science." In this paper I offer a number of brief, even schematic, hypotheses concerning the social determinants of political democracy in Chile, because I believe that the reasons why Chile historically has been a stable political democracy are of general theoretical relevance.

Why has a stable multiparty system, whose political parties range along an ideological spectrum from left to right, endured in Chile for the last 100 years or so? This question is merely a particular and limited formulation of the general theoretical question: what are the social and historical conditions that are responsible for the development and institutionalization of stable political democracy? Focusing our study on Chile is of particular theoretical relevance because she is a "deviant case" in Latin America not only in the significant sense that her parliamentary democracy is unique in Latin America, but for another reason as well: Chile would seem to deviate from much prevalent (if not dominant) theory concerning the social requisites of stable political democracy.

Contemporary Western students of political democracy and revolutionary (so-called "extremist") politics have more or less consistently linked what they consider to be the social requisites of political democracy—the conditions under which democracy arises and remains viable—to conditions opposite from those in which mass-based revolutionary movements (at least, ideologically speaking) subsist and grow. Thus, for instance, the existence of the

---

* From Maurice Zeitlan, "The Social Determinants of Political Democracy in Chile," James Petras and Maurice Zeitlan, eds., LATIN AMERICA: REFORM OR REVOLUTION? (New York: Fawcett Premier Books, 1968), pp. 221–234. Reprinted by permission of Fawcett Premier Books and of the author.

Anglo-American democracies is often "explained" in the same terms (and by the same general variables) used to explain these countries' lack of major revolutionary (anticapitalist) working-class movements. Stable parliamentary democracy and a gradualist reformist (non-Marxist nonrevolutionary) working class are alleged to be different sides of the same coin, minted of the same materials and having their causes in the same social processes and relations. "The instability of the democratic process in general and the strength of the Communists in particular" are seen to be directly related.

Such countries, for example, as France and Italy are alleged to be *un*stable democracies not only for the same reasons that caused the emergence and sustenance of their major working-class-based Communist parties, but even *because* of the presence of these parties. Thus, the political sociologist Seymour Martin Lipset, in his important article on "Some Social Requisites of Democracy," has gone so far as to define stable democracies in Europe as those characterized by "uninterrupted continuation of political democracy since World War I *and the absence over the past twenty-five years of a major political movement [Fascist or Communist] opposed to the democratic 'rules of the game.'* " By this approach, as if by conceptual prestidigitation, a major theoretical problem is obscured: namely, the circumstances that cause (allow) self-proclaimed revolutionary socialist working-class political parties to coexist with (and exist within) a stable political democracy.

Chile, of course, is precisely the case in point: it is a country characterized not only by stable political democracy, but also by the presence of a Socialist-Communist "proletarian front" (FRAP [Frente de Acción Popular]) that received 38.9 percent of the presidential vote in the 1964 election and 28.9 percent in 1958. The combined Communist-Socialist vote has not gone below 20 percent in any of the congressional elections of the past two decades. If not for the low women's vote for the FRAP candidate, Salvador Allende, in 1958, Chile would have been the seat of the first revolutionary socialist government to gain power through elections in a capitalist political democracy. Among all voters Allende lost by less than three percent; but among the men he actually won a majority by about the same margin by which he lost the election in the electorate as a whole!

Neither particular "explanations" of the stability of political democracy in Chile nor general theories of stable political democracy that are widely accepted seem to me to be adequate to the Chilean case. A number of simple "explanations" for Chilean political democracy found in the writings on Chile are not really explanations at all: the "genius of Diego Portales," the fact that the people respect the constitution, that Chileans are moderate, legalistic, and pragmatic, that the government is legitimate, that democracy is a "tradition," that the parties (although there are many of them) have been able to form coalitions easily, that the military has not interfered (except for a brief interlude 1925–31) in politics, etc. Most of these "explanations" are less explanations than low-level *descriptions* of some aspects of the Chilean political system that denote it as a stable political democracy. These confuse noting a syndrome with explanation, much like saying that the reason that someone feels inferior is because he has an inferiority complex. My focus in this article is on identifying the aspects or features of the social structure as a whole that underlie or determine the stability and democracy of the Chilean political system.

There are also some general theories of political democracy that, while explaining something, still explain far too little and assume too much. For example, the theory that political democracy is rooted in a high level of economic development tends to be *ahistorical*. First, when a country is "developed" is not specified, but rests on an eclectic selection of indices of development, shorn of their historical and class content. The emergence of political democracy in the essentially agrarian nation of postcolonial and frontier United States, for instance, is left completely unexplored and untouched by such a theory. Also Britain, for example, evolved most important democratic rights and liberties, such as habeas corpus, a good deal of freedom of expression, etc., long before she became a "developed nation." German Nazism, on the other hand, came to power in a highly developed capitalist country—perhaps the most developed in Europe. Secondly, even a cursory look at the kinds of statistics adduced to "explain" stable democracy shows that Chile falls in different rank order depending on which indices are used. A theoretical rationale for given indices is usually lacking. More important, *on many strategic indices Chile falls well below some countries in which instability and dictatorship have been characteristic*. Thus, for example, while Chile's per capita income was $360 (U.S. dollars), two countries not noted either for stability or democracy in the past three decades, Argentina and Venezuela, were well above Chile, with per capita incomes, respectively, of $460 and $540. The only other country with a per capita income over $300 was Batista's Cuba, at $310.

Using a variety of indices of economic development, we find that Chile's rank in Latin America is not consistent with the simple theory that economic development *ipso-facto* allows a country to be a political democracy. A theory that fails to specify what interconnections there are supposed to be between economic development and democracy is no theory at all. Correlation is hardly explanation, especially when even many correlates are "wrong!"

Any theory of the relationship between economic development and political democracy must go beyond the mere demonstration of a close association between the level of development in a country and the probability that it will be a stable political democracy. Usually, once specification of the theory begins, a multiplicity of variables is introduced which have little to do with the level of economic development per se. Lipset, for example, explores the impact of religion, "key" historical events, the *rate* of development, the governmental structure itself as it feeds back into the larger political system, questions of legitimacy, and the reactions of the ruling or conservative classes, etc.

Beyond a certain level of economic development necessary to sustain any political structure, there is a vast realm of uncertainty about the type of political system that will emerge. *What is crucial about economic development, as far as its effects on politics is concerned, is its interrelationship with given types and patterns of social conflicts and their resolution.* Neither, in fact, can be understood without the other. "Democratic rights," as Lipset, Trow, and Coleman have put it, "have developed in societies largely through the struggles of various groups—class, religious, sectional, economic, professional, and so on—against one another and against the group that controls the state." It is this general idea, sometimes referred to as the "conflict theory of politics," that has guided my research into the sources of Chilean political democracy. My leading question may therefore be put as follows:

What *struggles* in Chile between what *interest groups* (regional, class, intraclass, international), in what *phases* of the country's development, led to the *legitimization* and institutionalization of formal political democracy?

I suggest the following very schematic working hypotheses concerning the question:

> *1.* The conflict between British and American political-economic interests in the first decades of national Chilean history was relatively two-sided.
>
> (*a*) In the period after Chile won her independence, British alliances with one sector of the ruling classes and the United States with another sector split the ruling classes internally and created conflicting centers of power within it, each interested, therefore, in legitimizing the right to differ. (O'Higgins, for example, was more closely allied with England, Carrera with the U.S. O'Higgins won his conflict with Carrera. The division lingered on after their deaths as an important basis of political alliance and disalliance.) Contrast this

to the situation in the Caribbean, especially the role of the U.S. in Cuba. Spain's incompetence, the U.S. intervention in the Cuban War of Independence, and its imposition of the Platt Amendment transformed Cuba into a political protectorate. This happened, moreover, when the major leaders of Cuba's independence struggle had already died, and the leading colonial families, who had been pro-Spanish and not pro-independence, could easily *attach themselves* to the new foreign power in Cuba, rather than have to *secure their own base* in the country.

(*b*)   In Chile the conflict between British and American interests, combined with Chile's own relatively developed economy and *independent* military strength (see below) prevented her from becoming either a direct colony or political protectorate of either power—the result of which would have been to prevent her democratic development, as is clear from the history of American intervention and occupation of the Caribbean. Toppling "incompetent," "insolvent," or "unfriendly governments at will scarcely serves to implant either stability or respect for constitutional order (or one's own rulers).

(*c*)   Chile's internally based ruling classes thus had sufficient *time* after achieving independence from Spain and the *economic basis* (see below) to demonstrate their own effectiveness and reinforce their legitimacy, a legitimacy they had never lost, since many of their representatives had played a leading role in the independence movement itself. Their legitimacy as rulers was never put in jeopardy, as was the legitimacy of "ruling classes" in the Caribbean—which classes often didn't rule and were in covert or open alliance with and dependent upon a foreign government and foreign-owned industries. The Chilean Constitution of 1828, the first after independence, may be said to have reflected the thought of the so-called Liberal "party" in the *Chilean* ruling classes; the Constitution of 1833, destined to last almost a century, reflected the so-called Conservative "party." The 1901 Constitution of Cuba was written during the first United States occupation and, therefore, reflected *United States* influence and could hardly be revered as a symbol of *national* order or the embodiment of the *national* will. In Chile the legal order was identified with a legitimate national government and could serve as a strong source of authority. In Cuba the legal order was identified with the interests of an imperialist exploiter.

2.   The *early* breadth and *rapid pace* of Chilean economic development gave her ruling classes unbounded confidence in themselves and their country's "destiny in Latin America," and thus enhanced their ability to rule on a subjective and objective level (the nature of the resources they had available). They had the might to secure their rule and to define the rules of the political game, and their demonstrated "success" enhanced their prestige and secured their legitimacy among the citizenry. Their success also helped them develop an ideology of "freedom" and laissez faire not only in the market proper but also in the political arena.

(*a*)   Chile's own imperialist policies were critical both in her early sustained economic development and in reinforcing her already stable political institutions. The War of the Pacific (1879-83), in which Chile got Antofagasta from Bolivia and Tarapacá from Peru provided her ruling classes with secure control of the richest source of nitrates in the world, made possible significant public works in the 1880's, and provided seemingly inexhaustible funds for the national budget.

(*b*) The rulers of Chile *demonstrated their capacity to rule effectively* in the "nation's" behalf, maintaining order at home and competently directing a victorious and immediately enriching war against two nations double her population. By demonstrating their prevented the rise of an independent military elite within the country effectiveness, Chilean *civilian* rulers further enhanced their legitimacy, as a possible threat or even a competing center of prestige or power, and, in fact, reinforced the subordination of the military to the civilian authority.

(*c*) The mineral resources (nitrates and copper) acquired in the War also served to enlarge and strengthen the base of the newly developing banking-industrialist-mining stratum in the ruling classes, which joined its forces to those of the opposition parties, Liberal and Radical, in their competition for power with the Conservative Party based on the older landed aristocracy and mercantile elements centered in Santiago and Valparaíso.

(*d*) The imperialist war also furthered the development of a sense of national identity and national "destiny," and a renewed jealousy of her independence. Moreover, the United States now appeared as a concrete threat in its attempts to prevent Chile from securing her control over the newly won territories, and thus provided a negative stimulus to Chilean nationalism. The War also served to strengthen a national quasiracist sense of uniqueness and superiority in Latin America.

3. Foreign economic investment was never predominant in Chile's agricultural sector, so that the Chilean aristocracy was not weakened or displaced by a foreign absentee-ownership class, as was true, for instance, in Cuba, where any genuinely landed aristocracy was impossible because of American penetration of agriculture.

(*a*) The pattern of economic development in Chile was also such that the agrarian social structure and therefore the base of the *terratenientes* as a class was left largely intact. Traditionalist and paternalistic relations had been maintained in the countryside within the haciendas until recently with little change. Isolated, localized, and few in number within the haciendas, the peasants and inquilinos formed a secure base for the power of the landlord class. In Cuba, in contrast, the development of foreign-owned large-scale units of production in the sugar sector based on the employment of masses of wage laborers destroyed traditionalism and paternalism, while, in addition, displacing the native ruling class. Present in the midst of the agricultural laborers and peasants of Cuba also were the "factories in the field," the sugar mills, employing industrial workers proper, who became an early threat to the political and economic order in Cuba and an ever-present potential revolutionary force, whose influence radiated throughout the country. In Chile the mines early became important centers of working-class power (see below) and exerted influence on the development of militance among certain peasants, especially the communal peasantry of the North; but these were essentially isolated from the peasantry as a whole and posed no threat to stability of the social order.

(b)   Despite the importance of early British economic investment in Chile, the copper and nitrate mines continued to provide a developed Chilean base of entrepreneur-industrialists with a secure economic base (more or less) of their own. This enhanced their early nationalist and "antiimperialist" ideology (with the additional impetus of the War of the Pacific and the ensuing diplomatic difficulties with the United States), and their loyalty to Chilean sovereignty and the Chilean political system. Their demonstrated nationalism, in turn, helped to sustain their rule and their legitimacy with the citizenry. Contrast Cuba, where when a certain level of "business nationalism" began to develop in the 1920's, it was under American tutelage and encouraged by the U.S. as a means of bolstering a cooperative businessman's government with a facade of self-assertive nationalism.

4.   The pattern of early economic development in Chile was also such that within a short period after independence was gained a genuine industrial working class appeared that demanded and won the right to organize and whose leaders were the bearers of democratic ideology.

(a)   The strength of industrial working class organization was in the South and the North of the country and centered in the copper mining, coal, and nitrate areas outside of the big cities and far from the capital. These were, then, major independent and autonomous centers of social power countering to some extent the power of the ruling classes and encouraging the legitimatization of the workers' right to organize.

(b)   Dispersion of these centers of working-class strength served as sources of countervailing power without posing a real threat to the power of the ruling classes, because local and regional struggles tended to remain confined to (and be dissipated in) these areas rather than grow into national struggles between the classes as a whole. In Cuba, in contrast, the sugar *centrales* were scattered throughout the country and located in the midst of the countryside; there was regular contact between agricultural laborers and mill workers, and coordination of strikes in the nationwide industry inevitably became a national struggle. Moreover, the proportion of workers involved in and/or dependent on the sugar industry made them a national force, in contrast to the situation of the Chilean miners, who always constituted a numerically insignificant minority of the working class, even including those in associated processing plants.

(c)   In the struggle for influence between the new mining industrialists and the old landed aristocracy, the workers in the mining areas were initially courted by both electorally and they apparently played a significant role in support of the mid-nineteenth-century political movement of the mining industrialists (represented by such men as Pedro León Gallo, Urmaneta, Vicuña Mackenna, Matías Cousiño, Gregorio Ossa, Agustín Edwards Ossandón). This helped to secure the latter's entry into the ruling classes while also enhancing the political organization and consciousness of the workers.

5.   The combination of the apparent strength of the new labor movement, based on the miners, the rapidity of economic development

and the attraction of the new fortunes to an aristocracy many of whose members had recently been impoverished by the depression of 1858-60, the fact that mining was rooted in the countryside, and the foreign origins of many of the new wealthy helped to integrate the new wealth into the old ruling classes by familial, social, and economic bonds.

(*a*)   The legitimacy of the aristocracy (old "names") and the wealth of the new industrialists tended to lend themselves to each other and to stabilize the new hybrid ruling class.

(*b*)   Introduction of so many new men with new ideas and talents also probably contributed to securing the *stability* of rule of the new ruling class amalgam, while the endurance of divisions and competing centers of power based on early conflicts tended to reinforce an ideology of political compromise and legitimize the right to organize and compete for political power.

(*c*)   Since the old aristocracy had itself participated directly in party politics, entered government service, and elective office, so too did the newer elements in the ruling classes. Men of ability and energy, therefore, of whatever social origins, looked on politics as a respectable career and, often after serving an apprenticeship in private affairs that provided them with a fund of common experience and values, took to politics as a vocation. In Cuba respect for elective office was lacking, fundamentally because such office carried with it little authority over the nation's destiny, controlled as it was by a foreign power. "Politics" was a dirty word; opportunism, corruption, and gangsterism were identified with public office; and men of quality either spurned politics as a career or were deformed in the process of becoming seasoned "politicians."

6.   Regional economic differentiation between sectors of the ruling class also probably made it easier to live and let live politically and to believe in it, since within these zones of the country different sectors of the ruling class could hold sway; on the other hand, all would have to defer to each other on the national level in order to conciliate and form coalitions and alliances to accomplish their ends and protect their perceived interests.

(*a*)   Zonal or regional loyalties, moreover, crisscrossed class lines and reinforced the bases of different political parties and factions within these parties.

7.   Ruling class economic and social integration was accomplished to a great extent, its legitimacy secured and the party system established, before the working class became an independent political force having its own leaders who articulated, at least, a revolutionary *ideology*. Therefore, the political formula or ideology of the peaceful struggle for power, while severely tested in the period of social crisis, 1925-31, could survive and be reinvigorated in the following years. The institutional patterns for the resolution and *containment of social conflict* had been set, and the rule of the rulers was sufficiently secure to allow them to be flexible in dealing with the working-class demands (though even here the Alessandri-Ibañez epoch [1925-1938] indicates the frailty even of the Chilean system).

(*a*)   The ideology of the peaceful struggle for power was of such sufficient strength in Chile, in fact, that it impressed itself directly on even the early prebureaucratic phase of the so-called revolutionary Socialist and Communist movement. The Popular Front then inaugurated an epoch of the participation of the Left in *institutionalized social conflict,* and of parliamentary socialism as a method of containing conflict within acceptable channels, that has endured until the present.

(*b*)   In fact, the Popular Front period served to implant an institutionalized working relationship between so-called revolutionary parties (Socialist and Communist) and the party representing the newer elements in the capitalist class (Radical Party), as a mode of trading the political support of the Left and its containment of working-class demands in exchange for "policies of national development" desired by both the Left and the capitalist-industrialists. Politically, a major consequence of this alliance was the stabilization of ruling-class rule and the reinforcement of parliamentary democracy during the critical period following the demonstration of the fragility of even the Chilean political structure in 1925-31. Moreover, this was also a period of sustained economic development, which saw the rapid growth of the working class.

(*c*)   The essentially parliamentary nature of the Chilean Left has rested on a working class that is *organizationally* fragmented and, therefore, could form little else but an *electoral* base. So long as its leaders opted only for parliamentary and "peaceful" methods of struggle, and failed even to put its resources into a sustained drive to organize the unorganized, the working class, *as a class,* did not and could not really present a threat to Chilean stability. Apart from the copper, coal, and nitrate mines, and the steel and textile plants, in fact, Chilean unionism is even today essentially craft in nature, localized, isolated, and politically, even economically, impotent. (Of 296 municipalities in Chile, only 20 of them, or 6.7 percent, have as much as 25 percent of the labor force organized. Ten of these are in mining communities. All told, less than 15 percent of the entire labor force is organized.) Thus, the paradox and the basic weakness of the Chilean Left is that while it has deep political roots in the working class—and this class is in many senses very politicized—the working class has been organizationally unable to act with sufficient cohesiveness to destabilize the system.

(*d*)   Chilean political democracy has rested until the present, therefore, on an equilibrium of social forces more or less in stalemate, more or less willing to act toward each other in the political arena on the tacit assumption that each would respect the "rights" of the others concerning their fundamental interests as they define them. None has been willing or able to upset this equilibrium and risk the consequences. The result of this equilibrium, however, and of the Left's unwillingness to challenge it and risk a genuine confrontation of social interests outside the parliamentary arena, has been that, as Frederick Pike has recently put it so well: "What we have praised as democracy in Chile since 1920 has amounted to little more than a system in which a small, privileged class has been gentlemanly in determining, through very limited electoral processes, which of its members would rule the country."

In turn, this equilibrium of interests has meant that "Chilean democracy and Chilean capitalism have gone hand in hand toward producing outrageous social injustice . . . and [the] political hierarchy control that characterizes Chilean politics."

The Christian Democratic government, however, under the leadership of Eduardo Frei, seems to be breaking with this past and upsetting the equilibrium—an equilibrium that may, in fact, have already been upset or in jeopardy at least since the 1958 presidential elections. Many cadre of the Christian Democratic Party speak in a revolutionary idiom about changing the old structure of power, of making a fundamental agrarian reform, of the dignity of the *campesino*, and of the defense of Chilean independence. At the same time, their government has launched a severe attack on FRAP (the Socialist-Communist alliance) as the scapegoat of the nation's ills, is trying to establish a dual union movement under its tutelage and to break the power of organized labor, especially in the copper mines, and to outlaw the right to strike under explicit government approval. The government is also trying to organize its own mass base in the working-class neighborhoods, especially among the most impoverished slum dwellers, where under its program of "Promoción Popular" it is establishing what it calls "nonpolitical" neighborhood associations, women's clubs, and so on. Unions of peasants are also being organized in the countryside under its tutelage. The middle strata have displayed increasing mass support for the government, including attendance at mass rallies supporting its repressive policies against the mining unions. The present slogan of the Frei Christian Democratic government is "la mano dura," but against whom is still the big question. At the moment it seems clear that it is not against the large landowners, the bankers, the industrialists, or American investment in the copper mines, and throughout the economy, but rather against the old and institutionalized Left that had essentially accommodated itself to the existing political system of bargaining and trading. The question is whether the system of political democracy in Chile will survive the Christian Democrats' refusal to play according to the established rules of the game.

2

Revisionist history only recently gained a foothold in the literature of American scholars of Latin America. In the next selection Professor Fredrick B. Pike offers his revisionist interpretation of the Aprista party in Peru. In traditional literature APRA represents a reform movement condemned by the ruling oligarchy, and its leader, Raul Haya de la Torre, represents a persecuted reformer. Pike dissents from this view of one of Latin America's oldest "leftist" political groups. He believes that the Apristas, far from advocating reforms opposed by the old regime in the 1920s and 1930s, actually fought governments dedicated to enlightened modification of the status quo. He finds of dubious merit the claim of Apristas, and specifically of Haya de la Torre, that they spoke for democracy and self-government.

Fredrick B. Pike:
The Old and the New
APRA in Peru*

THE OLD APRA: AN INTRODUCTION

The Aprista movement celebrated the fortieth anniversary of its founding in May of 1964. The now venerable APRA (*Alianza Popular Revolucionaria Americana*) was, during its youth, one of the most important Latin American renovation attempts initiated since World War I. Even in its mature years when it has largely given up its pretensions to wield hegemony over all Latin America, it continues as a political power to be reckoned with in Peru, the native country of its founders and of all its important leaders. It is important, then, to inquire if the APRA movement, now beginning its life at forty, has been adequately understood and impartially described in United States publications. . . .

* From Fredrick B. Pike, "The Old and the New APRA in Peru: Myth and Reality," INTER-AMERICAN ECONOMIC AFFAIRS, XVIII (Autumn, 1964), pp. 3–25, 27–28, 30.

MYTHS OF THE OLD APRA

1. *In the midst of a conservative ambient characterized by blind devotion to the "status quo," the APRA arose as a unique and necessary voice of reform.* In reality, just before the turn of the century with the administration of the "democratic *caudillo*" Nicolás de Piérola (1895-1899) a strong reform movement originated in Peru. In the early twentieth century it rapidly gained momentum. The intellectual and political figures who contributed one important element to this movement can best be described as neo-Spencerians.

Strongly influenced not only by Herbert Spencer but also by Auguste Comte and positivism, Peru's neo-Spencerians believed in the empirical approach to all problems. They were highly optimistic that science could provide them with quick-progress formulas. They fully ascribed to the notion of social evolution. At the same time, they were much more tender, kind-hearted, and humanitarian in their concept as to how this evolution would be carried out than were their English master and many of his disciples. The Peruvian neo-Spencerians did not believe that their country could advance only through the elimination of the "unfit." Instead, they were satisfied as to the possibility of rendering fit those who because of historical and social circumstances had been made to appear unfit. Totally unlike the followers of Comte and Spencer in Mexico, Peru's neo-Spencerians believed whole-heartedly in the need for and the possibility of redeeming the Indian masses and assimilating them into society. They advanced the cause of Indian education and in general sought to free the native from the servilism that had been imposed by an unjust agrarian system and social order. In addition, they advocated the protection of urban workers through the enactment of a wide variety of labor and social security laws. Unlike the more publicized spokesman of change, Manuel González Prada, the neo-Spencerians did not maintain that society's downtrodden and dispossessed could be given an adequate place in a new Peru only if the presently directing and well-to-do classes were liquidated. The neo-Spencerians were reformers, not iconoclastic anarchists or total revolutionists. Precisely because of this they exercised a far greater and more constructive influence upon the Peruvian directing classes than did the immoderate González Prada and his handful of disciples.

Before the turn of the century Javier Prado y Ugarteche, one of the most revered university teachers that Peru has ever produced, had begun to write eloquently about the potential of the

Indians and the need to assimilate all of Peru's citizens, rural and urban, into meaningful participation in the nation's life. Not only in the classroom and in publications but in the Peruvian Senate as well, Javier Prado urged enactment of laws that would protect labor and curb the abuses of capitalism, in addition to measures that would be conducive to the emergence of a strong middle class. Similar views were voiced by such outstanding university and political figures as Manuel Vicente Villarán and Juan Capelo. The fathers of Peruvian sociology and perhaps the greatest sociologists that the country has produced, Mariano H. Cornejo and Carlos Lissón, were also dedicated champions of reform and penetrating critics of the *status quo*. Both were vitally concerned with turning Peru into a nation racially and geographically integrated. Prado, Villarán, Capelo, Cornejo, and Lissón were likewise concerned with eliminating political vice, looking forward to a genuinely democratic as well as socially open Peru.

In the same category with these men was Victor Maúrtua, who prided himself on being Peru's leading Spencerian but who also subjected Spencer's principles to far-reaching humanitarian revisions. From the same intellectual and political school came José Matías Manzanilla and Luis Miró Quesada whose indefatigable joint campaign in behalf of Peruvian workingmen culminated during the World-War-I period with the passage of important social legislation, including laws regulating woman and child labor and providing for the eight-hour work day. Even in traditionally conservative Arequipa, Santiago Mostajo (father of the renowned contemporary liberal *pensador* Francisco Mostajo) exercised widespread influence as the first important orator who emerged from the ranks and defended the cause of manual labor. Long before the national law, he introduced the eight-hour day in the carpentry shops of which he came to be the proprietor. The improved working conditions which he provided for his employees served as a model that came to be extensively followed in Arequipa's industrial establishments.

Peruvian presidents by no means remained outside of the reform current. José Pardo (son of the first *Civilista* president, Manuel Pardo, 1872-1876), twice chief executive of the republic (1904-1908, 1915-1919), was responsible for massive expansion of educational facilities and undertook important public works and health programs. During his second term, Pardo's cooperation was instrumental in securing passage of the social reforms sponsored by Manzanilla and Miró Quesada. From 1908 to 1912 Augusto B. Leguía, serving for the first time as his country's president, won genuine and widespread popular support not only by his convincingly expressed hopes for the future development of Peru which aroused patriotic fervor but because he worked effectively to improve conditions of education and labor. The extremely popular Guillermo Billinghurst who succeeded Leguía in the presidency was so enthused with his political and economic reform plans, which Mariano H. Cornejo had been instrumental in formulating, that he resorted to unconstitutional means to secure adoption of his program. Billinghurst's assault upon constitutional procedure in his haste for reform gave rise to a revolution which removed him from power in 1914. Still, the program he had advocated was largely incorporated into the 1920 Constitution, in the framing of which Cornejo and Manuel Vicente Villarán played leading roles.

If the men alluded to above mitigated the social harshness of Spencer's doctrines they were just as obsessed as their English tutor with the need for rapid material development. Although insisting upon political and business morality, they were little concerned with things purely of the spirit. Priding themselves upon their rational and utilitarian approach to the problems of Peru, they were staunchly opposed to what they regarded as the superstitious obscurantism of the Spanish colonial tradition. If they were not anticlerical to the virulent degree of atheistic González Prada they were still anxious to curtail the temporal influence of the Church and most of them were in the vanguard of the struggle that led in 1915 to Peru's law of religious toleration (President Prada unsuccessfully opposed this legislation). On the whole, the neo-Spencerians did not assign a role of great importance to the Catholic Church, or spiritual forces in general, in the restructuring of Peru. Their primary concern was to achieve tangible effects in reforming the economic and political structure. Science, reason, and natural virtue were adequate in their minds to bring about the desired transformations.

Another group of intellectual and political figures quite distinct from the neo-Spencerians contributed notably to Peru's early twentieth-century reform movement. This group was formed by men who tended to regard spiritual values as taking precedence over economic considerations. They were convinced that only a spiritual revival, based probably on a strong supernatural underpinning, would lead to the just, the integrated, the democratic and politically moral nation. Economic success, they maintained, would not suffice to bring about the redemption of Peru. Members of this school found much that was worthwhile in the Spanish tradition, and were strongly influenced by the Uruguayan *pensador* José Enrique Rodó and his plea as expressed in his best-known work, *Ariel y Calibán,* to protect the cultural and spiritual legacies of Latin America. For this reason they were frequently referred to as the Arielists (*Arielistas*).

A notable contribution of the Arielists was their reaction against the pessimistic tendency of the González Prada school to dismiss the entire Peruvian past as worthless. With patriotic and at the same time scientifically-disciplined zeal the Arielists turned to the study of the Peruvian past, pre-colonial, colonial, and republican, rightly convinced that they could thereby discover much that was worthwhile and that should be incorporated into plans for the future development of the nation. The preoccupation of the Arielists with their own nation, their desire to free themselves from blind imitation of foreign intellectual currents and to construct hypotheses based upon unique Peruvian circumstances, led to an impressive flowering of sociological and historical studies. For the first time in Peruvian intellectual circles it became fashionable to seek a deep and integrated understanding of the national reality.

However much they were convinced of the primacy of spiritual values, many of the Arielists had broken with the Catholic Church by the time they began their higher education. By the early 1930's, though, almost all had reentered the ranks of practicing Catholics. Two of the Arielist leaders who went through this process were the outstanding historian José de la Riva Agüero, one of the greatest masters of non-fiction prose that Latin America has produced, and the statesman, politician, orator, internationalist and sociologist, Victor Andrés Belaúnde. Exceptions to this pattern among the Arielists were Francisco and Ventura García Calderón, who remained agnostics to their death even though stressing the primacy of spiritual considerations.

The Arielists were preoccupied with the Indian problem and the need for the reincorporation of the aborigines into Peruvian society. Their concern with the Indian was based more on their conviction of his spiritual worth and dignity than on the utilitarian desire of the neo-Spencerians to see the native become an effective means for expanding economic productivity. At the same time the Arielists fully realized that the spiritual potential of the natives could never be fulfilled so long as they continued to be harshly exploited in the material order.

It has often been charged, and probably with considerable justification, that in their approach to Peru's social and economic problems the Arielists were paternalistic and more interested in reform as administered by a spiritually renovated elite than in attaining a genuinely open society. Still, given the conditions obtaining in early twentieth-century Peru it is likely that the only feasible reform would have necessarily been based upon a considerable degree of paternalism and enlightened tutelage.

Frequently uniting their efforts in the quest for a balanced and all-inclusive Peruvian renovation, the Arielists and neo-Spencerians were jointly responsible for the extremely important university reform movement that assumed significant proportions in 1919. Closely following the lines of Argentine developments during the same period, the Peruvian university reform succeeded ultimately in opening higher education to members of the middle and even lower classes, eliminating much professorial dead wood, and giving to students a voice, perhaps too much in university government. From this time on Peru's universities ceased to be bastions of the oligarchy. To a considerable degree the universities in the reform period were a microcosm of Peruvian society: as higher education became more open in the 1920's, the entire Peruvian social structure began to show unmistakable signs of increasing openness.

The most encouraging aspect of the two streams of reform in early twentieth-century Peru, Arielist and neo-Spencerian, was the manner in which both contributed to the creation of a consensus, a broadly-shared pattern of national values. Obviously until such a consensus emerges, no ideological or political force, unless it is totalitarian, can contribute fundamentally to the integration of a thoroughly heterogeneous population, transforming it into a nation. Significantly, both Arielists and neo-Spencerians agreed that the great need for Peru was *mestizaje*, that is the creation of a new nation through the amalgamation of European and Indian ethnic groups and values. Extremists of the González Prada school by urging the salvation of the Indians through the virtual destruction of the old directing classes and their culture had only fostered implacable cultural and racial animosity in Peru, moving the country ever farther away from the possibility of consensus.

One of the most eminent Peruvian intellectuals to give voice to the theme of *mestizaje* and the need for consensus was the historian Jorge Basadre, who represented the fusion of Arielist and neo-Spencerian ideology that appeared in the attitudes of many of the young *pensadores* of the 1920's. Beginning in this decade Basadre urged, as he has continued ever since to do, the need for an integral Peruvian patriotism, incorporating all the values of the nation, and not stressing some at the expense of others.

Arielist and neo-Spencerian initiated concern with reform led to an impressive literature of moderate *indigenismo*. Representative of this moderate approach were the works of José Uriel García, the best known of which is *El Nuevo Indio* (Cuzco, 1930). While praising the old aboriginal virtues in this book, Uriel García insists that the new Indian must be one who has gone through the process of *mestizaje* and assimilated into his nature the benefits, virtues, and lessons of European civilization.

If Peruvian reform currents in the early twentieth century were proceeding toward consensus on the racial and cultural question, glorifying neither Europeans nor Indians at the expense of the other, they were headed in the same direction in regard to the Church-state issue. Gone was the blatant anticlericalism of the preceding century. However much they were personally indifferent to the Catholic Church and inclined to seek their spiritual succor in Masonic lodges, the neo-Spencerians recognized the importance of Catholicism in Peruvian society and did not overtly attack it. The Church was quick to respond to the new moderation of the groups representing the rational, empirical school and purporting to be the heirs of nineteenth-century liberalism. In his pastoral letter of 1918 upon being elevated to the archepiscopal see of Lima, Emilio F. Lissón y Chávez lamented the confusion from which Peruvian churchmen had often suffered in distinguishing between what was spiritual and political.

The military was another of Peru's traditional institutions that had previously been the focus of seemingly irreconcilable conflict. In the recent past some of the more extreme civilian proponents of reform had regarded the military as a group that must be extirpated before Peru's salvation could be achieved. Realistically, the Arielists and neo-Spencerians recognized that, good or bad, the military was an institution destined to endure for many a year. They sought, therefore, to encourage the tendency toward reform and renovation that was beginning to appear in military circles, rather than blindly attacking all things pertaining to the armed forces. Thus, the way was opened for arriving at a consensus on the role of the military in a modern Peru.

Arielists and neo-Spencerians were also reconciled to the continuation of the class structure in Peru, at the same time that they sought to remove its more exploitative and artificial features and to work toward the emergence of an aristocracy of talent that would be constantly renewed. Rather than lashing out in fury at all members of the directing classes, from whose ranks many of them came, they preferred to arrive at reform through class cooperation. Here again, the two chief elements of early twentieth-century Peruvian reform contributed to the formation of a program and set of values acceptable to divergent classes and interests.

Finally, both Arielists and neo-Spencerians regarded capitalism, which was showing encouraging vitality in the early part of the century as well as the late World-War-I period, as the economic system through which Peru's transition and renovation would be achieved. There was no need, in the opinion of either school, to destroy capitalism and replace it with exotic systems imported from abroad. As a result, many of Peru's successful capitalists rather than being alienated by the Arielist, neo-Spencerian reform program decided that cooperation with it was possible and advisable, even though this might entail the modification of various aspects of the capitalist structure.

There was no absence of a promising reform movement when the APRA was officially founded. An intellectual evolution was underway that seemed to herald the appearance of a reformed, integrated, and reinvigorated Peru. Already it had produced considerable tangible results. More than at any time in its history, the country seemed to be on the verge of achieving through peaceful, evolutionary means an intellectual consensus, the necessary prerequisite of a modern nation.

The instigators of the APRA, who launched their party in Mexico on May 7, 1924, found themselves in exile for one very important reason. In their approach to reform they were dangerously and radically outside of the main stream of the formidable Peruvian renovation movement that had originated with the administration of Nicolás de Piérola. The role that they had chosen to play was not that of loyal or constitutional opposition aimed at correcting the various flaws and evils to which they could justifiably object. They sought instead to tear down the whole Peruvian social, economic, and political structure so as to replace it with one based exclusively on their own esoteric theories, rather than on a consensus of national opinion. . . .

It would be a considerable oversimplification to say that the APRA was alone responsible for ending the promising movement that was proceeding toward a consensus in regard to issues involved in Peruvian reform. Certainly, though, Apristas must assume considerable responsibility. While the APRA's founder Víctor Raúl Haya de la Torre did not personally identify the Indian as the sole possessor of virtue in Peru (he did, though, once say that the Incas had made the only worthwhile accomplishments in Peru), many of his more intemperate associates tended to do so. The appearance of this new extremist group with its strong element of exclusivistic *indigenismo* was naturally detrimental to the cause of reform. The directing classes which had come to recognize the need to aid and cooperate with the Indians in a process leading toward *mestizaje* were antagonized when fiery orators and publicists began to proclaim that reform meant not *mestizaje*, not fusion and integration of existing values in Peru, but the total obliteration of one set of values, the European, and the unilateral elevation of another, the Indian. This, combined with the widespread Andean violence that erupted in southern Peru in the 1920's, a repetition of the sort of racial disturbances that had appeared with the Túpac Amaru uprising of 1780 and have reappeared at intervals ever since then, alarmed the upper classes which had been growing more accommodating and hardened the lines of the adversaries on Peru's racial-cultural question.

In its avowed Marxian materialism and its proud claims to be the intellectual heirs of atheistic González Prada, the APRA antagonized the Church and undid the constructive work that had been carried out toward forging a consensus on the Church-state issue. The intransigent antimilitarism that Aprismo came to acquire in the 1930's served also to arouse old antagonisms that early twentieth-century reformers had almost succeeded in laying to rest.

APRA insistence that reform could only be attained through elimination of the upper classes, as accomplished by a combined middle class and proletariat, destroyed the evolving basis for class cooperation by alarming the upper and feeding the greed and envy of the middle and proletarian sectors. Typical of the APRA approach to the class question was a 1926 letter of Haya de la Torre to the Peruvian Communist José Carlos Mariátegui. "Now," wrote Haya, "the old ruling classes will disappear once and for all."

By introducing extremes into the discussion of the country's socio-politico-economic issues, by contemptuously dismissing as hopelessly inadequate and hypocritical all earlier reform movements, Aprismo drove the traditional aristocracy, many of whose members had sincerely cooperated with laudable innovation programs, as well as Church and military leaders, toward a more closed attitude, inducing them to regard reform advocates as likely enemies. APRA's anticapitalist position naturally contributed also to making the moneyed classes wary of reform movements, and just at the time when their cooperation had to a considerable extent been won by the moderate approach to innovation of the Arielists and neo-Spencerians.

2. *APRA's main contribution toward Peruvian reform was its emphasis on the immediate protection and redemption of the downtrodden, proletariat classes.* From the very outset the main endeavor of the APRA was to win the support of the Peruvian middle sectors, beginning to emerge in the 1920's as a potentially important source of political and economic power. The proletariat assumed only secondary and proximate importance in the APRA plans, in spite of the much-publicized, sentimental plank in the

party platform calling for the union of the downtrodden, proletariat classes throughout the world.

Writing on the Peruvian proletariat, Haya de la Torre referred to it as a "class still in formation; it has no class consciousness. In its great majority it is comprised of rural laborers who are illiterate. It lacks both the consciousness of class and the cultural level which have characterized the proletariat of more advanced capitalist countries." Haya then revealed where his immediate hopes lay.

> On the other hand, there is a middle class, made up of artesans and peasants who own means of production, mining and industrial workers, small capitalists and land-owners, and merchants. To this class belong also the intellectual workers, the professionals, the technicians, as well as private and state employees.
>
> It is this middle group that is being pushed toward ruination by the process of imperialism. . . . The great foreign firms extract our wealth, and then sell it outside of our country. Consequently, there is no opportunity for our middle class. This, then, is the abused class that will lead the revolution. . . .

Aprista emphasis on the plight of the middle class and the need to bring security to its members was nothing new in Peruvian ideology. In a more detailed and statistically documented study than Aprista leaders ever made of the situation, Victor Andrés Belaúnde, beginning with his 1914 address at San Marcos University, brilliantly described how the insecurity and impoverishment of the Peruvian middle class underlay many of the nation's fundamental problems. When Aprismo began ten years later to propagate Belaúnde's thesis as its own, adding to it a new ingredient of revolutionary violence, the picture of middle-class impoverishment was no longer in accord with Peruvian reality.

Augusto B. Leguía, ruling in dictatorial manner during his second presidential period extending from 1919 to 1930 (the *oncenio*), was fundamentally concerned with weakening the control which a traditional aristocracy had exclusively wielded over national destinies, and balancing the old directing group with a new middle class. Like Haya de la Torre and the Apristas, Leguía sensed the potential importance of the middle sector. To a surprising degree, thanks in large part to the foreign loans and investments which spurred rapid economic expansion, Leguía so succeeded in strengthening and augmenting the incipient middle sector that it became a counterweight to the old and established directing classes.

In presiding over this social transformation, Leguía wisely refrained from frontal attacks against the traditional aristocracy. More constructive and realistic in his approach than the Apristas, Leguía was not out to destroy the old-style rulers. He sought only to balance their power with a new force, and thereby initiate the process that would modernize the Peruvian social, political, and economic structure. The dishonesty of some of his political friends and more importantly the disastrous consequences of the depression, prevented Leguía's policies from attaining an even fuller measure of success.

As Peru made rapid economic headway under the Leguía regime, the middle sectors gained in numbers and strength. At the same time that their economic status grew less precarious, they benefited socially and politically from the many favors and special concessions extended them by an administration consciously set upon currying their favor. Consequently, the middle sectors did not respond to the APRA cry to lead the proletariat in an anticapitalist, anti-imperialist revolution that would topple the aristocracy. Owing to the vision, the political moderation and sagacity of Leguía, the middle and traditional upper classes had begun to cooperate in Peru and both seemed to be prospering from and enjoying the experience.

APRA's preoccupation with Peru's middle sectors explains why Leguía was so harsh a foe of Haya de la Torre and his disciples at the same time that he was relatively tolerant of Peruvian Communists, such as José Carlos Mariátegui and Ricardo Martínez de la Torre. Leguía's hope to continue as the dominant political power in Peru, a position which apparently he wanted to occupy indefinitely, depended to a great degree upon the support of the middle elements. This was the very socio-economic group which the APRA was seeking to proselytize. Leguía therefore rightly regarded the APRA as his most immediate and dangerous enemy. Communists purposely alienated the middle elements, contemptuously dismissing them as the petit *bourgeoisie* and advocating their liquidation by the proletariat. As a result, communism did not loom as an immediate challenge to Leguía; apparently it could not become a serious menace until some time in the distant future when the proletariat had become a more formidable and self-conscious force. Meanwhile, communism could even be welcomed as an ally in a common battle against the APRA.

If Leguía would not for a moment tolerate Aprista activity in Peru, his methods of suppression were mild indeed compared with those which were utilized following his ouster in 1930. The rapid growth of the APRA in the 1930's has, in fact, been sometimes attributed to a public reaction against the excessively severe measures to which the Luis M. Sánchez Cerro (1931-1933) and Oscar R. Benavides (1933-1939) regimes resorted in attempting to suppress the party. This is at best a partial explanation for the amazing rise of APRA popularity in Peru some ten years after the party's founding.

In the 1930's the analysis of middle-class impoverishment made first by Víctor Andrés Belaúnde and later incorporated by Haya de la Torre into APRA ideology was in accord with reality. Menaced by the effects of the depression, the traditional Peruvian aristocracy ceased its tolerant acceptance of and cooperation with new social elements, thinking only of protecting its own limited interests largely through alliance with the military. With its impoverishment a bitter fact in the 1930's, Peru's middle groups grew increasingly hostile toward the aristocracy. At the same time they developed a sharp antagonism toward foreign capital. Once the depression began, tough-worded demands for repayment of loans accompanied by tariff discrimination and worsening terms of trade, rather than large capital inflow, seemed to characterize Peru's relations with the world of foreign capital. Middle groups began to look on foreign capital not as the necessary source of economic development and opportunity, as it had appeared to be in the 1920's, but as an instrument of exploitation, as Haya de la Torre and other members of the Marxist-Leninist school of economics had always described it.

More and more the whole sum and substance of APRA economic theory seemed vindicated. Not only was foreign investment synonymous with exploitative imperialism, but imperialism must indeed be the last stage of capitalism, a Leninism that had been diffused widely in Peru through APRA and communist propaganda. This theory explained the sudden collapse of the capitalist nations at the moment when their imperialism had apparently reached its peak. If capitalism was moribund even in the great world powers, obviously Peru must reject the system and seek its redemption through socialism, destroying in the process the aristocracy which was the natural enemy of the middle class that was to guide the process of revolutionary change.

3. *Communism exercised an overwhelming influence on APRA ideology.* In the first twenty years or so of its political life, the APRA was often pictured by an extremist opposition as a direct agent of international communism. The myth thereby created never won serious credence in the United States. This is one instance in which North American writers have painted a realistic picture of

the APRA. They have correctly observed that the APRA was a force not only independent of but also directly opposed to international communism.

It is true that Aprista leaders had originally appeared to be friendly to the early communist movement in Peru, led primarily by Mariátegui and defended in the pages of the influential journal *Amauta* which he founded in 1926. Writing to Mariátegui from London on November 2, 1926, Haya de la Torre extended fulsome praise to the Peruvian Communist:

> You, companion Mariátegui, have begun the work of bringing the workers, intellectuals, men of letters, artists, critics, and poets together in the vanguard. You have begun the realization of our great goal which is the unification of these elements and the formation of the *frente único* of manual and intellectual laborers . . . *Amauta* is the greatest possible contribution in the move to unify the intellectuals, laborers, and artists of Peru.

Probably Haya's favorable response to and the publication of articles by Aprista leaders in the early numbers of *Amauta* was not due to the desire of the Aprista high command to flirt with communism, but rather to the agonizing, soul-searching attempt of Mariátegui to make up his mind as to whether or not he was a Communist. In this respect, Mariátegui was something of a Hamlet. Perhaps his position vis-à-vis communism was similar to that of Brazilian *pensador* Jackson de Figuereida in regard to Catholicism. Describing his Catholicism, the Brazilian once stated: "I am a twilight being; though torn by an infinite doubt, I am still a believer."

During its initial period of publication, *Amauta* reflected the indecision of its director. In its various editions appeared articles representing a broad intellectual cross-current, ranging from purely Marxian concepts to those of Christian mysticism. The goal of the journal in its early days, Mariátegui stated, was to arrive at the true policy for saving Peru by considering and publishing the recommendations of all reform-minded individuals. By late 1928, however, Mariátegui had finally made up his mind as to what were the true means of redemption and *Amauta,* having become an avowed mouthpiece of communism, was engaged in bitterly assailing the APRA. Once the directors of *Amauta* had opted for communism they were bound to clash with Aprismo, if for no other reason than the Aprista glorification of the Peruvian middle class and the desire to accomplish social revolution through the instrumentality of this class rather than through the proletariat.

Responding energetically to the communist-launched attack against them, Apristas by 1930 were doing all in their power to vilify their new foe. At the same time they sought on dispassionate ideological grounds to show why their movement, although influenced by Marxism, was entirely distinct from international communism. Haya de la Torre began now to stress his space-time concept, which allegedly achieved the fusion of Marxian theories and Einstein's relativity. The essence of the space-time concept, which more recently has been inflated into the so-called space-time-history philosophy, was the assertion that although the economic analysis of Marxism-Leninism was basically correct, the fall of capitalism and the rise of the proletariat would proceed differently in Latin America than in Europe. This was because differences in space and differences in the stage of development of the historical evolutionary process in which civilizations found themselves prevented the simultaneous, world-wide application of a single pattern of events. Instead, there had to be relative differences in the unfolding of basically similar patterns throughout the world.

For all the talk about space-time-history and relativity, much of Aprismo's ideology was not only similar to but apparently directly copied from Marxian-Leninist analysis. Haya de la Torre, for example, throughout the 1920's professed the imminent collapse of the capitalist system and the consequent need for Peru to proceed with the establishment of socialism. In 1926 Haya asserted that the success of the United States would not continue forever, and the sooner that the oppressed people of the world awakened and took steps to prevent North American capitalism from feeding on the misery of workers in all oppressed areas, the sooner Yankee economic hegemony would come to an end.

In analyzing imperialism and asserting the creation of wealth exclusively by labor, Haya de la Torre was more often than not quite orthodox in his Marxism. Quoting Marx to bolster his contention, Haya in 1926 asserted that it is labor, and labor alone, which creates wealth. From this he advanced to the theory that the wealth of the United States was based upon its exploitation of cheap labor in Latin America and other areas of the world. United States imperialism, he held, was fast converting Peru into a colony, and neither the problems of the Indian nor of the middle class could be resolved until the imperialist yoke had been cast off. As might be expected in the light of this analysis, Haya complained indignantly about the fact that between 1917 and 1928 United States investments in Peru had more than doubled. He bitterly attacked the Leguía administration for having given additional concessions in 1924 to the International Petroleum Company, and in general for having delivered Peru to the agents of United States imperialism.

In exploring the question as to what was the proper name for those who populated the region south of the Rio Grande, Haya de la Torre again revealed this blatant anti-imperialism. Ibero-American, he stated, was an apt enough term to apply to them during the colonial period, while Latin American was the appropriate name in the early independence period. On the other hand, placing these people within a bloc that was denominated Pan-American was tantamount to describing them as the victims of Yankee imperialism. Indo-America would be the glorious name for the future people of South and Central America, when United States imperialism had been forever destroyed.

By the late 1920's communism and Aprismo were engaged in a running dispute as to which was the most authentically and uncompromising anti-imperialist. Communists and Apristas alike urged the immediate undertaking of Latin America's second emancipation movement, aimed against United States imperialism. Both groups agreed that the relations of an economically underdeveloped with a powerful and advanced capitalist country inevitably worked to further impoverish the weaker nation; that imperialism fixed upon Peru a system of economic exploitation in which its raw goods were drained off at ever lower prices, and prevented the accumulation of native capital necessary to resolve national problems; that no social or economic progress could be made until the forces of imperialism had been ousted.

There was, however, an inconsistency in the APRA line toward imperialism. At the same time that he and other Apristas called for a concerted effort to oust imperialism so as to make possible the introduction of socialism and the attainment of social and economic reform in Latin America, Haya de la Torre was revising Marxism-Leninism along the following lines. True, said Haya, imperialism is the last stage of capitalism, but only in the developed, highly-capitalized countries. In contrast, the imperialism to which underdeveloped countries are subjected is the first stage of their capitalism. Hence, the weak nations must encourage the imperialist process, for it will create the capitalism which will generate a powerful proletariat which will in turn lead the socialist revolution. "Before the socialist revolution which will be led by the proletariat," wrote Haya, "the APRA sustains that our people must pass through previous periods of economic and political transformation . . ."

Just how Haya de la Torre proposed to cooperate with United States imperialism, which in effect he had identified with Yankee investments, as a means of developing capitalism in Peru and thus hastening the socialist revolution, while at the same time urging the immediate end of imperialism, which he so often did, is not quite clear. Nor is it clear how United States imperialism could be encouraged as the first stage of capitalism while at the same time the effort was made to nationalize the means of production, as Haya advocated, and the middle class was being encouraged to lead a revolution that would emancipate Peru from foreign imperialism. Moreover, if Haya welcomed imperialism as the first stage of capitalism it is difficult to explain why he was so alarmed about the doubling of United States investment in Peru within a ten-year period and the concession of additional petroleum reserves to the International Petroleum Company. It is even more incomprehensible how Haya could have asserted in 1927 that the major struggle in Peru was between incipient capitalism and socialism, and that only the prompt introduction of socialism provided the way out for the nation; or how he could have praised as heroic and worthy of emulation the actions of an Aprista in fighting with Augusto César Sandino in Nicaragua to bring an immediate end to Yankee imperialism. Further, in his last stage-first stage theory, Haya seemed to have placed himself on a very tight and critical time schedule. If imperialism is in one instance the last stage of capitalism, then the wealthy nations whose investments should foster Latin American capitalism were already moribund. What guarantee was there that their wealth would endure long enough to allow adequate investment to create first-stage capitalism in Latin America?

Probably because the last stage-first stage theory was so glaringly inconsistent with the rest of his ideology, Haya de la Torre never stressed it in the early years of Aprismo. To the contrary, Aprista leadership emphasized the need for the prompt anti-imperialist revolution and the introduction of socialism into Peru and all Latin America.

In their acceptance of economic determinism, Apristas were more consistent Marxist-Leninists. Haya de la Torre boldly asserted that all Peruvian history, including the heroic events of the emancipation period, was purely the result of economic forces. Further, an early member of the APRA who is still very influential in the party and in Peruvian national politics, Carlos Manuel Cox, strongly attacked César Antonio Ugarte's book, *Bosquejo de la historia económica de Perú* (1926) on the grounds that the author did not realize "material determinism is in charge of the entire economic process." Ugarte, charged Cox, committed a serious error in his attempt to give some role to the so-called "whole man," thus denying the total domination of economic factors.

In virtually none of his writings does Haya de la Torre allow spiritual considerations to creep into his interpretations. There is a certain hardness, a tendency simply to regard men as so many ciphers to be manipulated in the game of clashing economic forces, rather than as beings possessing innate dignity and inalienable human rights. It is significant that never in his opposition to Yankee imperialism does Haya express fear, along the lines of Uruguay's José Enrique Rodó and his legion of Latin American disciples, that the worst danger of the United States might lie in the tendency of its influence to destroy the cultural and spiritual attainments and values of Latin America. The horizons of Aprismo seldom extended beyond economic considerations. . . .

Nor does the APRA leader concern himself with ethical considerations to the extent that Mariátegui often did. Deeply indignant over the charge that Marxism destroys ethics, Mariátegui argued that the zeal for the class struggle when it fully possessed the proletariat turned him into a true ascetic, more thoroughly morally cleansed and more ethical than any product of bourgeois morality. The allegedly ethical foundation of communism was all important to Mariátegui, while the founder of Aprismo did not seem concerned about providing such a basis for his party. In some respects, Haya seems more and Mariátegui less like the stereotype image of the Communist that exists in the minds of many in the United States.

4. *The early APRA advocated nonviolence and democratic processes as the means of bringing reform to Peru.* The APRA has often been pictured as championing, from its very origins, the use of nonviolent, democratic means to achieve reform in Peru and Latin America as a whole. Haya de la Torre, it has been said, was a great admirer of Ghandi and his school of nonviolence. Here is what Haya actually wrote about Ghandi in 1930:

> Time will continue to demonstrate that the nonviolence of Ghandi
> is more apparent than real. . . . If Ghandi completes his task,
> then will come others who will initiate the second epoch with
> new methods and new tactics. The work of Ghandi will remain
> . . . as the firm base of revolutionary action in India. It does not
> matter that his original program bore the banner of peace. In
> its essence it is war, violence, and forceful struggle.

Haya went on to say that if a certain element of nonviolence had been necessary in India because of British dominance, the situation was different in Indo-America.

Europe and the United States, in the opinion of Haya de la Torre, had been able frequently to avoid violence in their internal development because of a continuing integral evolution. No such evolution had occurred in Latin America, where feudalism still existed beneath a superimposed and weak capitalist structure. Under these circumstances, with the institutions of different ages and civilizations existing side by side, violence might be inevitable. Again, when acknowledging in 1927 his adherence to much of the philosophy of Hegel, Haya accepted the use of violence. According to the APRA's maximum leader, violence was a necessary ingredient in the working out of the thesis, antithesis, synthesis cycle. "Within all societies the classes and systems evolve, denying each other mutually [in the process of thesis and antithesis]. Out of the conflict emerges the new society [synthesis], the fruit of violence. Contrary forces can only be overcome by revolution."

Writing also in 1927, Aprista leader Carlos Manuel Cox claimed that the principles of humanitarianism and charity were superannuated and would be swept aside by revolution. In a book published the year before this Manuel Seoane, who until his death in 1963 was the number-two man in the APRA, called the people of Indo-America to action and combat. The same Seoane was bitingly sarcastic in considering whether reform might come to Peru through democratic processes.

> The task of governing a nation each day becomes more and more the work of science, of specialists, of men of high and solid culture. People cannot vote conscientiously if they do not possess the least knowledge of economic and political events. It is ridiculous to think, therefore, of curing our ills by giving the vote to the person who has had one year of school . . . there is a difference between the quantitative criterion of elections and the qualitative criterion of government: the two are mutually opposed.

> There must first be the work of culture; but since this is the province of government, it is necessary first to capture control of the government. . . .

> To speak of a Peruvian transformation based on suffrage is laughable. . . . Our formula must be another. We should be interested in the end and not in the means. . . . When society has changed, then you can think of extending suffrage. For then, if each citizen acquires knowledge, suffrage would become the expression of the reasoning will of the majority.

Seoane's conviction that only a few, initiated intellectuals could lead the Peruvian transformation was fully shared by Haya de la Torre. Inquiring if within the theory of economic determinism there was room for the hero, the strong man, the great man, Haya replied, "All the room in the world. The hero interprets, intuits, and directs the vague and imprecise aspirations of the multitude; but these aspirations arise only from economic considerations."

Given this ideological background, the reaction of Aprismo to its electoral defeat by the immensely popular Sánchez Cerro in late 1931 was predictable. Hypocritically, though, in order to justify the violence to which they were able to resort, APRA's leaders actually invoked the principle of democracy. The October presidential elections, they claimed, had been unfair, and the APRA had been unjustly deprived of victory. In reality, almost every responsible Peruvian political analyst who has bothered to study the proceedings agrees that these elections were scrupulously honest. Moreover, the military junta which presided over the electoral process was strongly hostile to successful candidate Sánchez Cerro, so much so that for a considerable period prior to the voting he found it necessary to live in exile. APRA complaints about the non-democratic features of the electoral defeat were only a smoke screen, because Aprista ideology scorned the use of democratic means in bringing about its revolution. . . .

It is quite clear that following the 1931 elections the APRA was unwilling to play a role of constitutional opposition to the triumphant party. Further, given the content of the Aprista program, the wave of violence to which the party soon resorted was to be expected. In March of 1932 an eighteen-year-old Aprista, Melgar Márquez, attempted to assassinate Sánchez Cerro but only succeeded in wounding the president. Beginning in his published pronouncements now to pose as the foe of violence, Haya de la Torre made a pathetic effort to explain the act of the would-be assassin. The boy, said Haya, realizing that the strict discipline of the APRA did not permit violence, had temporarily separated himself from the party before attempting the assassination. Perhaps the convenient out-and-in again trick explains how another member of the nonviolence Aprista party, Abelardo Mendoza Leiva, succeeded in killing Sánchez Cerro in April, 1933, and how still another young APRA militant, Carlos Steer, in 1935 assassinated both Antonio Miró Quesada, director of the violently anti-APRA daily *El Comercio,* and his wife.

If it is justifiable to assume on the basis of the evidence that the APRA shunned democratic means and opted for violent revolution in its quest for power, it remains to be seen whether once their hoped-for command of the country had been achieved the Apristas intended to work toward the evolution of genuine democracy.

The party structure organized by Aprismo did not seem to be of the type that was suitable to operate in a democratic environment. Learning probably both from the Communists and Fascists with whom he had contact, as well as from the experience of the

Mexican Revolution in developing a one-party system, Haya de la Torre insisted, in the first place, on iron-bound discipline for all Apristas. Membership cards were awarded only after a close scrutiny of the applicant and after party chiefs were satisfied that the prospective member would follow party discipline and ideological pronouncements with the same blind loyalty of a Communist Party cardholder. The attempt of Luis Heysen to explain the rigors of APRA discipline is revealing: "Its [the APRA's] internal life does not suffer in the slightest respect from the vicissitudes of other parties where the ideology and the discipline are not shared unanimously. Within the APRA the accord of the militants is complete and the discipline is accepted with pleasure and responsibility." ...

Obviously influenced by the corporate-state features of Fascism as well as by the attempt of Plutarco Elías Calles to forge an all-dominant, single party in Mexico on the basis of the corporate state, Haya added the following to his description of the ideal Peruvian state: "There will be a functional system beginning at the municipal level and extending up through the regional to the national parliamentary level. Parliament will be made up of the representatives of all sectors of production. Also represented will be professionals and technicians, whether they work for the state or not."

APRA emphasis on the corporate state was something new in the 1930's. It had not been a part of the original ideology formulated in the 1920's. Its subsequent addition seems to have been the result of Haya's admiration for the success with which the system was being utilized by two men who held democracy in disdain, Mussolini and Calles.

Perhaps more censurable in the early APRA program than the antidemocratic features was the desire to discard every feature of the past, both good and bad, in order to experiment with vague reform innovations which were assumed to be good primarily because new. The authoritarian regimes of Leguía (1919–1930) and the military dictatorships of Sáncho Cerro and Benavides in the 1930's were in their over-all effects constructive, because they combined an emphasis on order and authority with a utilization of traditional methods of capital formation and development. The Leguía period was marked by an incredible economic expansion, which by no means could be attributed exclusively to foreign loans, while the great contribution of Sánchez Cerro, and much more of Benavides, was to salvage in a period of extreme crisis all that could be salvaged from an economic system that although on trial had in it still much life and much that was good. By their authoritarian-administered use of pragmatically tested measures of capitalism,

Sánchez Cerro and Benavides saved Peru from the totalitarian-administered utilization of vague and utopian schemes concocted by a handful of dilettante philosophers totally lacking economic and political experience. This may be one reason why Sánchez Cerro and Benavides more and more assume a mounting stature in the appraisal of a large number of Peruvians.

3

Only three countries in Latin America have tasted the heady wine of revolution. Bolivia, perhaps the poorest of the Andean republics, is one of them. Until 1952 little had occurred to disturb the rule of a mining-landlord elite that dated from colonial times. Still, as Richard W. Patch writes, the old foundations stood on shaky ground. The catastrophe of the Chaco War had heightened nationalist sentiment and exacerbated popular discontent with status-quo-minded regimes. The Revolution of 1952 developed in response to the demands for change but only, Patch believes, after peasants had already taken the initiative into their own hands. Patch wrote this article during the euphoric period of the Revolution before the military coup of 1964. The situation, therefore, has changed since the publication of his essay. Yet, no one can deny that Bolivia today is different from the country of the tin czars. Patch makes the reasons for these changes abundantly clear.

Richard W. Patch:
Bolivia*

The word "revolution," like many another in our insufficient vocabulary of terms describing complex political and social movements, is overused and underdefined. Particularly with reference

    * From Richard W. Patch, "Bolivia: The Restrained Revolution," THE ANNALS OF THE AMERICAN ACADEMY OF POLITICAL AND SOCIAL SCIENCE, Vol. 334 (March 1961), pp. 124–132.

to Latin America, the word has been so often used that it has become synonymous with a range of changes from the relatively insignificant trading of power between leaders at the pinnacle of a stable political pyramid to profoundly significant upheavals in which social and political institutions mutate to new and unexpected forms.

Since the wars of independence, there have been few changes of the latter type in Latin America. Such a revolution did occur in Bolivia in 1952, and its consequences will continue to work themselves out in new social, political, and economic adjustments for many years to come. The Bolivian revolution has been little reported, and such reporting as has been done has been confined to economic aspects. But events in this Andean country, where a former depressed majority of persons speaking Indian languages have achieved not only emancipation but power, carry a vital message to students of Latin-American nations in which an economic segment's political power is likely to be inversely proportional to its numbers.

The revolution is also worthy of note because events subsequent to the shift of power in 1952 do not conform to the stereotype of revolutions in underdeveloped nations. The Bolivian revolution is genuine in its irreversibility. It took place rapidly, both in actual fighting and in the destruction or reform of long-standing institutions. Its leaders were early forced to extreme measures, from nationalization of the tin mines to destruction of the army and partition of the estates among Indian tenants. Yet this complete, rapid, effective revolution has remained in the hands of men who are essentially moderates—at least in comparison with any conceivable leadership which might have arisen in their place. The reign of moderates during periods of revolutionary change is notoriously brief, but this nation, in spite of its hectic history as a republic, emerged from its most critical trial under the leadership of men who accept the responsibilities of government, who use feelings inspired by nationalism to achieve domestic integration rather than to promote external strife, and who subject themselves to the rigors of a policy of austerity rather than seek the easy popularity of utopian promises. In this sense these men are moderates. And they are still in power.

THE MEASURE OF REVOLUTION

Before 1952 Bolivian society and its power structure were cast in the mold of the Spanish colonial institutions which persist in many Latin-American republics. In Bolivia, the mold was particularly rigid because over half the population spoke the Aymará and Quechua languages and, thus, were considered Indians. In this tight society in which exploitation was justified by social distance, it was the function of institutions such as the *latifundio* to define the status of these persons as serfs—beyond the pale of the urban, Spanish-speaking society; without hope of mobility. They were unpaid laborers in an agricultural system which supported the status symbols of the few while yielding a meager subsistence to the mass of tillers. The revolution not only placed the land in the hands of the men who cultivated it, it also destroyed the institution of *latifundio*, and went far towards replacing the castelike status of the Indians with a class concept of *campesino* in which mobility is possible.

Taking the long view, this is the crucial aspect of the revolution. No modern nation finds it easy to bring an alien culture with a long and conscious history, speaking a different language, and with an attributed racial identity into a national, urban, Westernized society. Consider how much more difficult the feat is when the culture apart is not a minority, but a majority with the potential for wielding not strategic but absolute power. The Bolivian revolution accomplished the formal integration with such success that true social adjustments to the new laws and decrees are proceeding with surprising rapidity.

But, as in all revolutions, the social adaptations are the most difficult to detect. Much nearer the surface are the economic results of the changes. In Bolivia, the economic catastrophes have been so dramatic as to obscure all else. An inflation of 6,000 per cent in four years, the conversion of the tin mines from the nation's greatest asset to its most persistent liability, the decline in agricultural production—all are undeniable and important consequences of the revolution and its reforms. But they are not the only measure of the revolution.

Nor are the originally avowed goals, the ideology, the intent of the revolutionary leaders reliable explanations of the revolution as it took place. Superficially, the drastic changes might be seen as the work of a single man, Victor Paz Estenssoro, the founder of the revolutionary party, its durable conspirator; and the compelling leader who has twice been elected president of the republic. But, if he and his party have left their stamp on the changes, they have also been borne along in the current of events and ideas which for many years swept the nation to revolutionary change. To give credit—or blame—for the revolution to Paz Estenssoro and the Nationalistic Revolutionary Movement (MNR) is to ignore that current. And the early pronouncements of the MNR now seem to bear little relation to actual policy as it has developed.

THE ROAD TO REVOLUTION

The country's recent history begins in 1920 with the fall of the self-styled Liberal Party. The Liberal Party and its predecessor in power had maintained a stable and strongly conservative government for thirty-six years. The principal platform of these governments was constitutionalism—respect for law and established order above all else. It was a period of financial equilibrium, expansion of the railroads and mining industry, but nearly complete disregard for the welfare of the impoverished urban population, of the tin miners, and of the 60 per cent of the population who were called Indians and who lived in abject dependence and poverty. The Latin-American phenomenon of *cansansio*—a popular tiredness with the existing government, a desire for change under the impression that any innovation would be an improvement—undermined the long conservative reign. At the same time, no coherent ideology emerged to fill the void after the regime fell. But two related propositions gained wide acceptance: first, that nationalism in the sense of a basic attack on national problems and the protection of territorial integrity was desirable and inevitable; and, second, that revolution was a legitimate and perhaps necessary means of political and social reform. These ideas were undoubtedly distilled from imported doctrines of Marxism and the ultranationalistic socialism of fascist Germany and Italy. No party, however, managed to give the themes sufficient clarity, and they remained in ferment until they crystallized in the crisis of the Chaco war.

THE CHACO WAR

Many threads led to Bolivia's unfortunate war with Paraguay over the disputed area of the Chaco. Bolivia still smarted from its defeat in a war with Brazil in which it lost valuable rubber lands and its ignominious loss of the War of the Pacific in which Chile seized Bolivia's coastal strip, intensifying the country's isolation in its mountain fastness. Cut off from the Pacific, Bolivia began to look toward the Atlantic and the river ports which would give access to it. Such river ports existed in the Gran Chaco where national jurisdictions were poorly defined. Bolivia began to arm. As part of its preoccupation with national socialism, it imported a German general staff officer who trained and equipped a modern army which was believed to be superior to anything Paraguay could produce. Petroleum was discovered in lands bordering the Chaco. Ardent nationalism appeared to coincide with patriotism, with a new outlet to the sea, with economic advantage, and with the possibility of a quick and decisive victory over a neighbor for the first time in over a century of lost wars.

Revolutionary reform was forgotten when war was declared in 1932. Unfortunately for Bolivia, its German chief of staff had calculated without knowledge of the inhospitable Chaco—a desert during the dry season, an impossible quagmire after the sudden rains. The Paraguayans became practiced guerilla fighters and subjected the Bolivians to defeat after bloody defeat. Casualties were heavy on both sides. Bolivia was forced to impress thousands of Indians to supplement its elite corps. Officers attempted to impose some unity by repeated discourses on the Indians' duties and obligations, and, incidentally, his rights, his citizenship, his equality before the fatherland. The war and the territory of the Chaco were lost to Paraguay by 1935, but it was the new experience and vision of the Indian veterans and the disillusionment with the senior army officers which would most profoundly affect Bolivia's future by clearing the way for revolution and by preparing a mass of people who would take advantage of the change when it came.

SECRET MANEUVERS

The junior army officers, circumventing normal government and party channels, organized secret lodges in a movement called RADEPA (Razón de Patria, or Reason of the Fatherland) and dedicated to fascist ideals and revolutionary means. The lodges became infiltrated with Nazi ideas as fascism gathered force in Germany and Italy. The RADEPA installed Colonel David Toro as president in 1936. Toro responded to the pressures of nationalism and direct action by expropriating United States oil properties and creating a state petroleum monopoly. His successor, Lieutenant Colonel Germán Busch, 33 years old, took banking power from private hands to create the state controlled Central Bank. He declared himself dictator in 1939 and moved to require mine owners to surrender to the government all foreign exchange earnings from the sale of tin. However, before the measure took effect Busch was killed or committed suicide under mysterious circumstances.

This secret political maneuvering by a part of the military was not an outstanding success. Governments dominated by RADEPA attempted to increase the power of the state according to their ideas of socialism, but they were unable to stir popular support or maintain effective public order. The political vacuum began to be filled in the early 1940's by the formation of half a dozen parties of varying tendencies, from the Nationalistic Revolutionary Movement, which was able to reach an understanding with the RADEPA, to a Bolivian Communist Party. The MNR, founded by intellectuals such as the university professor Víctor Paz Estenssoro, was able to combine the popular themes of nationalism and revolution with a program of government which included, in the beginning, the RADEPA's ideals of a powerful centralized state headed by the military.

In 1943 the RADEPA and the MNR deposed a president sympathetic to the Allies and installed Lieutenant Colonel Gualberto Villarroel. Paz Estenssoro became Minister of Finance. But the alliance was unstable and became increasingly unpopular after the defeat of the Axis. Finally, Villarroel was killed in his palace by street mobs, and his body was hung from a lamppost in the Plaza Murillo. The RADEPA was discredited, and the MNR was driven underground and into exile.

POLITICAL INSTABILITY

One government rapidly followed another in the succeeding five years. New liberals tried makeshift reforms which were frustrated by landowners, mine owners, and parts of the army. Traditional governments enacted repressive legislation which could not be enforced by an atrophied administrative arm, but which did arouse new restlessness in the Indians and miners. Two presidents in succession resigned their posts and fled into voluntary exile. Bolivia was fast approaching anarchy through the failure of one faction after another to master the art of governing. A presidential and congressional election was held in 1951. Paz Estenssoro, in exile, and many MNR congressional candidates received a plurality. But the army annulled the election in a last desperate move. A military junta governed briefly, then fell apart.

THE REVOLUTION

In April 1952, it was plain that if Bolivia did not have an MNR government it would have no government. The party had planned a revolution later in the year, but the defection of one of the military junta to their ranks made revolution an immediate necessity. For this reason, and despite the radical propaganda of the MNR, the actual fighting of the April revolution was not a spectacular struggle between strong partisans of the old regime and the revolutionaries. The old regime no longer existed as a group with faith in itself and power to enforce its beliefs; it was a shattered conglomerate of special interests without the force or talent to impose the principles which supported their privilege. Fighting in La Paz was led by Hernán Siles Zuazo, rebel son of a former president, and Juan Lechín, a labor leader who calls himself a Trotskyite. Civilian irregulars and a portion of the army quickly defeated loyal army forces, and the MNR was suddenly in power.

The revolution did not follow the rules. There was no class struggle. There was little loss of life. There was little fighting outside La Paz. There was no accession of the extremists, no reign of terror, no Thermidor. The keynote of moderation was struck by Siles Zuazo who named himself provisional president at the conclusion of the fighting, but he held the post only during the time it took Paz Estenssoro to fly to Bolivia. Paz assumed the presidency to which he considered himself elected by the invalidated balloting of the previous year. Siles became vice-president during Paz's term, then was himself elected president in the regular elections of 1956.

AGRARIAN REFORM

The important question was what the permanent results of the revolution would be. The mines were nationalized, but property once expropriated can be returned to private hands. The army was neutralized, but armies can be re-created. The unexpected and irreversible feature of the revolution was the organized emergence of the *campesinos* as a political and social force. The Indian population had taken no part in the fighting which installed the new government. For several months in 1952, there was little change in their lot on the *latifundios*. The MNR had plans for an eventual agrarian reform, but no planned reform could have been as sweeping as the one initiated by the Indians themselves and only formalized by the government decree-law of August 2, 1953.

The Indian organization which forced the reform upon the government had begun in the Indian villages of the upper Cochabamba valleys in the mid-1930's. It was another result of the Chaco war. The Cochabamba valleys contained Bolivia's densest population of Quechua speakers. It was in this area that the colonial institution of *reducciones*, the forced resettlement of Indians into new population centers dominated by a Spanish town, was pushed with vigor in the time of the viceroy Francisco de Toledo. The *reducciones* entailed many difficulties, and they were violently opposed by the *encomenderos* and by the superintendents of mines deprived of men for their labor levy. The institution of the *reducciones* had a brief existence in the Cochabamba valleys as in the rest of Alto and Bajo Peru. It rapidly gave way to the new *latifundios*. But, in Cochabamba, a pattern had been set. The serfs lived in hamlets or villages, not scattered over wide areas as before and as they do today in many parts of Peru. These villages continued to be as strongly influenced by the Spanish towns in the twentieth century as they were in the sixteenth century. Indian interaction with the Spaniards was greater than, for example, on the Aymará-inhabited altiplano or in the Peruvian sierra. In all probability, the aspirations of the Quechua speakers in Cochabamba to the status of mestizo—to which they were certainly entitled by race—was more keenly developed than in other parts of the Andes.

The experiences of the Quechua speakers in the Chaco war, the assurances of equality, the description of their rights and duties, were sown in minds already prepared for a new status. After the war, the veterans returned to the *latifundios* as serfs, on land which was theirs only at the pleasure of the *patrón*, for which land they labored three days each week without pay, and for which the entire family owed many other obligations: a period of domestic service in the house of the *patrón*, a levy of firewood and wool, care of the livestock of the *patrón*, and a cash payment, the ancient *canon*. The head of the family, the *colono, peón,* or *pegujalero*, as he was variously called, could be rented out as any other chattel by the *patrón* when the serf was not needed for work on the *latifundio*.

The Chaco veterans rebelled and formed an agrarian syndicate for the purpose of renting land for cash and escaping the feudal obligations of the *colonos*. At first they were successful, then the landowners also began to organize. They drove the syndicate members from their lands and homes. But this only strengthened the Indian organization. Able leaders arose. The syndicates spread slowly through the Cochabamba valleys before 1952, then rapidly throughout Bolivia after the revolution—with little help from the government. By late 1952 an organization existed, headed by a Quechua speaking *jefe maximo*, which united most of the Quechua speakers and some of the Aymará speakers of Bolivia. It owed nothing to the government and could act independently of it.

By 1953 the Quechua speakers began attacking rural landowners. The *patrones* and administrators of *latifundios* were driven from the countryside into the cities. Land, buildings, seed stocks, animals, vehicles, and machinery were seized and divided among syndicate members. It became dangerous to use the word "Indian," and the substitute, *"campesino,"* came into vogue. Civil war became a menacing possibility when the *campesinos* threatened to attack small towns. The government was forced to act and to act drastically. The result was the decree-law of the agrarian reform, signed in the Indian village of Ucureña under the watchful eyes of fifty thousand *campesinos*.

The agrarian reform has not accomplished all that some had hoped. Agrarian reform, like revolution itself, carries the magical aura of miracles worked overnight. But, in this hard world of realities, agrarian reform in Bolivia, as in other countries, meant temporarily lower production, greater consumption by the producers and a smaller surplus for the towns, an unwieldy bureaucratic administration, and long delays in placing the actual title in the hands of the new property owner. But the agrarian reform, together with an extended franchise without a literacy test, placed the seal of government recognition on the *campesinos'* new status as small farmers. They are still the lowest class of a class conscious society. But they now have the potential of upward movement in that society, which they did not have when they were members of the caste-like group of Indians.

MASS VS. INDIVIDUAL CHANGE

It would be a mistake to overstate the present extent of the change from Indian to mestizo. There are still many families on the altiplano and in the more remote areas of the sierra and *puna* who consider themselves Indians. Their cultural world remains much the same as in the seventeenth century. They live a wretched existence which can be called subsistence only by virtue of an extraordinary physical adaption to a grossly insufficient diet. They still maintain themselves in dogged isolation from the rest of the world they have come to fear.

Even in the more accessible areas where colonial *reducciones* established a tradition of interaction between Indian and Spanish speakers and where agrarian syndicates flourish, the new *campesinos* have not suddenly been integrated into the society of Western-oriented townspeople. The former Indians are, instead, a new class which gives a different shape to the new society.

The *campesino* class is not a mass of individuals eager to leave their relatively poor agricultural lands and to ape the manners and mores of mestizos, as in a process of simple social mobility. Particularly in the Cochabamba valleys, the *campesinos* are undergoing a genuine process of acculturation in the sense that entire communities are beginning to display behavior characteristic of the dominant Spanish-speaking culture. This is more unusual than it sounds, because a normal pattern of change in the Andes is for the individual to become a mestizo by leaving his highland community of birth, rejecting his Indian background, and assuming all possible mestizo status symbols. The individual who becomes a mestizo by this route, however, finds himself part of a despised "cholo" minority in a world dominated by urban upper classes to which he cannot aspire. This is properly described as a process of social mobility—an individual affair in which neither the Indian nor the mestizo communities are importantly affected.

In the formerly Indian communities of Bolivia, on the other hand, the group itself is the agency regulating the adoption of mestizo traits. The individuals within the group proceed at the same pace, with few persons standing out as "more mestizo" than the others. Neither is there strong motivation physically to leave the commuuity nor to reject identifiably Indian behavior patterns. Rather, the individuals are participating in a true cultural change, as a group, which promises to create a new culture retaining some indigenous features but, as a whole, closely resembling present small-town mestizo patterns. From this group, which now has the characteristics of a lower class, mobility within the next generation to any level of national society will be possible, especially for persons taking advantage of the public school system.

Education has become a basic aspiration of *campesino* communities. Most persons hold the aspiration not for themselves but for their children. Many communities have accepted the national government's offer to provide teachers for any village which builds a school. The situation and the potentialities of the *campesinos* have changed radically since the revolution. But, as stated before, this change is not apparent in ways which immediately strike the eye. The *campesinos'* houses are the same, their food is the same, although there may be more of it, their clothing changes only slowly towards the Western styles of the mestizos, although school children now use the purchased uniforms once the prerogative of the Spanish-speaking children. There is no rush to acquire status symbols, because there is a deep sense of the ridiculousness of a person wearing a necktie, for example, when that person is unable to speak Spanish. Sewing machines, bicycles, and Italian accordions are becoming common possessions among the *campesinos,* but they are only weak indicators of the change which has taken place.

THE LEVELED SOCIETY

The revolution has leveled Bolivian society in two ways. The bottom mass has moved upward, and the upper class has virtually disappeared. Ownership of land through a period of time was once a prime indication of aristocracy. Expropriation of the *latifundios* put an end to the badge and to the income which accompanied it. The hyperinflation of 1952–1956 wiped out much other accumulated wealth. Commerce came to a near standstill. Opportunities for renewing wealth dried up. The economic climate and public opinion were such that these persons found it more comfortable outside Bolivia. Large numbers left the country voluntarily, some were exiled, few have returned. The exodus has left a critical lack of professional and managerial personnel. It has also left a void which will eventually be filled by a class in which status is achieved rather than ascribed.

NATIONALISM AS INTEGRATION

One of the reasons for the present moderation of the MNR is the realization of the power which resides in the organized bloc of *campesinos*. The agrarian syndicates on occasion have taken measures in their own hands with dismaying consequences. But the MNR government has been largely successful in its courtship of the *campesinos* and in maintaining a counterbalance of power in the militias of the miners and the urban MNR Political Control Posts. But civil war between *campesinos* and townspeople remains a disturbing possibility. This, perhaps as much as the government's dependence on foreign aid, has dictated a policy of restraint and avoidance of extreme measures which might place salaried workers in conflict with the largely subsistence *campesinos*.

The MNR gave new impetus to sentiments of nationalism in a country with a long history of nationhood but in which nationalism is a new phenomenon. The banner of nationalism was raised in the 1920's after the fall of constitutionalism. The new philosophy called for a new approach to national problems which would supposedly transcend the legalisms of the old order. The emphasis on national problems permeated the universities, but it did not capture the popular imagination. It remained for the MNR to revive and direct the sentiment after national socialism proved to be a dead end.

The MNR aroused and used feelings of national pride to broaden its base of popular support, to identify the national good with the good of the party. It has been successful to the point where the only opposition to the MNR is the numerically small Bolivian Falange originally inspired by Antonio Primo de Rivera's Spanish movement. Since the MNR revolution, the Falange has mounted a number of limited but sanguinary revolts, none with any chance of success, which the MNR used to convince the population that opposition to the party is treason to the state.

PROBLEMS OF INTERNATIONALISM

In spite of the ardent talk of nationalism, the country is actually undergoing a remarkable experiment in submitting national interests to international supervision. The MNR is able to pursue its moderate course because of very substantial aid given by the United States. The United States has made the aid conditional on acceptance of economic recommendations of the International Monetary Fund (IMF). In 1956 the IMF drew up a detailed stabilization plan which the government found itself forced to accept. The plan achieved foreign exchange stabilization by freezing wages, allowing prices to seek their level, sharply restricting credit, and eliminating subsidies which the government had given to offset the effects of inflation. The stabilization is somewhat illusory because the effect of domestic policies is small compared with the effect of the United States contribution to the national budget. There is no illusion, however, in the fact that the stabilization plan has created large political problems for the government. The tin miners had lived more from subsidies than from wages, which remain insufficient. Salaried workers suffered from the disparity between the price level which increased some ten times and the new wage level which only approximately doubled. Worst of all, credit operations nearly ceased, industries closed their doors when allowed to do so by the government, and the prospect for economic development receded. Bolivia's experiment with international supervision of its economic policies has not been an unmixed blessing.

The cloud in the sky is that continued austerity imposed by the stabilization plan on the salaried workers—an economic stability unrelieved by economic development—may at last provoke the townspeople to more radical and probably ill-advised approaches to the unsolved problems of massive poverty and national dependence. The most popular and least responsible partisan of extreme measures is Trotskyite Juan Lechín, recently elected vice-president of the republic. The Bolivian national revolution is unique in Latin America, both in having wrought great change with a minimum of violence and in maintaining close ties with the United States. But those ties have not yet produced the dramatic results for which Bolivians continue to hope. Bolivia has weathered eight years of revolution without recourse to the crude machinery of totalitarianism. But a revolution within a democratic structure needs all the help and understanding it can get.

4

Since 1928 Venezuela has been the world's leading exporter of petroleum. Petroleum financed the dictatorship of Juan Vicente Gómez but also provided revenue for the political and social gains of recent years. Free of a foreign debt that limits other Latin American republics and possessing a strong and stable currency, Venezuela can afford urgent but expensive reforms. Michael Bamberger, an Englishman who lives in Venezuela, writes that it is not surprising that the petroleum industry and particularly the foreigners who control it pose a ubiquitous and controversial issue in the national life of the country.

Michael Bamberger:
Venezuela*

Recently *El Nacional,* one of Venezuela's most influential newspapers, arranged a series of interviews with experts on the oil industry to discuss a petroleum policy for Venezuela. All but one

* From Michael Bamberger, "Venezuela 1: Brittle Democracy," VENTURE, XVIII (July–August 1966), pp. 9–12; "Shall Venezuela Nationalize?" VENTURE, XVIII (September 1966), pp. 19–22.

stated that the government must establish a much stricter control over the foreign companies who at present run almost the whole of industry, and several suggested the nationalisation of the whole oil industry must be the ultimate aim. A similar opinion is expressed in most other Venezuelan papers. The government itself has just published a plan stating that the state must increase greatly its participation in the oil industry.

At the same time a battle is in progress between the oil companies and the Venezuelan government over a claim for approximately £50 million of back taxes. Another dispute between the governments of Venezuela and the United States concerns the quotas for Venezuelan oil entering the United States.

What are the reasons for these discussions? At present over 90 per cent of Venezuela's foreign exchange comes from oil, and the future of the industry is obviously vital for Venezuela. However, the problem of oil is closely related to a number of other political and economic developments which have been taking place in recent years. The significance of the oil discussions can thus only be understood against the wider background of Venezuelan development.

At the turn of the century Venezuela was still an agricultural and ranching country with almost no industry. Oil had been discovered at the end of the nineteenth century but was not being exploited on a large scale. By 1928 however Venezuela was the world's largest oil exporter. All the oil was being produced by foreign companies who were paying royalties to the government. At the time of the oil boom, the country was ruled by Juan Vincente Gómez, one of the long line of dictators to come from the mountain state of Tachira.

For Gómez, oil promised to be a source of immense wealth. As long as the money continued to pour in, his interference with the oil companies was minimal. Although some of the money was used to start a large public works programme, little was done to promote the general welfare of the population.

The political decisions of Gómez laid the pattern of development of Venezuela for many years, and are still being felt. There was a large population shift to the oil producing areas and to the towns, and away from the agricultural regions. From this time onwards, Venezuela, potentially a very rich agricultural nation, has been a net importer of many basic foodstuffs, with the result that the cost of living has risen steadily.

The need for skilled labour led to an encouragement of immigration mainly from Europe. The pattern, until recently, has been to encourage foreign labour to enter, rather than to train the local labour force.

The new-found wealth resulted in a steep price inflation. This had particularly severe effects on those sectors of the labour force which were not participating in the oil boom. It also resulted in a rise in land prices, and a building boom.

On the positive side, the oil revenue eliminated the foreign debt and created a strong currency. It also made possible a public works programme, which provided a good system of roads. The most fundamental effect of the policy was to tie the country's destiny to the fortunes of the oil industry, and to give foreign capital a dominating effect.

The period up to 1945 saw a continuance under Contreras and then Angarita, of this policy, of predominant *laissez faire*. The policy was rudely interrupted in 1945 by Venezuela's first social revolution. Romulo Betancourt, and the left of centre party Acción Democrática, were brought into power by a revolt of young, discontented army officers. Betancourt's government played a much more active role in the economy and ploughed back the profits of oil to benefit the nation as a whole. He put into effect a contract whereby the government would receive 50 per cent of the profits made by the oil companies (the "50-50 rule").

He also pressured the companies to invest some of their earnings in the Venezuelan economy, and insisted that they must accept greater responsibility for the welfare of their employees. Another radical change was his refusal to grant any more exploration concessions to the oil companies, and his stated intention of starting a state owned company to extract and market oil.

With the revenue from oil, the government began to develop broad-based programmes of social and economic development. This included a campaign against illiteracy and ill health (particularly contagious diseases), a house building programme, the creation of the Venezuelan Development Corporation to coordinate overall planning, an attempt to stop the population flow into Caracas, and a stimulation of agriculture. Associated with the last of these was a programme of land reform, but the government was overthrown in 1948, by yet another army coup, and the land reform had to wait until 1960. The military and the large land owners had become alarmed at the radical nature of the programme and decided to end the regime. Between 1945 and 1948 the government had confiscated property which had been illegally obtained, worth $120 million.

MILITARY JUNTA

A three-man military junta came into power and was replaced four years later by Perez Jimenez (PJ). Politically the ten years up to 1958 were characterized by savage repression of AD and later of the other two main parties, COPEI and URD. The powerful trade unions were broken and the government maintained itself in power by extravagant bribes to army officers and to trusted party officials.

In the economic field there was a policy of support for foreign business interests. The oil companies were allowed to begin exploration again, union demands for higher wages were suppressed, and very few advances made in social welfare. Foreign investment was encouraged by low taxes and stern labour laws. The Gomez type public works policy was reinstated, with particular emphasis on the development of Caracas as an international showplace. (During the PJ era the Caracas population trebled to 1,100,000.) Although many useful projects, such as the Caroní dam, and the freeway to the capital, were completed, huge amounts of money were also spent on frivolous and expensive projects such as a mountain-top hotel complete with ice-rink, which did little or nothing to solve the pressing problems of the nation as a whole. Apart from this type of conspicuous waste, Jimenez is estimated to have accumulated a personal fortune of $250 million during his period in power.

THRIVING

As a counterbalance to the completely negative impression created by many writers, however, one must recall that in many ways both the agriculture and the industry of the country were thriving under a *laissez faire* policy.

Jimenez was overthrown in 1958 in a revolt led by Rear Admiral Wolfgang Larazabal. Larazabal was appointed head of a junta created in an attempt to rescue the country from the political and economic crisis which it was undergoing. Jimenez had, among other things, incurred international debts to the amount of $500 million. The immediate measure taken by the junta was to increase taxes on foreign firms and to cancel many of the construction projects, thus causing widespread unemployment and political unrest. To counteract the latter, all unemployed workers were paid unemployment benefit of approximately £1 (10 Bolívares) per day. This "plan de emergencia" resulted in a further influx of workers into Caracas. Finding nowhere to live, they invaded private land on the hills surrounding the city, and built shacks of whatever materials they could find; wood, bricks, zinc, or even cardboard. Although many bloody battles with landowners and police ensued, the settlements continued to grow at a fantastic pace. It is estimated that there are now, in Caracas alone, some half million people living in these shanty settlements or "barrios."

Despite the many criticisms which can be levelled against the government of Larazabal, it did achieve its main purpose, which was to prepare the country for a democratic election. In February 1959 Romulo Betancourt was re-elected President of the Republic. The government was formed of a coalition of all the major parties except the communists, but with AD having an overall majority.

During his previous term of office Betancourt had been overthrown because he had alienated large and influential sectors of the community; the landed aristocracy, the army and much of the business community. By 1958 he had come to realise that for any form of democratic government to survive in Venezuela, it must be able to count on at least the passive support of all the important sectors of the community.

The most clear example of his changed thinking can be seen in his attitude to the army. In the previous government, Betancourt had attacked the privileged position of the army. He now went out of his way to praise the army on every possible occasion, and to condone the excessive army appropriations in the budget. Betancourt had learnt that he only stayed in power as long as he had the support of the armed forces, and that he could only move as fast as they would permit him to.

Within this limitation, AD continued their previous policy of trying to achieve more equitable distribution of the national resources. National resources include human resources, and this was the area which had been most seriously neglected. The educational budget was doubled, and emergency teacher training and school building programmes were started. An attack was made on adult illiteracy (it was estimated that the illiteracy rate was 57 per cent in 1958). A hospital and health programme were also started. The main area in which no real progress was made was housing. When Jimenez was overthrown there was an estimated shortage of a half million permanent housing units. During the following years this shortage became steadily more acute as the population continued to increase at more than 3 per cent per annum, and people continued to pour into the towns. (The proportion of the population living in towns rose from 53 per cent in 1950 to 67 per cent in 1961.)

The policy of land reform was now put into practice. During the first year in office, land was sometimes simply invaded by the peasants but in 1960 the National Agrarian Institute was established to organise the redistribution of public and private land. Land which was not being used efficiently was bought at a fair market price, or was expropriated if the owners would not cooperate. By 1964 some 75,000 families had received over five million acres under the scheme. Land reform was an extremely political issue, since it attacked the position of the rural aristocracy. The peasants had traditionally provided the greatest part of the support of AD and the party was therefore anxious to keep its election promises, so as to maintain this support.

The effects of the land reform were less spectacular than had been hoped. The main reason for this was that a whole rural infrastructure of roads, houses, water supply, agricultural training centers etc. has to be provided before the benefits of a more efficient type of land holding can be felt. (It is still hotly argued by COPEI, the Christian Democrat party, that this form of land tenure is not in fact efficient.) Despite the many valid criticisms of the programme, however, since 1960 agricultural output has begun to keep pace with the population increase.

DIVERSIFY

In the field of economic policy an attempt was made to diversify the economy, to restore the strong bargaining position of labour, and to avoid dependence on a narrow base of foreign owned companies. This again had strong political motives. In the oil field, no further exploration rights were granted to foreign oil companies, and the first moves were made to set up a national oil company, the CVP. An attempt was also made to establish an international organisation of petroleum exporting countries to maintain prices in the face of increasing production. As far as Venezuela was concerned this was a failure as the low-cost production countries of the Middle and Far East had no interest in trying to keep prices high.

In 1960 the Guayana Development Corporation was established to create a whole new industrial complex in the Guayana, based initially on metallurgy. It was intended to diversify into other products and to create an industrial zone around the newly created town of Cuidad Guayana. It is estimated that by 1968 this town will have a population of 130,000. The development of new industrial centres in Valencia, Maracay, Barcelona and several other new towns was also encouraged, to try to diversify the resources of the country as far as possible and to divert the population drift away from Caracas.

So we find ourselves in 1966 with AD still in power, but with serious internal divisions, and with the coalition on the point of collapse. The country, however, is politically more stable than it has been for many years, and is now probably the wealthiest country in

Latin America (the per capita income of $724 was the highest for Latin America in 1964). Venezuela is still, however, facing all the problems of an under-developed country. Politically and economically there is still a dangerous dependency on revenue from oil. In 1964 this still accounted for 92 per cent of foreign exchange, and was budgeted to produce 63 per cent of the country's revenue in 1966. The future of the oil industry is uncertain and the race to diversify the economy will be the major determinant of the future progress of Venezuela. The future patterns of ownership and control of these foreign-owned industries is a continual subject of political debate. The obvious evidence of dependence on foreign business also results in various types of manifestations against the influence of foreigners on the direction of the country. A growing nationalism can be seen in other areas as well, for example in the conflict over Guayana Esequiba (the part of ex-British Guiana claimed by Venezuela). This is a major issue in Venezuela although hardly mentioned by the British press.

DEPENDENCY RATIO

In the social field, Venezuela is still faced with an annual population growth of over 3 per cent. According to the 1961 census over half of the population was under the age of 19. This creates a very high dependency ratio (i.e. the proportion of the population which is not in an age group which can be usefully employed). It also places a great strain on the educational resources. In every area the economy has to work hard to maintain the standard of living, let alone raise it. Large numbers of children are still not attending school and it is estimated that in Caracas alone, at least half a million people are living in the hillside barrio settlements where the majority of the houses are substandard, often not having access to running water or electric light or provided with proper sewage disposal systems.

STRUGGLING DEMOCRACY

In the political field democracy is still struggling to establish itself. The dictator Jimenez was overthrown only eight years ago. Since then the life of the president has been threatened many times. In 1960 Betancourt narrowly escaped a bomb attack by agents of President Trujillo of Dominica. In 1962 the FALN (Armed Forces of National Liberation) killed or wounded over 80 policemen; in

1963 they threatened to shoot anyone who went to the polls. Betancourt also had to overcome several rebellions by sectors of the armed forces. Even today, rebels partly control some outlying areas of the country, and the government is obliged to spend 10 per cent of the national revenue on the maintenance of armed forces. Against this background there are constant accusations of political arrests, suppressions of individual liberties and, occasionally, of assassinations.

The political parties, which maintained a coalition during the first few years after the overthrow of Jimenez, are beginning to realign themselves and to suffer serious internal splits. Serious thought is being given to future party structures, and some writers see the splits as providing a grave threat to democracy.

In the light of the present political situation it can be seen that the debate on the oil industry is not an isolated event, but part of a long term development which affects social and political policy as well as the economic life of the country. . . .

In the Venezuelan budget for 1966, the oil industry, either through royalties or through income tax, is to contribute 63 per cent of the government's revenue. The real contribution is substantially higher than this when one takes into account the spending of the oil employees, the system of "fines" for oil spillage (a device for raising revenue), and the various other forms in which the companies contribute to the economy. Venezuela relies on the sale of oil to produce well over 90 per cent of her foreign exchange.

Until the early 1960s the Venezuelan oil industry had enjoyed, with short recessions, a long sustained boom. During and immediately after the second world war, oil was a vital and scarce product and prices were maintained at a high level (this was interrupted only during the earlier part of the war by a shortage of tankers to transport the oil). During the early '50s another boom was caused by the Korean war, and the nationalisation of the oil industry in Persia under Mossadeq. In the later '50s when it appeared that world oil production was going to rise rapidly, Venezuela again benefited, this time from the disruptions caused by the Suez crisis. Thus Venezuelan gross national product rose between 1950-57 at the amazing annual rate of 9.4 per cent.

However, since 1958 the situation of the industry has begun to look less optimistic. The main changes have been brought about by the coming into production of areas of production in the near and far east, in Russia and more recently in Africa. Production costs in these areas are in many cases substantially lower than in Venezuela, and the productive possibilities seem almost unlimited. As well as the low cost areas there is likely to be a substantial increase in production within the continent of South America. In 1965 Venezuela was responsible for over 80 per cent of the production of the sub-continent, but recently there have been substantial discoveries in Brazil and Colombia.

There may also be a decline in demand. Venezuelan oil is largely of the heavier varieties, used for domestic and commercial heating. Within the next 20-30 years there is likely to be a major shift to nuclear energy, and perhaps also to natural gas. Already prices are being quoted in the United States which suggest that to compete with nuclear energy for heating purposes, a discount of 80 per cent would have to be offered on the present price. This is approximately twice the current trade discount. Venezuela could also run into problems over the United States' anti-smog campaign. This may mean that the maximum sulphur content of fuel oil will be 2.2 per cent. Much Venezuelan oil is above this level, and some very expensive blending and refining might be necessary. There are also indications that the United States may reduce her quota of Venezuelan oil. Until now the quota has been maintained, as a matter of policy, at a generous level.

These difficulties come at a time of rising nationalism and increased national awareness of dependence of the country on foreigners. What have been the reactions to this situation? The policy of Acción Democrática since their return to power in 1959 has been "sowing the petroleum", getting the maximum benefit for the country from the earnings of the petroleum industry. This has taken two main forms, first raising the level of taxes on the industry, and second persuading the companies to invest more of their money in the country. There has also been a gradual increase in the direct participation of the government in the production and distribution of petroleum through the state owned Venezuelan Petroleum Corporation (CVP). The company is still small, producing in 1964 some 2.3 million barrels, compared with a total national *daily* production of 3.4 million barrels. However, the government is making substantial investments in the CVP and its production and sales are likely to grow.

IN 1983

Ultimately it is intended the state should completely take over the ownership of the industry. This policy is being carried out by refusing to grant any more concessions for exploration to the oil companies. The present concessions run out in 1983. If the policy is continued, the whole industry would accrue to the state in that year. No major party even considers an earlier date.

Despite the tax increases, produced after bitter negotiations with the companies, the revenue available to the government is not increasing fast enough to provide for all its plans and programmes. New ways have to be found to raise money, and these inevitably have to be closely related to the petroleum industry. Towards the beginning of this year the government tried to raise revenue from the oil companies in the form of back taxes, amounting to some £50m. On a slightly wider front the government has proposed a bill for a complete national tax reform. This would affect individual income tax, as well as company revenue.

The bill proposes that during the next financial year, a further £2m should be raised from individual income tax, £5m from companies other than the oil industry, and £30m from the oil industry.

On the international level the Venezuelan government tried unsuccessfully to maintain world petroleum prices at a high level through the Organisation of Petroleum Exporting Countries (OPEC). It has failed because the other countries see it in their interest to sell a greater volume at a lower price.

GOVERNMENT PAMPHLET

In April 1965 a pamphlet was put out by the Central Office of Information entitled "The national market for hydrocarbons and derivatives", in which the government's case on nationalisation was stated. The first argument complains against "ruinous competition". It is claimed the major companies are concerned only to fight each other and take no account of the national interest, that they build far too many petrol stations and that their policy is generally irresponsible. This free enterprise policy has continued since the time of Gómez (30 years ago), and the government claims the evil effects are now clear for all to see. Although the internal market has no economic significance compared with exports, this argument has a strong emotional appeal.

The second complaint is that the companies construct oil stations which are far too large and which are designed purely as "monuments" to the oil companies. The third argument is that until recently the foreign companies have not really been developing the internal market but have been more concerned to export. Recently, with the development of high octane petrol, a large number of stations have been growing up and with the profits from this, export prices have been subsidised. "Thus with Venezuela's own money we are contributing in part to the export of petroleum". The conclusion is drawn that the government must refuse to grant any new concessions for exploration to the oil companies, and that the CVP must come to take an increasingly active part in the extraction, processing and marketing of oil.

The other major argument which is expressed by politicians and the press, but which the pamphlet does not stress, is the purely nationalistic angle. The belief that national industries ought to be in the hands of the nation, and the claim that the foreign companies are not concerned with the national interests, and that therefore they should not be left in control of this vital sector of the economy. This is an argument which has been constantly expressed since the 1940s. In Britain such an argument comes only from the left wing, but in Venezuela, as in many other Latin American countries, the support for nationalisation comes from the right wing as well. This is because the enemy, the capitalist, is the foreigner, and thus nationalists of the right and the left are able to join forces.

The final argument which is brought up by the economists and sociologists arises from the very one-sided development of the country. There is a small section of the economy which is related to the oil industry, and which is developing very rapidly. The rest of the economy has been lagging far behind. There is a great need to diversify investment. It is argued that private companies will not be prepared to do this, they will either invest only in the sector where the profits are to be made the most rapidly or they will take their money abroad to invest. The state, it is argued, must therefore step in to redirect investment.

IDEOLOGICAL

Looking at the argument in the context of British discussions of nationalisation, and thinking in particular of steel one or two notable differences appear. First, the Venezuelan debate appears to be much more ideological and less factual.

Although the British debate has been far from completely objective, a number of reasonably hard facts, relating to price trends, production rates, etc., have been brought forward. In Venezuela the facts are less in evidence. The debate is more that the industry *ought* to be nationalised (or ought not to be, depending on your politics). No-one discusses economies of scale (the idea that the state with all of its resources could make one big industry which by its size could enjoy facilities that a number of small industries could not afford), because the companies involved are so large and operate in so many different countries, that they can call upon a range of resources much greater than the government could. Nor does one hear arguments about the technical advantages of pooling research. Again the companies are so large and have such vast experience that they can call upon more research experience than the government could ever hope to obtain.

In fact if you follow the argument fairly carefully there is no mention of any technical or operating improvements which could be brought about by state control. The argument is half put forward that marketing within Venezuela could be made more effective, but no real force is given to this and no real evidence is brought forward.

THEMES NOT HEARD

Nor, except from the extreme left, does one hear about workers control. The workers of the industry, with the support of the government, have been able to negotiate far higher wages than any other sectors of the economy, and they would not be likely to obtain further improvements simply by state ownership. In fact the state would probably prefer to give the workers moral support in their fight to obtain more money from the foreign companies, than to be in the position of ownership and have to refuse the wage increases.

One of the most fundamental points of rethinking in Britain, namely the distinction between ownership and control, has hardly entered into the thinking in Venezuela yet, except in the writings of some of the COPEI (the party which enjoys the support of large sectors of the business community) economists, who are arguing for a modification of the "no concessions policy". The real arguments are therefore reduced to the belief that state control would bring in more revenue, that a wider section of the community would benefit from investments, and that the interests of the country as a whole could be better served by the government.

The critics reply that the internal market for petroleum is almost negligible. The revenue comes almost entirely from international sales, through the big companies who have marketing and shipping arrangements throughout the world. Doubt is shown whether the Venezuelan government would be able to sell substantial quantities of oil. It could not hope to set up a system to compete with the big companies, and it would probably have to sell to them. The companies are not likely to give very generous terms, both because an extra link has been introduced into the distribution chain, and because the companies can probably buy cheaper else-where. Revenue is likely to take a substantial drop. As the critics are quick to point out, 70 per cent of large profits (about the pro-portion the government receives) is more use than 100 per cent of small profits.

The critics go on to argue that the government does not have any very efficient central planning agencies which would be capable of reallocating investments (CORDIPLAN is still having teething problems). It is also claimed that there are so many political con-siderations in government investment, that it is not possible to put into practice any efficient overall investment plan.

NOT INTERESTED

The argument that the country as a whole would benefit from state ownership is a little more complex. Lieuwen, one of the lead-ing authorities on the Venezuelan petroleum industry, was of the opinion in 1957 that the oil industry had never of its own free will made any concessions or made any attempts to improve social con-ditions, except where they had been forced to by the government. A lot of changes have come about in the last nine years, but there is still a strong feeling that the companies have very little interest in the welfare of Venezuela.

On the other hand there is a strong feeling on the other side, that the state is not capable of carrying out any effective large scale planning, nor is it able to direct particular industries (the example is quoted of the difference in efficiency of the privately owned Avensa, and the state owned LAV airline). There is also a rapidly growing feeling that Acción Democrática is not able to represent the nation any more and that until some "United Front" party which can enjoy a wider base of national support, is returned to power, it is meaningless to talk of the government representing the nation.

Considerable doubt is also expressed as to the ability of Ven-ezuela to provide the necessary managerial and technical skills re-quired to run the industry. Although a great advance is being made in technical training (particularly through the Instituto Nacional de Cooperacion Educational) there is still a great shortage of skilled labour and management. The oil companies bring their own man-agement and technicians with them. If the companies go their skills go with them.

The argument against nationalisation of oil is not conclusive,

but for Venezuela to survive, the argument must be based on expediency rather than ideology. A relatively young democracy, with
limited experience of administration and international marketing,
may just have to accept that large, powerful and experienced international companies can do a better job of running an industry than
any national organisation could. The companies must be prodded
and cajoled when they lag in their social policies, but it may just
have to be accepted that the hard foreign currency they earn in
such large amounts, is more important to a struggling country than
the national pride to be gained from owning the industry.

Suggestions for Further Reading

For a survey of Chilean politics, see Federico G. Gil, *The
Political Systems of Chile* (Boston, 1966). Gil takes a generally
favorable view of the Chilean domestic situation. An exciting,
provocative analysis of Chile's development and the character of
its society is provided by Fredrick B. Pike, *Chile and the United
States, 1880–1962; The Emergence of Chile's Social Crisis and the
Challenge to United States Diplomacy* (Notre Dame, 1963). An-
drew G. Frank, *Capitalism and Development in Latin America:
Historical Studies of Chile and Brazil* (New York, 1967) provides
a marxist's interpretation of economic development, while in *Nationalism and Communism in Chile* (Cambridge, 1965) Ernst Hal-
perin, an anti-communist scholar, takes the opposite view. Robert
R. Kaufman explores the role of conservative Chileans in *The
Chilean Political Right and Agrarian Reform* (Washington, 1967).
On the Apristas in Peru, Harry Kantor offers an interpretation
with a perspective different from that of Pike in *The Ideology and
Program of the Aprista Movement* (Berkeley, 1953). A brief history of Peru can be found in Ronald J. Owens' *Peru* (London and
New York, 1963). For a short survey of Bolivian history see Harold Osborne, *Bolivia, a Land Divided* (London and New York,
1964) ; Cornelius H. Zondag, *The Bolivian Economy, 1952–65: the
Revolution and Its Aftermath* (New York, 1966), explores the impact of the revolution on the local economy. Edwin Lieuwen's two
books on Venezuela provide a good foundation for an evaluation
of Michael Bamberger's essay. His *Venezuela* (New York, 1961)
is a short history; in *Petroleum in Venezuela* (Berkeley and Los
Angeles, 1954) Lieuwen looks carefully at the petroleum industry
and its role in local society. The political scene is covered by Robert
J. Alexander, *The Venezuelan Democratic Revolution; a Profile of*

the Regime of Romulo Betancourt (New Brunswick, 1964) which, as the title indicates, lauds Betancourt and *Acción Democrática*. The novelist and politician, Rómula Gallegos, wrote the classic Venezuelan interpretation of foreign capital and local development in *Dona Bárbara,* translated by Robert Malloy (New York, 1931).

Latin American Issues: The Problems of a Continent

VI

Latin American Issues: The Problems of a Continent

Although differing in a multitude of ways, the Latin American republics share common problems, among which is the agrarian question. On a continental scale, just 1.5 percent of the population controls 65 percent of the arable land; the great majority of peasants are landless. Many of the large estates are inefficiently operated with outdated equipment and methods that produce low yields per acre: cheap peasant labor makes them economically profitable. No republic, not even Mexico and Cuba who have experienced social revolutions, claims to have solved the problem that results from the unequal distribution of land. The agrarian issue varies from country to country. Land concentration in Argentina and Uruguay, where mechanized, large-scale agricultural methods are employed on the *estancias,* cannot be compared to that of the backward *latifundias* in Peru and Ecuador. Nor do landless Mexican Indian peasants voice the demands of mulatto *guajiros* in Cuba. The essential features of the agrarian problem can be surveyed on a hemispheric level, but any analysis in depth requires a detailed examination of the problem in each republic.

As the history of Venezuela demonstrates, the economies of Latin America depend on the exports of raw materials to the industrialized nations of Western

Europe and increasingly to the United States. The terms of trade determine the degree of prosperity—the price that raw materials command on the international market in comparison with the price of manufactured products which must be imported while Latin American efforts to industrialize remain in their infant stage. Industrialization rests on exports, because the income derived from the sale of raw materials and agricultural goods must pay for the purchase of capital goods—the machinery and equipment which manufactures the products now imported. Latin American economists and government leaders devote a great deal of their time and effort to the search for formulas that will maintain high export prices. To escape from the need to rely on exports is the ultimate goal of every republic. Latin American economists believe that industrialization will lead to economic independence. Is their interpretation valid? Can Latin Americans emulate the industrialized nations and free themselves of their reliance on outsiders? Is economic autonomy in the twentieth century a feasible or realistic goal?

To many observers the military represent a formidable barrier to progress in Latin America. Since the wars for independence when the need to defeat the Spanish Royalist armies led the patriots to organize militias of their own, political generals have hampered the process of orderly political development. No country has avoided the evils of militarism; the *cuartelazo* and *pronunciamiento* have shaped the historical outlines. The military, usually in league with landlord and cleric, has defended the status quo, particularly in the more underdeveloped republics. The military, however, is not a homogeneous body. From its ranks rose such men as Lázaro Cárdenas of Mexico and Juan Domingo Perón of Argentina who, despite the controversial nature of their administrations, attempted to implant reforms. No politician in the history of Mexico ever matched Cárdenas' endeavors or equalled his accomplishments in the area of reform. The character of the military varies by country, reflecting the peculiar social and economic conditions of each.

In the republics with large middle sectors, the military often has an ambivalent role, speaking both for itself as a separate institution and for the middle sectors. To understand the military mind, therefore, requires a careful analysis of the character and goals of the middle sectors from which the military springs. Obviously, if the middle sectors simply aspire to join the elite, the military will have a role different from that which they would perform if the middle sectors serve a function comparable to that of the middle classes in the United States or in Western Europe. If the military identifies with a "middle class" that stands for modernization, it may represent a force for change. But if the military reflects the goals of middle sectors that mimic the rich and powerful, is it an institution that encourages the transformation of society?

In the nineteenth century the *caudillo* provided the political leadership of the Latin American republics. Only in a few exceptional cases—Argentina, Chile, and Uruguay—did political history surmount the *caudillo*, but then only temporarily and perhaps superficially. In the twentieth century, the periods free of the more blatant evils of *caudillaje* have increased both in frequency and in length, especially in the progressive republics. However, a relapse is always possible as the recent histories of Argentina and Brazil amply demonstrate. Despite some progress towards more representative governments in a few countries, the institution of the *caudillo* remains strong. Even in Mexico, where one party has controlled the government since 1928, the president, for all intents and purposes, is a *caudillo*. Thus, any study of political power in Latin America must focus on the *caudillo* and the forces that make him both possible and necessary. To what degree is he a voice from the past or a political institution in the process of transformation? Will industrialization and the growth of urban middle sectors eventually eliminate him?

Attempts to overcome socio-economic difficulties in Latin America are as old as the republics themselves. Reform movements swept nearly all of the republics in the nineteenth century. Still, despite some accomplishments, old problems persisted; the stability and orderly development envisaged did not materialize. Outside of Argentina, Uruguay, and perhaps Chile, the majority of the population continued to live in the patterns of yesteryear: too few had land of their own to till, only a tiny minority enjoyed access to schools, and political troubles matched in intensity the lack of economic progress. The population boom in the years since the end of World War II attests to the partial success of previous socio-economic reforms, but has aggravated old inequities. With the advent of rapid and mass means of communication, millions of Latin Americans have become aware of the disparity between their way of life and that of more prosperous peoples. Militant reformers, frequently of Marxist bent, increasingly propose revolution as a remedy for what ails Latin America.

To combat the evils of dictatorship and the chaos and suffering that violent revolution brings, moderate reformers urge an evolutionary approach to change. The Alliance for Progress, an American-sponsored developmental program, speaks for the moderate approach. Inagurated in 1961, the Alliance, based on the ideal of self-help, promised aid to Latin Americans in their battles against illiteracy, substandard housing, and poor health conditions, and in their attempts to implant much needed programs of tax and agrarian reform. Supporters of the Alliance believe that it offers a practical alternative to the violence of revolution. Its Latin American critics, however, condemn the Alliance as an American attempt to preserve the status quo. In their opinion, the Alliance offers token change in recognition of that well-known axiom of politics that governments must "grant some change in order that there be no change." Are the critics mistaken in their evaluation? Is evolution a way out for Latin America? Can American-sponsored reforms succeed in the highly nationalistic climate of public opinion in Latin America?

1

The great majority of Latin Americans till the land for a livelihood; in 1960 more than half of the population lived in rural villages, yet only a tiny fraction owned land. Though the indices of industrialization and urbanization grew rapidly in the era after World War II, more people lived in rural areas in 1960 than ever before. The population explosion, among the severest in the world, has simply exceeded the flight of people from country to city. The rural population not only has to feed itself, often on arid and overpopulated lands, but must also provide larger amounts of food for the new urban dwellers. Among the solutions offered to meet the challenge is land reform, the distribution of land to hungry peasants who in their exploited state represent a potential source of political unrest. In the next essay, Oscar Delgado, a Mexican economist, surveys the steps taken to solve the agrarian question and, in his conclusion, presents a somber and pessimistic evaluation of the results.

Oscar Delgado:
Revolution, Reform,
Conservatism*

Latin America had a population of 199 million in 1960, according to a United Nations estimate. Of this total, 108 million or 54 per cent live in rural areas, and of these 28½ million are economically active.

All rural dwellers who are economically active have family and social responsibilities, but almost all of them are underemployed and many are victims of seasonal unemployment. Their income is extremely low, and considerable numbers of them live only on the margin of money economy. Generally speaking, they work the soil in a primitive or almost primitive fashion. The average percentage of rural Latin America is around 80; but vast areas have no schools at all and an illiteracy rate of 100 per cent.

Indians form some 15 per cent of Latin America's rural population. The majority of them speak only an Indian language, though some of them are bilingual. The Indian policy of Latin American governments generally aims to keep them isolated from the white peasantry of their countries. Moreover, Indian communities benefit very little from government aid or not at all, and it is an open secret that such programs have been a complete failure because of inadequate funds and lack of any real interest on the part of the governments concerned.

In spite of these obstacles, some Indians have established contact with the white peasants. These have adopted the cultural patterns of that peasantry. Wherever such cultural contacts take place, the Indians suffer from exploitation not only by the white bourgeoisie but also by the white and *ladino* (mestizo) peasants.

These 28½ million have to produce food not only for themselves but also directly for their 70½ million dependents and, more indirectly, for the 91 million urban dwellers. Moreover, in terms of the national economy, they have to produce a surplus for economic development. And yet, 63 per cent of them—18 million adult farmers—have no land at all. Some 5½ million have an insufficient

* From Oscar Delgado, "Revolution, Reform, Conservatism: Three Types of Agrarian Structure," DISSENT, IX (Autumn 1962), pp. 350–357.

amount of land; 1.9 million have enough land, and 100,000—mostly absentee landlords—have too much land.

One out of every 185,000 Latin Americans—or one out of every 100,000 rural Latin Americans—owns over 1,000 hectares. For 107,955 landlords, or 1.5 per cent of all landholders, own 471 hectares, or 65 per cent of all land in private hands. Each of them owns an average of 4,300 hectares; but many have more than 10,-000, and some have hundreds of thousands—even millions.

So much for individuals. But properties belonging to several members of a family can be registered under the name of its head. There are Latin American families who own more land than is occupied by a number of sovereign nations. In fact, there are families or groups of interrelated families in the Argentine, Brazil, Chile and Venezuela, of which each has more land than several countries put together. This is a situation with no parallel elsewhere. Statistically speaking, Latin America has the highest index of concentrated accumulation of rural property in the world.

Latin America is now beginning to develop, however, slowly. Its indices of urbanization and industrialization are progressively rising. However, this progress is generally unnoticeable because the population rapidly increases at one of the highest rates of growth in the world. Internal migration to the cities is constant and growing, but it does not absorb the rural population explosion caused by the rising birth rate and the falling death rate. This migration, a product of urbanization and industrialization, makes the rural population decrease relatively, in proportion to urban population; but it does not decrease it absolutely.

It is estimated that the percentage of rural population will fall from 54 to 46 in 1970. However, the rural population as a whole and hence also the number of actual and potential agricultural workers, will actually rise by that date from 108 million to 133 million. . . . There can be no question that the rural—and agricultural—population of Latin America is increasing today in a geometrical progression. Every year, every month and every day there are new mouths to feed and new hands to be provided with work, land, tools, and money. Given an annual rate of increase of 3 per cent, this means about 6 million new mouths and new pair of hands every year in all Latin America, and 3.8 million in the rural sector.

"PARCELLATION" AND COLONIZATION

How can this problem be solved? The answer is simple and can be reduced to four words: Economic and social development.

We can deal here only with one aspect of this urgent problem: The different agrarian policies which can become stimulants or obstacles to the improvement of agricultural production and productivity, and to the white, mestizo, and indigenous rural population which participates—or is unable to participate—in growing crops and raising cattle.

In three countries of Latin America, a political revolution produced an agrarian policy of redistributing the property and tenancy of land: Mexico (1915), Bolivia (1953), and Cuba (1959). In these countries, new ruling groups and new ideologies replaced the old and changed the traditional values. The old ruling groups had governed with the support of traditional ideas, and their rule was tolerated by the masses who lived in utmost ignorance, submission, and political apathy.

In two other countries, conservative governments, representing a bourgeois-landlord-military-clerical coalition, have introduced a land reform: Venezuela (1959) and Colombia (1961). This reform has meant a "parcellation" of cultivated land or a "colonization" of virgin soil.

"Parcellation," as used in this article means:

> *a.*   The acquisition by a government agency of land used for crops or cattle by purchase from its private owners paid in cash and at once and
>
> *b.*   the subdivision of this land for resale as private property to landless or landpoor peasants by payment of an amount of money equal to or similar to that laid out by the government agency on the installment system, with a fixed term and a low interest rate.

Similarly, "colonization" means here the opening or preparation of new agricultural, cattle-raising, or forest land owned by the government or of no definite ownership, and the settlement in it of rural population.

In all the remaining countries of Latin America, there has been no serious program of redistribution or parcellation. The countries which tried colonization in the course of the present century were successful only as regards a few fortunate individuals; for the rest, colonization completely failed to solve their agrarian problem.

Parcellation, as a method of land reform, leaves the large estates practically intact. The concentration of land in a few hands is not affected by it, and it leaves the problems of the rural population unsolved. This is why it is the favorite method of land reform in "rural conservative" countries.

This phrase also requires some explanation. At first sight it seems strange to apply the label of "rural conservative" to seventeen countries which differ so much economically, socially, and politically. They include two countries at the very extremes of economic and social development: Argentina and Haiti. This is also true of political development: They include, on the one hand, the Central American republics dominated by "strong executives" and custodians of foreign interests and, on the other, a country like Uruguay, with its markedly developed democracy. Nor is it easy to include in the same group countries which never had any significant colonization or foreign immigration with others which have intermittently tried out colonization ever since the beginning of the 19th century, though on a small scale in relation to their open spaces and settled population.

Still, it is convenient to group together the countries of recent parcellation (Venezuela and Colombia), those of colonization (Argentina, Brazil, Chile, and Uruguay), and those dominated by large estates (the rest of the seventeen). They have something in common—rural conservatism—which distinguishes them from the countries of revolutionary land reform, which we may call countries of "agricultural transformation."

A closer look at the three countries where a revolution occurred with a broad popular participation will reveal certain distinctions which will require separate categories.

In Cuba, the large estates and ranches were not divided by the Castro Revolution; they continue in operation by either a government agency or a peasant cooperative. Both in Mexico and in Bolivia, land reform marked a notable social progress, though it was limited to only a part of the rural population. The national economy of these two countries benefited somewhat from the land reform, but the benefits were limited by an excessive fragmentation of the estates which were distributed. Also, neither country made a sufficient effort to foster government, collective, or cooperative operation of agriculture and cattle-breeding.

We can now classify the Latin American countries as follows:

  I. *Agricultural Transformation:*
      1. Agrarian revolution (Cuba)
      2. Land reform (Mexico and Bolivia)
 II. *Rural Conservatism:*
      2. Parcellation (Venezuela and Colombia)
      2. Colonization (Argentina, Brazil, Chile, and Uruguay)
      3. Rural conservatism, in the narrower meaning of that phrase (the remaining countries).

The countries of agricultural transformation have a dynamic agrarian situation: Their agricultural population—or at least a large part of it—has a genuine opportunity to raise its standard of living. The countries of rural conservatism have a static agrarian situation; such an opportunity is limited or non-existent in them. . . .

The reason Cuba falls into a different category from Mexico and Bolivia is that the transformation happened there with surprising efficiency and speed. This is no longer land reform; it must be called an "agrarian revolution." In Mexico and Bolivia, the rhythm of change has been much slower than in Cuba, for all the positive achievements of their land policies. But it has been very fast by comparison with Venezuela and Colombia.

LAND REFORM LAWS

In Mexico today, 47 years after the Land Reform Law was signed, 106 milion hectares remain in private hands, and 71 million (76%) belong to private individuals who own more than 1,000 hectares each. In Bolivia, land reform has moved at a faster pace than in Mexico; but even here, 9 years after the law was passed, 28.5 million hectares—87 per cent of all utilized land—are still in the hands of landlords who own more than 1,000 hectares each.

The land reform laws of Cuba, Mexico, and Bolivia stipulate that the former owners of expropriated land be indemnified with long-term bonds. But, in actual practice, none of these countries has paid the compensation required by the law. The small payment was made in money, not in bonds. How else would it have been possible to redistribute 61 million hectares (52 in Mexico, 5 in Cuba, 4 in Bolivia)?

The laws of Venezuela and Colombia, on the other hand, authorize the expropriation of land, with payment partly in cash and partly in medium-term bonds. Both, however, have actually preferred parcellation.

The Venezuelan government has bought about half a million hectares, at market prices, from landlords who sold their land voluntarily. They actually received payment, almost full and immediate. This land has not been given to the peasants, as happened in Cuba, Mexico, and Bolivia. It was sold to them at cost price, which included the value of improvements and the wages of the officials in charge of the transactions. The peasants pay in annual installments for a medium-term period.

In Cuba, the large estates and ranches were taken from individual owners and national and foreign companies. They were not subdivided, but continue to be operated as wholes by the government or by peasant cooperatives.

In Mexico and Bolivia, on the contrary, they were subdivided into very small farms—an average of 4 hectares of unirrigated lands—and handed over to the peasants. But the beneficiaries of the land reform were, in both countries, abandoned to their fate. Because of financial stringency or for other reasons, they have received hardly any credit, technical assistance and other services needed for efficient farming.

Among the different types of rural conservatism, parcellation deserves special treatment. In most of the literature on the subject, "land reform" actually means parcellation. This is because, for many people, parcellation means an "agrarian transformation," and so they associate what is happening in Venezuela and Colombia with what happened in Mexico, Bolivia, and Cuba.

Several Latin American countries are planning to start a parcellation program in 1963. Only they are careful to call it "land reform." (This is also true of Venezuela and Colombia with their "land reform" laws.) The Congresses of two "colonization" countries (Brazil and Chile) and of two "rural conservative" countries (Peru and Ecuador) are now studying several "land reform" projects. If they are approved in the form they were presented, they will certainly not provide the legal basis for an agrarian transformation, but only for parcellation. And their practical efficiency will depend on the amount of public funds assigned to buy land from private owners.

We stated earlier that parcellation permits preservation of the traditional structure, based on large estates. The case of Venezuela will prove this. That country is now engaged in the most expensive "land reform" ever made in the world, even more expensive than those of Italy and Japan, with their special difficulties.

Venezuela has financial resources unmatched by any Latin American country. Its annual per capita income is, through the revenue derived from petroleum, the highest in Latin America—$500, as against $92 in Bolivia, and a general average of $292. Also, Venezuela has an unusually small number of agriculturally active population—only 705,000, as against 10,300,000 in Brazil and 28,500,000 in all of Latin America. No other Latin American country could afford to invest the equivalent of 750 million dollars in a program devoted exclusively to parcellation and its auxiliary agricultural services.

The sum seems disproportionately high when compared with the cost of land reform in Japan and Italy. Japan spent 390 million dollars to distribute 2 million hectares among 4 million beneficiaries. Italy spent only 120 million to give to over half a million beneficiaries 750,000 hectares of redistributed land and 28½ million hectares of improved and colonized land.

The Venezuelan Four-Year program proposes to settle 200,000 peasants on the parcelled land; but in its first three years (1960–1962) only 50,000—a quarter of the number planned—have been actually settled. This means 7 per cent of the active agricultural population, as opposed to 41 per cent in Mexico and 32 per cent in Cuba. The Venezuelan beneficiaries occupy 1.5 million hectares of land: One-third taken from public lands (colonization); one third bought by the government from private owners (parcellation); and one third confiscated from the friends of the deposed dictator Perez Jimenez who had obtained it illegally when in power.

Venezuela has 29.6 million hectares of land used to raise crops and breed cattle. Before parcellation was started, 22 million hectares were occupied by large estates, over 1,000 hectares. Three years later, when the four-year plan is coming to its close, this figure has fallen to only 21.5 million.

Another difference between parcellation and agrarian transformation is that the latter limits the amount of land a person may legally own, and the former doesn't. Thus, in Cuba the limit, for a private person or a corporation, is 403 hectares; in Mexico, 100 hectares of irrigated and 200 of unirrigated land; in Bolivia, the limit varies according to the geographical zone. No other country has such restrictions.

The amount of money Venezuela spent on its "land reform" would seem fabulous if we didn't compare it with the cost of agrarian transformation, truly insignificant by comparison: 133,000 dollars in Bolivia for 4 million hectares; 14.5 million dollars in Mexico for 52 million hectares; and 8.9 million dollars in Cuba for 5 million hectares. (In all three cases, the land was expropriated.)

In Colombia, the government assigns annually, from 1962, 12 million dollars for "land reform," some 3 per cent of the national budget. (Venezuela makes an annual assignment of 187.5 million dollars; the Peruvian draft law foresees one of 11.5 million dollars or about 3 per cent of the budget.) In the year since the Colombian law was passed (November 1961), the Colombian Institute of Land Reform has so far parcelled out only 15 thousand hectares, which were handed over to 750 persons. The two-year plan of the Colombian Ministry of Agriculture for 1962–3 proposes an expenditure of 18 million dollars for the purchase of land to be distributed to tenant farmers and sharecroppers.

Colombia and Peru have an active agricultural population of 2,023,000 and 1,546,000 respectively, i.e. roughly three times and twice that of Venezuela. Colombia has 27.7 million hectares of agricultural land. Of this, 7.4 million is owned by landlords with over 1,000 hectares each.

POLITICAL AND JUDICIAL RESTRAINTS

Some "colonization" and "rural conservative" countries are preparing a parcellation for 1963. In Brazil and Chile there is a hope, still vague and distant, that parcellation may be transcended and a genuine land reform achieved. This hope is based on changes in the composition of their Congresses (Brazil will have elections in October 1962) and on the election of a new president of Chile.

As things are now, Brazil and Chile cannot be expected to go beyond a modest parcellation. Any serious land reform there is blocked by juridical considerations—always the most conservative and change-resisting in Latin America. The constitutions of these two countries bar any expropriations without a cash payment in advance for the property to be expropriated, and at market prices. Large parts of Brazilian and Chilean public opinion believe that such constitutional provisions make land reform impossible and they are pushing for constitutional amendments which would permit a deferred payment of the indemnification. In the present pre-election campaigns they are concentrating upon obtaining more representative Congresses so as to neutralize—to say the least—parliamentary domination by big land owners and their allies.

It is worth recalling that, in the last 10 years, 208 projects of land reform laws or relevant legislation have been presented to the Brazilian Congress. Not one of them was able to pursue its normal course through the commissions appointed to "study" them. None of these laws were actually rejected; they were simply buried in the commissions.

Much the same thing happened in Peru and Ecuador. And yet a conference of agricultural economists agreed that "the majority of the tenancy contracts now prevalent in Latin America are archaic, unequal, rigid and unsuitable for the full utilization of human and natural resources."

Generally speaking, in the countries of agrarian conservatism, the big landowners have exercised a powerful political and economic influence ever since Independence. Conditions vary from country to country; but, except in one or two cases, the landed interests have been completely successful in blocking any structural change.

Their resistance is certainly not without a logic of its own.

An agrarian transformation may well make the landlords feel "lost." Their lands would be confiscated outright or they would receive an indemnity which they consider too small for investment in business. Moreover, they would not receive it in cash but in long-term bonds. They would lose their political power and their social status, which they derive from the ownership of land. Not only would they lose their prestige, but they would fall into the depths of unpopularity and be blamed by society as a whole for having prolonged a fundamentally unjust situation. From the point of view of defending their interests, the resistance of landlords to the land reform is perfectly logical, even if it is irrational in the present historical situation.

But whether they resist or not, the landlords are doomed to lose the fight for the retention of their long-held privileges. Since society asked them to give up their lands, they have won many skirmishes and even some technical battles. But they are losing strategically and the fortress of their privileges—inherited rather than acquired—is beginning to succumb.

The more intelligent among the landlords will adapt themselves to the new situation. They will try to forget a lost world which had seemed ideal to them but which was too unjust to resist the passage of time. That ideal world, in which they had been the center of attention and power, is now colliding with industrial civilization.

The landlords will find a refuge in the big cities (or will remain in them if they are absentee owners). They will be shareholders in industrial, commercial, and service enterprises. Some of them will stick to their old values, and would rather become the victims of the hurricane of social transformation than give up an inch of their land. This type of landlord will die with his boots on and with his gun cocked.

2

In the opinion of many Latin American economists, the terms of trade have worsened in recent years. The agricultural and raw-material producing nations cannot compete on an equitable basis with the industrialized peoples of the world because the prices of their goods have dropped while those of manufactured articles have risen. As a result, the profits from Latin American exports are less today than before, and thus national incomes stagnate and economic development slows because of a lack of capital. The unfriendly terms of trade mean lower standards of living for Latin Americans with no promise of improvement in the future unless they turn from the production of raw materials to a program of self-sufficiency based on local industry. Victor Urquidi, a Mexican economist, questions some of these assumptions. He believes that trade with the industrial countries encouraged development in Latin America. To quote Urquidi, "When more advanced nations no longer need food and raw materials from Latin America, the latter's 'dependence' will cease, but so will the drive behind its development."

Victor L. Urquidi:
The Challenge of
Development*

It is pointless simply to go on repeating, as is so common, that Latin America is subject to the fluctuations of international trade; the situation must be analyzed and defined in all its complexities. To state that Latin American economic development has been or is being helped or hampered by the behavior of foreign markets is to say a great deal without really saying anything. It is hardly conceivable that the Latin American economy could have reached its present stage of development without foreign trade. International trade is not an accident but a means by which an economy develops. The degree and scope of its contribution to economic growth and welfare depend on whether buyer or seller is in the stronger position, but as long as there is development, there will be trade.

Development had to begin somewhere in the world, and throughout history its acceleration or deceleration in different countries has brought about changes in the volume and composition of international trade. The less developed countries inevitably tend to

* From Victor L. Urquidi, THE CHALLENGE OF DEVELOPMENT IN LATIN AMERICA, trans. by Marjory M. Urquidi, Foreword by Frank Tannenbaum (New York and London: Frederick A. Praeger, Publisher, 1964), pp. 15–29.

link their economies to those of the more advanced countries, which both need their products and are better able to supply their requirements.

Then, is it not more accurate to say that the Latin American economy is subject, not to the fluctuations of international trade, but to the rate and pattern of economic development in the rest of the world, especially in countries with higher per capita income and thus greater demand and purchasing power? If so, attention should be focused on how countries with a high standard of living have evolved and where they are headed. For such an analysis, the traditional "theory of international trade" is hardly useful. It is an analytical method that has prevented consideration of the problem as a whole and as a dynamic process.

Obviously, it is essential to look for the long-term, basic trends. As long as the European economy was predominant and its structure and growth permitted its needs to be met from its own resources, the goods it imported from Latin America created very little real wealth; the precious metals were a means of exchange and an object of greed, but not a raw material for European industry or an article of direct consumption. The industrial revolution, its technical advances, better transportation, and the acceleration of population growth caused shifts in demand and changes in the structure of supply that compelled Europe to import food and raw materials. In responding to Europe's new demands, Latin America entered a new stage of development, which owed much of its momentum to the introduction of modern means of transportation. Next came the impact of the raw-material requirements of United States industrialization. Meanwhile, Latin America benefited from improved techniques—for instance, in the treatment of industrial ores—and changing food habits, especially the growing taste for coffee.

Clearly, industrial countries could not buy from Latin America what it did not produce—manufactured goods—but only the food and raw materials for which it had ample resources and the possibility of establishing adequate means of production. Thus, development in Latin America was a response to that of the more advanced countries—directly, in foreign investment in the production of primary products and exportable foods, and indirectly and less apparently, in the use made of increased domestic income. This process, in no way related to the theory of comparative costs, can be analyzed only in terms of development trends.

Unfortunately, there does not exist, at least to my knowledge, a general study of Latin America's economic evolution since the nineteenth century correlating the growth of exports with the expansion of different branches of industry in Europe and the United States, or with particular shifts in consumer demand. Such a study not only would be interesting in itself, but would give substance to the often repeated thesis of Latin American dependence. Once these relationships, and their cyclical behavior, have been documented, it will be much easier to understand how Latin America's exports are tied to the world economy. Students concerned with the external factors in Latin America's economic growth should worry less about excessive dependence on other countries—these bonds will always exist—and more about the danger that countries of higher productivity and income might become self-sufficient and either halt or reduce their purchases of Latin American products. When more advanced nations no longer need food and raw materials from Latin America, the latter's "dependence" will cease, but so will the drive behind its development.

The foregoing does not condemn Latin America to an endless future of simply trading primary products for manufactured goods. Its own structure of output is changing and will continue to do so, just as the structure of demand in the more advanced countries is being transformed. But it will be many years before an appreciable reduction can be made in the gap between the average level of Latin American productivity and that of Western Europe, the United States, and Canada. Granted, world development should be directed toward narrowing this gap, but as long as it exists, its influence on the nature of international trade must be recognized.

None of the above implies that errors and injustices have never existed or do not exist today in the industrialized nations' trade policy toward the less-developed countries, or that conspiracies, unfair competition, damaging actions by international monopolies, control of transportation media, and the like are unheard of. But in the background, there has always been the reality of an economic evolution that induces uneven development. In addition, anxiety about the international political situation has prompted many countries to create their own source of supply rather than depend on distant producers. Also, important technological changes have affected the relative use and value of different products. Obviously, protectionism is not the result of purely economic causes.

It is interesting to analyze how all these elements have been reflected in the trends and structure of world trade. Until the beginning of this century, the United Kingdom accounted for more than one-fifth of all world imports and, with the rest of Western Europe, absorbed about 60 per cent of the total. Meanwhile, the United States and Canada together received less than 10 per cent. After World War I, the United States and Canada increased their share, which reached 14 per cent in 1937, while the United Kingdom and the rest of Western Europe reduced theirs. . . . By 1953, the North American share in imports had grown still larger and that of Western Europe, especially the United Kingdom, still smaller. Thus, during the almost 80 years from 1876 to 1953, the center of gravity of world import demand shifted from Western Europe to the United States—from countries with few natural resources, such as Great Britain, to those with almost limitless potential resources and therefore less need of imports. Nor did the emergence of other industrial powers counteract this phenomenon. The Soviet Union can draw on its own many resources for its industrial development; furthermore, it has never unleashed its latent consumer demand for such articles as coffee and tropical fruit. Japan, like the United Kingdom an importer of food and raw materials, has never had the latter's purchasing power.

Despite these changes in the structure of world trade, Latin America's share of exports rose only slightly over the years. The exports of Western Europe, including the United Kingdom, steadily declined, from almost one-half of the total at the beginning of the century to little more than one-third in 1953. The change in the origin of world exports, particularly the relative drop in European exports, makes it surprising that Latin America's share did not increase faster. Between the start of World War I and 1937, it went up from 8 to 10 per cent of the total; by 1953, it had expanded very little more. . . . The shares of Africa and Oceania grew faster, and Asia, despite the setback in Japanese trade, also gained ground. Thus, Latin America benefited less from the transfer of the center of gravity to the great United States purchasing area.

The analysis may be carried further by separating trade in primary products from trade in manufactures. In 1913, Latin America supplied nearly 13 per cent of world exports of primary products, and in 1937, this proportion was 16 per cent. In 1953, the ascent was continuing. . . . But during the same forty-year span, the combined share of Africa and Oceania almost doubled. In terms of quantum, the growth of Latin American exports lagged considerably behind those of other underdeveloped areas. World trade tripled in volume from 1876 to 1913, but increased by only 50 per cent between 1913 and 1953. Thus, the evolution of the world economy in the latter period was less favorable to exporters of primary products than in the first forty years.

This over-all picture makes it apparent that the United States and Canada, with almost one-fifth of the aggregate, have supplanted the United Kingdom as the principal importer of primary products. Again the question arises: Why has Latin American export trade lagged behind that of other less-developed regions? This is part of the problem, posed earlier, of how the Latin American economy is specifically linked to the economies of industrial countries, a problem that obviously should be studied product by product.

A few hints can be gathered from information already at hand. In 1913, Latin America carried on 21 per cent of the world trade in food, and by 1953, this proportion had grown to 25 per cent. . . . But because the income-elasticity of the demand for food is low, the slow rise in European income necessarily had a less favorable effect on Latin America. Practically the only foods imported by the United States were coffee, bananas, and sugar. Latin America advanced only in beverages (that is, coffee) and sugar, and by 1953, it led the world in exports of these, with 64 and 51 per cent, respectively, of the total exports. There is a serious surplus of both these commodities on the market today.

Latin America slid downward mainly in its share of world exports of cereals, livestock products, oilseeds and fats, and fruits and vegetables—precisely the items in which the United States and Canada increased their share of imports between 1913 and 1953. . . . This means that Latin America was not supplying either North America's growing needs or Europe's relatively low demand. It may be noted that in 1953–54, the volume of Argentina's wheat exports was only 8 per cent higher than its 1909–13 average forty years earlier, and that it exported 44 per cent less corn and 30 per cent less meat than before World War I. . . . Meanwhile, the United States multiplied its meat imports almost by nine, and Italy, Belgium, Holland, the Soviet Union, Sweden, Germany, and other countries became meat importers.

The volume of Latin America's exports of oilseeds and vegetable oils also shrank during these forty years, in both absolute and relative terms (again the case of Argentina), while world imports doubled.

In a discussion of agricultural raw materials—which have become less important in world trade—it is well to remember that the products that have made the most progress in world exports since 1913 are rubber, wood pulp, lumber, and tobacco. Latin America has traded very little in rubber and wood pulp. World interchange in textile fibers, which account for nearly half the total of agricultural raw materials, has declined in absolute terms. Nonetheless, Latin America considerably increased its share of total fiber exports, up to nearly 18 per cent in 1953, as against only 6 per cent in 1913. . . . Wool exports, which continue to be more important than cotton, remained stationary in Argentina and Uruguay; these two countries, handicapped by hoof-and-mouth disease and Australian competition, actually exported less wool in 1953 than in 1913. . . . Significantly, world imports of wool did not rise during those forty years. The plight of cotton has been equally bad or worse. World imports of cotton in 1953 were 13 per cent less than in 1913, owing to reduced purchases by England, Germany, and other countries. But of this declining market, Latin America substantially augmented its share, with exports from Mexico and Brazil displacing those from the United States, Egypt, and India.

The output of minerals and fuels, which play a major role in Latin American exports, has expanded dramatically until recently. Trade in these products in 1953 showed a tremendous increase over the 1913 level, especially in petroleum, tin, zinc, lead, copper, and iron. . . . Iron was supplied primarily by Sweden, followed by France and North Africa, but Venezuela by 1953 already had reached fourth place and today is probably second. Thus, Venezuela, together with Brazil, has captured for Latin America a sizable share of the growing world demand for a product that is beginning to be in short supply in many industrial countries. Copper is an import necessity for both the United States and Europe. Chile, the world's second-largest exporter of copper after central Africa, continues to expand its output and is the mainstay behind Latin America's present production of one-third of the world total. The increase in Chilean exports has scored a substantial gain for Latin America. Similar advances have been made in lead; over the forty-year period, exports have been shifting from Spain to Mexico and lately Peru.

Latin America produces 25 per cent of the world's zinc, which is chiefly imported by Europe and the United States in the form of zinc concentrates. From 1913 to 1953, Mexico and Peru increased their exports of zinc concentrates at the expense of Australia. The swiftly rising demand for zinc is expected to continue for some time to come. On the other hand, the weak trend in tin has had an adverse effect on the export trade of Latin America and its leading tin producer, Bolivia.

The spectacular expansion of petroleum—1955 world imports of crude oil were six times the 1929 level and those of refined oil were three times that level—has caused an extraordinary change in Latin America's trade structure. In 1955, Latin America, mainly Venezuela, accounted for 44 per cent of all refined-oil exports and 40 per cent of all crude-oil exports. However, in the last fifteen to twenty years, Europe, which has always been the principal customer for both crude and refined oil, has turned to the Middle East for its supply.

The foregoing data are important not only as historical background but as a basis for appraising the future. Of the total value of Latin America's exports, more than 25 per cent is represented by petroleum and derivatives; 18 to 22 per cent by coffee; 9 per cent by sugar; 4 per cent by cotton; 2.5 per cent by copper; and 2.4 per cent by iron ore. . . . These six products make up almost two-thirds of the value of all exports. Add twelve more products— meat, hides, and skins, cacao, wheat, corn (maize), tobacco, wool, quebracho, lead, tin, zinc, and nitrates—and almost three-quarters of the total value is accounted for. Every product on this list, with the possible exception of iron ore, faces grave market difficulties arising from serious maladjustments between world demand and potential world exports. Naturally, prices have reflected this situation. It is estimated that the export prices of 17 commodities, roughly those listed above, have declined an average of 9 per cent from their 1950 level and 16 per cent from their 1955 level. . . . The prices of tropical products, particularly coffee and cotton, and nonferrous metals, chiefly lead and zinc, have fallen more than 25 per cent, many of them below their 1948 level. These immediate factors of actual and potential instability must be considered along with the long-term growth rates and protectionist policies of the various industrial countries. At present, Latin America's economic prospects are threatened by a decline in price or by over-supply of most of its export products.

Nevertheless, the more distant future may be brighter, at least for some products. A primary factor in this is the outlook for the world economy and the repercussions it is likely to have on Latin America's trade, or more specifically, its leading products.

The United States spends about $4 billion a year to purchase almost one-half of Latin America's exports—chiefly petroleum and coffee, followed by copper, iron ore, lead, and cacao. . . . From 1946–48 to 1955–57, the United States economy expanded an average of 3.8 per cent per annum. Some projections assume a growth rate of 4.3 to 4.5 per cent until 1970. This implies that the United States will increase sizably its imports of certain Latin American products, especially minerals, such as iron ore and copper, in which its resources are approaching depletion, and petroleum, for which its demand will probably continue buoyant. . . . The prices of these commodities are expected to remain steady. On the other hand, United States purchases of coffee in the next decade are not expected to exceed previous levels. Its low rate of population growth makes it impossible for the United States to absorb any appreciable part of the coffee surpluses in the next few years. The United States demand for other products may increase, but these do not play so important a role. Although they may be crucial to certain countries, they do not count for much in the aggregate. At best, United States growth, which may not be so rapid as some projections indicate, will benefit Latin America only in its rising demand for minerals. . . . U.S. imports of coffee and a number of foodstuffs will expand slowly and with fluctuating prices.

An unfavorable trend for exporters of primary products is the declining ratio of consumption of raw materials to gross product experienced in industrial countries. In Canada and the United States, these ratios are estimated to have dropped from 8.19 and 6.07 per cent, respectively, in 1926–28 to 7.13 and 5.10 per cent in 1955–57, and they are expected to shrink to 6.30 and 4.71 per cent by 1980. . . . In the United States, this decline has been more marked in fuels, and in Canada, in lumber and pulp.

Western Europe, which takes 30 per cent of Latin America's exports, generally has shown a higher rate of economic growth than the United States. Its future impact on Latin America may be important in several products, including petroleum, iron ore, copper, zinc, sulphur, coffee, cacao, and wool. Again, prospects are better for minerals and petroleum than for other products. . . . But, despite their brisk over-all growth, European countries do not expand proportionately their purchases of agricultural primary products. Food has a low income-elasticity, agriculture is highly protected, and substitutes have been developed for many raw materials. In Europe, the outlook is not very promising for Latin American cotton, meat, cereals, oilseeds and fats, sugar, and fruits. In many instances, it will be difficult to overcome the preference given to African and Asian suppliers. Furthermore, Western Europe's population is expected to increase only 0.6 per cent per annum.

The 20 per cent of Latin American exports not sold to the United States or Western Europe is evenly divided between Latin America itself, on the one hand, and Japan and Eastern Europe, on the other. In the last few years, trade with Japan has expanded considerably, especially in cotton, sugar, and wool. But despite the very rapid growth forecast for the Japanese economy, the sum total of these figures does not alter the general outlook.

Although Latin America's exports to the Soviet Union and other countries of Eastern Europe have recently increased, their volume, at least until 1959, has not been significant. There is no basis on which to calculate their future growth. The Canadian market is also of little consequence.

Taking into account the various studies on the subject, the expansion of Latin American trade, as linked to the growth of other parts of the world—principally the United States and Europe, where it now sends nearly 80 per cent of its exports—can be anticipated as follows: a substantial increase in exports of minerals, metals, and petroleum; a slight expansion in food exports (in the long run, this will depend primarily on what happens to coffee) ; and a somewhat higher increment in exports of agricultural raw materials, which in any case represent only a small proportion of the total. . . .

These estimates usually omit the possible effect of tourism on Latin America's future foreign-exchange earnings. At present, tourism yields a net balance of nearly $550 million, which is not large in relation to total export trade, but considered as an individual earner, is in fourth place after petroleum, coffee, and sugar. Most of this income goes to Mexico (along its borders) and a lesser amount goes to Haiti, Panama, and Uruguay. . . . Argentina, Brazil, and Venezuela have negative travel balances. Tourism, at least in Mexico, is expanding faster than any export product, and in ten years will probably be a major element in the general picture of Latin America's external demand. It will be determined primarily by the rate and level of disposable income in the United States, although in time it should benefit significantly from tourism of other countries.

Latin America's dependence, through trade and tourism, on the economic development of other countries will continue indefinitely. It would be to Latin America's advantage to diversify both export products and markets and to send abroad products with a higher degree of processing, but these would not essentially alter the problem. For Latin America to increase sales to countries that have not been important customers, these countries must grow more rapidly and want Latin American products. This is even true of Latin America itself, as a market. Herein lies the value of the present free-trade zone and the future Latin American common market.

Dependence involves other problems: on the one hand, price fluctuations; on the other, foreign investments and credits. Price fluctuations are particularly serious because they discourage the investments necessary to augment exports, they frequently have very unfavorable repercussions on other aspects of the domestic economy, as well as on financial conditions, and they bring about production cycles that intensify the imbalance of supply and demand. It is evident that anything that can be done to avoid or moderate fluctuations will in the long run benefit Latin America. The practice of calculating what Latin America "loses" every time prices fall does not seem to be a very useful analytical method, since what is "no longer earned" is not always "lost"; an economic analysis would also have to estimate the effect that continued high prices would have had on the volume of output and exports. A sharp rise in export prices can be as harmful as a decline, because it may lead to inflationary disturbances and create incentives for production on a scale that is subsequently not justified. But it cannot be denied that the Latin American economy would be strengthened if prices were less erratic and if suitable international agreements were adopted to this end.

Another problem presented by Latin America's economic dependence concerns the terms of trade, i.e., the ratio of average prices of exports to those of imports. It is not exclusively a problem of underdeveloped countries. Great Britain is very sensitive to the terms of trade, as is natural for a country whose imports not only are essential to the functioning and growth of its economy, but also constitute a significant cost factor. Many objections of a statistical nature have been raised over the measuring of the terms of trade, chiefly on the grounds that changes in the composition of exports and imports influence indices and that the quality of products varies with the passage of time. But there is no question that over the last eighty years, export prices of primary products in general have dropped in relation to those of manufactured goods. Between 1876–80 and 1896–1900—that is, in about the final quarter-century—the prices of primary products declined by 26 per cent, and by 1913 they had not returned to their original level. In the same period, prices of manufactures fell by only 7 per cent, and by 1913 they had recovered to a level slightly higher than the original. In the forty years from 1913 to 1953, average prices of exports of primary products went up 136 per cent, but those of manufactures rose 175 per cent. Thus, for about eighty years the terms of trade have been moving against primary products, and in the last forty years alone they have worsened by 16 per cent. Latin America, of course, has been adversely affected by this trend; from 1953 to 1959, it suffered an additional drop of 21 per cent because of a slump in average export prices and an upswing in import prices. . . .

This problem has been widely discussed in recent years. In the United Nations, hundreds of man-hours and stacks of paper have been devoted to the question of whether there should not be more "just" or "equitable" terms of trade. Obviously, this kind of discussion leads to no solution and only turns the problem into a political issue. The problem of fluctuating export prices in world markets is more susceptible to treatment. But the terms of trade, which derive from the very structure of the world economy—the development rates of different regions and their relative levels of industrialization and technical progress—cannot be remedied by price regulation. Once again it is apparent that a country is at a disadvantage because it is insufficiently developed and not because it has to trade with the rest of the world.

Transportation is considered to be another factor in the dependence of the Latin American economy, because of the control exercised by the countries supplying most of the shipping and the protection accorded their fleets. There is no doubt that Latin American countries could economize on foreign exchange by employing their own merchant marines more extensively. Dependence could be reduced in this way. However—and this is not always recognized—the individual exporter does not necessarily save money by shipping under his national flag. In any case, he must pay freight charges that are usually fixed by international agreement. This is a subject that merits further study.

Finally, the Latin American economies are dependent on those of the rest of the world because they need to import equipment, machinery, raw materials, some consumer goods, and even basic foodstuffs. In this case, the relationship is of a different nature, because for Latin America the question is not whether industrial countries are interested in selling it equipment or machinery; in fact, the latter's elasticity of supply seems to present no difficulties. The problem for Latin America is that it must acquire foreign exchange, by exports or loans, to pay for its imports. If the amount is insufficient, economic development can be held back. Hence the basic importance of the roles played by all aspects of Latin America's foreign trade and by foreign financing in this region's future economic development.

3

Of the traditional problems of Latin America, the military question merits special attention in that soldiers have always enjoyed prominent roles in the political life of the republics. In 1969 nearly half of the republics were governed directly by generals or indirectly by them through politicians whose authority rested on the consent of the army. Until recently the military had attracted scant interest from scholars in the United States. In the last few years, however, a number of historians have explored the issue. Two schools of

thought have emerged from these studies. The traditional school
views military participation in politics in negative terms, concluding that only the elimination of the soldier from politics will
provide a healthy basis for the future. A new school of scholars,
the revisionists, insists that a realistic appraisal must accept the
military as an inevitable element in national life and believes that
soldiers can contribute to national development and stability. Lyle
N. McAlister, professor of Latin American history at the University of Florida, supports this interpretation.

Lyle N. McAlister:
Changing Concepts of the
Role of the Military*

During the past decade a substantial number of new or revised
interpretations, explanations, and prescriptions relating to the role
of the military in Latin America have appeared. In this paper I
propose to show how traditional views have been challenged or modified by recent writings. I will employ throughout the expressions
"traditional" and "revisionist" thinking or writing, not, however,
to indicate two clearly defined and opposing schools of thought, but
as devices for comparing older and still widely held beliefs about
the Latin-American military with what an increasing number of
scholars and observers believe or hypothesize today. For purposes
of clarity and manageability, the military are defined as the regular
armies, navies, air forces, and the nationally controlled permanent
constabularies of the several nations, as distinct from militias,
secret police, and irregular armed groups. This distinction is significant and will be discussed subsequently in more detail.

TRADITIONAL VIEWS

Traditional patterns of thinking about the military and their
position in the general society are deeply rooted in the Western intellectual heritage. Except for a few deviants, historians, social

* From Lyle N. McAlister, "Changing Concepts of the Role of the Military
in Latin America," THE ANNALS OF THE AMERICAN ACADEMY OF POLITICAL AND
SOCIAL SCIENCE, CCCLX (July 1965), pp. 86–94.

scientists, and literary men have regarded military establishments as the institutional embodiments of violence, and thus as representing the worst side of human nature. Machiavelli observed that "a military man cannot be a good man," and Voltaire described the soldier as the very archetype of the wicked, the manifestation of brute force in rationalized form. Somewhat later Auguste Comte and Herbert Spencer, the fathers of modern sociology, developed the concepts of "militarism" and "militaristic societies." The latter were regarded as inferior to modern industrial society, and nations in which the military performed an active political role were regarded as cruder or more barbaric than those in which they were apolitical. Moreover, the eighteenth-century rationalists and the nineteenth-century positivists believed firmly in the perfectibility of man and held that in the course of "progress" the military would wither away and disappear. In terms of classical political theory, antimilitarism appeared as a model of civil-military relations in which, by both objective and subjective devices, the military were subject to civil control and were politically neutral. Pragmatically, it was affected by the political experiences of the Anglo-Saxon and Scandinavian nations and, in the cases of many Latin-American writers, by brutalities, oppressions, and frustrations suffered at the hands of their own military.

Traditional thinking as applied to Latin America may be broadly sketched as follows. In the first two decades of the nineteenth century, the major territorial units of Spanish America created armies to fight for their independence. When liberation was achieved, these forces emerged as self-confident corporate interest groups which, because of their pre-eminent role in the creation of new nations, felt that they should have a major voice in determining forms of national organization and in the making of public policy. At the same time, the dissolution of the traditional social order left civilian groups weak, disorganized, and incapable of creating viable political systems. The national armies, therefore, moved into a power vacuum and proceeded to exercise the political authority which they believed was inherent in their status and mission, a role which has been aptly described as the military "supermission."

It has been a traditional belief, furthermore, that there was never a genuine need for regular military establishments in Latin America. The new nations created in the early nineteenth century were not burdened by ancient dynastic and territorial rivalries such as those which made armies and navies necessary evils within the nation-state system of Europe. Also, the Latin-American states had a common cultural heritage which served to limit nationalistic conflicts. Thus, rivalries and tensions which developed among them were of a low magnitude. They could be and generally were resolved by negotiation or arbitration. More recently, the Organization of American States is believed to be capable of settling international conflicts in Latin America, so that recourse to war is even less necessary. Finally, it is contended, with the development of complex and costly weapon systems during the last two decades, Latin America cannot maintain armed forces capable of fighting modern wars, and the defense of the Western Hemisphere against outside aggression must be left to the United States.

With no real military mission to perform, therefore, the Latin-American military establishments turned inward against their own people. Historically, they have been reactionary forces which, acting either alone or in conjunction with other conservative elements, have intervened in politics frequently and maliciously and by doing so have thwarted the development of democratic political systems, desirable social change, and economic progress. In the nineteenth and early twentieth centuries militarism was represented by the *caudillo* who, with the support of the army, overthrew the existing government and installed himself in the presidency. More recently, it has assumed a corporate form in which the armed forces pronounce collectively and rule through the military junta. Both types of intervention, however, are regarded as equally pernicious. A corollary to this proposition is that the United States bears a heavy responsibility for the continued vitality of militarism in Latin America because of its recognition and, in some cases, its support of military governments and its programs of military assistance to the Latin-American nations.

Implicit in traditional thinking is the assumption that the military is not really a component of the social order which created it. It is, rather, an alien and demoniac force which does not interact with other social groups but simply acts against them.

The ideal solution to Latin-American militarism, according to traditional opinion, is the abolition of regular military establishments, the relinquishment of the defense of the Western Hemisphere to the United States, and the delegation of internal security functions to constabularies. These moves would not only abolish militarism but would release for more constructive uses the excessive proportion of national budgets now being absorbed by armies, navies, and air forces. The examples of Costa Rica and Bolivia, which disbanded their regular armies in 1948 and 1952, respectively, are cited as examples of the practicability of these policies. An alternative to the ideal prescription against militarism holds that since it may not be practicable to demilitarize Latin America completely and immediately, its armed forces should be reduced in size and placed under civilian control, as was actually done in Mexico after 1920.

The traditional view is basically teleological. It interprets Latin-American history in terms of the "Struggle for Democracy" or "Progress toward Democracy," and maintained, at least until recently, that the depoliticization of the military in Latin America was, in fact, proceeding at an observable rate. This process is illustrated by citing clusters of occasions on which military *caudillos* or juntas were replaced by civilian governments, and by developmental typologies of civil-military relations. Thus, Professor Edwin Lieuwen groups the twenty Latin-American republics into three categories: those in which the armed forces dominate politics; those in which they are in transition from political to nonpolitical bodies; and those in which they are nonpolitical. Clusters of military interventions, on the contrary, are regarded as temporary deviations from the secular trend.

The forthcoming demise of militarism is explained historically by tracing changes both within the general society and the armed forces themselves. Since the late nineteenth century, Latin America has experienced accelerating economic development, the breakdown of highly stratified social systems, and the emergence of new and influential civilian interest groups, such as labor unions, student organizations, and programmatic political parties. The appearance of countervailing civilian forces makes it more difficult for the military to intervene, and the increasing complexity of governmental operations makes it more difficult for them to rule should they do so. During the same period, in the more advanced countries of Latin America and beginning with Argentina and Chile, the military have become increasingly professionalized. According to widely accepted theories of civil-military relations, professionalism reduces the inclination of the military to intervene in politics. Officer recruitment, moreover, has dipped deeper and deeper into social strata so that now most field, company grade, and junior officers are of middle and lower sector origin. Presumably, they retain some of the social values and attitudes of the groups from which they derived.

REVISIONIST VIEWS

As a more or less systematic set of explanations and prescriptions, revisionist views may perhaps be related to Burkean conservatism with its skepticism about the perfectibility of man, its concept of the organic society, and its philosophy of gradual, undirected evolutionary change. However, several more immediate and more direct intellectual influences may be detected. These include: first, a general reformulation of the classic theory of democracy which assumed that the neutrality of the military was an essential quality of democratic political systems. More recently a clearer concept of the institutional requirements for a democratic society has induced theorists to believe that a system of democratic consent must also include the military. Second, the influence of the concept of cultural relativism and of research on political systems of developing nations has convinced many Latin-Americanists that Anglo-Saxon constitutional norms are not automatically transferrable to nations with differing cultural heritages. Third, developments in the theory and method of political sociology permit a more objective view of the military, and provide more sophisticated tools for analyzing their political functions. Theoretical and methodological influences have been reinforced by empirical observations of changes in the attitudes and behavior of the armed forces in a number of Latin-American countries.

More specifically, revisionist thinking contends that the intervention of the Latin-American military in politics is but one manifestation of a more general phenomenon: the employment of violence for political ends. Violence includes not only the classic *cuartelazo* or *golpe de estado* executed by regular military units, but also the anomic riot, such as the *Bogotazo* of 1948; civil wars fought by armed civilian factions which were characteristic of Venezuela in the nineteenth century; and traditional dictatorships maintained by national guards, constabularies, and secret police. These several types of violence are inherent components in political systems which have not developed accepted rules and procedures for the conduct of government and the orderly transfer of power. Within this frame of reference, the military is not a "cause" of political instability but a manifestation of it; militarism is not a disease but a symptom in a syndrome characterizing a social ailment.

This proposition carries several corollaries. First, military interventions in Latin America have not always been what Professor Morris Janowitz terms "designed militarism," that is, deliberate and selfish grabs for power. Frequently they have represented "reactive militarism," that is, the expansion of military political activity resulting from the debility of civilian institutions; from the efforts of civilian politicians to suborn the armed forces for personal, factional, or party purposes; and from reactions to undemocratic or unconstitutional behavior on the part of civilian governments. Second, it is simplistic to assign any significant portion of the blame for Latin-American militarism to the United States. Latin-Americans will ultimately develop political systems in harmony with their cultural heritage and unique requirements. If militarism continues to flourish, it will not be because of ephemeral policies of the United States. If democracy is to triumph, it will be because of native will and political skill exercised over the long range.

In regard to the changing role of the military, revisionist thinking recognizes many of the trends identified in traditional analyses including the increasing complexity of Latin-American society, the emergence of countervailing sources of civilian power, changing patterns of officer recruitment and training, and increasing professionalization of the armed forces. However, it interprets them in a somewhat different way. Professionalism, it is argued, is no specific for militarism. Indeed, in recent years two of the most highly professionalized military establishments in Latin America, those of Argentina and Peru, have been very active in politics. Moreover, there is little evidence that the younger officers on whom the traditionalists pin their hopes are less inclined toward political action than their elders. Also, younger officers inevitably become older officers. Major trends in the general society and within the services do not presage the demise of militarism in the foreseeable future, but rather the emergence of new patterns of military political action. Anticipated resistance of civilian elements and the difficulties of administering complex governmental systems may deter the armed forces from overt forms of intervention and military rule, but they will continue to participate in political processes through more subtle methods of persuasion, pressure, and blackmail. Finally, because of their social origins, improved education, and greater awareness of national and international problems their political motivations will no longer be the maintenance of narrow corporate and class privileges but rather a desire to participate in and accelerate change. The role of the military as social reformers and promoters of economic development is frequently described as "Nasserism."

In normative and prescriptive terms, most revisionist thinking is basically antimilitarist. It does not, however, regard the abolition or substantial reduction of Latin America's armed forces as either practicable or desirable in the foreseeable future. With regard to practicability, in the first place the Latin-American military are highly self-conscious, privileged, and powerful groups which are not likely to acquiesce voluntarily to their own dissolution. In the two most recent instances where regular military establishments were "abolished"—in Costa Rica and Bolivia—it was only after they had been defeated in a species of civil war. In the latter country, moreover, a new army was formed almost immediately, and although the revolutionary government attempted to mold its political and ideological orientation, in fact an organic continuity was maintained between the old and new institutions.

Second, the Latin-American armed services and important segments of the civilian population are not at all convinced that they can rely on international agencies and the United States for their external security. Peruvians are quite aware that they possess boundaries with five different nations, at least one of which they regard as hostile. They remember also that because of the lack of an effective army and navy, they lost a valuable section of national territory during the War of the Pacific. Brazilians are not at all certain that some day they will not have to defend their southern boundary against a revitalized and possibly militaristic Argentina.

Third, more than any other national institution, the military serve as symbols of nationality, or, as Morris Janowitz puts it, as "marks of sovereignty." This is a particularly important function in nations still searching for true national identities and extremely jealous of their sovereignty. Moreover, in countries with military traditions, such as Chile, Peru, or Brazil, the armed forces command high prestige and are a source of national pride. Dr. Edward Glick records an interview with a Brazilian diplomat in 1963—not a military attaché—who took great pains to inform him that as the largest country in Latin America, Brazil must have a respectable military estabishment and "keep ahead of other nations and regions. If nothing else," he continued, "it is a matter of our national *prestige*."

Fourth, the military in many Latin-American nations are regarded by wide sectors of the public as the guarantors of internal order and as regulators which keep scheming civilian politicians in line. Professor John J. Johnson in his previously cited work, *The Military and Society in Latin America,* makes an extensive analysis of the public image of the military in Brazil and concludes that it is widely respected among most social groups, including intellectuals. Somewhat the same image appears to exist in Colombia, Peru, and Chile. In short, if plebiscites were to be held throughout Latin America on whether or not to disband regular military establishments, the champions of disarmament would not universally prevail.

Turning to the desirability of general disarmament in Latin

America, revisionist thinking includes substantial reservations. In the first place, in countries where viable political systems do not exist, where contending forces and factions are unable to achieve peaceful accommodations, the armed forces may perform a vital moderating function. Through the exertion of pressures or, if necessary, direct intervention, they can prevent swings to political extremes. Brazil is frequently cited as a case in point. It has even been hypothesized that in some countries it might be desirable to formalize this function by constituting senior officers of the armed forces as a superjudiciary with authority to judge the legality or desirability of executive and legislative acts.

Second, the rising threat of the Maoist-Castro type of insurgency, already serious in Venezuela, Colombia, and Guatemala, requires for counterinsurgency missions more elaborate military establishments than simple constabularies. On this point, a distinction must be made between the use of the military to protect the status quo against progressive reform, a role commonly imputed to them, and their employment to protect the state against Communist-inspired revolutionary movements.

Third, as suggested above, there is certainly a tendency among revisionist writers to believe that, in certain situations, civilian governments lack the power or the will to undertake essential economic and social reforms and that only an enlightened military can provide the necessary impetus. The junta which came to power in Ecuador in July 1963 is offered as an example of progressive military government.

Fourth, it may be argued that where violence is an accepted alternative to peaceful resolution of political issues, the means of violence will become available whether or not regular military institutions exist. Thus, at the same time that the old army was "abolished" in Bolivia after the revolution of 1952, civilian interest groups proceeded to create their own armed militias. It can be contended further that such forces which are political by virtue of the terms of their creation are much more dangerous to the state than professional armies. Historically, throughout the first decades of the nineteenth century, politically motivated violence in Latin America more often than not resulted from the actions of irregular and temporary armed groups led by civilians rather than from insurrections of regular forces. This interpretation is carefully developed and precisely documented in Professor Robert Gilmore's *Caudillism and Militarism in Venezuela, 1810–1910.*

In the case of the Costa Rican model of disarmament, labelistic distinctions between constabularies and armies are not really meaningful, particularly in Latin America where the two are sometimes deliberately confused. Dr. Glick writes:

> If a man wears a uniform, is trained to use weapons, and is under legal discipline, in practical terms it often makes little difference whether you call him a soldier, a policeman, a militiaman, or a member of the national guard.

Furthermore, it can be argued that police forces are intrinsically more political than armies. Their primary concern is with internal affairs, and their loyalty is owed to the government in power, which is temporary, rather than to the state, which is permanent. Even if it is insisted that constabularies are lesser threats to stability than armies, a government can transform one into the other by a simple change of name. This, in fact, was done in Panama when Colonel José Remón redesignated the national police as the national guard, increased its strength by 50 per cent, and provided it with improved weaponry. Finally, it is worthy of note that Costa Rica was represented at the Fourth American Armies Conference in 1963 by its Director of Public Security, and that it is among the countries to which United States Army military civic action teams have been dispatched.

The proposition most heavily stressed in revisionist thinking is that as long as the Latin-American military cannot be "talked or written away," their technical proficiencies and organizational formats should be exploited for constructive purposes. Historically, they have performed a wide range of tasks which are not primarily military in character. These include the construction of roads, schools, and sanitary facilities; primary and vocational education; colonization of underdeveloped national territory; and reforestation. More recently the public service functions of the armed services have been given a more formal and explicit definition in a number of Latin-American countries in the form of military civic action programs. Lieutenant General Aberto Ruíz Navoa, former Colombian Minister of War, recently defined civic action rather eloquently:

> Military-civic action has as its purpose to extend to vast sectors of the populace the government's help, especially in the field of social assistance, through the military organization of the nation. It is based on the premise that the use of military means to accomplish programs of economic and social welfare will awaken in the benefited population trust and sympathy toward the government and the military forces. These programs are developed without affecting the military efficiency of the armed institutions or compromising their principal functions.

As of July 1963, the date of the Fourth American Armies Conference, in ten of the Latin-American countries represented, the armed services were constructing schools and churches. In eight, they were conducting literary campaigns for adults. In at least four, there were reforestation projects sponsored by the military. Six had military personnel engaged in housing construction for civilians, including manufacture of basic materials. In twelve countries the military were involved on a large scale in preventive medicine and disease control. Finally, military involvement in primary education was the second biggest civic action operation in Latin America, surpassed only by the medical program. Revisionist thinking holds that the Latin-American armed forces can be induced to expand substantially such undertakings.

The style and emphasis of the preceding presentation have undoubtedly revealed that I support the basic propositions of the newer thinking about the role of the military in Latin America. Although I am temperamentally and intellectually opposed to military dictators and military juntas and hope fervently that the Latin-American nations will evolve in the direction of democratic, civilian-dominated political systems, I am not at all certain that this destiny has already been written into history. Furthermore, I do not think that Latin-American armies can be conjured away or that in the foreseeable future most of them can be reduced to civilian control by constitutional formulas, political action, or the termination of United States military assistance. In the meantime, I hope they can be employed for socially useful purposes.

I do, however, have some reservations about certain revisionist interpretations and prescriptions. In regard to the political activities of the military, it would seem risky to condone formally or to encourage or legitimatize military intervention. Such a policy includes a self-fulfilling feature. If it is generally and openly accepted that the military has the right and sometimes the obligation to intervene, it will certainly be encouraged to do so. In situations where the military, in fact, does perform a moderating role, perhaps the most appropriate formula is contained in a statement made to me by a Brazilian senior civil servant shortly before the overthrow of the Goulart government. "Our problem," he observed, "is to discourage the armed forces from intervening while at the same time maintaining their capability to do so."

Turning to military civic action, an expansion of such programs is a promising and even exciting prospect. If realized, it would not only make a substantial contribution to national development but also, hopefully, provide soldiers with a sense of service and participation in national efforts. One may speculate, however, on the extent to which expanded long-term civic action programs are feasible. In the first place, the defense of the national territory, internal security missions, or political considerations require the disposition of troops in certain ways and in certain places. This kind of deployment may not always be compatible with the troop distribution required for expanded civic action projects. Second, in some countries military personnel may have such low technical competence that they lack the capability to support them.

Third, armed forces may use such activities to claim larger portions of the national budgets. Further, expanded civic action may create dissensions within the military by disrupting power and status relationships existing among the several services and their component arms and branches. They certainly would seem to enhance the prestige of the Corps of Engineers at the expense of the traditional combat arms. Fourth, there is a question as to what extent civic action programs on a large scale are compatible with the military's concept of its primary role. Armies are created to fight wars and, when they are not fighting, to prepare for them. The military profession is built around a set of values and symbols —courage, honor, status, and privilege—deriving from a preindustrial age, which are not easily reconcilable with the bourgeois attitudes of sanitary engineers, foresters, and public school teachers. Perhaps this question raises phantom problems. As military organization, communications, and weapons systems become more complex, the gap between military and civilian skills and values narrows, and the military hero is increasingly replaced by the military manager, the fighting man by the military technician.

A fifth question relates to the attitude of civilian bureaucrats and politicians toward expanded civic action programs. There is scattered evidence that agencies charged with similar functions resent the intrusion of soldiers into their domains and argue that they could do the job better if the equivalent of funds allotted to the military were allocated to them. Moreover, there is also some random evidence that civilian leaders are not always enthusiastic about the creation of a more favorable public image of the military which, it is assumed, will emerge from civic action.

4

Caudillos, the legendary men on horseback, have ruled every country in Latin America at one time or another. Some republics have scarcely known any other type of government. Today, *caudillos* still predominate even in the more developed nations though in a subtler manner. *Caudillos* range from local chieftains who dictate policy in the municipalities to national figures who control the country-wide pyramid of petty and provincial bosses. The *caudillo* has survived every attempt to eliminate him, including social revolutions in Mexico, Cuba, and Bolivia. Fidel Castro, despite his Communist trappings, heads the list of today's strong men. To Frank Tannenbaum, an American scholar who devoted a lifetime of study to Latin America, the roots of the *caudillo* lie deeply imbedded in the social and political fabric of society. His thesis challenges the assertion that recent socio-economic changes make inevitable the disappearance of the *caudillo* from Latin American society.

Frank Tannenbaum:
The Political Dilemma in
Latin America*

I

There have been changes in Latin America in the past generation which have been complicated and obscured the political scene without really changing its character. The spread of doctrines such as Nazism, Fascism, Socialism and Communism, and their adoption as party names, has given foreigners and even some culturally Europeanized nationals the impression that something

* From Frank Tannenbaum, "The Political Dilemma in Latin America," FOREIGN AFFAIRS: AN AMERICAN QUARTERLY REVIEW, XXXVIII (April 1960), pp. 497–505, 511–515. Excerpted by special permission from FOREIGN AFFAIRS, April 1960. Copyright by the Council on Foreign Relations, Inc., New York.

strange has happened, that what was always a personal phenomenon in Latin America had become a matter of ideals—that the party, the ideology, has displaced the individual, that the slogan is more important than the leader, that law is now of greater significance than personal influence, that matters of principle now substitute for friendship, family and political clan. Those who have let themselves believe all this have simply lost their bearings and are reading their politics out of a European book and calling things by false names.

The one thing that has not changed has been the *caudillo*, the leader, he who has *la suma del poder*, who governs because he can, not because he was elected. There are many differences between Fidel Castro and Trujillo, but there is one thing in common between them: they govern because they can. The fact that Trujillo has himself elected and always receives 100 percent of the vote while Fidel Castro has had no election is irrelevant except as embroidery, or something that gives apparent sanction, or that satisfies critics in the United States or England who do not really appreciate what is going on. And what is going on has always gone on—if "always" is the wrong word, then we will have to say "what has gone on for a very long time." Leadership is personal. The basis of authority is customary rather than constitutional. The political unit is not the individual. It is the "gang," the extended family, the community, the Indian village, each with its own "natural" leader, each endowed with unlimited authority, each possessing the complete loyalty of his immediate followers.

The great leader by some magic, fraud or force has at his disposal all this power, which in his absence devolves to the local leaders. And because he has it, his power is absolute regardless of what the constitution may say. The power is absolute because it is all deposited in one person and he cannot divulge it, delegate it or refuse to use it. As a matter of simple fact, he cannot resign it —as Fidel Castro could not resign from being the "maximum leader of the Revolution" in Cuba. He could resign his office of Premier, but not his personal authority. The *caudillo* governs by his mere presence, and anything he says is an order; and if he refuses to say anything at all, then others will act in his name on the assumption that they are carrying out the orders he would have given, and he will be credited with them. The king could abdicate in favor of the legitimate heir to the crown. In Latin America the leader cannot abdicate because there is no legitimate heir to his power. When the successor appears, the power of the older leader evaporates. The power cannot be shared. It is absolute or it does not exist.

The case of Fidel Castro is particularly revealing. Cuba is not typical of Latin America. The Indian influence is nil. The Negro, on the other hand, is important in numbers, but more so even in over-all influence. The Negro has given the Cubans a gentle, friendly and optimistic attitude towards life. He has tended to emphasize the importance of the moment. He has filled the land with music, the drum and the dance. Cuba, too, is close to the United States and our impact upon Cuba has been great—greater perhaps than either they or we realize. There are therefore many reasons for arguing that politically Cuba should be less Latin American than it has shown itself to be. For what it has shown in Fidel Castro is that it likes to have a *caudillo* who stands above the law, above the constitution, because all authority, all justice, all good emanate from him.

The differences between Fidel Castro and Batista are many and great, but as administrators they both respond to the same demand, the same way. Batista was secretive, cruel, selfish and acted for himself and a small clique. But no one doubted who exercised the power. He depended upon the police and the army, and his power was absolute. All constitutional formulas were secondary. Fidel Castro uses the radio and television; he is devoted to the ideal of nationalism and a strong Cuba. Administratively, like Batista, he stands above the law, above the constitution, for he embodies them both. The uses the power is put to are different. The totality of its lodgement in a single hand is the same.

The power is put to different uses because the individual leaders are different and not because the "party" which carried them to power is different. In fact, there was no party in Batista's case and there is none in Fidel Castro's case. The Cuban people have Fidel Castro because they want him. They had Batista because they tolerated him—perhaps, until the last two years, wanted him —not because he was "good" or constitutional, but because he was strong, because he was a *caudillo*. If they finally overthrew him (and the active fighters against him were never very numerous) it was because he had become a tyrant, because he was misusing his power beyond reason, beyond the wide tolerance of human fallibility so characteristic of Latin America. He had lost what moral sanction he might have had or claimed. His overthrow by a revolution was accepted as good and the leader of the revolution was greeted with an outpouring of public joy.

It is difficult for people outside Latin America to understand the reasons for these repeated changes. They know only that Latin American governments are unstable, that revolutions are frequent, that tyrannies are a commonplace and occasionally, as the recent one in Colombia, bloody and heartless, and that constitutional government has remained an unsatisfied aspiration. This has now been the case for nearly 150 years and there is really no evidence that, politically speaking, the countries are closer to representative democracy now than they were in the nineteenth century. There are exceptions to these broad generalizations, but they are few and even so would be subject to qualification.

The pattern of dictatorship, then, is rebellion and again dictatorship, and it has not materially changed since 1900. Anyone who would make a count of the abortive uprisings and the rebellions that were successful in the last 59 years would convince himself that if there has been political change, it has not necessarily been in the direction of greater stability. This is so in spite of an almost universal commitment to the ideals of democracy among Latin American intellectuals and statesmen. Students, scholars, newspapermen and politicians have written an impressive public record in their striving for political democracy, and every constitution describes in detail the manner in which popular governments are to come to power, how long they are to last and how they are to be succeeded by another administration freely elected and resting upon the consent of the governed.

This contrast between what men say they want politically and what they do cannot be ascribed to malice or perfidy. That would be too simple. If the political difficulties were merely the product of evil intent, they could be dealt with. Politically active people in Latin America are on the whole neither better nor worse than their kind in other parts of the world. The trouble lies somewhere else. Politicians do what they do because they have only limited alternatives and it is not always clear that choices other than those they make would always be better.

II

The social and cultural matrix within which the politicians operate is such that popular democracy is not a feasible immediate alternative. The only really responsible question that the democratically minded observer can ask of a politician in Latin America is whether his conduct is conducive towards an increasing prospect of popular democracy, and an honest man would find it difficult to give an honest answer. For how can one be sure that the professed idealist in his enthusiasm for reform, in his stirring the passions and hopes of simple folk beyond his own ability to satisfy them, may not be sowing the dragon's teeth and preparing the ground for some conscienceless tyrant tomorrow, who will make all promises and fulfill none? The difficulty lies somewhere else. It is not personal. It lies in the absence of a universally accepted symbol of political authority. That is why Latin-American politicians cannot do what they would and lack the moral support to carry out the programs they do have in mind.

For the business of government is to govern. That is the first responsibility. If it fails at that, then the politicians in office will soon be fleeing the country and seeking exile in places where they will have no relentless responsibilities to fulfill. But to govern in Latin America is an unusually difficult matter.

General Lazaro Cardenas once remarked that the people of Mexico must learn that they can be governed without violence. Cardenas, however, had qualities of leadership which made violence unnecessary. He could govern Mexico that way but no one else had been able to do so before him. Violence has been an essential in Latin America because the governments have been unstable, and the governments have been unstable because violence is a traditional means of coming to office. And violence is traditional because there has generally been no other sure means of transferring political power from one administration to another. Here is the heart of the matter: how to come to power without violence, how to transfer it without revolution.

In other parts of the world which are familiar with the political miracle of entering upon and leaving public office peacefully, there is some universally accepted principle of legitimacy. A universal symbol makes the government of today just as much a government as it was yesterday in spite of a complete change-over in personnel. The king is dead, long live the king, is a perfect example of this kind of symbol of authority. As long as the accepted principle of descent is adhered to, there is never any question as to where authority resides and to whom the crown descends. The government is never without a recognized head. Everyone knows who the king is. No such universally accepted symbol exists in Latin America.

During the colonial period the question of where legitimate power resided never arose. The king was the king in all things and at all times. People might have notions about the wisdom, the stupidity or even the lunacy of the king or queen, but none about the legitimacy of the power he or she exercised. So universal was this acceptance that it seemed like a part of nature itself. Men had laid down their lives for "God and the King" for so many generations that the king's "divine" authority was beyond question. He filled every political and civil need and his law protected the innocent and punished the guilty. All offices, all honors, all men, all property, life itself were under his protection and held by his mercy. Even the church, because of the *Patronato*, was in many important ways subject to the king. The authority of the crown was everywhere, unquestioned and unopposed. The two things that were known even to the most humble were the power of the king and the mercy of God. It was therefore always simple to transfer power as long as the rules of succession were followed. The future king was known while the present king was still alive.

It is at this point that the independence movement served the people of Latin America poorly. It destroyed legitimate political power without providing an equally legitimate substitute. When the wars of independence were over, no one knew where political power resided. Who was the legitimate heir to the King of Spain —to his authority, influence, prestige, semi-sacred character, the embodiment of the will of the people, the protector of the poor, the fountainhead of justice?

The answer, of course, is that no one inherited those qualities of popularly endowed eminence; no one received the same degree of devotion from the populace and no one was looked to as the absolute father of his people. Latin America was left without a legitimate symbol of political authority. And that vacuum has remained unfilled. It has not been filled by "democracy," "federalism," "socialism," "Communism," "justiciatism, or what-not. The idea of the nation comes closer to being a substitute for the idea of the king than any so far. But nationalism in Latin America is relatively recent and many of the nations lack cultural unity. A considerable part of the population, the majority perhaps, in Guatemala, Peru, Bolivia and Ecuador, for instance, have but the vaguest notion of what the nation means. There is the other difficulty that nationalism has taken an anti-foreign turn and has become a slogan for demagogues and ambitious politicians. More serious, however, is the absence of a fixed rule of who is to represent the nation and how he is to be chosen.

The constitution has proved an insufficient influence to guide the political process. There have been too many constitutions and they have been disregarded with such regularity that they do not serve to discipline political behavior. In fact, the constitution has frequently been a personal political broadsheet used by the new *mandatario* as his own private declaration, and since it is private it need not be scrupulously followed. What ought to be protected and guarded as the embodiment of all public law and public will has become a matter to be changed, modified, suspended or abolished. What might have become an effective symbol of authority as a substitute for the awe-inspiring bearer of the Spanish crown has been perverted to personal use.

An American scholar tells the story somewhere that when as a young man he went to Venezuela to study its constitutional history, people in Caracas, when they learned of his purpose, said, "Why, he must be a poet!" The constitution in their mind had a literary, conceivably a theoretical interest, but certainly not a political one. The 19 constitutions that he studied showed no evolutionary principle and could not be classified on any rational basis. He finally grouped them under various rubrics including that of experimental constitutions. All of this merely goes to emphasize the point that there is no recognized basis of political authority universally accepted and universally respected. What does not in fact exist cannot be symbolized. This, however, is only one part of the difficulty.

Independence abolished the monarchy but retained what is natural to a monarchy—centralism, authoritarianism and aristocracy. These characteristics remained because the revolutionists were themselves reared in the Spanish tradition and knew no other. Centralism, authoritarianism and aristocracy were a part of life itself and no other way was known to either the leaders or the people.

Aristocracy was affected only in the degree that the Spanish aristocrats departed while the local *criollo* with his claims to nobility remained; and below him were the merchants, farmers, *mestizos, castas,* free Negroes, Negro slaves and Indians. To all appearances, nothing had changed socially except that a few *mestizos* had worked their way to public notice by their part in the Wars of Liberation and that a number of Negro slaves had been freed because they had been drafted into the revolutionary armies. Beyond that, the hierarchical structure survived more or less intact in most places throughout the nineteenth and in some areas to the middle of the twentieth century.

Natural to the hierarchical structure, too, was the survival of authoritarianism and administrative centralization. The existence of slavery, the survival of Indian peonage, the universality of the hacienda and the important role of the military all contributed to the maintenance of a political system which did not know how to share or divide political authority.

The contrast between an authoritarian and democratic society lies at this point. A democratic society finds it natural and logical to divide and distribute political authority in many places. No one person or institution is possessed of all the authority of the state.

Quite the contrary, in an authoritarian society, political authority is indivisible.

The president is all powerful but he has no heir. There is no effective machinery for transferring political power. And this is the most serious crisis facing the elected chief executive. If he does not decide who the next president is going to be, then he is sure to face serious difficulties. For someone is going to make that decision and anyone who can do that is stronger than the president. The chief executive soon discovers that all of his power has ebbed away and is now in the hands of him who was able to pick the next president. The prospects are that a revolution will be inevitable unless the occupant of the presidential chair is completely pliant. There is a story about Ortiz Rubio which does not have to be true to be important. The fact that it could be told and believed is sufficiently revealing of the political process in an authoritarian and centralized tradition. The story is that Ortiz Rubio heard on good authority that General Plutarco Elias Calles was going to start a revolution against him. Ortiz Rubio called General Calles on the phone to inform him that he, the president, was going to join the revolution against the government. If, on the other hand, the president decides upon his successor and can make the decision effective, he still has the prospect of revolution against his decision. He is surely going to be accused of imposing the next president against the will of the people. Where there is no institutionalized and universally acknowledged basis of public power, then violence becomes a "natural" means to public office.

In the Spanish tradition, however, political authority requires a moral basis. Power over other people is something that can be exercised only with divine sanction. It must have a moral basis and serve moral ends; otherwise it cannot be considered legitimate. Violence is not the route to legitimacy even if it is successful. The dictator, even when in office, even when he imposes obedience by terror and cruelty, will be held to have no moral basis for this authority. That explains the frequent resort to elections by dictators who have come to office by violence. If they hold an election they will become legitimate in their own minds and, they believe, in those of the populace. The old saying that the will of the people is the voice of God is here taken literally even if the will of the people has to be invented before it can be recorded. But such instances (and they are numerous, if not as extreme as in Santo Domingo) merely illustrate that even the tyrant is seeking a moral basis of power because sheer violence even if successful does not legitimize public office.

The dictator will be obeyed of necessity and opposed secretly or by conspiracy on the grounds that his power is immoral and tyrannical. The opposition may ultimately triumph as it did in Venezuela, Argentina, Colombia and Cuba. As soon as the revolution is over and the tyrant is no more, the old dilemma reappears as "The king is dead—who is the king now?"

Who shall be the next—what? Not a tyrant, not a dictator surely. Who shall be the next executive who will exercise all power but will remain a democrat, a gentle human being who will have all the power of the government without restraint, without limit, but will not use it to evil ends? He cannot divide his authority or delegate it. The populace will not permit that. The president must be president. On that point there is general agreement. But on what ground does he become president? How does he achieve power? How does he retain it? What is his mandate? Who is he responsible to? To these questions there is really no answer because there is no institutional basis for the political process. There is no prerequisite which determines how the candidate for the highest office is to be chosen, how once designated he is to be selected, how once selected he is to remain in office for the period set by the constitution. Nor is there anything absolute and sacred about how and to whom he is to transmit power when his legal term of office draws to a close. These questions had to be faced recently in Argentina, Colombia, Venezuela and Cuba and in none of them is the answer irrevocable; in none is the occupant of the highest office certain of his post or certain that he can transmit it peacefully at the end of his term. . . .

In the absence of a political party system, the president must be his own party and maintain himself in office by his own ingenuity and political skill, by dependence upon the loyalty of his immediate followers, by compromise, blandishment and, if these fail, by force and fraud. What this really means is that the president is not only the chief executive but also the most active politician, almost the only politician. For under the circumstances no one else may be allowed to have political influence. Politics is the act of keeping your political enemies from depriving you of the presidency. What is really involved is not your policy but your power. Under the circumstances, the government must do everything because every act has political significance and no one but the president can indulge in political activities. When the power of the government is in daily question, every public act, no matter how small, has political implications.

Any activity which the president does not control is a threat to his influence. He can have power only if he has all the power. If any escapes him, all of it will. This is so because his power is not institutionalized but belongs to him personally. The government is his government. He conquered it. He must be the whole government, executive, legislative, judicial. Never mind what the constitution says. The constitution is not the instrument of government. It is only the name in which the government is carried out. The president must be his own head of the army, his own cabinet, and in these days of planning he must be his own planner. He must be all of this because he cannot delegate really effective powers to anyone else. He governs without a party. There are only the president and his friends, and his friends must be real friends—unconditionally, who will take orders and do what they are told, politically speaking.

The tradition of centralization and the absence of effective party organization define the role of political leadership. The leader must do everything, have the answer to all problems and the remedy for every ill. Jose Antonio Paez once wrote to Bolivar: "I do not know why, but the people bring me all their problems, how to build a house, whom to marry, how to settle a family dispute, and what seeds to plant." He was their leader because they turned to him in need, expected to be helped. If he had refused to listen he would soon have lost his leadership. This dependence upon the leader converts the ministry, cabinet, legislature and courts of justice into his appendages. The poorest citizen refuses to abide by a decision of any intermediate and will take his case to the president personally.

Under the circumstances, there are no bases either for democracy or monarchy. It is interesting to recall that Bolivar recognized that the American milieu would erode any monarchy established in America. He was equally skeptical, after much experience, that the former Spanish colonies would lend themselves to democratic government. In his disillusionment he predicted that America was ungovernable, a prophecy that proved itself true in many places over a long time.

For one thing, the government seems foreign and the law it enforces looks like an imposition. This was true in the colonial period and has continued to be true since. In the colonial period the government and the law were foreign in the literal sense of the word. In spite of their best intent, the officials of the crown remained Europeans and Spaniards, with the natural consequence that the law they wrote reflected their local allegiance and training and remained an empty gesture. The good intentions written into the law proved unenforceable. The law was one thing, the customary ways another. . . .

This Spanish tradition of a government apart from and strange to the people has survived in Latin America to this day. The "elected" official government is not part of the real substance of custom, common law and local order. The locality follows local traditions and the representatives of the "government" collect taxes and chase smugglers if they can. The government was not chosen by the people and does not represent them. This is obviously true of areas where there are large Indian populations, which govern themselves to the extent allowed by the "official" government. The same may be said about large Negro communities and areas. Government here, too, is foreign and local order is made by custom and tradition. In their degree this is true of the regions where the local *caudillo* is the real ruler of the area and the "government" a tolerated but suspected meddler in things beyond its "legitimate" jurisdiction. The people in Yucatan, Cuzco, Cartegena or Amazonas have never been converted to the idea that the governments in Mexico City, Lima, Bogota or Rio de Janeiro are their governments. This is true of the *mestizo* and *criollo* and especially true of the Indian and Negro. Political instability and political revolutions are preoccupations of the central government.

At the local level there is little instability for on the whole the same people will govern because the effective loyalty and power are theirs regardless of who is the new president of the country or who are his agents. "Elected government" is important at the center; in the locality, he who governs has always governed. In fact, at the local level the "election" is unnecessary for everyone recognizes who the "real" governor is regardless of the election. If the president at the center interferes by imposing his own "governor," the emissary finds the task difficult because he can do only what the police or the army will do for him, and he discovers for himself an old Napoleonic dictum that the one thing you cannot do with bayonets is to sit on them. He may be the designated governor but the real ruler of the district is the locally accepted leader whose power and influence have come to him "naturally."

What we are really saying is that the central government and the localities are two worlds apart; that the lack of legitimacy, the absence of popularly endowed authority, applies to the center a great deal more than it does to the locality. The prospect of political stability rests on the possibilities of identifying the locality with the center, for that would be one way, perhaps the only way, of making the central government "legitimate." This can be done only in a democratic world through effective political parties, and no such parties are in existence.

General Lazaro Cardenas once remarked that "when all of the land belongs to the villages then the government will rest on the villages, but at present it depends upon the army." The reason why the government in Mexico rested upon the army was because there was no other institutionalized basis sufficient for the purpose. This statement can be generalized for all of Latin America. The only exceptions possibly are Costa Rica and Uruguay. So far as the other Latin American countries are concerned, and this includes Brazil, the government's ability to survive to the end of the presidential term and its prospects of passing on the government to the next administration in peace are determined by the army's willingness to stand back of the president. Beyond the army there is no really effective underpinning for the government.

III

In democratic countries such as Great Britain, the United States or Switzerland, the government at the center comes into being in response to a consensus of the localities. . . .

None of this political complex exists in Latin America. There is no effective local self-government. The school, the roads, the police, the tax collector, the agents of *formal* government are in the central administration. The governors are appointed or are removed by the central administration. The intervenor in Argentina and Brazil, the authority to declare that a state has lost its constitutional powers in Mexico, are illustrative of the central government's control over the state even in countries where there is a constitutionally established federal system. Most of the income from taxes is taken by the central government, the state, counties and townships being left with a pittance. I have seen a village that had built its own school out of local materials with the free labor of its own residents wait for months for the money to buy the windows which they could not make. A community will send a delegation to the capital to sit for months in the antechamber of the president to beg for a pipe or small gasoline engine to bring water to the community. All of this follows from the traditional principle of authoritarian and centralized rule. The president must make every decision and he must provide for all needs. He must do this because there is no effective local government; and in the absence of that, there is no means of developing a political party that can provide the needed support to make the presidency independent of the army.

In spite of the ancient and honorable tradition of the Spanish *cabildo*, there is really no way of organizing a political party with strong roots in local government. Beyond the reach of the large urban center, the hacienda, with its enclosed community of *encasillados* living inside the boundaries of a private estate, has no local self-government. For them the government is what local tradition has grown up to define the relations between the *hacendado* and his laborers. The hacienda community, no matter how large, has no civic status. If the population happens to be Indian, there is normally the added barrier of language difference to make political communication most difficult. These communities are comparable to our own mill "village" organized about the southern textile mills until a few years ago, where the mill owner hired the policeman, the schoolteacher and the preacher, and where the local factory "hands" had neither a vote nor a voice in the arrangement of the minutest affairs of their community.

In the case of the village—in Guatemala, for instance—if it is large enough, the central government will control the local administration through one of its own appointed agents who may have the compulsory assistance of a given number of villagers. But the real government, apart from taxes and purely legal imposition, will be in the hands of traditionally recognized authority completely alien to the central government. The central government may be ignorant of its existence or contemptuous of its doings, considering them foolish Indian ways. But the effective authority in these Indian communities is with the traditional government and not with the agents sent down from the center.

An interesting example of this can be seen today in Peru, in the *barrajes* (shanty towns) which have sprung up all around Lima. Where the recent migrants in these communities are of Indian origin, a locally improvised democratic government traditional in the Indian village automatically comes into being. This government takes on the problems of the new community as best it can. All male members vote in the election of the community officers and frequent public assemblies discuss community needs. Actually this government is legally non-existent, since local communities in Peru are run by delegates from the center. Here in the capital of the country is an interesting example of two systems of administration, one legal and *mestizo* and centrally controlled, the other democratic, Indian and legally non-existent.

If the Latin American governments had really been prepared to build a democratic society, here was (and still is in many places) a good foundation based upon custom and traditional folk law. But no political administration has ever contemplated such a possibility. The theory of individualism and the practice of organizing everything from above have made it impossible for all practical purposes to incorporate the remnants of democratic practices and customs that still survive among Indian communities. These communities, like the hacienda, are not really part of the civic organization of the state.

This leaves the *mestizo* and Negro communities, other than those on plantations. These will be under the influence of a regional power system that will exist independent of central government. The central government will be represented by appointed officials, except in those areas where there are elections for local office. Where there are elections, the central government will manage to win all elections, including the local one, for it cannot permit the locality to escape from its control. Even in Mexico no governor of a state could be elected against the will of the president or against his known opposition. The governor of the state has to be a friend of the president. Furthermore, no governor could survive in office if he made it clear that he opposed the administration's policies or that he would not accept the decision about who the next president should be. Any governor who could defy the president on these matters would be stronger than the president and would end by driving the president from office. These are not elements out of which a political party independent of the executive can be built.

In the large urban centers the situation is more complicated. In a number of places the most important local interests are in the hands of foreigners. Or control may lie in the large nearby haciendas, as, for instance, in Trujillo in Peru, in which case urban political life is dominated by the rural. Cities like São Paulo, Lima and Santiago have increased in size so recently that the effective control still lies with the older oligarchic members dominated by strong family allegiances, the same element to which the government belongs. The oligarchy is one aspect of the extended family which reaches back into the regions. It certainly does not provide an effective basis for a political party system. As for the middle class and the workers, these have not discovered their interest or their power and are so dependent upon favors from the government that an independent party composed of these elements is either make-believe for political window-dressing or is inspired with the panacea that lies hidden in the aurora of a possible revolution. They may become elements out of which a party grows, but the time when that will happen has not yet arrived.

The president who comes to office has none of the assurance and strength provided by a political party with deep roots in the thousands of communities that form the nation. That is why he has to be the architect of his own power.

This brings us back to Fidel Castro. During the days when he was in the Sierra Maestra with a handful of followers fighting to overthrow the Batista régime he had, on the report of those who knew him best, no ambitions other than the reëstablishment of political freedom in Cuba. He himself wanted neither power nor office. His task would be completed when the dictatorship had fallen and a new democratic government had taken office. Both he and his friends should have known better. But Latin Americans, like others, enjoy living in a make-believe world. They talked as if Cuba were a democracy with political parties and elections and as if the president were chosen by a majority of the people. The facts are quite different. The president either has been a *caudillo* himself or has been imposed by one. The successor to Machado was Batista, the intervening governments were largely his creatures and the successor to Batista is Fidel Castro.

He does not have to be elected. He does not need a Congress. He does not need them because his power would be as equally unrestrained after an election as before one. What passed for political parties has disappeared because they were not parties. They were groups of office seekers in search of a leader who would, by becoming president, authorize their misuse of public funds for private ends. Castro has no need of a political party because the people expect him to govern, to make every decision, to lead them, to impose his will on any and every one who opposes him. If he makes a social revolution, it is good because he makes it. If he did not make one, that would also be good because he did not make one. I am not arguing the merits of his program. That is beside the point in this discussion. This kind of program could have emanated from a popularly elected legislature. What is at issue is that the power, the program, the policy, are personal. He is the executive, the legislative and the judiciary. Every statement he makes is the law of the land. That is what the people want. They know who their government is—Fidel Castro. Not only that, Fidel Castro claims a moral sanction for his power. He destroyed the tyrant and is now bringing justice and liberty to the people. As long as the people believe that his intent is good, that his purposes are to protect and help them, then he will continue to be a national hero, a very prince returned to rule with divine power. He is the king come to office again.

His difficulty will arise if and when his actions become suspect as being motivated by personal ends, when he becomes suspicious, arbitrary and tyrannical. When the people become fearful and no longer trust him, should that misfortune befall him, he will be driven to become a tyrant as happened to Calles in Mexico. He will find that he cannot resign his power, cannot transfer it, cannot abandon it. If elections are held, his party will have to win and he will govern as he governs now. To be able to transfer his power he would have had to come to office through a political party which had strong deep roots in every community, that had chosen him and might have chosen someone else. The party would have brought him to office temporarily and when the time came would pass the office on again temporarily to someone else. But there is no such party, nor can it be created overnight.

Fidel Castro would make an important contribution to the democratic development of Cuba if in his intent to democratize the country he would devolve and decentralize the government, give the provinces, towns and villages power of self-government, reform the tax structure so that most of the income from taxes would go to the smallest political units, allow the localities to elect their own officials without interfering, permit the localities to spend their money as they thought best and allow the courts to deal with infractions of the law. But that kind of program would largely strip him of his role as active leader, his followers would not approve of it and the people themselves would in all probability consider that he was weak because he permitted others to do what was clearly his own responsibility—to govern all things.

That is the dilemma of Latin American politics and it reappears in every administration. Democracy requires local self-government and local power independent of the center and beyond its realm. Centralization requires just the opposite, no local power and nothing beyond the reach of the chief executive. How the contemporary Latin American statesmen who believe in democracy can move to increase local power and independence without at the same time undermining their own position is the unanswered question.

5

In the early 1960s no international aid program received more publicity in Latin America than President John F. Kennedy's Alliance for Progress, Washington's answer to the challenge of revolution. It would provide the incentive and the funds for major reforms to eliminate the continent's ills. The measures proposed included tax and financial schemes, land reform, and public education. In Latin

America, the Alliance received a mixed reaction; many supported its goals but others openly opposed it. In their opinion, the Alliance did not promise a viable remedy for the problems of Latin America. In particular, critics viewed the Alliance as an attempt by the United States to preserve its political and economic hegemony over Latin America—an interpretation that the noted Mexican economist, Alonso Aguilar, develops in the next essay.

Alonso Aguilar:
Latin America and the
Alliance for Progress*

ECONOMIC TRENDS IN LATIN AMERICA

Latin America emerged from the Second World War with many unresolved problems and many unsatisfied aspirations. Prior to the economic collapse of 1929, most Latin American countries believed that industrialization alone would help to strengthen and diversify their economies, assure independence, and raise the overall standard of living. However, the Depression and the economic decline of the 1930's hampered any progress in terms of economic development. It was the temporary absence of the great powers from the shrinking world market of the war years which, although it caused confusion in the supply of capital goods, acted as a factor stimulating the industrial development of the principal Latin American countries. If the benefits of the period were accompanied by errors, difficulties, and a certain disequilibrium, nevertheless production grew rapidly (the rate of growth surpassing 6 percent per annum during the years 1942-1951), and Latin America experienced a brief spell of prosperity. There was an increase in population as well as an increase in investment and employment; industrial production expanded, as did foreign trade, both in terms of value and volume; the balance of payments was favorable; prices rose in the domestic market; and commercial ventures of every kind mushroomed.

* From Alonso Aguilar, LATIN AMERICA AND THE ALLIANCE FOR PROGRESS, trans. by Ursula Wasserman (New York: Monthly Review Press, 1963), pp. 6–9, 15–32. Reprinted by permission of Monthly Review Press. Copyright © 1963 by Monthly Review Press.

but practically everywhere the system of taxation, and of public finance in general, shows the same defects: Revenue is inadequate and depends, in large measure, on direct taxation, leaving ample oportunity for tax-evasion; budget control is insufficient; most public expenditure can hardly be termed productive; the public debt tends to grow in an inflationary spiral, and monetary policy is not designed to promote economic development.

Educational expenditure represents but a tiny part of the national income and, in addition, is badly distributed from a geographic, economic, and social point of view; illiteracy is widespread and there exists an overall lack of schools on all levels.

Public administration is defective and is characterized by gaps and maladjustments which result in bureacracy and inefficiency.

Some countries boast of no labor legislation of any kind to protect workers and grant them certain fundamental rights; in others, including those where relatively progressive legislation has been passed—as, for example, in Mexico—such laws have become a dead letter.

In many other fields basic reforms are, of course, needed on which the OAS experts surely never—or hardly ever—reflect. To list only a few, there are the system of credit, the stock market, the organization and operation of foreign trade, the distribution of income, and the principles of government intervention in the national economy.

A peculiar situation has arisen with regard to the need for basic reforms, although at bottom the situation is not difficult to understand. At the beginning of the Alliance for Progress, many persons believed that reforms constituted a prerequisite for the benefits promised at Punta del Este. This left the conservatives aghast, but pleased those who had long been convinced of the necessity of adopting certain reforms. Matters, however, became clarified little by little; and little by little, too, the premature fears vanished together with the unjustified hopes.

Faced with the apprehensions of those who owe their wealth and privileges to the survival of anachronistic social structures, ALPRO officials have had to be very outspoken: Structural reforms, the Committee of Nine has stated, are not a prerequisite to foreign aid. The Ad Hoc committees are, therefore, to confine themselves to "an appreciation of good will wherever it exists [sic] to carry out needed reforms and to determine at which points . . . existing conditions may be adapted to suggested objectives." . . . The Committee itself, nevertheless, considers the realization of reforms to be an obligation deriving from an international statute which makes the OAS the principal arbiter of Latin American life and relegates our constitutions a rank below, or at most equal to that of the Charter of Punta del Este.

With regard to most reforms, we once again come across the same contradictions we have already encountered in connection with national development programs. The opportunity to carry out one of the proposed reforms hardly arises when innumerable and often insurmountable obstacles are put in the way of any contemplated economic or social change; when this occurs, the authorities begin to temporize, and the most solemn pronouncements turn into hollow phrases; a little later, more limited reforms are proposed, and despite the fact that they are indispensable even within the narrow framework of the Alliance, they too become expendable, as they begin to arouse the hostility of all who might be adversely affected, from officials charged with bringing them about, to obstinate national and foreign investors who see their interests threatened.

An American periodical recently quoted the revealing opinion of a Chilean economist: "To try to modify from one day to the next a class system which has existed for centuries is to play with fire. Any hurried attempt to reduce the contrast between rich and poor must produce serious difficulties." (*U.S. News & World Report*, February 14, 1962). Since ALPRO, naturally, does not pretend to modify, but rather intends to preserve the "class system," the opinion quoted is of some significance. The *Post Gazette* of Pittsburgh wrote on the same subject in August of last year, "as in other parts of the world, those in Latin America who enjoy special privileges frequently oppose any social change, especially if such change implies material losses." Teodoro Moscoso himself has recognized that the "extremely rich and powerful minorities . . . refuse to relinquish even an ounce of their comfort or the smallest part of their virtually tax-exempt incomes." The French journalist, Claude Julien, scrutinizing the work of the Alliance 14 months after its initiation, noted that "the large landowners do not wish to hear of agrarian reform, just as other privileged groups do not cherish the mention of fiscal reform. Moreover, they denounce as Communists anyone who asks for such fiscal or land reforms as are advocated by Mr. Kennedy." (*Le Monde*, quoted in *Comercio Exterior*, December, 1962.) In the same way, we might add, that Mr. Kennedy would label "Communist" anyone who proposed the breakup of the large estates or touched the other interests of North American investors in Latin America.

The conclusion is telling: Every day they talk more and more of the need for such and such a reform, and every day they move further away from any possibility of carrying out any type of reform. Eighteen months after the Alliance was launched, we must ask ourselves: Where is the land reform which was going to modify the tenancy system, reduce exploitation, split up the large estates, and establish the basis for a new type of agriculture? Where are the fiscal reforms which were to result in a new and less unjust system of taxation? Where is the monetary policy which was to combat the "evils of inflation" and defend the purchasing power of the many? Where is the just basic wage and the respect for the independence of labor organizations? Surely few, if any, of the highfalutin phrases of Punta del Este have been translated into policy. The agricultural structure of Latin America has not changed in the past two years, nor the unwillingness on the part of the ruling cliques to carry out any type of reform, except the kind of superficial and bureaucratic reforms which respect vested interests and have been imposed from above, financed from abroad, and approved of by the landowners in Venezuela, Colombia, and Peru. Nor has the tax system been modified, except to an insignificant degree in Mexico and two or three other countries—modifications which leave the system as unfair, regressive, and anti-popular as before. Monetary policy continues to suffocate within the orthodox and inefficient framework of the International Monetary Fund's recommendations; and so-called programs of stability and austerity paradoxically serve only to intensify stagnation, inflation, and the impoverishment of the majority. Workers in rural and urban areas alike continue to live on miserable wages, often suffering the arbitrary restraint of their organizations, ironically imposed by officials and businessmen in the name of freedom.

What of the degree of economic integration achieved to date? Without going back to the Treaty of Montevideo, which would lead us too far away from our central topic and would require much fuller treatment, it might be well to examine two or three questions briefly. Economic integration, the Committee of Nine points out, "must be examined within the general context of the Alliance for Progress," since it is closely tied up with "the national development programs and the possibilities of rapid growth in Latin American productivity." . . . Integration should, moreover, primarily be considered "as a problem of investment and secondarily as a problem of trade."

These views seem worth examining for a moment. Why should integration be considered within the context of ALPRO? Only because it is intimately tied up with the process of national development programs? The basic problem surely is how to achieve integration and in what direction to guide it, to know whether integration is to be conceived as a Latin American alliance destined to facilitate the development of our countries and their interchange in the face of the great powers which in one way or another always succeed in putting new obstacles in our way, or whether integration will take on the character of a joint effort within the framework of the Alliance, which ignores the basic contradictions between Latin America and the United States. Integration within the system of ALPRO will strip the Latin American Free Trade Association (LAFTA) of its basic *Latin American* character and convert it into one more inter-American instrument, which for obvious reasons will be unable to accomplish the tasks posed at the time of its establishment.

Here we are faced with another danger: Unless the members of LAFTA take prompt and effective measures to make certain that any benefits which may accrue from it should go to their own respective national enterprises, the concessions already granted will result in heavy and unjustified advantages to foreign, and in particular North American, investors.

If some who may be over-optimistic with regard to integration, see a possible line of defense in membership in LAFTA, others will point to contradictions which show the true position of the United States. Washington's attitude toward LAFTA has undergone an evolution, passing from an original state of indifference, dislike, and even isolated instances of hostility, to one which conditionally recognizes the need "to support any type of economic integration which favors the expansion of markets and offers wider scope for competition." (*En Camino de la Integración,* supplement to *Comercio Exterior,* Mexico City, September-October, 1962.)

It will be appreciated that the United States, conscious of its power and loyal to its established commercial policy, does not support the type of integration which tends to strengthen the competitive position of Latin America vis-à-vis the great powers, but supports rather a "wider scope of competition" as such.

This position on the part of the United States will obviously be very difficult to change and constitutes one of the factors which condition the rhythm and above all the direction of economic integration. The proofs are manifold: Only a few weeks ago, the United States criticized Brazil's decision to diversify her foreign trade and to establish closer contacts with the socialist countries. It also criticized the "discriminatory" character of Brazil's exchange policy with regard to members of LAFTA, a position which essentially coincided with that which Douglas Dillon had recently outlined at the latest session of the Inter-American Economic and Social Council.

All this shows that economic integration, which in fact has

made little progress, is faced with an inevitable dilemma. Yet, on its solution depends the fate of LAFTA and the Central American Common Market. Either integration will develop into an instrument strengthening, consolidating, and helping to coordinate the economic and commercial development of the associated countries, and will be combined with an active policy of diversification in terms of foreign trade; or integration, within the context of the Alliance, will mask a policy which subordinates Latin American interests to the demands of continental solidarity—which means at bottom to the demands of American interests. In the latter case, the hopes raised by the prospect of integration will soon be converted into new frustrations.

In this connection, we cannot pass over a recent occurrence which clearly reveals the dangers of the wrong kind of integration: When Cuba recently applied for membership in LAFTA, integration was put to its first test and came out poorly. For instead of accepting Cuba's application, LAFTA argued that it could not grant membership to a country "whose economic system was incompatible with the Treaty of Montevideo." The position of the Mexican government was even more explicit: "In view of the principles of free enterprise and free competition on which the Treaty of Montevideo is based," it declared, "a country where policy, foreign trade, and production are in the hands of the government is ineligible for membership, since this constitutes a case which the Treaty did not foresee." If in effect Cuba's case was not, and could not have been, foreseen—although in the exercise of sovereignty each country may choose the economic and political system it prefers—the truth of the matter is that LAFTA on this occasion acted as the tool of OAS, adding alleged "economic incompatibility" to the "political incompatibility" which some months previously at Punta del Este had served as a pretext to exclude Cuba from that organization.

Let us now examine the part played by foreign financial aid which, as we know, is another pillar of the Alliance for Progress.

At the beginning of the Punta del Este conference, American leadership underwent a mental change similar to that which we have already noted in connection with economic development programs and social reforms. The change expresses itself in recognizing the need of appreciably augmenting the volume of foreign financial aid and of admitting, on the basis of resolutions passed shortly before at the Inter-American conference at Bogota, the necessity of more adequate and more flexible conditions of financial assistance. In accordance with these concepts, Latin America was offered credits and investments to the extent of at least $2,000 million annually, and the United States alone promised to contribute a minimum of $1,000 million during the first year of the Alliance.

What is the meaning of a contribution of $2,000 million per annum? Certain circles in America, as well as in Latin America, believe that foreign financial aid will prove the decisive factor in our economic development during the coming decade. There are also some who believe that the rate of investment is in large part dependent on foreign aid and that with increased aid it will *ipso facto* rise above the levels of previous years. ALPRO's experts estimate that Latin America, in order to achieve the rate of growth blueprinted at Punta del Este, will require a total investment of $140,000–$170,000 million during the first ten years, which would leave foreign financial aid with a participation of roughly between 12 and 14 percent of gross capital formation.

Here, however, we need to keep several facts in mind. In the first place, contrary to what might be assumed, total foreign investment has been considerable during the past few years. It has been running at between $1,500–$1,700 million annually, figures which are very close to the promises held out at Punta del Este. In the second place—and here we must be careful to reflect on the factors which determine Latin American development—even this substantial rate of foreign investment has been unable to free Latin America from economic stagnation, which, on the contrary, has become more pronounced. Last, considering the role played by foreign aid, we must not forget that even if the international movement of capital generates additional financial resources, it simultaneously causes a drainage of funds which almost always exceeds the rate of inflow.

According to available estimates, direct foreign investments in Latin America during the decade 1950–1960 amounted to $6,179 million, while profits transferred abroad totalled $11,083 million. In other words, Latin America suffered a net loss of $4,904 million on foreign investment account. For the years 1950–1955 these figures include only profits transmitted to the United States. If we add remissions to Europe, the aggregate loss would surely surpass the $5,000 million mark. The exactions of foreign investors are of such proportions that the United Nations Economic Commission for Latin America calculated that they amounted to $680 million in 1947, $940 million in 1951, and to more than $1,200 million annually during the years 1955–1960.

In view of these figures, it may seem somewhat surprising that the President of the United States, reviewing the measures taken by ALPRO, laid most emphasis on the fact that one out of every four children of school age "received supplementary rations out of U.S. agricultural surplus"; that one and a half million textbooks had been distributed and 17,000 classrooms constructed; that "to a large degree the Alliance encourages our neighbors to help themselves and to adopt various reforms on their own initative; that the Alliance will provide new housing, and hope, better health and dignity for millions of forgotten human beings." (*El Dia*, February 17, 1963.) Douglas Dillon, summing up the achievements of the Alliance during its first year of existence, pointed out coldly —like the banker he is and without President Kennedy's rhetoric —that the main achievement was that the United States was granting the financial aid promised at Punta del Este.

During the first year, Latin America received a little over $1,000 million in loans from institutions controlled by, or under the influence of, the government of the United States. Out of this sum, $600 million were Export-Import bank credits, with strings attached—the Bank's mission being to further the export of U.S. goods—and $150 million were furnished in the form of surplus food, under the "Food for Peace" scheme, a program which frequently operates on the basis of dumping, causing incalculable harm to local producers. Even though credits and investments were obtained elsewhere in smaller quantities, the total amount of private investment declined and the total influx of funds never sufficed to compensate for the outflow of profits on foreign investments or the losses coming from deterioration of the terms of trade, which vastly exceeded the figure of $2,000 million per annum. Added to this are hundreds of millions of dollars which wealthy Latin Americans transfer each year to Swiss, American, and Canadian banks.

Where then is the acceleration of economic development and the improvement in prices for Latin American exports? Instead of a rising standard of living, stagnation and prostration continue to dominate the Latin American scene; rather than receiving higher prices for our exports, we receive less every day and in exchange pay more for whatever we purchase abroad. Even the modest aim of an annual 2.5 percent increase in the rate of economic growth is beginning to be considered too ambitious, and they already tell us that it will be more realistic to think in terms of more than ten years and of an annual per capita increase of only 2 percent. Even 2 percent, however, is almost twice as high as the increase Latin America has been able to achieve during the past two years. To sum up, the fruits of the Alliance have been meager and it has failed not only to "capture the imagination or kindle the hope of millions of human beings from the Rio Grande to Patagonia," as Teodoro Moscoso lyrically put it (*"Problemas de la Alianza para el Progreso"* in *Comercio Exterior,* February, 1962), but has disappointed even its most ardent partisans, such as Kubitschek and Lleros Camargo, and has failed in the sense that its initial proposals have been drowned in the mire of bureaucracy, inefficiency, a lack of understanding, and an abundance of contradictions—submerged by the weight of an oppressive reality which, contrary to predictions, does not seem to show any signs of improvement.

It is, indeed, interesting to observe how the idea has taken root, both in the United States and among our "democratic oligarchies"—to use the picturesque expression of a Mexican Senator—that the fundamental need consists in obtaining more money and in stimulating private investment rather than in transforming the economy with a view to widening its horizons and opening up new vistas of progress.

"The premature exhaustion on the part of the Alliance," said a recent report of the Morgan Guaranty Trust Company (Associated Press release, February 15, 1963), "is in part simply the weariness caused by words rather than deeds, words which have not yet been translated into action. . . . The prerequisite for better results must be the Alliance's reorientation along lines which will induce private capital . . . to enter into action." The *Wall Street Journal* opines that aid on an inter-governmental basis has retarded development and that it is necessary to encourage private investment (*Excélsior,* February 12, 1963). The periodical *U.S. News & World Report* (August 20, 1962) considers that the Alliance's defects lie in its "lack of stimulus to private enterprise." And Senator Javits recently declared in a speech that "Latin American progress will depend on successful investment in private enterprise." (*El Dia,* January 30, 1963.)

Similar views can be heard every day. "The Alliance," said the Chairman of the Grace Line early this year, "can be saved only on the basis of a substantial increase in aid, coupled with the encouragement of private investment and private enterprise." (*Excélsior,* February 3, 1963). The attitude of U.S. Secretary of Commerce Luther Hodges and prominent American bankers, headed by David Rockefeller, has been the same, when they suggest that "American aid should be utilized to persuade the nations of Latin America to adopt policies favorable to American financial investments." (*El Dia,* February 3, 1963.)

THE TRUE SIGNIFICANCE OF THE ALLIANCE AND ITS PERSPECTIVES

This brings us to our last point, an attempt to establish the true nature and scope of the Alliance for Progress.

The advocates of ALPRO show a perceptible, and at times exceedingly suspicious, desire to define the Alliance as "multilateral," "Latin American," and "revolutionary." "Let us once again transform the American continent," said President Kennedy in launching the Alliance, "into a vast crucible of revolutionary ideas and efforts. . . . Let us once again awaken our American revolution," and put our faith in the "rule of courage and freedom and hope for the future of man." Raúl Prebisch, for his part, has at various times stressed the Latin American origin of many of the Alliance's features and has expressed the fear lest such ideas be regarded as having been "conceived in the United States."

The indefatigable and ingenious Teodoro Moscoso, who never stops insisting that the Alliance represents a "peaceful revolution," has stated emphatically: "The Alliance, if successful, will produce far-reaching changes in the life of Latin America. The traditional class structure will not survive. The profound contrast between the few who live in abundance and the many who live in misery has no more place in our time." And the Committee of Nine always maintains that the Alliance is not a program imposed by the United States but an entity of Latin American ideas accepted by the United States. "The Alliance for Progress," the experts of the OAS never tire of repeating, "is of a revolutionary nature and recognized as such by the United States."

To what extent is this, in effect, the true nature of the Alliance? To begin with, it is perfectly true that the Alliance was not imposed by the United States, but originated from an agreement between the government of that country and the governments of the Latin American republics. It is further true that the Alliance poses problems that are pertinent and recognizes the legitimate aspirations of our people. But as to its "revolutionary" character or its "multilateral" mechanism, that is another matter. "During the first year of the Alliance," says the Committee of Nine, "except for the case of Bolivia"—whose program, we are bound to note, was never even examined by the OAS—"all aid has been accorded on the basis of bilateral agreements, without complying with the more formal procedures foreseen by the Charter." . . . Where then is the Alliance's multilateral nature?

And what of its profoundly "revolutionary" implications, and the manner in which these implications are recognized? The revolutionary nature of the Alliance, states the Committee of Nine, has not been understood by the people of Latin America. It has not been understood "because the leaders of Latin America have never presented it as such to their people." . . . Is it possible that ALPRO experts would consider it sufficient if the leaders of Latin American public opinion hailed the Alliance as revolutionary? Are the people to accept even the OAS as a revolutionary body and admit that imperialist policy as well has suddenly turned revolutionary?

In Mexico, to take an example, leaders of employers' groups and of the trade unions, as well as public officials of different ranks, repeat at every opportunity that ALPRO pursues aims identical to those of the Mexican revolution. Who is supposed to believe this? Who can compare the deeply democratic movement—anti-imperialist and anti-feudal—which arose in our country in 1910 with the designs of the continent's ruling classes to preserve their political and economic privileges in exchange for some insipid reforms imposed from above? Who would confuse Emiliano Zapata and the peasants who initiated our land reform under the slogan "Land and Liberty" with Teodoro Moscoso, Muñoz Marin, and the experts of the OAS?

United States policy toward Latin America always follows the same track. After the era of the Good Neighbor policy, which President Roosevelt introduced within the framework of a democratic domestic program and a determined fight against fascism, all we have received from North America is pressure, interference, low prices, McCarthyism, gifts with strings attached, investments which pervert our development and put brakes on our progress, as well as rhetoric in defense of free enterprise and the so-called Free World. In 1946, at the very moment when the bloodiest war in the history of mankind had come to an end, Winston Churchill launched from the United States the policy of the Cold War. Its effects upon Latin America soon became evident. In 1947 the Cold War made its triumphal entry at Rio de Janeiro and gave birth to the Inter-American Treaty of Reciprocal Assistance. One year later the Cold War made itself felt at Bogota, and in 1951 the struggle against an alleged international Communist conspiracy acquired new forms in Washington, only to culminate in 1954 in Foster Dulles' and Castillo Armas' "glorious victory" over the Guatemalan revolution.

Demands for financial aid and higher prices for raw materials always rise in equal proportion to Washington's insistence—echoed by the governments of various Latin American republics—on the gravity of the twin dangers of "Communism" and "internal subversion." Most Latin American governments are inclined to support United States policy, but in exchange they demand economic and financial aid. Prior to 1958, prevailing conditions were not such as to oblige the United States to offer aid to all claimants, let alone concede it. The triumph of the Cuban Revolution changed matters. American pressure increased with a view to opposing Cuba and strengthening the OAS. In mid-1959 a conference held at Santiago de Chile reiterated the principles of "representative democracy." The following year, in Costa Rica, the Cuban Revolution was denounced as a form of extra-continental intervention, posing a threat to the security of the Americas. The principal ideas of the so-called "Operation Pan-America" were recognized in the Act of Bogota, and some months later the Charter of Punta del Este led to Cuba's expulsion from the OAS, its socialist government being pronounced "incompatible" with the system of "representative democracy" prevalent throughout the Hemisphere.

This was the process which shaped the pattern of the Alliance for Progress—an instrument in defense of the ruling classes, an expression of Monroeism and an outpost of anti-Communism, an answer to popular discontent, a barricade against any desire for emancipation, an alternative and a check to the Cuban Revolution, and a new Holy Alliance directed against the revolutionary struggle of our people. And yet ALPRO is not the same old weapon which the United States has traditionally used to protect her interests. The Alliance constitutes a vast new attempt to convince Latin America that her only road to progress is the one indicated by the United States. The road is paved with hitherto unknown materials. ALPRO does not mechanically repeat the same outworn phrases which never meant anything and never attracted anybody. The Alliance indicates a significant change, for until recently the United States openly defended the interests of the most conservative groups, while now she takes a stand against the large landowners and opposes the inequitable distribution of wealth. The Alliance has, indeed, employed a new idiom, undoubtedly incorporating some ancient Latin American demands. The problems to which the Alliance refers are real enough and remain unresolved. Recognition of the need for social reform is also new, as is the acknowledgment of the need for ample long-term credits at low rates of interest in order to stimulate economic development. The Alliance is not the coarse instrument of a blind and insensitive policy, but an ingenious device, far more intelligent than the Marshall Plan and of wider scope, with which the governments of America have chosen to defend themselves against the real danger of revolutionary change and the profound social transformation which threatens their vested interests. In synthesis, the Alliance does not pretend to cope with the principal historical causes of backwardness, nor with the poverty of Latin America, but merely attempts to preserve law and order and to apply the brakes to any popular movement which might cause damage to the powers that be. In this attempt, the Alliance puts forward certain more or less superficial measures which will hardly change the face of the continent.

It seems difficult to remain in doubt as to the Alliance's true nature. "We consider this Alliance," José Figueras said recently, "as a realistic and defensive measure on the part of the United States government. . . . We are satisfied that the United States has taken up this struggle in the protection of her liberties and with a view to her own interests, in the manner of a productive investment rather than a mere handout." Dean Rusk, for his part, has written: "The Alliance constitutes a concrete part of an invisible whole . . . it rests on the concept that this Hemisphere is part of Western Civilization which we are pledged to defend." Within the framework of American anti-Communist policy, the Alliance will obviously not permit the violation of the interests of privileged groups. Moscoso made this abundantly clear when he said: "In supporting the Alliance, members of the traditional ruling class will have nothing to fear. . . . The Alliance deserves their support, for is it not a call to their conscience and their patriotism and at the same time their very means of self-defense?" The privileged groups, he added, "must choose between the objectives of the Alliance and exposing themselves to the destructive type of revolution of a Fidel Castro." Romulo Betancourt, the Venezuelan president who has gained the dubious distinction in Washington of being "one of the outstanding anti-Communist leaders in the Americas," in trying to explain the Alliance's role, has been even more explicit: "We must help the poor," said he, "in order to save the rich." *The Times* of London commented with good reason (August 10, 1962) that "the Alliance has been the object of that instinctive suspicion Latin Americans possess for North American motives."

The true nature of the Alliance, its antecedents, its projection, and its scope explain why it is failing. As we have seen, the Alliance does not try to tackle the basic problems of Latin America. It projects itself into secondary fields and evades decisive issues, such as the problem of imperialism; its discussions take place within the framework of profound contradictions, and it is based on utopian principles. Its failure is due not to its disorganization or its bureaucracy, but to its inner contradictions, to the obstacles which block the realization of its programs, to the greedy illusions which cause Latin America's privileged minorities to substitute "firmness, austerity, dedication, and sacrifice" for the betterment of the majority's living conditions.

What may we then expect from the Alliance? Has the ambitious scheme drawn up at Punta del Este had no repercussions throughout the continent? In our view, there have been certain conflicting influences which are, however, not mutually exclusive. The Alliance for Progress cannot help but have a certain impact on Latin American development; in fact, its impact is already being felt. In some countries, it has helped to improve the financial situation, even if on a short-term basis, raising the rate of investment or accelerating the rhythm of development; in others, it has to a certain extent stimulated the construction of housing, schools, and health centers. The Alliance is very likely encouraging a number of institutional reforms; and many Latin Americans who live on the margin of privilege defending their own class interests, have begun to believe in all good faith that such reforms are of substantial significance in terms of Latin America's evolution.

In conclusion, ALPRO can point to a certain amount of success and may, for another few years, stem the tide of social and economic change for which the people of Latin America have begun to clamor. What seems equally evident, however, is that the Alliance will not be able to solve any basic problems, if only because of its dependence on forces abroad, a dependence which has been one of the decisive causes of our backwardness. Within the framework of the Alliance, this dependence cannot be broken but can only be reinforced.

Suggestions for Further Reading

In recent years a wealth of information has appeared on the subject of agrarian reform. A thoughtful and factual account of the problem is Thomas F. Carrol, "The Land Reform Issue in Latin America," in Albert O. Hirschman, ed., *Latin American Issues* (New York, 1961), pp. 161–201. In *Meeting of High Level Experts in Agricultural Problems* (Washington, 1962), pp. 16–23, the Inter-American Committee for Agricultural Development probes the complexities of the question. For an idealistic interpretation of the meaning of land reform, see Clarence Senior, *Land Reform and Democracy* (Gainesville, 1958). Nathan Whetten, "Land Reform in a Modern World," *Rural Sociology*, XIX (December, 1954), pp. 329–337, also bears reading. The problem of economic development in Latin America is discussed with an insider's point of view by Celso Furtado, *Development and Under-development,* translated by Ricardo W. de Aguiar and Eric C. Drysdale (Berkeley, 1964), and from an international perspective by the United Nations, *Towards a Dynamic Development Policy for Latin America* (New York, 1963). Of particular interest to the student of ideas in economic development is Albert O. Hirschman, "Ideologies of Economic Development in Latin America," which is in his *Latin American Issues* (New York, 1961). For the military in its traditional role, see Edwin Lieuwen, *Arms and Politics in Latin America* (New York, 1960). In *The Military in Society in Latin America* (Stanford, 1964), John J. Johnson assigns the soldier a new role as the spokesman for middle-class aspirations. The most provocative and fresh picture of the military is provided by the Argentine scholar, José Nun, in "The Middle-Class Military Coup," in Claudio Veliz ed., *The Politics of Conformity in Latin America* (London, New York, Toronto, 1967), pp. 66–118. Cecil Jane's *Liberty and Despotism in Latin America* (Oxford, 1929), though published four decades ago, remains a classic study of the forces that explain dictatorship in Latin America. For a recent intellectual approach to the nature of *caudillaje* read Richard R. Morse, "Toward a Theory of Spanish American Government," *Journal of the History of Ideas,"* XV (1954), 71–93. Another essay of value is Robin A. Humphreys, "Latin America: The Caudillo Tradition," in Michael Howard, ed., *Soldiers and Governments: Nine Studies in Civil-Military Relations* (Bloomington, 1959), pp. 149–165. A strong case for the Alliance for Progress (but with suggestions for strengthening it) is made by Hilmer S. Raushenbush, *The Challenge to the Alliance for Progress* (Washington, 1962), while the Kennedy's administration view can be found in Arthur M. Schlesinger, Jr., *A Thousand Days* (Boston, 1965), ch. XIII. In *Five Years of the Alliance for Progress* (Washington, 1967), Simon G. Hanson presents a harsh judgment of the program's failures.

Index